the MODERN BAKER

The MODERN BAKER

TIME-SAVING TECHNIQUES *for* BREADS, TARTS, PIES, CAKES, *&* COOKIES

Nick Malgieri

PHOTOGRAPHS BY CHARLES SCHILLER

DK

London, New York, Melbourne,
Munich, and Delhi

Executive Editor Anja Schmidt
Assistant Editor Nichole Morford
Creative Direction & Art Director Dirk Kaufman
Managing Art Editor Michelle Baxter
DTP Coordinator Kathy Farias
Production Manager Ivor Parker
Executive Managing Editor Sharon Lucas

Design & Art Direction Gary Tooth/Empire Design Studio
Photography Charles Schiller
Food Styling Karen Tack
Prop Styling Pamela Duncan Silver

FOR SANDY LUSTIG

First American Edition, 2008

Published in the United States by
DK Publishing
375 Hudson Street
New York, New York 10014

08 09 10 11 12 10 9 8 7 6 5 4 3 2 1
CD199—September 2008

Copyright © 2008 DK Publishing
Text Copyright © Nick Malgieri
All rights reserved

Without limiting the rights under copyright reserved above, no part of this
publication may be reproduced, stored in or introduced into a retrieval system, or transmitted, in any form, or by any means (electronic, mechanical,
photocopying, recording, or otherwise), without the prior written permission
of both the copyright owner and the above publisher of this book.

A catalog record for this book is available from the Library of Congress.

ISBN 978-0-7566-3971-6

DK books are available at special discounts when purchased in bulk for
sales promotions, premiums, fund-raising, or educational use. For details,
contact: DK Publishing Special Markets, 375 Hudson Street, New York, New
York 10014 or SpecialSales@dk.com.

Color reproduction by Colourscan, Singapore
Printed and bound in China by Hung Hing

Discover more at www.dk.com

Contents

6   Introduction

10   Ingredients

24   Equipment

34   Techniques

39   **1. Quick Breads**

65   **2. Breads**

93   **3. Yeast-Risen Specialties, Sweet & Savory**

121   **4. Savory Tarts & Pies**

155   **5. Sweet Tarts & Pies**

193   **6. Puff Pastries**

219   **7. Cakes**

269   **8. Cookies, Bars, & Biscotti**

312   Sources

313   Bibliography

314   Index

320   Acknowledgments

I love to bake,

and I love teaching others to bake too.
Home baking is a way to enjoy all the best baked goods at a fraction of what you'd spend at a bakery —and, as an added bonus, home baked goods are fresher. But I don't love to bake as a cost-saving measure. I love to bake because it's fun and relaxing, and because baking, to me, is all about sharing something special with family and friends.

This book focuses on showing you how much fun baking can be, and encouraging you to make it an everyday event in your home, rather than something you reserve for special occasions. That's why I've incorporated many techniques that I've developed over the years to shave some time and work from the baking process. Not every single recipe incorporates time-saving strategies, but most do. In fact, this whole book is very technique oriented, with explanations about the hows and whys of what you'll be doing at the beginning of every chapter.

Yet while the recipes are quicker and easier, you'll find their results are as good as—and often better than—baked goods prepared

8 using standard recipes. I think everyone who knows me, my books, and my classes is aware that I attach a lot of importance to great flavor and texture. Of course, anything baked also has to look neat (but not necessarily decorated to death), too. If you're a beginning baker, you'll be surprised at the good results you get from a first-time try with a pastry crust or cake layer. If you're an experienced baker, you'll learn new techniques, since everyone likes to save some time in the kitchen, and you'll enjoy trying some of the more challenging recipes that require a little more practice to master.

For example, my new method for preparing bread doughs involves very little mixing and kneading—instead, after the ingredients are stirred together or mixed quickly by machine, the dough rests for a few minutes, allowing it to come together smoothly with a minimum of effort on the baker's part. This not only provides good results but it actually provides *better* results than the standard long mixing and kneading method. The flour retains its fresh flavor rather than losing it through lengthy manipulation. And you'll love pressing pastry dough into the pan instead of rolling it out, or mixing a cake batter without folding in whipped egg whites at the end.

Baking should be a joy, not a chore, and my new recipes guarantee excellent results of a quality as good as or superior to anything that takes twice as long or more. And who doesn't need more joy in his or her life? When you've tried a few of these streamlined recipes and tasted the results, I think you'll discover that you love baking too.

Nick Malgieri
New York City, February 2008

Ingredients

The following alphabetical list of ingredients is drawn entirely from the ones used in this book. Ingredients specific to a certain category appear in the appropriate chapter. Though the ingredients described are my personal favorites, they were not chosen because of any bias toward them on my part, but they reflect the ones I have determined the best over the past more than thirty years of developing, testing, and teaching baking recipes.

12 CHOCOLATE & COCOA: Many books have been devoted solely to chocolate—including my own *Chocolate*—attesting to its popularity as a flavoring, beverage, and confection.

CHOCOLATE: Made from the fruit of the cacao tree, *Thobroma cacao*, chocolate has been used mostly as a beverage throughout its more than 3,000-year history. The fruit, or pods, contain several dozen large beans as well as a tangy pulp that isn't used. After the pods are split open, the beans are separated from the pulp and placed on the ground (usually on banana leaves), covered with more leaves, and allowed to ferment. This period of fermentation brings out their chocolate flavor. After fermentation, the beans are dried to stop the fermentation and roasted, further developing the chocolate flavor. Crushed into nibs (see Cocoa Nibs) and winnowed to remove the skin, the cocoa beans are finally ready to become chocolate. They are crushed between stone rollers, and sugar, cocoa butter (the natural fat in the beans), vanilla flavoring, and lecithin—an innocuous soy-based emulsifier that keeps the mixture from separating—are added. The proportion of each ingredient determines whether the chocolate will be sweet, semisweet, or bitter-sweet. Chocolate's percentage of cocoa solids refers to the amount of cocoa beans in the mixture. Milk chocolate is made by adding reduced milk in paste or powdered form.

UNSWEETENED CHOCOLATE (CHOCOLATE LIQUOR): Made from cocoa nibs and nothing else besides some lecithin, unsweetened chocolate is used in some older baking recipes for cakes and brownies. In chocolate terminology, sometimes the term *liquor* or *chocolate liquor* (really ambiguous since it is neither liquid nor does it contain alcohol) is used interchange-ably with *cocoa solids*.

HIGH COCOA SOLID BITTERSWEET CHOCOLATE: The public's taste for more bittersweet chocolate has increased in the course of the past 20 years, and chocolate manufacturers are catering to this taste both by labeling chocolate as to the actual percentage of cocoa solids it contains and by offering a variety of percentages in their lines of chocolate products. Percentages of 70 percent and higher are considered high and can function well in recipes where there is sufficient sweetening to support the chocolate's intensity. Good "all-purpose" chocolates fall into the slightly lower range of bittersweets, from 60 to 70 percent cocoa solids. Chocolates in the 50 to 60 percent range are considered semisweet.

COUVERTURE: A term used to describe chocolate that can be tempered (see Tempering on page 15) and used for making confections, it means "covering" in French and denotes the fact that the chocolate has enough extra cocoa butter added to make it fluid enough to use for dipping. Much of the high-quality chocolate available now is couverture quality, though it isn't labeled as such.

COCOA NIBS: Cocoa nibs, one of the newest additions to the chocolate pantry, are roasted cocoa beans that are husked and coarsely chopped. Their toasted nutlike flavor and crunchy texture add an extra dimension to chocolate desserts.

COCOA POWDER: I use alkalized (Dutch-process) cocoa exclusively. Alkalization neutralizes some of the acidity of the product and I think the flavor is far superior. It also lends a richer color to baked goods. The package will either have a Dutch-sounding name or will say "alkalized" or "Dutch process" on it. There are different levels of alkalization that give slightly different results: The more alkalized the powder, the darker the color.

VARIETAL CHOCOLATE: As is the case with wine and coffee, it is now possible to purchase chocolate according to its varietal, meaning the type of cocoa bean used to make it. You can also find single-origin chocolate that is made from the cocoa beans of just one plantation. Both of these can be excellent, but as always, much depends on the reputability of the brand and the quality of the chocolate they produce. In the Sources, on page 312, I recommend my favorite place to shop for varietal chocolate.

WORKING WITH CHOCOLATE

CHOPPING: Use a sharp serrated knife to shave the chocolate from one end on a cutting board, making ¼-inch (6-mm) pieces. Or use a 4-pronged, pointed, forklike ice pick. Just remember not to use the ice pick on a good cutting board.

MELTING: Cut the chocolate into ¼-inch (6-mm) pieces. Place the chocolate in a glass or stainless-steel bowl. Half-fill with water a saucepan large enough for the bowl to sit in without the water getting inside it. Bring the water to a full boil. Turn off the heat and place the bowl on the pan. Stir occasionally until the chocolate is melted and smooth. For milk and white chocolate, stir often. If over-heated, the sugar and milk solids in milk and white chocolate can form lumps. To micro-wave, cut the chocolate as above and place in a glass bowl. Microwave for 20 seconds and stir, then repeat. It will take 2 or 3 times for the chocolate to begin melting, then once it does it will go quickly. Repeat the 20-second microwaving and stirring until the chocolate is melted. For milk and white chocolate, decrease the time to 15 seconds at a time after the chocolate has started to melt.

TEMPERING: Tempered chocolate has a beautiful finish. To temper 1 pound (450 grams) of chocolate, cut off and reserve a 2-ounce (50-gram) piece, then cut the remaining chocolate into ¼-inch (6-mm) pieces. Place the cut chocolate in a heatproof bowl. Half-fill a medium saucepan with water, bring the water to a boil, then remove the pan from the heat and place the bowl of chocolate on it. Stir the chocolate with a metal spoon until it has melted and is very warm, 115° to 120°F (46° to 49°C). Remove the bowl from the pan and dry the bottom, then set it aside and allow the chocolate to cool to about 90°F (32°C). Add the reserved 2-ounce (50-gram) chunk of chocolate and stir it in to lower the melted chocolate's temperature to the low 80s. While the chocolate is cooling, reheat the water in the pan. When the choco-late has cooled enough, remove the chunk of chocolate. Replace the bowl of melted chocolate over the hot water for a second or two, then remove it. Continue heating briefly over the water until the chocolate tempera-ture reaches 88° to 91°F (31° to 33°C), then use immediately for dipping or decorating. For milk or white chocolate, reheat the chocolate to 84° to 88°F (29° to 31°C).

DAIRY PRODUCTS

Milk and its derivatives—butter, milk, cream, sour cream, yogurt, and cheese—make up these dairy ingredients. Although goats, sheep, and other animals are often sources of dairy foods in other cultures, the dairy industry in the United States is based on cow's milk.

BUTTER: One of the keys to great baking is to use ingredients that are perfectly fresh, but nowhere is this rule more important than when it comes to butter. To test for freshness, unwrap a stick of butter and scratch the surface with the point of a table knife. If the butter is lighter-colored on the inside than on the outside, it has oxidized and become stale. Such butter won't impart anything but a stale flavor to whatever you bake with it.

If you stock up on butter during a sale, store it in the freezer. If you intend to keep butter for more than a month or so, wrap the packages in plastic wrap and then foil to keep them as airtight as possible. I use unsalted butter exclusively in this book.

In the past, butter was usually made with slightly fermented cream, imparting a height-ened flavor to it as well as to the buttermilk, the liquid that separates from the fat when the butter solidifies during churning. Nowadays, cultures are added to butter while it is being churned to approximate a little of that acidity that defines butter's flavor. Many European butters and some American specialty brands are still made with slightly fermented cream and have wonderful flavor. High-fat butters, also called "European butters," have extra fat in them and won't yield the same results as supermarket butter, especially in cookie batters and pastry doughs, which will spread more than they would with standard butter. They work well in cake batters and buttercream, however.

BUTTERMILK: Buttermilk used to be the liquid that was left over after churning butter. Today, however, most American butter is made from sweet cream, so the buttermilk has no acidic flavor. As a result, modern buttermilk is made much the same way yogurt is—by slightly souring milk with bacteria—and becomes a tangy liquid that adds excellent flavor and consistency to baked goods.

CREAM: All cream called for in this book is heavy whipping cream with a fat content of 36 percent—what you'll expect to find in the supermarket. If you have 40 percent cream available, by all means use it; it won't change anything in the recipe.

MILK: For baking, I almost always use whole (full-fat) milk. Milk—which is available in whole, low-fat, and nonfat versions—is amazingly versatile. In addition to serving as an ingredient itself, it is used to make cheese, yogurt, and other dairy products. And while in this country when we say milk we always mean cow's milk, other cultures use goat's and sheep's (ewe's) milk as well.

Milk sold in stores is pasteurized throughout the western world in order to kill bacteria (and to give it a somewhat longer shelf life). In addition to being pasteurized, most milk is homogenized, which is a way of keeping the cream from separating to the top. While this is convenient, it does remove some of the flavor from the milk.

SOUR CREAM: Sour cream used to be made, as its name implies, by letting heavy cream sour naturally. Today, an acidic agent is added to help the process along and the cream is actually half-and-half, not heavy cream. Sour cream cannot be boiled or it will curdle, but otherwise it is easy to use in a cake batter or filling. Unless otherwise indicated, when I call for sour cream I mean the full-fat kind.

SWEETENED CONDENSED MILK: The process of condensing milk was actually invented to preserve milk for long periods before the advent of refrigeration. The milk is heated in a strong vacuum until almost all of the liquid

15

evaporates, leaving a very dense, syrupy substance. It is then sweetened and canned.

THAI COCONUT CREAM: See entry on page 19.

YOGURT: During the last 20 years, yogurt has become big business and many different types are available. For baking, however, you always want plain, unflavored yogurt. Yogurt is available in low-fat, fat-free, and full-fat varieties. If they will work interchangeably in a recipe, I've indicated that. The flavor and consistency of yogurt varies widely by brand, so taste around and pick your favorite, but avoid those with artificial thickeners such as gelatin. The only ingredients should be milk and live cultures. If you can get Greek yogurt, use it—it is infinitely superior.

Some recipes call for draining yogurt to thicken it. To do this, place a coffee filter (or a piece of cheesecloth) inside a strainer and set the strainer over a bowl. Then simply dump the yogurt into the coffee filter, set the whole thing in the refrigerator, and let some of the liquid drain off overnight. Drained yogurt has a consistency similar to cream cheese.

EGGS

Probably the most versatile of a baker's ingredients, eggs are primary in the production of cakes, custards, buttercreams, and pastries such as *pâte à choux*. Whole or separated, eggs perform many tasks: they bind together other ingredients such as flour, sugar, and butter in a cake; they act as leaveners, either on their own or in combination with leaveners such as baking powder; they enrich foods, rendering them moist with a golden color; they thicken mixtures such as custards and buttercreams; they emulsify liquids, holding fats in suspension so that ingredients hold together rather than separate; and they glaze pastries and doughs.

The egg white, or albumen, makes up about $\frac{2}{3}$ of the total weight of the egg, providing over $\frac{1}{2}$ the total protein. (When whipped, egg whites increase in volume 6 to 8 times.) The yolk comprises the remaining $\frac{1}{3}$ and all the fat and less than $\frac{1}{2}$ the protein.

Eggs are categorized by grade and size. Grade is based on the inner and outer quality of the egg, while size is determined by the average weight per dozen eggs. There is no difference in quality or nutrition between brown and white eggs, or between eggs with deep golden or pale yellow yolks. All my recipes are based on eggs graded U.S. large: 24 ounces (675 grams) per dozen. Remember that within the dozen there might be slight variations, and that individual eggs may differ slightly from each other in size. When an exact amount of egg (or white or yolk) is crucial to a recipe, the amount is given in terms of volume, as in "1 cup whole eggs (about 5 large eggs)" or "⅔ cup egg whites (about 5 large egg whites)." Some recipes, notably those for some meringues, call for egg whites that are just heated, but not completely cooked. If you are concerned about this, substitute pasteurized egg whites, now available in supermarkets.

When selecting whole eggs, choose those that have clean, uncracked shells. Store eggs large end up in their cartons in the refrigerator for maximum keeping quality and use them before the expiration date on the package. Because eggs absorb odors, they should be kept away from strong-flavored foods. Egg whites can be stored covered in the refrigerator up to 10 days. Yolks should be carefully covered with a sprinkling of water with plastic wrap pressed directly against their surface in a covered container before being refrigerated up to 2 days. No matter how fresh your eggs are, it's always wise to crack them one at a time into a small cup before adding them to the full amount in a larger bowl. Otherwise, if you get one bad egg (and if you've never had the opportunity to smell a rotten egg, don't worry—you'll know) you'll ruin the whole mixture, waste the other eggs, and be forced to start over again .

FLAVORINGS & EXTRACTS: Understanding the nature of flavorings makes it possible to create delicate desserts with subtle and delicious tastes. Sometimes flavorings dominate a preparation, as in a chocolate buttercream or lemon mousse. In other cases, they accentuate the dominant flavor of a preparation, deepening it or adding contrast.

BALSAMIC VINEGAR: True artisanal balsamic vinegar costs upward of $100 for a tiny bottle and is doled out carefully with an eyedropper. Poor-quality imitation balsamic is usually colored and flavored, but not aged at all. I aim for the middle ground and purchase commercial balsamic vinegar from Modena in Emilia Romagna, the home of balsamic vinegar. The price ranges from $20 to $35 for a bottle, and the flavor is still quite good, if not as exalted as the taste of the truly pricy and hard-to-find artisanal varieties. I also like Forum vinegar from Spain, which has a complex flavor and consistency, similar to mid-range balsamic vinegar.

INSTANT ESPRESSO POWDER: Espresso powder is intended to be dissolved in hot water in order to make instant espresso. While it makes terrible coffee, it can be very useful as a flavoring agent that provides a jolt of coffee flavor. Instant espresso tastes best when diluted with brewed coffee, so save some leftover coffee in a jar in the refrigerator for up to a day if you know you are preparing something that calls for instant espresso.

EXTRACTS: Essential oils are made by distilling a combination of aromatic substances and water and then blended with ethyl alcohol to make flavoring extracts. Although pure extracts may seem expensive, their flavor is so concentrated that only a small amount is needed. Because alcohol evaporates, extracts should be bought in small, tightly capped bottles and stored in a cool, dry place.

VANILLA EXTRACT: One of the most valued and widely used flavorings, vanilla deserves a special mention. It is used as a primary flavoring or as a flavor enhancer to other ingredients, such as chocolate or coffee. Although vanilla is native to the Americas, most of the vanilla sold today comes from Madagascar. Avoid vanilla/vanillin blends and imitation vanilla. Purchase vanilla in small quantities and store for up to a year.

FLAVORING OILS: Flavoring oils—the most common are lemon and orange oils, mint oils, and anise oil—offer an even more intense flavor than extracts. They are used in small amounts, only a few drops at a time. Any more would be overwhelming.

MUSTARD: Mustard is a condiment made from mustard seeds and vinegar. There are a number of mustards available. I like the brown Dijon type and also tarragon mustard, which are a far cry from the bright yellow "hot-dog mustard." Store in the refrigerator once opened; it will keep almost indefinitely.

ORANGE FLOWER WATER: This distillation made with the blossoms of a variety of bitter orange has a light, perfume-like (in fact, orange flower water is used in perfumery) scent that blends well with delicate pastries and syrups.

VANILLA BEANS: These long, coarse-skinned pods are dark in color and have a strong vanilla scent. Typically, I add vanilla beans in the form of whole or split beans or their scrapings. The essence can also be released by steeping a bean in a hot liquid such as milk or cream for 10 to 20 minutes. Beans that have been used to flavor a hot liquid can be rinsed, wiped dry, and reused a couple of times.

....

FLOURS, THICKENERS, GRAINS, & GRAIN FLAKES

These starchy substances are the cornerstones of baking.

FLOURS: Each wheat berry is composed of three parts: the starchy endosperm, from which white flour is made; the outer covering, or bran; and the oily germ. To produce flour, the berries are milled and sifted to remove the bran and germ. Flour is milled from wheat that may be hard or soft-kerneled. Hard wheat has a higher proportion of the proteins that will eventually form strong gluten strands in dough when the flour made from it is moistened and mixed. For this reason, flours made from hard wheat are referred to as strong flours. Soft wheat has a lower percentage of gluten-forming proteins and is used to make weak flour. Weak flour also forms gluten when moistened and mixed, though the gluten it forms is weak and tender. Bread flour is a strong flour and cake flour a weak one. All-purpose flour falls right between the two.

A word on gluten: Whenever flour is moistened and even gently stirred, gluten develops. Proteins in the flour change shape (denature) and form elastic strands of gluten. It's easiest to see in a bread dough, but gluten develops even if you stir a spoonful of flour into a glass of water—the difference lies in the fact that the bread dough gluten is strong and the glass of water gluten is very weak. Different doughs call for specific strengths of gluten and work successfully when the gluten is at just the correct strength.

ALL-PURPOSE FLOUR: All-purpose flour (standard white flour) is a mixture of strong and weak flours and, as its name implies, can be used for everything. It appears, in large or small amounts, in almost every recipe in this book. All-purpose flour has a $10\frac{1}{2}$ to $11\frac{1}{2}$ percent protein content that makes it suitable for almost all uses, as the name implies. Stored at room temperature in an airtight container, it will keep for one year or longer (I like to transfer it from the bag to a large glass container when I get it home from the store).

BLEACHED ALL-PURPOSE FLOUR: Bleached flour is whiter in color and slightly lower in protein content than unbleached flour. In some recipes you must use bleached flour in order to achieve the correct soft texture. Recipes that require bleached flour say so. Unbleached flour lightens in color naturally as carotenoid pigments in the flour oxidize during aging. Bleached flour is treated with chlorine gas to lighten its color quickly.

BREAD FLOUR: Bread flour is high in protein, which means that it results in bread doughs with a strong gluten, lending chewiness and resistance, exactly the qualities you would *not* want in a cake or pastry. Bread flour also usually incorporates some barley flour or malt, which provides food for yeast. I call for unbleached all-purpose flour in all of my bread recipes.

CAKE FLOUR: This flour has a very low protein content and a high starch content, making it useful when you are baking a cake with a delicate, tender crumb resulting from a weak gluten. Cake flour is also acidified to help batters containing it to set quickly, thus helping to avoid cakes falling during baking.

CORNMEAL: Dried corn kernels are ground to make cornmeal, sometimes used in doughs and fillings for its distinctive flavor and pleasantly gritty texture. Look for stone-ground cornmeal, which has more flavor because it hasn't had the germ removed. Store cornmeal in the refrigerator.

RYE FLOUR: Rye is a hearty grain that grows in cold weather, which explains why rye bread is more commonly found in northern European cultures. However, a bread dough made purely of rye flour would have virtually no gluten developed, so more commonly rye and white flours are combined. Pumpernickel flour is a dark and coarsely ground rye flour used to make pumpernickel bread.

SELF-RISING FLOUR: Self-rising flour is simply (usually bleached) white flour with baking powder and salt added to it. I prefer not to use self-rising flour, both because adding my own salt and baking powder to flour gives me more control and because baking powder tends to eventually lose its potency, so self-rising flour cannot be stored for as long as all-purpose flour.

SEMOLINA FLOUR: Semolina flour is made from hard durum wheat ground to a fine but not powdery state. It is most commonly used to make dry, factory-made pasta, such as spaghetti. It can be a flavorful (and colorful—it has a lovely golden hue) addition to a bread dough, as well as to some puddings and desserts. It has a pleasantly chewy texture and a delicious wheaty flavor.

WHOLE WHEAT FLOUR: White flour has been refined, which means the bran and wheat germ have been sifted out of it after the wheat was cracked, just before it was ground. Whole wheat flour contains both the bran and the germ, which means it is more nutritious, but also darker in color and heavier in texture. Very few items, including whole wheat bread, consist of 100 percent whole wheat flour. An all whole wheat loaf has a heavy, cakey texture we usually don't associate with good bread. The part whole-grain breads in this book utilize those grains for their flavor and texture. Once they are mixed with a significant portion of white flour the resulting bread does offer the same nutritional benefits of a 100 percent whole-grain bread.

Always store whole wheat flour in the refrigerator, where it will keep for six months or longer. (If you have doubts, taste a tiny amount of raw flour to test for bitterness or off flavors.) Do not confuse whole wheat flour with whole wheat pastry flour, which sits at a kind of halfway point between white flour and whole wheat flour.

THICKENERS: Thickeners, as the name implies, are added to liquids to make them gel slightly—a classic example of a preparation that is thickened is the filling for a fruit pie, so that the filling won't simply leak out of the crust. Thickeners are generally bland and are used in small amounts so that they are not particularly noticeable.

CORNSTARCH: A pure starch with negligible protein content, cornstarch is the result of a long milling and purifying process. Two properties make it ideal for use in some cake batters: Its fine grain produces a feathery crumb, and its high absorption power in very liquid batters sets them more efficiently and ensures better air retention and lightness.

CRUMBS: The idea of using crumbs in baking originated for economic reasons: Saving trimmings and unusable cakes and loaves is a tradition still observed today by many bakeries. Dry bread and cake crumbs are often used to replace flour or other starches as a binder in batters. You can buy fine dry bread crumbs in the supermarket; just be sure they are unflavored. Fresh bread crumbs (as opposed to dry) are made by removing the crusts from fresh bread, dicing the bread into manageable pieces, then reducing it to crumbs by pulsing it in the food processor. Both types may be stored in the refrigerator up to one week, or frozen up to one month.

GELATIN: A substance commercially derived from pigskin, gelatin is used to set liquids. Once the gelatin is rehydrated, heated, melted, and dispersed in a liquid, that liquid will become semisolid when cooled. Gelatin is available in both granulated and leaf forms. Granulated gelatin is packaged in bulk and in the more familiar envelopes. Leaf gelatin is sold in bulk by weight and in smaller packages of several leaves. I recommend granulated gelatin only. One envelope of granulated gelatin contains 1/4 ounce (7 grams) or approximately 2 1/2 teaspoons.

GRAINS AND GRAIN FLAKES: Rolled oats are the most familiar grain flakes, but health-food stores stock flakes made from all types of grains, including barley and wheat.

MUESLI CEREAL: Muesli (the word is Swiss German) is similar to granola, except that the rolled oats and other grain flakes in it are not toasted. Muesli is available in health-food stores and often in the cereal aisle of general

grocery stores. When purchasing Muesli cereal to use in a recipe, look for Familia brand, the only one made with the approval of the heirs of Dr. Bircher-Benner, the inventor of Muesli.

ROLLED OATS: Sometimes labeled "old-fashioned oatmeal" or "oat flakes," rolled oats are made by steaming the oat grains, then passing them between rollers. Oat flakes should be stored in the refrigerator. When you are buying rolled oats, make sure you do not mistakenly pick up steel-cut oats or instant oatmeal.

WHEAT BERRIES: The outer hull has been removed from grains of wheat to make hulled wheat berries. They are off white in color and cook fairly quickly.

....

LIQUORS & LIQUEURS: This is an area where false economy can really influence the flavor of what you are preparing. If a large bottle of good imported rum is expensive, buy a smaller bottle rather than a lesser brand. This is true whether you are purchasing liquors or liqueurs. The latter, also called cordials, are alcoholic beverages that combine a spirit—such as brandy or grain alcohol—with flavorings and sugar syrup. Liqueurs are sweet and sometimes thick on the palate as a result of their high sugar content. Store in a cool, dark cupboard almost indefinitely—some liquid may evaporate, but the flavor will not deteriorate.

Fruit brandies or *eaux-de-vie*, such as Kirsch (cherry brandy), Framboise (raspberry brandy), and Poire William (pear brandy), are distilled from a mash of fermented fruit and are colorless because they have not been aged in wooden casks as Cognac, whisky, and dark rum have been. *Eaux-de-vie* can add a distinctive perfume to all sorts of dessert preparations, but must be used with caution because the high alcohol content can impart a bitter flavor if too much was used.

NUTS & SEEDS: In general, nut meats with the skin still on are referred to as "natural" or "unblanched," and those with the skin removed are referred to as "blanched" or "skinless." Store nuts and seeds in plastic bags in the freezer.

NUTS: Nuts derive most of their flavor from the oils they contain. These oils, like other fats, have a tendency to become rancid and render the nuts stale. Buying nuts in their shells usually means they will be fresh. (But if they make a noise when you shake them, they are apt to be stale.) Good-quality shelled nuts, especially those in vacuum-packed containers, are perfectly suitable for baking. If you are buying nuts from bins, be sure to frequent a store with high turnover.

For storage of a month or less, nuts should be kept in airtight containers in a cool, dry spot away from direct light. Freezing is recommended for long-term storage, between one and six months.

To chop nuts into coarse pieces, place them on a jelly-roll pan and press down on them with the bottom of a small saucepan, rocking it back and forth. If you need the nuts finely chopped, use a knife after crushing them first. To be finely ground, nuts must be at room temperature. Nuts cold from the freezer will only reduce to damp cubes, and nuts that have just been toasted and not cooled will immediately turn to nut butter. Use rapid pulses in the food processor to grind nuts, stopping and scraping the inside bottom of the bowl occasionally with the edge of a metal spatula to keep the ground nuts from sticking. Do not grind or finely chop nuts until just before using.

To blanch (remove the skin from) almonds and pistachios, place the nuts in a saucepan and cover them with 2 inches (5 cm) of cold water. Place over medium heat and bring to a full rolling boil. Drain immediately and pour the nuts onto a towel. Fold the towel over the nuts (be careful, they're hot) and rub to loosen the skins. Then separate the nuts from the skins. You'll need to pop the almonds out of their skins. Pistachios might require a little extra rubbing to remove every trace of skin. Place the nuts in a small roasting pan and bake them at 325°F (160°C) for 5 minutes, then cool them on the pan to evaporate the excess moisture they absorbed in the water.

To blanch hazelnuts, place the nuts in a small roasting pan and bake them at 325°F (160°C) for about 15 minutes, or until they are lightly toasted and the skins are loose. Test one by removing it from the pan and rubbing it in a towel. If the skin flakes away easily, the nuts are ready. Pour all the nuts onto a towel and rub vigorously to remove the skins. If you get ⅔ of the skin off the hazelnuts, consider the blanching to be very successful. Never skin hazelnuts by boiling them in baking soda.

To toast nuts, place them in a small roasting pan and bake at 325°F (160°C) for about 15 minutes, stirring 3 or 4 times, until they are golden. Immediately pour the nuts from the pan onto a cold pan or directly onto the work surface to cool.

ALMONDS: Oval-shaped almonds come in both sweet and bitter varieties. The sweet almond is found at the retail level and used in baking and confections. The bitter almond is primarily used in making almond extract and cannot be eaten out of hand due to its high level of toxic prussic acid. Virtually all the almonds in American grocery stores are from California. They are readily available year-round, fresh and packaged. They are sold in or out of the shell; blanched (skinned) or unblanched (sometimes labeled "natural"); halved, sliced, slivered; toasted, buttered, or salted. Almonds ground for light-colored batters or doughs should be blanched first.

ALMOND PASTE: Almond paste is available in 7-pound (3.2kg) cans from wholesalers or in 8-ounce (225-gram) cans in retail stores. If you cannot find almond paste, substitute 1 cup whole blanched almonds and ½ cup sugar finely ground in the food processor for 8 ounces (225 grams) almond paste. There is, however, no substitute for canned almond paste when making marzipan. If you have an opportunity to purchase a large quantity of almond paste, divide it into 8-ounce (225-gram) pieces, double wrap in plastic, and freeze for up to one year. Thaw before using.

CHESTNUTS: Chestnuts are available canned, sweetened or unsweetened, whole or puréed; dried (soak in water for several hours or overnight before using); or pulverized into flour. Fresh chestnuts are available in their shells from mid-September to March. When choosing fresh, look for hard, shiny brown shells free of scars and soft spots. Store loosely covered in the refrigerator for up to 3 weeks.

COCONUT: Fresh coconuts are generally sold in the shell, stripped of its fibrous husk. Choose coconuts that are heavy for their size. The shell should be devoid of wet "eyes" and should sound full of liquid when shaken or gently tapped. An unshelled coconut will keep at room temperature for several months.

THAI COCONUT CREAM: Richer than coconut milk, coconut cream is sold canned and sometimes frozen in Asian groceries and gourmet specialty stores. Do not confuse it with sweetened canned "cream of coconut," which is used to make tropical cocktails. Coconut cream is the thick liquid that floats to the top after a freshly grated coconut is first moistened with water; coconut milk is skimmed from the second moistening of the coconut.

UNSWEETENED COCONUT MEAT: This is the closest thing to fresh coconut meat and is sold in vacuum-packed cans. The meat is usually grated or shredded, but you will also find toasted coconut flakes, which make a nice garnish for coconut desserts. Be sure to look for unsweetened coconut rather than the shredded or flaked sweetened coconut.

HAZELNUTS: Hazelnuts (also known as filberts) are often toasted to bring out their pro-

19

nounced flavor and aroma. They have less oil than almonds and pecans, and are therefore somewhat harder. Ground hazelnuts are mixed with caramelized sugar to form praline paste. It is unnecessary to blanch hazelnuts if they will be used ground, unless a light-colored dough or batter is desired. Hazelnuts for chopping should be blanched first; the skin becomes brittle and unappetizing when left in bigger pieces.

MACADAMIAS: Rich in oil, macadamias are available whole and in pieces. For baking, look for unsalted macadamia nuts. The most expensive of these are the whole, fully processed nuts. Macadamia pieces, if available, are less expensive and are adequate for baking. If you can only find salted macadamias, rinse them in a strainer under hot running water and let them dry, or dry them for a few minutes in a moderate oven and cool them before using.

NUT BUTTERS: The most common nut butter on American supermarket shelves is, of course, peanut butter, but almond, cashew, and other nut butters are also available. For cooking and baking, I much prefer the natural nut butters, which consist only of ground nuts. The only inconvenient aspect of natural butters is that the naturally occurring oil in the nuts tends to separate and rise to the top of the jar. Simply stir the oil back down into the nut butter before proceeding with a recipe. Store natural nut butters in the refrigerator for up to six months.

PECANS: Fresh pecans are in season from September to November. Of the processed forms, whole halves are the most expensive but also the most appropriate for decorative purposes. Pieces are adequate for many uses, but do not remain fresh as long as the larger halves or unshelled nuts. Pecans bought fresh or packaged in the shell should be free of cracks and scars and should be tested to see if they rattle loosely in their shells (a sign of age and staleness).

PINE NUTS: The term *pine nut* refers to the edible seeds from certain pine-tree cones in many parts of the world. They are widely available, usually packaged with their shell and inner skin removed. They are also sold under their Italian name, *pignoli.*

PISTACHIOS: Pistachios are commonly used in Middle Eastern pastries and desserts. In European baking, they are often used as a garnish because of their subtle green color, although their cherry-like flavor is also valued. The red coloring sometimes added to pistachios is purely decorative and has nothing to do with the taste of the nut meat itself. Undyed pistachios, often labeled "natural," are less processed, better for culinary purposes, and less expensive. Pistachios keep best unshelled.

WALNUTS: Walnuts are available in two varieties: strong-flavored black walnuts and the milder English walnuts, which are the ones I use in baking. A walnut shell contains a two-lobed nut meat that does not need blanching. Shelled walnuts are usually sold in the form of whole halves or in pieces. The pieces are less expensive but do not keep as well as whole halves or unshelled nuts.

POPPY SEEDS: Round black poppy seeds are tiny—there are about 900,000 of them in a pound. Poppy seeds appear in many pastries and cakes, especially those from Central and Eastern Europe. Poppy seeds used in this book are whole, but the fillings made from them require they be ground first.

PUMPKINSEEDS: Pale green pumpkinseeds are integral to Mexican cooking and may be known by their Spanish name, "pepitas." They are sold either roasted or raw. For baking, always purchase hulled seeds, as removing each one from its shell would be extremely tedious work.

SESAME SEEDS: Sesame seeds add a subtle nutty flavor to the crusts of some breads and cookies. Use white sesame seeds for this purpose.

SUNFLOWER SEEDS: Shelled sunflower seeds are sold both raw and roasted and are a good addition to whole-grain bread.

....

OILS: Oils are used in baked items in place of or in addition to butter, and frequently they are used to coat pans so that a cake or tart will lift out easily once it is baked.

OLIVE OIL: Olive oil comes in three categories: extra virgin, virgin, and pure (sometimes now simply labeled "olive oil"). For dressing a salad or drizzling on vegetables, you want extra virgin olive oil, but in baking its distinctive flavor isn't desired, and since its flavor will be muted anyway, its higher price isn't warranted. I use pure olive oil for baking. Look for cold-pressed oils and store at a cool room temperature.

VEGETABLE OIL: My preferred vegetable oil for baking and cooking is canola oil (made from rapeseeds). It has a mild flavor that doesn't overshadow the main ingredients. Store in the refrigerator to guard against rancidity.

VEGETABLE COOKING SPRAY: Occasionally I call for greasing a pan with vegetable cooking spray, which is simply vegetable oil in a spray can.

SALT: I usually use fine sea salt for both baking and salting the food I am cooking. When a coarse salt is needed, I use the kosher salt available in the supermarket. Occasionally, especially when I receive it as a gift, I use French *fleur de sel*, a high-quality, coarse-textured, natural, unadulterated sea salt. It's best for sprinkling on things when you want the crunch of a fine-tasting salt crystal.

....

SPICES & HERBS: In the days before refrigeration, herbs and spices were needed to mask the flavor of food past its prime. Today, herbs and spices are valued for the flavor nuances they provide. Store all dried herbs

and spices in a cool, dark place, away from heat. The flavor in herbs and spices comes from volatile oils that dissipate over time, taking the flavor with them. If you know you have had spices or dried herbs around for more than a year, it's probably time to discard them.

SPICES: Spices, from tropical areas, are the seeds, bark, nuts, and roots of certain plants. Most desserts use spices rather than herbs for flavoring. Although whole spices last longer than ground spices, most pastry making relies on the ground version. For best results, buy small quantities of ground spices.

BLACK PEPPER: Black pepper, ground from black peppercorns, is used in most savory dishes. You may want to keep a dedicated pepper grinder in your kitchen to freshly grind black pepper as it is so commonly used.

CINNAMON: Cinnamon is tree bark, available either in stick form or already ground. Until recently, cinnamon used to be just cinnamon, but today there are many varieties available, and they are very distinct from each other in flavor. Cinnamon breaks down into two categories: Cassia cinnamon and Ceylon (Sri Lanka) cinnamon. Ceylon varieties are much less sweet, with a hint of citrus, and are often used in Mexican and English baked goods. Cassia cinnamon, more commonly used in North America, is also native to southeast Asia and includes Saigon cinnamon and Chinese varieties, as well as mellow Korintje cinnamon from Sumatra. Saigon cinnamon is the strongest flavored of these—use it only when an assertive cinnamon flavor is needed. This cinnamon, as its name implies, is produced solely in Vietnam, so it was not available in the United States for close to 20 years due to trade restrictions implemented after the Vietnam War. Vietnam began exporting it to the United States again in the early 21st century.

GINGER: Knobby roots of fresh ginger are common ingredients in Asian cuisines. When fresh ginger is called for in a recipe, break off

a knob from the "hand," as the gnarled tuber is called, and peel it with a small, sharp paring knife. Use a grater with medium, diagonally set holes to grate the ginger. A fine-holed grater will only produce juice and no pulp. Failing all else, coarsely dice peeled ginger and chop it finely on a cutting board with a stainless-steel chef's knife. Purchase ground ginger (which is dried before it is ground) in small amounts. Its sharp flavor adds a welcome edge to many sweet baked items. See Candied Fruit on page 159 for information on crystallized ginger.

NUTMEG: Nutmeg is not a nut, but a seed. You can purchase whole nutmeg and grate a little bit as needed, which is preferable to buying ground nutmeg. The spice mace is made by grinding the membrane that surrounds the nutmeg and it has a milder flavor.

TURMERIC: Turmeric is a root similar to ginger, but with a very vivid yellow-orange color. Turmeric gives prepared mustard its yellow color. It is used in small amounts, as too much of it can impart a bitter flavor.

HERBS: Herbs are the leaves, and sometimes the stems, of plants that grow in temperate climates. Whenever possible I like to use fresh, as opposed to dried, herbs. Fresh herbs have become much more available, even in winter in the supermarket, in the past few years. If you use dried herbs, make sure they have a lively fragrance when you bruise some between your thumb and index finger.

Thoroughly rinse and dry herbs before chopping. Separate leaves from stems and gather the leaves into a bundle on a cutting board, holding them together with one hand. Cut across one end with a sharp knife, continuing to cut through the bundle every ⅛ inch (3 mm). Chop through the whole pile of fragments to make them finer.

BASIL: Basil is a key herb in Italian cooking. It has a distinctive anise-like flavor and is a tender annual, so it grows only during warm

weather. It is highly perishable once picked. Store basil in a plastic bag in the refrigerator, but don't expect it to last more than a day or two at the most. Never cut basil with a knife or it will blacken and lose its flavor. Tear basil leaves into ½-inch (1-cm) pieces.

CARAWAY SEEDS: Caraway seeds are the seeds of an herb plant that is related to parsley. Ground caraway imparts the distinctive flavor we associate with rye bread.

CILANTRO: Coriander leaves, or cilantro, appears in Asian and Latin American dishes. Cilantro looks similar to parsley, but it has a different taste. Some people have a genetic "cilantro sensitivity" that makes them unable to digest the herb; in extreme cases it may nauseate even them.

FENNEL SEEDS: Fennel seeds are available whole or ground and are used both in desserts (such as Italian cookies, where they lend a licorice-like taste) and in savory preparations.

PARSLEY: Parsley is the closest thing to an all-purpose herb—it is used in many countries around the world, and its flavor is refreshing yet mild enough to complement almost anything. I prefer flat-leaf parsley (sometimes called "Italian parsley") over the curly variety for its stronger flavor. Rinse and dry parsley carefully before using to remove any grit.

ROSEMARY: Rosemary has a long history, stretching back to ancient Rome, as a medicinal herb, but today it is used more for cooking. Rosemary has long thin leaves that resemble pine needles, and it also has a faintly piney taste and smell. It may be used fresh or dried. Make sure any dried rosemary you purchase is vividly fragrant. Rosemary particularly complements savory baked goods containing olive oil and/or garlic.

TARRAGON: Most commonly used in French cooking, tarragon has long, thin leaves and an anise-like flavor. It is one of the herbs in the French mixture known as *fines herbes*.

SWEETENERS: Sucrose, or granulated sugar, is a disaccharide, or double sugar, that enables its molecules to form crystals. Liquid sugars, such as glucose and corn syrup, are monosaccharides, simple or single sugars. I never use artificial sweeteners, which do not provide the same structure, moisture, and flavor that real sugar does.

During sugar production, sugarcane is ground, then pressed to release its juice. This liquid is heated and spun in a centrifuge to produce sugar and molasses. The sugar is redissolved and purified with granular carbon, which is then filtered out along with the impurities it traps. Once purified, the sugar is processed to form crystals. The crystals are dried to remove any remaining moisture. Finally, the sugar is passed through a succession of sieves to separate the coarse from fine crystals. Sugar is hygroscopic, that is, it absorbs water in the air. Therefore, it should be stored as airtight as possible. It will last indefinitely if properly stored.

BROWN SUGAR: Brown sugar is made from still-liquid refined sugar blended with molasses before crystallization. The molasses coating remains on the crystals, providing moisture and flavor. The degree of molasses added determines whether the sugar is light brown or dark brown. Brown sugar has a tendency to collect air between its crystals, so pack it firmly for accurate measuring. Also, brown sugar can dry out and harden into a block if left uncovered. Once opened, store it tightly covered, preferably in a plastic bag, in the refrigerator. If it hardens, you can soften it in a few seconds in the microwave.

CONFECTIONERS' SUGAR: Also known as "powdered" sugar or "10X" sugar (because it is approximately ten times finer than granulated sugar), confectioners' sugar is made from granulated sugar that has been ground to a powder. In the United States, it incorporates a small amount of cornstarch to prevent caking. For this reason you cannot use confectioners' sugar in any kind of cooked

sugar solution—the cornstarch may burn. For the same reason, it should never be used in whipped cream, where it can impart a chalky flavor from the starch. It is often dusted on baked products as decoration. Sift after measuring it to eliminate lumps.

CORN SYRUP: After syrup is extracted from corn, it is treated with enzymes to produce corn syrup. Light corn syrup is clarified and milder in flavor than darker corn syrup, which contains a proportion of molasses for color and flavor. Corn syrup is sometimes used as a glaze, producing a transparent, varnish-like sheen. It is also added to sugar syrups that will be cooked to temperatures beyond the boiling point—as in certain icings and confections—to control crystallization. However, when mixtures of corn syrup and sugar are heated past boiling point, stirring must be kept to a minimum; excess agitation may nullify the effect of the corn syrup and cause crystallization to occur after all.

GRANULATED SUGAR: All recipes in this book use granulated sugar—regular white sugar—unless otherwise specified. Besides adding sweetness to baked products, granulated sugar provides structure, helps to retain moisture, and contributes tenderness. It also aids in crust color and formation because it caramelizes during baking. One cup of granulated sugar, scooped and leveled, weighs 7½ ounces (212 grams).

Granulated sugar is added gradually to most preparations, especially egg mixtures. Unbeaten egg yolks to which sugar is quickly added may lump and "burn," a phenomenon in which sugar absorbs so much of the yolk liquid on initial contact that the remaining yolk hardens, preventing the sugar from dissolving completely. Also, when you whip egg whites with sugar, a large quantity of sugar falling on the egg whites at one time can force air out of them. Granulated sugar should be stored as airtight as possible, and, if stored properly, will last almost indefinitely.

HONEY: Produced by certain bee species for food, honey is derived from the nectar of flowers, as well as from the fluids of other non-flowering plants. The flavor of honey is influenced by the predominant plant, such as orange blossom, lavender, clover, or pine, tapped by the bees. Once extracted from the comb, honey is heated, refined, and strained. Honey is best used in recipes where its distinctive flavor will enhance, rather than overpower, a baked product. In addition to flavor and sweetness, honey is valued for its ability to retain moisture, thus extending the freshness of baked goods. Store honey in an airtight container in a cool place to minimize crystallization, which makes it prone to fermentation and spoilage. If your cupboards are very warm or if the honey will be stored for a long time, keep it refrigerated. Liquefy both crystallized and refrigerated honey each time you use it by heating the jar of honey in a pan of hot water.

MAPLE SYRUP: Maple syrup is the concentrated sap of the sugar maple tree. It is made by boiling down the sap to as little as $\frac{1}{40}$ of its original volume and skimming off the impurities. The resulting amber-to-brown syrup is principally used to impart its unique flavor to baked goods. When purchasing maple syrup, select pure syrup as opposed to "maple-flavored syrup." Maple syrup is classified as AA, A, or B, but, strangely, the AA and A grade syrups, which are the most expensive, have less flavor than the darker B grade that I prefer for baking. Once opened, store maple syrup in a nonmetallic container in the refrigerator.

MOLASSES: I use unsulfured molasses, which tends to be milder in flavor than the other type available, which is usually marked "robust flavor." However, most recipes that call for molasses use so little that I doubt it would make a difference if you substituted one for the other.

23

Equipment

General baking equipment follows, as well as specifics on items needed to prepare the recipes in this book. As with any other type of hard goods, keep in mind when purchasing baking equipment that a quality product is often not the cheapest available in its category. The best quality equipment, whether a rolling pin or a stand mixer, lasts a lifetime and over time is an economical choice, since such items won't need replacement.

26 BAKING PANS: It's important to have the correct size baking pans for a recipe, since a smaller pan might not hold all the batter to be baked and a larger one would spread the batter too thin. I try to limit the sizes I use for my recipes so that you can have the correct pans without going to great expense.

BAKING MOLDS: Baking molds are decoratively shaped bakeware, usually metal. They include everything from Bundt pans to pans in the shape of everything from buildings to cartoon characters. Kaiser and Nordicware are two well-known manufacturers of a wide variety of baking molds.

CAKE OR LAYER PANS: These are round pans usually 2 inches (5 cm) deep most commonly used for baking cake layers. I call for 8-inch (20-cm), 9-inch (23-cm), and 10-inch (25-cm) diameter pans in this book.

COOKIE SHEETS: A cookie sheet is useful for more than just baking cookies. Rolls, free-form pastries and pies, and even some individual pastries may be baked on them. They are also useful for holding pieces of dough or whole cakes in the refrigerator. Sheets with three open ends can also be used as spatulas, moving large pieces of dough which may have stuck to the work surface. Open-ended pans are the real cookie sheets, while the ones with sides are called jelly-roll pans (see at right).

Insulated cookie sheets are worthwhile if your oven gives strong bottom heat and has a tendency to burn things on the bottom. Use them only in the bottom of the oven, though. You can produce the same effect by stacking two uninsulated cookie sheets together for baking in the bottom of the oven.

FLEXIPANS: Flexipans are flexible fiberglass and silicone bakeware that are absolutely non-stick, although they do need to be buttered or oiled. While expensive, they are also long lasting. Because flexipans are flexible, they need to be placed on a cookie sheet or other flat pan before filling and baking.

GUGELHUPF PAN: A Gugelhupf pan is a fluted tube pan with an 8- to 10-cup capacity used to make a Gugelhupf cake (Viennese coffee cake). You can substitute a tube or Bundt pan, although the cake might not be as tall as it would be in a Gugelhupf pan.

JELLY-ROLL PANS: Also called "sheet pans," these are similar to cookie sheets but have one raised edge. They come in 10 x 15-inch (25 x 28-cm) or 12 x 18-inch (30 x 45-cm) sizes. The latter are "half-sheet" pans and are available at restaurant supply stores in heavy-gauge aluminum that is less likely to warp in the oven.

LOAF PANS: I use 9 x 5 x 3-inch (23 x 13 x 7-cm) and 8½ x 4 ½ x 2¾-inch (21 x 11 x 7-cm) loaf pans for the recipes in this book. These are the most common sizes, although you may see others called for in other books. A loaf pan is just what it sounds like: a rectangular pan used to bake a loaf of bread. Many quick breads are baked in loaf pans. For the most part, metric loaf pan sizes go by length only, since European manufacturers tend to limit the number of sizes they make.

MUFFIN TINS: I use 12-cavity muffin pans and 24-cavity mini-muffin pans. These also make good substitutes for individual tart and tartlet pans in a pinch. Remember, if you ever make a recipe for, say, 10 muffins in a 12-cavity pan, you should fill the empty cavities with a small amount of water to keep them from burning.

PANIBOIS: Panibois are wooden bakeware—mostly basket-like rectangular or loaf pans—made of thin poplar wood lined with silicon, and they come with a paper liner as well. The glue used to seal the corners is resistant to even very high heat. As disposable bakeware goes, panibois look a lot prettier than aluminum foil pans, and they're a particularly nice way to package a gift.

PIE PANS: I always use a 9-inch (23-cm) Pyrex pie plate or "pan" with gently sloping sides. The glass makes it easier to see the degree of doneness on the bottom crust, and the glass heats better than metal, ensuring a well-baked bottom crust.

PIZZA PAN: Used to make pizzas (and in this book, at least one semi-free-form tart), pizza pans are round, flat metal pans, usually 12 to 14 inches (30 to 35 cm) in diameter.

RAMEKINS: Porcelain ramekins are available in various sizes and, in all the recipes in this

book, may be substituted with disposable foil cups. I find the 4-ounce (100-gram) size the most useful for individual desserts.

RECTANGULAR BAKING PANS: A 9 x 13 x 2-inch (23 x 33 x 5-cm) pan is useful for many different recipes, in this book and elsewhere. A metal one can double as a roasting pan. I like glass "pans," too, for chilling pastry cream or other fillings I don't want to come into contact with metal. A rectangular glass dish is also a good pan for deep-dish pies.

ROASTING PAN: A roasting pan is useful for toasting nuts, as the higher sides make it easier to stir the nuts without spilling them into the oven.

SPRINGFORM PANS: A springform pan consists of two parts: a bottom and a side rim with a clamp that fits into a groove in the bottom. I prefer the newer design from Kaiser, which has a completely flat bottom. They make it easy to slide your cake or pastry off the pan onto a platter. For recipes in this book I use a 9-inch (23-cm) round springform pan with 2½- to 3-inch (6- to 7½-cm) sides.

TART PANS: The French fluted-edge tinned removable bottom pan is used in all of my tart recipes. Some of my recipes call specifically for a 10-inch (25-cm) tart pan, while others indicate that either a 10- or 11-inch (25- or 28-cm) size will work well. In either case, it should be 1 inch (2½ cm) high.

TARTLET PANS: The ones I use most often are about 2½ inches (6 cm) in diameter, have sloping sides, and are made from tinned base metal. To season the pans before using them for the first time, bake them for half an hour at 350°F (180°C). You may butter them the first few times you use them, but after that it won't be necessary. Just wipe the pans well with a dry cloth or paper towel after each use. Don't wash them, or you'll have to season them again. Mini-muffin pans make an adequate substitute.

TUBE PANS: A tube pan can be a 1- or 2-piece 12-cup (10-inch/25-cm) tube pan, or a scalloped Bundt pan also with a 12-cup capacity.

PANS FOR COOKING: Enameled cast-iron pans are good for dessert preparations because of their nonreactive interiors. I especially like enameled iron for a large Dutch oven and also for smaller saucepans and covered casseroles for making syrups and pastry cream. The pans are heavy-bottomed, so delicate mixtures such as pastry cream cook through well without scorching. Try to avoid aluminum pans and all-stainless pans, as the aluminum may discolor acid or egg yolk preparations. All-stainless pans heat very unevenly. Bimetal cookware (stainless-steel pans with an aluminum core) is a good choice, since it combines the even heating of aluminum with the nonreactive property of stainless. Copper pans lined with tin or nickel give excellent results, but unfortunately are very expensive.

Useful sizes for saucepans include 1-, 1½-, 3-, and 4-quart. A 10- and a 12-inch (25- and 30-cm) sauté pan are good for a variety of jobs, and a small 8-inch (20-cm) sauté pan can be handy for smaller quantities.

DOUBLE BOILER: You can buy a double boiler—which consists of two pans, one underneath for the water and one on top for the ingredients—or you can improvise one pretty easily by resting a heatproof bowl over a saucepan. Just be sure the bowl doesn't sit so low that the bottom rests in the boiling water.

HAND TOOLS AND UTENSILS: Some tools and utensils can be approximated with regular kitchen implements, for example, you can purchase a roller docker if you feel you must have one, or you can pierce your doughs with a fork. I really like the Oxo

Good Grips series of tools and utensils, which have fat rubber grips.

COOKIE CUTTERS: Cookie cutters are used to cut out rolled doughs. The most common and therefore the most useful size is a round 2- or 2½-inch (5- or 6-cm) cutter. Cutters are also available with a fluted or a straight edge and in various other shapes and patterns. Be aware that the bottom of a cookie cutter can be almost as sharp as a knife. Obviously, that's what helps it cut so neatly through your dough, but you can accidentally cut a finger on the edge rather easily. Cutters are usually made from tinned metal or good quality hard plastic, but some are stainless steel or copper.

FOOD MILL: Mostly outmoded by the food processor, this tool is still useful for making purées and removing the seeds from mixtures such as raspberry purée. Foley and Mouli are the most commonly seen brand names.

FORK: You can use a regular table fork for piercing dough.

GRATERS: Graters make quick work of reducing everything from cheese to citrus zest to small pieces. Just be sure to watch your knuckles and fingers when you get close to the surface. I tend to avoid the kinds of graters that look as if they were formed by a nail piercing sheet metal. I prefer the openings that are set into the grater at an angle so that delicate materials do not stick in them. Best of all are graters with holes that are photo-etched rather than stamped. The two brand names for these are Cuisipro and Microplane®, both of which make a range of sizes and types. These truly shave foods into small pieces rather than simply tearing them the way that lower quality graters do.

BOX GRATER: A box grater has four or six sides with sharp holes of different shapes and sizes.

FLAT GRATER: A flat grater has a handle and is usually held over a bowl or a piece of wax paper to allow the grated material to collect.

ROTARY GRATER: A rotary grater consists of a stainless-steel drum that turns while using the handle. These are usually used for grating hard cheese, such as Parmigiano-Reggiano.

KITCHEN SCISSORS: Kitchen scissors are just what they sound like: scissors you use in the kitchen to snip herbs, slash breads, and more.

KNIVES: Buy the best knives available and they will last a lifetime. So many tasks in baking are accomplished more easily and more accurately with the help of a strong, sharp knife. Knives with stainless-steel blades are best because, unlike carbon-steel blades, they do not react with the acidity of certain fruits and vegetables.

Look for full-tang knives—ones where the blade and handle are one continuous piece of metal with the wooden handle riveted on. These are less likely to come loose from their handles than cheaper knives where the blade extends only partially into the handle.

Store knives in a dry place, making sure that they are perfectly clean and dry before putting them away. A knife rack is helpful in preventing damage to the points. Use a carborundum stone for sharpening, or have your knives professionally sharpened every six months or so, depending on use. A steel helps keep the knife edge in good shape between sharpenings.

As for the types of knives you will need, a bread (serrated edge) knife, a chef's or chopping knife, and a paring knife are all essential. I also like to use an offset serrated knife (sometimes labeled a "sandwich knife") for slicing through cake layers. A thin-bladed slicing knife or boning knife is useful for slicing cakes and other desserts when serving.

PASTRY BRUSHES: Flexible natural bristle brushes are used for applying egg wash, glazes, and syrups. A range of sizes from ½ inch to 3 inches (1 to 7 cm) in width is useful. New silicone brushes are fine for applying glaze—I prefer the ones with pointed bristles rather than the ones with bristles that end in little spheres, which are better for basting. To clean pastry brushes, stand them, bristles upward, in the utensil rack of the dishwasher. Remove, dry them off, and straighten out the bristles as soon as the rinse cycle is over and allow them to air dry.

PASTRY WHEEL: Also labeled a "pizza wheel," a sharp, metal pastry wheel helps achieve straight, accurate results when cutting dough into strips or trimming large pieces of dough. It is available in straight and serrated versions; sometimes you will find a single tool with both types mounted on one handle. Use the serrated wheel for sweet doughs only; it could compress the layers in puff pastry or other flaky doughs.

PEELER: A swivel-bladed peeler, like the one used for potatoes, is useful for peeling fruits and vegetables and making chocolate shavings.

ROLLER DOCKER: A roller docker consists of a small spiked wheel on a handle. Run it over a piece of rolled dough to pierce it more regularly and thoroughly (not to mention easily) than you could using a fork. Roller dockers may be made of steel or plastic.

ROLLING PINS: A straight boxwood pin, about 16 inches (40 cm) long and 2 inches (5 cm) in diameter, is a good all-purpose rolling pin. I prefer the type without handles. For heavier work, such as large batches of puff pastry, a 14- or 16-inch (35- or 40-cm) ball-bearing pin is useful. The newer nylon rolling pins will not stick to dough.

SCRAPERS: A bench scraper has a rectangular stainless-steel blade—usually about 3 x 5 inches (7 x 13 cm)—and a rectangular wooden handle. Indispensable for working with dough, a bench scraper is used for keeping the work surface free of stuck bits of dough, as well as for cutting through thick pieces of dough. A rubber or plastic scraper is sometimes called a "corne" (it used to be made from horn which is *corne* in French) and is useful for scraping the inside of a mixing bowl, filling a pastry bag, or smoothing a batter or filling with a flat edge.

RUBBER SPATULAS: The professional type of spatula with a hard plastic or rubber handle is best. These range in length from 8 to 14 inches (20 to 35 cm). An assortment of different sizes is recommended, and the heat-proof silicone spatulas now available are handy as well.

SINGLE-EDGE RAZOR BLADE: Single-edge razor blades are sometimes used to slash doughs that can't be cut with a knife or kitchen scissors without deflating. Obviously, the fact that only one side of the blade is sharp makes it safe to hold in your hand.

METAL SPATULAS: Small and large offset spatulas are essential for finishing cakes, spreading fillings on dough, and spreading batters in pans. An offset spatula has a blade that is offset an inch (2½ cm) or so lower than the handle. These come in very small (3-inch/7-cm blades) and large (8- to 12-inch/20- to 30-cm blades) sizes. Straight metal spatulas (as opposed to offset) are used for finishing cakes and transferring finished cakes and pastries. Those with 8- to 12-inch (20- to 30-cm) blades, about 1½ inches (4 cm) wide, are best.

WOODEN SPOONS AND SPATULAS: Boxwood spoons and spatulas are best, since the wood is hard and less likely to splinter. An assortment of graduated sizes is good, from 8 to 12 inches (20 to 30 cm) long. Wooden spatulas have a straight bottom edge and are best for stirring mixtures that are likely to scorch while cooking, since the flat edge covers the bottom of the pan more efficiently than a curved one.

29

METAL SPOON: A large metal kitchen spoon is often used to test the runniness of a glaze or syrup. A large slotted spoon is also useful.

STRAINERS: Several different round-bottomed strainers with very fine to coarse mesh are useful for sifting dry ingredients, straining liquids, and removing seeds from purées. A conical mesh strainer, called a *chinois* in French, is also good for large quantities of liquids. A skimmer—a small mesh strainer on a long handle—is useful for scooping items out of boiling water or oil. A colander is best for rinsing fruits and vegetables. A sieve is a drum-shaped strainer used for making purées or sifting dry ingredients; a strainer with a handle is not a sieve.

WHISKS: Thin-wired whisks (sometimes called "whips") are best for most purposes. Their flexible wires are good for incorporating mixtures that are not too dense. A small (8-inch/20-cm) and large (12-inch/30-cm) whisk will be sufficient for most recipes. Choose a sauce whisk, one that is somewhat narrow and pointed, for general mixing and for whisking mixtures while they are cooking. Its pointed end easily reaches into the corners of a pan to prevent dense mixtures such as pastry cream from sticking and burning there. When whipping cream or egg whites by hand, a large round balloon whisk, with a wide spherical space in the middle, incorporates air more quickly.

ZESTER: A zester removes the zest from citrus fruit in long, thin strands. It has a short wood handle surmounted by a metal blade with a row of tiny, sharp circular blades at the end. Look for a zester with sharp openings on top and a securely attached handle. A stripper is similar to a zester, but will remove single ¼-inch (6-mm) strips of rind.

MEASURING TOOLS: As a minimum you will need at least one set of dry-measure cups, one set of liquid-measure cups, and one set of

measuring spoons, but I like to have multiples on hand so that I'm not always rinsing and drying them while I'm baking. For dry measure, I use stainless-steel measuring cups and spoons made by Foley. To measure liquid, I use Pyrex measuring cups. This should not be construed as a brand endorsement, though I recommend you use the same measuring devices I do to get the same results. Such national brands are calibrated to strict standards of accuracy—cheap generic measuring cups may not be.

LIQUID-MEASURE CUPS: Though I prefer glass liquid-measure cups over plastic, I like the new-style plastic measuring cups that allow you to read the quantity from the top, rather than the side, of the cup—a definite improvement. I have several each in 1-, 2-, 4-, and 8-cup sizes. Try to avoid placing liquid measure cups in the dishwasher—eventually the numbers will wear off.

DRY-MEASURE CUPS: These are for measuring dry ingredients such as flour, confectioners' sugar, or cornstarch. I keep them in ¼-, ⅓-, ½-, 1-, and 2-cup sizes. If you buy a set that also includes ⅔-, ¾-, and 1½-cup sizes, use them to hold paper clips or stamps, or relegate them to the potting bench. They are too similar in appearance to other sizes and will lead to mistakes in measuring.

MEASURING SPOONS: Graduated metal measuring spoons are essential. A standard set includes ¼-teaspoon, ½-teaspoon, 1-teaspoon, and 1-tablespoon sizes. Some include a ⅛-teaspoon size as well.

SCALE: There are any number of fairly inexpensive, battery-operated scales available. These make quick work of weighing chocolate or other ingredients.

MELON BALL SCOOP: I like to use a scoop for coring apples and pears after they have been halved. I find this more accurate and less wasteful than using a corer or knife.

THERMOMETERS: Thermometers are used to measure the temperature of various items, and there are a variety of kitchen thermometers for each purpose.

OVEN THERMOMETER: An oven thermometer is usually a metal thermometer with a lip at the top and bottom so that it can either hang from an oven rack or sit on one. Oven thermometers are inexpensive, so it's not a bad idea to replace yours every year or so. Oven temperatures can differ from the number on the dial by as much as 100 degrees. You can also have your oven professionally calibrated to correct the difference, but eventually it will probably begin to waver again.

INSTANT-READ THERMOMETER: A small, sensitive thermometer, an instant read has a metal skewer surmounted by a temperature dial or a digital readout. To gauge the temperature of foods, you plunge the skewer into the item and then simply read the number. This is very useful for monitoring the internal temperature of baked bread.

DIGITAL THERMOMETER: Like a paperweight with a digital readout, this type of thermometer has a wire probe for taking the temperature of the item being cooked or baked. Better ones even monitor changes in temperature. Many of these also incorporate timers.

CANDY THERMOMETER: A candy thermometer is used to gauge the temperature of liquids, usually syrups or oils that are being brought to high heat. A candy thermometer comes with a clip so it can be attached to the side of a pot and left there to monitor the temperature. The clip prevents the bulb from touching the bottom of the pot and giving an inaccurately high reading. A candy thermometer goes to much higher temperature levels than a cooking thermometer; the more modern ones can be set to beep when the correct temperature has been reached. I prefer the ruler-type over the kind with a round dial at the top.

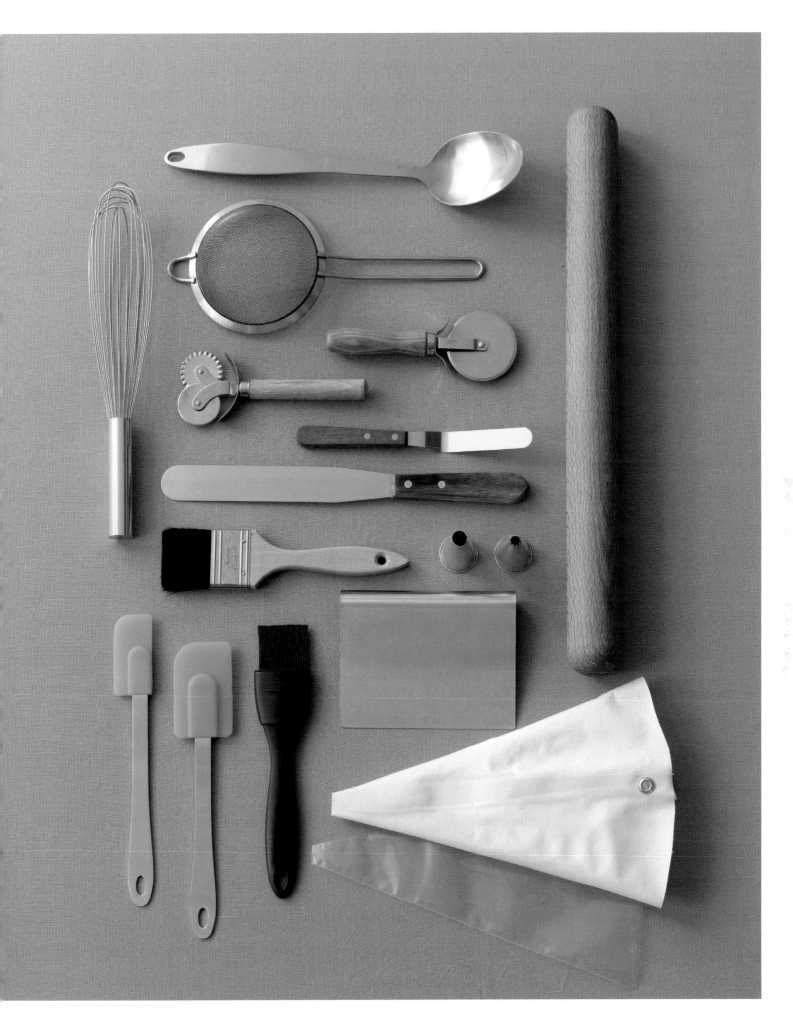

OVEN ITEMS: Know your oven! By this I mean you should be aware of its "hot spots." When baking something on the bottom shelf, check that it is not coloring too deeply on the bottom. If it is, insulate the bottom by sliding another pan under the baking pan being used.

OVEN RACKS: Most home ovens come with movable metal racks that fit into grooves in the sides of the oven. In all my recipes I give precise instruction for placement of oven racks. Be sure to adjust the racks before you preheat the oven; there's nothing more annoying than going to slide in a pan, only to discover the rack is too high or too low.

BAKING STONE: A baking stone is useful for making free-form breads that rest directly on the stone rather than in a pan, and it's not expensive. I like the large rectangular stones. The one I have is about 14 x 16 inches (35 x 40 cm). Just remember to place the stone on the oven rack when you turn the oven on, as it needs to preheat.

OVEN MITTS: You probably buy a new pair of oven mitts every few years without giving them much thought. I like the slightly longer kind that cover a little more of your arms, and I look for mitts that can be machine washed and dried.

TOASTER OVEN: I don't bother baking in a toaster oven, but it's ideal for reheating certain baked goods or for toasting small quantities of nuts.

ELECTRICAL EQUIPMENT: I'm not a gadget-crazed baker, but I do use an electric stand mixer and a food processor frequently.

ELECTRIC MIXER: Instructions for all recipes in this book are for tabletop mixers. Low speed on an electric mixer is the first setting; medium, the one that falls between the lowest and the highest; and high, the highest. I use a heavy-duty KitchenAid mixer, and as

long as you've got the counter space for it, I highly recommend owning one. A heavy-duty mixer comes with a paddle attachment for general mixing, a wire whip for aerating (whipping cream or egg whites), and a dough hook to use on heavy doughs, such as some bread doughs. If you are investing in a stand mixer, go all the way and buy an extra bowl and whisk. They will save you so much time that they will more than pay for themselves in the first year.

A hand mixer or lightweight tabletop mixer has rotary blades, and while they do a good job of mixing batters and whipping cream and egg whites, they tend to get stuck on thicker mixtures and should never be used on bread doughs or other heavy mixtures.

FOOD PROCESSOR: The food processor has become a standard piece of kitchen equipment. Aside from puréeing, grinding, grating, and chopping, a food processor can perform most of the functions of a heavy-duty mixer.

A food processor comes with a metal blade for puréeing, grinding, and making pastry doughs, and a plastic blade that is used for kneading yeast doughs. It may also come with a grating blade.

BLENDER: The blender has been mostly replaced by the food processor, but I still think a blender does a faster and more efficient job than the processor when it comes to puréeing fruit for sauces or fillings. A handheld blender takes up less room than the traditional countertop variety.

WAFFLE IRON: An electric waffle iron plugs into the wall, and you pour your waffle batter into its grid, then close the lid and let the waffles cook. There is no substitute for a waffle iron.

PAPER GOODS, TOWELS, AND LINERS:
ALUMINUM FOIL: Foil can also be useful for lining pans. I tend to stock up on extra-wide foil, so I can cover a large pan with one piece rather than piecing together a foil patchwork. The new nonstick foil is great for cookies.

KITCHEN TOWELS: I like to keep a variety of types of kitchen towels around, not just for drying my hands and dishes, but also for covering doughs when they are rising and for other uses. I prefer to use flat-weave towels when the towel will be touching food, and steer clear of fuzzy terry-cloth types, which would be more inclined to stick to dough.

PARCHMENT PAPER: After years of production work in professional kitchens, I always use large sheets of parchment paper (18 x 24 inches/45 x 61 cm) that come in a box of 1,000 sheets. These are easy to obtain from paper wholesalers. You can share a box with several friends who also like to bake, and it's so much more convenient and economical than using boxes of narrow paper on a roll.

PLASTIC WRAP: Plastic wrap is most useful for covering foods to keep them fresh. I prefer to let most still-warm cooked foods cool before covering them with plastic wrap.

SILICONE BAKING MATS: Silicone baking mats, sold most commonly under the Silpat brand, are a reusable replacement for parchment and other pan liners. They are completely nonstick. In addition to using them to line pans (they are resistant to even very high heat), you can use them on a surface when you are rolling out a particularly sticky dough. Just remember not to cut dough on your Silpat, and don't put it in the dishwasher.

WAX PAPER: Buttered wax paper is my least favorite choice for lining pans, but it does work if you have no parchment paper.

DECORATING EQUIPMENT: A surprisingly small number of tools are required to decorate the vast majority of desserts in this book. Even without pastry bags and tubes, you can make chocolate shavings using a vegetable peeler, or marbleize frosting with the tip of a knife. If you are interested in piping rosettes and other decorations with buttercream, however, you will want to invest in the following.

PASTRY BAGS: I prefer plastic-coated canvas bags. Nylon and disposable plastic versions are also available, and all types should be easy to find in cookware stores or, failing that, by mail order. Remember to snip the narrow end of a new bag to allow the end of the tube to protrude sufficiently. Wash bags with soap and water and turn them inside out after each use; stand them upright to dry. Every few weeks, machine-wash the bags with other kitchen wash, using detergent and bleach, to prevent them from becoming rancid from accumulated traces of fat. An 8-inch (20-cm) bag is good for piping small amounts of whipped cream or buttercream; 12- and 14-inch (30- and 35-cm) sizes are good for pâte à choux and fillings. I think a 14- or 16-inch (35- or 40-cm) bag makes the best all-purpose choice.

PASTRY TUBES: There are hundreds of different shapes of tubes or nozzles used for decorating. The one most commonly called for is a plain tube with a ½-inch (1-cm) opening for most general piping; the next is a star tube with a ½-inch (1-cm) opening for whipped cream and meringue. The best star tube for piping whipped cream and meringue has six or eight large triangular teeth and is open at the end. Teeth that are too small, too numerous, and too close together will not make a sufficiently deep impression in soft materials such as whipped cream and meringue, although they are excellent for firmer mixtures such as buttercream. A small plain tube with a ¼-inch (6-mm) opening is useful for piping thin lines. Ateco is the more or less universal supplier of tubes and the brand you'll most likely encounter when you shop for them. Many writers of recipes, myself included, include the specific Ateco number for the tip you should use. Just make sure you are using the 1½- to 2-inch (4- to 5-cm) pastry tubes, not the tiny decorating ones.

DECORATING COMB: This is a thin piece of metal or plastic, usually triangular, with serrated edges like saw teeth. Draw the comb gently across the top or side of a cake to leave a grooved pattern on the surface. For cake tops, the same thing can be accomplished using the edge of a serrated knife.

OFFSET SPATULAS: Offset spatulas are used for filling and finishing cakes. See Metal Spatulas on page 29 for more information.

BOWLS: Stainless-steel bowls in graduated sizes—from 1 to 6 quarts (1 to 6 liters)—can hold different parts of the same recipe and be used for mixing as well. Pyrex bowls come in graduated sets and are useful as well as inexpensive. A copper bowl should be used only for whipping egg whites since the copper can react with fat and produce mildly toxic results. Though I use plastic containers for storage, I don't like plastic bowls for mixing—no matter how carefully they are washed, they can retain fat and odors.

SURFACES: When I indicate a "work surface" in this book, I mean your kitchen countertop. It might be butcher block, laminate (Formica), stone, or ceramic. All of them are fine. A marble surface is more important for working with cooked sugar, not a technique featured in this book.

CUTTING BOARDS: After years of back and forth, it turns out wooden cutting boards are better than plastic. I like the very smooth, hard, fused wooden cutting boards that are thin and lightweight, made by Epicurean. Wash cutting boards thoroughly with hot water by hand; never put a wooden cutting board in the dishwasher or eventually it will warp.

COOLING RACKS: Metal cooling racks with strips of metal arranged in a grid, concentric circles, or parallel lines are my choice for resting many items as they cool. Some recipes instruct you to cool items in a pan on a rack, and others instruct you to unmold the item immediately and cool it on a rack. You will want to have several racks on hand, because some cakes are unmolded upside down and then inverted again to cool right side up. A good standard size is a round rack with a 10- or 12-inch (25- to 30-cm) diameter.

CARDBOARDS: Cardboards are available in various sizes and shapes. Round ones the same diameter as your cake will make cake finishing a breeze. Rectangular ones can make unmolding large cakes or tarts easy, and can also be used to slide loaves of free-form bread onto a baking stone in the oven.

STORAGE ITEMS: Long-term storage almost always requires freezing, but with a few good storage items, you can keep certain baked goods fresh for quite a long time. See the individual recipes in this book for specific storage instructions.

CAKE DOME: A cake dome, consisting of a plate and a lid, is often the best place to store a cake. I like the type with little swiveling tabs that hold the lid in place.

CONTAINERS WITH TIGHT-FITTING LIDS: Plastic or metal containers with tight-fitting lids are ideal for storing most cookies and bars. I also like the glass containers with plastic lids, which are harder to find. Simply arrange the items in layers with wax or parchment paper between them to prevent them from sticking.

33

Techniques

Rather than being arranged alphabetically, the techniques here follow a logical progression from processing ingredients before use, through measuring, mixing, shaping, baking, cooling, and finishing. Many techniques are described in depth within the chapter where they are most used.

MAKING A DRY CARAMEL

a. Once the sugar begins to melt, avoid stirring it too much or it will recrystallize.

b. As the sugar starts to turn amber, decrease the heat to low.

c. Test the color of the caramel by letting some fall from the spoon back into the pan, as it always looks darker in the pan.

36

MEASURING

VOLUME MEASURE FOR DRY INGREDIENTS: For fine, powdery ingredients, such as flour, confectioners' sugar, and cocoa powder, gently spoon into a dry-measure cup, without shaking the cup, until it is overflowing. Use any kind of a straight-edged tool to level off the top of the cup. I don't bother to do this with granulated sugar—I just scoop up the sugar and level it off. If cocoa, confectioners' sugar, or any other ingredient you need to measure this way is lumpy, crush the lumps with a spoon first, but don't sift until after you are done measuring.

LIQUID MEASURE: Use clear glass or plastic cups for liquid measure. Don't measure small quantities in a large cup. If you need ¼ cup of milk, use a 1-cup measure, not a 2- or 4-cup one. Stand the cup at eye level to get an accurate reading, or use one of the new liquid-measure cups that allows you to read the quantity from above.

WEIGHING: Use a good quality battery-operated digital scale for measuring ingredients, such as chocolate, that need to be weighed. Use a scale that registers pounds, ounces, and fractions of ounces, not one that registers decimal quantities of pounds. A good scale has an on-off button so you can conserve battery life and won't need to leave the scale turned on over a long period of time. The best way to use a scale is to turn it on and place a lightweight bowl on the weighing plate. Press the on button again or the tare button to bring the weight back to zero, then

weigh the ingredient. Tare (bring back to zero) the scale again every time you place an empty bowl on it, even if you are repeatedly using the same bowl.

SIFTING BEFORE MEASURING: None of the recipes in this book require you to sift a dry ingredient before measuring it, because measuring sifted ingredients is less consistent than first measuring and then sifting. If you encounter a recipe needing this elsewhere, it will state "X cups of sifted flour." Use a strainer or sifter to sift the flour into a bowl or onto a sheet of wax paper, then spoon the flour into the cup as described above.

USING YOUR OVEN

PREHEATING: Preheat the oven for 15 to 20 minutes before you are going to bake something, except when using a baking stone, which should preheat for 30 minutes. All recipes indicate an appropriate position for the oven rack(s), so arrange these before preheating the oven.

RACK POSITION FOR DIFFERENT BAKED ITEMS: Breads and cakes go in the middle. Pies, tarts, focaccia, and anything that requires a well-done bottom crust go in the lowest level. Tube and Bundt pans go in the lower third, and if your oven gives very strong bottom heat, stand the pan on a jelly-roll pan for added insulation. For cookies, use an insulated cookie sheet on the bottom rack of the oven, or double two pans together.

Leave the second pan in place if you switch positions from top to bottom and vice versa during baking. All the recipes in this book indicate correct rack position.

ROTATING AND CHANGING RACKS DURING BAKING: This keeps baked goods in multiple pans baking evenly. Even if I'm baking a single cake or tart, I turn it back to front once or twice during baking.

UNMOLDING AND COOLING

QUICK BREADS AND BREADS: Cool in the pan for fewer than 5 minutes, then unmold onto a rack. Cool loaves on their sides to avoid compressing the crumb.

TARTS: Cool on a rack and unmold by standing the tart pan on a low, wide cylinder, such as a can of tomatoes. The side of the pan should fall away. Slide a large spatula under the pan base and slide the tart onto a platter.

PIES: Cool in the pan on a rack, then serve from the pan.

CAKE LAYERS: For everything but sponge layers, cool in the pan for fewer than 5 minutes, then invert onto a rack and remove the pan, leaving the paper stuck to the cake. Invert another rack against the bottom of the cake, then invert the stack of rack/cake/rack and remove the top rack. Cooling the cake right side up and leaving it on the paper makes it easier to handle afterward. Unmold sponge

fig. a

fig. b

fig. c

layers immediately after removing from the oven or they will shrink and fall.

CAKES BAKED IN DECORATIVE MOLDS: Cool in the pan for under 5 minutes, then invert onto a rack and lift off the pan.

BAR COOKIES: Cool in the pan on a rack. Unmold between two racks as in Cake Layers, opposite. Transfer to a cutting board to slice into bars.

COOKIES: Except for the second baking of biscotti, slide the paper or foil from the hot pan onto a rack to cool cookies. Leaving them on the pan to cool might make them dry. Leave biscotti to cool on the pan, since they are meant to be dry.

UNMOLDING FROM A SPRINGFORM PAN: Run a thin knife between the inside of the pan and the cake, scraping into the pan, not the cake. Unbuckle the side of the pan and lift it away. Use a wide spatula to ease the cake off the pan base onto a rack.

COOKING SUGAR

MAKING A "DRY" CARAMEL: Moisten the sugar with a little lemon juice or water as specified in the recipe. Acids work best, but if the caramel is to be diluted with milk or cream later on, using an acid during this phase will result in a curdled final mixture. Work the liquid evenly into the sugar—it should look like wet sand. Place over medium heat and wait until the sugar starts to melt—you'll see a wisp of smoke coming from the center of the pan. Use a large metal kitchen spoon to stir the sugar a little after it starts to melt. Avoid stirring too much, or the sugar will begin to recrystallize and form lumps. As the sugar melts more, decrease the heat to low. Test the color of the caramel by letting some fall from the spoon back into the pan—it always looks darker in the pan. If the caramel is still very light, slide the pan off the heat and let it continue cooking from the heat retained by the pan. Dilute (see below) or use the caramel as soon as it is a deep amber color—if it is too light it won't have enough caramel flavor; if it is too dark it will be bitter.

DILUTING CARAMEL: Only add a hot liquid to caramel. When the caramel is ready, cover the back of your hand and forearm with a towel or oven mitts and use a ladle to add the liquid to the pan. The caramel will splatter and bubble up, so always remember to avert your face. Continue adding the liquid until it is all incorporated. If some of the caramel has solidified, return the pan to low heat and stir occasionally to melt the hardened pieces of caramel before adding the liquid.

42 Fennel Fig & Almond Bread

45 Chocolate Spice Bread

46 Whole Wheat Currant Bread

47 Date Walnut Bread

48 Whole Grain Apple
Raisin Bread

50 Spicy Jalapeño Cornbread

51 Pecorino & Pepper Biscuits

52 Real Welsh Scones

54 Ginger Scones with
Almond Topping

55 Butterscotch Scones

57 Triple Chocolate Scones

58 Blueberry Crumb Muffins

59 Irish Soda Bread Muffins

60 Cocoa Banana Muffins

62 Sweet Rusks for Dunking

I.

Quick Breads

Quick breads are a fairly recent addition to the baking repertoire, dating only from the middle of the 19th century, when baking powder first became widely available. Before that, there were quick breads leavened only with baking soda, since bicarbonate of soda was in general use for baking already toward the first half of the 19th century. See page 41 for more information on baking powder versus other leaveners.

There are several categories of quick breads, all of which are represented by recipes in this chapter: Loaves baked in a rectangular loaf pan and meant to be sliced and spread with butter or cream cheese when served; biscuits, the classic quick bread of the American South; scones, sweetened dough similar to that for biscuits, but shaped as a disk and cut into wedges before baking; and, finally, muffins, individual breads often enriched with fresh or dried fruit. This chapter also includes a recipe for fancy rusks, the plainer versions of which are usually made with yeast. As their name implies, quick breads require a minimum of time. Most can be in the oven in less than 30 minutes, and many are best served right after they've cooled a little, making them one of the best sources of instant baking gratification.

When a quick-bread recipe calls for mixing all the liquid ingredients into the dry, use a large rubber spatula to fold them only until absorbed so that the batter or dough doesn't become too elastic, rendering the baked quick bread tough and chewy. Use an ice-cream scoop for uniform results when transferring muffin batter to tins. To shape scones, gently pat out the dough and use a bench scraper or a knife to divide it into wedges. Use a wide spatula to transfer them to the pan.

To prepare decorative molds and Bundt pans for quick breads, butter them with soft butter, cover with a coat of dry bread crumbs, and then apply a coat of vegetable cooking spray for a perfect nonstick finish. Do this even with nonstick pans, especially those that have a black nonstick coating, which seem to make cakes stick like crazy.

To test for doneness, use a thin-bladed paring knife plunged into the center of the cake or muffin. It should emerge dry or with only a few crumbs clinging to it, as specified in recipes.

LEAVENERS

BAKING POWDER: Chemical leaveners, such as baking powder, produce carbon dioxide when an acid and alkali are combined in the presence of a liquid. Baking powder includes both the alkali and the acid: The alkali is almost always baking soda. Starch, usually cornstarch, is also mixed into baking powder, both to stabilize it and to neutralize the chemical reaction, as well as to absorb the excess moisture in the air, which would cause caking and lack of potency. Almost all the baking powder available today is double-acting, meaning that it creates two chemical reactions that promote rising: one when the baking powder is combined with liquid, and the second when it is exposed to heat. Keep baking powder in a dry spot and replace the container every six months or so, as it does lose potency as it ages.

BAKING SODA: Baking soda, or sodium bicarbonate, is an alkali only, so it requires the presence of an acid in the dough or batter to begin the leavening process. Acids that are paired with baking soda in recipes include buttermilk, yogurt, sour cream, molasses, honey, cocoa, chocolate, and cream of tartar. Always use only the amount of baking soda called for in the recipe, sift it over the other dry ingredients, and stir it in well to avoid an excess of alkalinity and pockets of undissolved baking soda. This eliminates the possibility of a chemical aftertaste. Any batter made with baking soda needs to be placed in a preheated oven immediately, because baking soda reacts on contact with moisture and immediately begins producing the carbon dioxide that will leaven what you're baking. Baking soda, too, loses its potency as it ages, so keep it in a cool, dry spot and replace it every six months or so.

CREAM OF TARTAR: Derived from the acidic sediment that develops on the sides of wine casks, cream of tartar was once the most widely used acid in the manufacturing of commercial baking powder. Although it can still be combined with baking soda to form a rudimentary single-acting baking powder, cream of tartar is now more commonly used in sugar cooking because its acidity helps to prevent unwanted crystallization.

....

2 cups all-purpose flour
(spoon flour into a dry-measure cup and level off)

2 teaspoons baking powder

½ teaspoon salt

2 teaspoons fennel seeds, crushed

6 tablespoons (¾ stick) unsalted butter, softened

⅔ cup sugar

2 large eggs

¾ cup milk

1½ cups (8 to 9 ounces/225 to 250 grams) stemmed and diced white or black dried figs

1 cup (about 4 ounces/100 grams) slivered almonds, lightly toasted

One 9 x 5 x 3-inch (23 x 13 x 7-cm) loaf pan, buttered and the bottom lined with a rectangle of parchment or buttered wax paper cut to fit

Fennel Fig & Almond Bread

This delicious bread was inspired by a fragrant golden raisin, fennel, and cornmeal bread created by my friend Amy Scherber, owner of Amy's Bread in New York City. The touch of fennel is a perfect foil for the figs and somehow emphasizes their sweetness. To crush the fennel seeds, place them in a jelly-roll or small roasting pan and press on them with the bottom of a heavy saucepan.

1. Set a rack in the middle level of the oven and preheat to 350°F (180°C).

2. Combine the flour, baking powder, salt, and fennel seeds in a medium bowl and stir well to mix.

3. In a large bowl, beat the butter until smooth, then beat in the sugar. Beat in the eggs, one at a time.

4. Beat ½ the flour mixture into the butter and egg mixture, then gently beat in the milk, about ⅓ at a time. Beat in the remaining flour mixture. Use a large rubber spatula to fold in the figs and almonds.

5. Scrape the batter into the prepared pan and smooth the top. Bake the bread until it is well risen and a toothpick or a narrow-bladed knife inserted into the center of the bread emerges clean, about 1 hour.

6. Cool the bread in the pan on a rack for 5 minutes, then unmold it and cool it completely on a rack. Transfer the bread to a platter or cutting board before serving.

SERVING: Cut the bread into thin slices and serve with butter or cream cheese.

STORAGE: Keep the bread under a cake dome or loosely wrapped in plastic wrap on the day it is made. Wrap in plastic wrap and aluminum foil and keep at room temperature for up to 3 or 4 days. Freeze for longer storage.

Makes one 8½ x 4½ x 2¾-inch (21 x 11 x 7-cm) loaf, 12 to 16 slices

....

1½ cups all-purpose flour
(spoon flour into a dry-measure cup and level off)

⅓ cup, alkalized (Dutch process) cocoa powder, sifted after measuring

1 teaspoon baking powder

½ teaspoon salt

½ teaspoon ground cinnamon

½ teaspoon freshly grated nutmeg

½ teaspoon ground ginger

2 large eggs

½ cup granulated sugar

⅓ cup dark brown sugar

5 tablespoons unsalted butter, melted

⅔ cup sour cream

One 8½ x 4½ x 2¾-inch (21 x 11 x 7-cm) loaf pan, buttered and the bottom lined with a piece of parchment or buttered wax paper cut to fit

Chocolate Spice Bread

For those of us who can never get enough chocolate, here's an easy quick bread that's packed with chocolate flavor. Watch this carefully toward the end of the baking time and make sure to remove it from the oven as soon as it's ready. Overbaking will make the bread very dry.

1. Set a rack in the middle level of the oven and preheat to 350°F (180°C).

2. Combine the flour, cocoa, baking powder, salt, and spices in a mixing bowl; stir well to combine.

3. In a large bowl, whisk the eggs to break them up, then whisk in the granulated sugar and brown sugar. Continue whisking for a minute, or until the mixture lightens. Whisk in the butter and sour cream.

4. Add the dry ingredients to the egg mixture all at once and gently whisk until smooth.

5. Scrape the batter into the prepared pan and smooth the top. Bake the bread until it is well risen and a toothpick or a narrow-bladed knife inserted into the center of the bread emerges clean, 35 to 40 minutes.

6. Cool the bread in the pan on a rack for 5 minutes, then unmold it and cool it completely on a rack. Transfer the bread to a platter or cutting board before serving.

SERVING: Cut the bread into thin slices and serve with preserves or marmalade. Raspberry preserves or ginger marmalade are especially good with it.

STORAGE: Keep the bread under a cake dome or loosely wrapped in plastic wrap on the day it is made. Wrap in plastic wrap and aluminum foil and keep at room temperature for up to 3 or 4 days. Freeze for longer storage.

....

2 cups whole wheat flour
(spoon flour into a dry-measure cup and level off)

2 teaspoons baking powder

½ teaspoon salt

2 large eggs

⅓ cup granulated sugar

⅓ cup dark brown sugar

⅓ cup vegetable oil, such as canola

¾ cup milk or buttermilk

2 cups (10 ounces/275 grams) dried currants

One 8½ x 4½ x 2¾-inch (21 x 11 x 7-cm) loaf pan, buttered and the bottom lined with a rectangle of parchment or buttered wax paper cut to fit

Whole Wheat Currant Bread

Whole wheat flour gives this easy bread a deep rich flavor and a tender crumb. Feel free to substitute other types of raisins or diced dried fruit for the currants. I sometimes add about ½ cup coarsely chopped pecan or walnut pieces to the batter along with the currants.

1. Set a rack in the middle level of the oven and preheat to 350°F (180°C).

2. Combine the flour, baking powder, and salt in a bowl and stir well to mix.

3. In a large bowl, whisk the eggs to break them up, then whisk in the sugar and brown sugar. Whisk in the oil and milk, one at a time, whisking until smooth after each.

4. Use a large rubber spatula to fold the flour mixture into the egg mixture. Quickly fold in the currants.

5. Scrape the batter into the prepared pan and smooth the top. Bake the bread until it is well risen and a toothpick or a narrow-bladed knife inserted into the center of the bread emerges clean, 45 to 50 minutes.

6. Cool the bread in the pan on a rack for 5 minutes, then unmold it and cool it completely on a rack. Transfer the bread to a platter or cutting board before serving.

SERVING: Cut the bread into thin slices and serve with butter or cream cheese.

STORAGE: Keep the bread under a cake dome or loosely wrapped in plastic wrap on the day it is made. Wrap in plastic wrap and aluminum foil and keep at room temperature for up to 3 to 4 days. Freeze for longer storage.

Makes 1 short 10-inch (25-cm) tube or Bundt cake, about 16 servings

....

1 pound (450 grams) pitted dates, checked carefully for pits and snipped in half

1 tablespoon unsalted butter

1½ cups boiling water

2 large eggs

1½ cups sugar

1 teaspoon vanilla extract

3 cups all-purpose flour
(spoon flour into a dry-measure cup and level off)

2 teaspoons baking soda

1 teaspoon salt

2 cups (about 7 ounces/200 grams) walnut pieces

One 12-cup tube or Bundt pan, buttered, the buttered surface coated with fine bread crumbs, and sprayed with vegetable cooking spray

Date Walnut Bread

This is a classic of the 1950s and incredibly easy to prepare. My aunt Rachel Malgieri Rocco used to make this loaf every week and served it when her friends dropped in for coffee in the afternoon.

One note of caution: Pitted dates often have a pit or two still lurking inside them—check them carefully before you start the recipe.

1. Place the snipped dates in a heatproof bowl and add the butter. Pour the boiling water over the dates and butter and let the mixture stand for 1 hour.

2. Set a rack in the lower third of the oven and preheat to 325°F (160°C).

3. Whisk the eggs in a large mixing bowl to break them up. Whisk the sugar into the eggs in a stream and continue whisking until the mixture lightens in color, about 1 minute. Whisk in the vanilla.

4. Use a large rubber spatula to fold the date mixture into the egg mixture.

5. In a separate bowl, mix the flour with the baking soda and salt. Gently stir the flour mixture into the date and egg mixture along with the walnuts.

6. Scrape the batter into the prepared pan and smooth the top. Bake the bread until a toothpick or a narrow-bladed knife inserted halfway between the side of the pan and the central tube emerges clean, about 1 hour.

7. Place the pan on a rack for a minute, then invert the bread onto the rack to cool completely. Transfer the bread to a platter or cutting board before serving.

....

SERVING: Cut the bread into thin slices and serve with cream cheese. Or, slice the bread thinly, spread with cream cheese and top with another slice of the bread. Cut into 3 to 4 narrow rectangles for tea sandwiches.

STORAGE: Keep the bread under a cake dome or loosely wrapped in plastic wrap on the day it is made. Wrap in plastic wrap and aluminum foil and keep at room temperature for up to 3 to 4 days. Freeze for longer storage.

Makes one 8½ x 4½ x 2¾-inch (21 x 11 x 7-cm) loaf, 12 to 16 slices

··

⅔ cup all-purpose flour
(spoon flour into a dry-measure cup and level off)

⅔ cup whole wheat flour

¾ teaspoon baking soda

½ teaspoon ground cinnamon

2 large eggs

½ cup light brown sugar

⅔ cup vegetable oil, such as canola

2 large tart apples, such as Granny Smith

½ cup dark raisins

½ cup (about 2 ounces/60 grams) walnut pieces, coarsely chopped

One 8½ x 4½ x 2¾-inch (21 x 11 x 7-cm) loaf pan, buttered and the bottom lined with a rectangle of parchment or buttered wax paper cut to fit

Whole Grain
Apple Raisin Bread

The whole wheat flour in this recipe gives the bread a nutty flavor that's a perfect background for the apples and raisins. I use the largest holes on a box grater for the apples, and I peel and grate them immediately before incorporating them into the batter.

1. Set a rack in the middle level of the oven and preheat to 350°F (180°C).

2. Combine the flours, baking soda, and cinnamon in a bowl and stir well to mix.

3. In a separate large bowl, whisk the eggs to break them up and whisk the sugar into the eggs. Whisk in the oil and set the bowl aside.

4. Quickly peel and grate the apples into a shallow bowl—you should have about 2 cups of grated apple.

5. Use a large rubber spatula to fold the flour mixture into the egg mixture. Quickly fold in the apples, raisins, and walnuts.

6. Scrape the batter into the prepared pan and smooth the top. Bake the bread until it is well risen and a toothpick or a narrow-bladed knife inserted into the center of the bread emerges clean, 35 to 40 minutes.

7. Cool the bread in the pan on a rack for 5 minutes, then unmold it and cool it completely on a rack. Transfer the bread to a platter or cutting board before serving.

SERVING: Cut the bread into thin slices and serve with butter or cream cheese.

STORAGE: Keep the bread under a cake dome or loosely wrapped in plastic wrap on the day it is made. Wrap in plastic wrap and aluminum foil and keep at room temperature for up to 3 or 4 days. Freeze for longer storage.

Makes one 10-inch (25-cm) round cornbread, about 12 generous wedges

....

1 tablespoon vegetable oil

4 fresh jalapeño chiles, stemmed, halved, seeded, interior ribs removed, and sliced

6 scallions (green onions), white parts and an equal amount of the green, rinsed, roots removed, and thinly sliced

2 cups stone-ground yellow cornmeal

1½ cups all-purpose flour
(spoon flour into a dry-measure cup and level off)

2 tablespoons sugar

2 tablespoons baking powder

2 teaspoons salt

2 large eggs

2 cups light cream, half-and-half, buttermilk, or milk

8 tablespoons (1 stick) unsalted butter, melted

¼ cup fresh cilantro leaves

One 10-inch (25-cm) round pan, 2 inches (5 cm) deep, buttered and the bottom lined with a disk of parchment or buttered wax paper cut to fit

VARIATIONS

OLD-FASHIONED CORNBREAD: Omit the chiles, scallions, and cilantro. Increase the sugar to ¼ cup.

FOR STUFFING: Add 2 tablespoons poultry seasoning or 4 tablespoons finely chopped fresh sage leaves.

CORN MUFFINS: Use the jalapeño batter or the plain batter above to make 12 muffins. Line muffin pans with paper liners and bake them for about 20 minutes.

Spicy Jalapeño Cornbread

This qualifies as more of a Southwestern American version of cornbread than a Mexican one, but it does embody some of the typical flavors of Mexican food— namely jalapeños, scallions, and cilantro. The cornbread can stand alone without these seasonings; you may also increase or decrease any of them according to your own taste. Jalapeños vary widely in heat: some have none at all; others are fiercely hot. The only way to determine this is to taste a little bit of each one you cut up— if they're mild, add a little more. Please remember to wear gloves or to wash your hands several times in succession after handling the chiles. You don't realize how often you unconsciously touch one of your eyes until you do so with hot chile juice on your hands.

1. Pour the oil into a small sauté pan and add the chiles and scallions. Place over medium heat and cook just until slightly wilted, about 2 minutes. Set aside.

2. Set a rack in the middle level of the oven and preheat to 375°F (190°C).

3. Combine the cornmeal, flour, sugar, baking powder, and salt in a mixing bowl and stir well to mix.

4. In a large bowl, whisk the eggs to break them up and then whisk in the cream, butter, the cooked chiles and scallions, and the cilantro.

5. Add the dry ingredients to the egg mixture all at once and use a large rubber spatula to fold them into the liquid. The batter will be very thick.

6. Scrape the batter into the prepared pan and smooth the top. Bake the cornbread until it is well risen and a toothpick or a narrow-bladed knife inserted into the center of the bread emerges clean, about 30 minutes.

7. Cool the cornbread in the pan on a rack for 5 minutes, then unmold it onto a plate. Peel off the paper if it is stuck to the bottom of the cornbread. Invert the cornbread back onto the rack, then remove the plate, and cool the cornbread on the rack. Slide the cornbread onto a platter or cutting board to serve it.

....

SERVING: This makes a great accompaniment to eggs for brunch, or to a substantial salad for lunch. To serve the cornbread warm, slide it onto a cookie sheet and cover it loosely with aluminum foil. Heat at 325°F (160°C) for about 15 minutes. Slide onto a platter or cutting board and serve immediately.

STORAGE: Keep the cornbread under a cake dome or loosely covered with plastic wrap on the day it is baked. Wrap in plastic wrap and foil and keep at room temperature for 2 to 3 days. Freeze for longer storage; defrost and reheat as in Serving, above.

Makes about twelve 2½-inch (6-cm) biscuits

....

2¾ cups all-purpose flour
(spoon flour into a dry-measure cup and level off)

1 tablespoon baking powder

1½ teaspoons coarsely ground black pepper

¼ teaspoon salt

3 ounces Pecorino Romano, finely grated, about 1⅓ cups

8 tablespoons cold unsalted butter, cut into 12 pieces

¾ cup milk or buttermilk, plus 1 to 2 tablespoons, if needed

1 cookie sheet or jelly-roll pan lined with parchment or foil

VARIATIONS

PARMIGIANO-REGGIANO BISCUITS: Substitute Parmigiano-Reggiano for the Pecorino Romano. Decrease the pepper to ½ teaspoon or leave it out—too much pepper will drown out the delicate flavor of this cheese.

GRUYÈRE BISCUITS: These are a personal favorite. Substitute real Swiss Gruyère for the Pecorino Romano. Pepper or not, as you wish; they're excellent either way. If you use these for ham sandwiches, add a thin smear of Dijon mustard.

OLD-FASHIONED, BAKING-POWDER BISCUITS: Omit the cheese and pepper and increase the salt to ½ teaspoon. Pulse the dry ingredients in the food processor first, then add the cut-up butter and proceed with the recipe from the middle of step 4.

Pecorino & Pepper Biscuits

Baking-powder biscuits and cheese are a natural combination, but I like the cheese to be completely absorbed into the dough rather than appearing as little lumps in the baked biscuits, as it often does in traditional cheese biscuits. Grating the cheese finely and then giving it a spin in the food processor with the butter does the trick. By the way, resist the temptation to try any kind of blue-veined cheese in this recipe, unless you really like gray biscuits. Also, the amount of salt in this recipe is purposely small to compensate for the saltiness of the cheese.

1. Set a rack in the middle level of the oven and preheat to 400°F (200°C).

2. Combine the flour, baking powder, pepper, and salt in a mixing bowl and mix well.

3. Combine the grated cheese and butter in the bowl of a food processor fitted with the metal blade. Pulse several times to mix the butter and cheese together. You might need to scrape down the inside of the bowl with a thin metal spatula once or twice and pulse again to make sure they are thoroughly mixed. The whole process should take about 30 seconds—you don't want to soften the butter too much. Use the metal spatula again to scrape the cheese and butter mixture off the side and the bottom of the bowl.

4. Add the flour mixture and pulse 6 or 8 times to combine the butter and cheese mixture thoroughly. Add the milk and pulse again 3 to 4 times until the dough is thoroughly combined but does not form a ball.

5. Invert the dough onto a floured work surface and carefully remove the blade. If there are dry areas in the dough, sprinkle with up to 2 additional tablespoons of milk. Use a bench scraper to fold the dough over onto itself several times to make it a little smoother.

6. Lightly flour the dough and press it into a rectangle about ½ inch (1 cm) thick. Use a floured plain round cutter up to 2½ inches (6 cm) in diameter to cut out the biscuits. Press straight down with the cutter— twisting it as you cut prevents the biscuits from having straight, even sides when baked.

7. Arrange the cut biscuits on the prepared pan about 1 inch (2½ cm) apart. Press the scraps together and cut more biscuits, then discard the remaining scraps.

8. Bake the biscuits for about 20 minutes, or until they are well risen and nicely golden.

9. Serve the biscuits immediately or cool them before serving.

....

SERVING: These are excellent with baked ham—split the biscuits and fill each one with a small piece of ham. They're also very good with a hearty soup, such as minestrone.

STORAGE: Keep the biscuits loosely covered with plastic wrap on the day they are baked. Double wrap in plastic and freeze for longer storage. Defrost and reheat at 375°F (190°C) for about 5 minutes before serving.

Makes 16 scones

....

2¼ cups all-purpose flour
(spoon flour into a dry-measure cup and level off)

⅓ cup sugar

1 tablespoon baking powder

1 teaspoon cream of tartar

½ teaspoon salt

8 tablespoons (1 stick) cold unsalted butter,
cut into 12 pieces

1 large egg

½ cup milk

1 cookie sheet or jelly-roll pan lined with parchment or foil

Real Welsh Scones

One of my dearest friends, Kyra Effren, lives in Dallas but spends part of every year with her mother in Cape Town, South Africa. While Kyra is there, she bakes scones for her mother, who was born in Wales and knows good scones, almost every day. These are easy to mix in the food processor—up to a point. I like to pour the powdery mixture into a bowl before adding the liquid so the dough doesn't get overworked and tough in the machine.

1. Set a rack in the middle level of the oven and preheat to 450°F (230°C).

2. Combine the flour, sugar, baking powder, cream of tartar, and salt in the bowl of a food processor fitted with the metal blade. Add the butter and pulse until the mixture is mealy but dry and powdery (figure a).

3. Invert the bowl of the food processor over a mixing bowl and carefully remove the blade.

4. Quickly whisk the egg and milk together and use a fork to toss the egg mixture into the flour mixture, continuing to toss until all the flour mixture is evenly moistened (figure b).

5. Gently knead the dough 3 to 4 times, until it is smooth (figure c). Divide the dough in half and press and pat each half into a disk about 6 inches (15 cm) in diameter (figure d). Place the two disks of dough a couple of inches apart on the prepared pan.

6. Use a floured bench scraper or knife to mark each disk of dough into 8 wedges, pressing straight down, and cutting no further than halfway into the dough disk (figure e).

7. Bake the scones until they are very deep golden and firm, 12 to 15 minutes.

8. Slide each disk of baked scones onto a platter and use a knife to cut them completely along the markings into wedges.

....

SERVING: Serve the scones with butter, whipped cream, and jam for tea. They're also excellent for breakfast or brunch.

STORAGE: If you don't serve the scones immediately after they are baked, you may reheat them at 375°F (190°C) for a couple of minutes to warm them. If you wish to prepare them in advance, wrap and freeze them. Defrost and reheat as above.

....

VARIATIONS

CURRANT OR RAISIN SCONES: Stir ½ cup of dark raisins, golden raisins, or currants into the dry ingredients immediately before adding the liquid.

ROUND SCONES: Use either the plain or raisin dough for these. Pat the dough out about ¾ inch (3 cm) thick on a floured surface and use a 2½-inch (6-cm) diameter plain round cutter to form them. Place the scones about 1 inch (2½ cm) apart all around on the prepared pan. Press the scraps together and cut more scones, continuing to press the scraps together until you have used all the dough. Bake these for only 8 to 10 minutes.

fig. a

fig. b

fig. c

fig. d

fig. e

STEPS

a. After combining all of the dry ingredients in the food processor, add the butter and pulse until you reach a dry powdery consistency (step 2).

b. Use a fork to toss in the egg and milk mixture (step 4).

c. Gently knead the dough 3 to 4 times until it is smooth (step 5).

d. On a lightly floured surface, divide the dough in half and press and pat each half into a disk (step 5).

e. After transferring the disks to the prepared pan, use a bench scraper to mark each disk of dough into 8 wedges (step 6).

Makes 18 scones

SCONE DOUGH

3½ cups all-purpose flour
(spoon flour into a dry-measure cup and level off)

⅓ cup sugar

1 tablespoon baking powder

½ teaspoon salt

1 teaspoon ground ginger

6 tablespoons (¾ stick) cold unsalted butter,
cut into 12 pieces

⅔ cup (about 4 ounces/100 grams) crystallized
ginger, cut into ¼-inch (6-mm) dice

2 large eggs

¾ cup milk

ALMOND TOPPING

1 tablespoon egg white (liquefy egg white by beating
with a fork, then measure)

¾ cup (about 2 ounces/50 grams) blanched
sliced almonds

⅛ teaspoon ground cinnamon

⅓ cup sugar

1 cookie sheet or jelly-roll pan lined with parchment or foil

Ginger Scones
with Almond Topping

The crunch of the slightly sugary almond topping is perfect with the spicy tenderness of these scones. When you purchase crystallized ginger for your scones, make sure it is tender and moist, not dry and hard, since it can't be plumped like raisins without losing much of its flavor. See Sources on page 312 for mail-order ginger products.

1. Set a rack in the middle level of the oven and preheat to 400°F (200°C).

2. Combine the flour, sugar, baking powder, salt, and ginger in the bowl of a food processor fitted with the metal blade. Pulse several times to mix.

3. Add the butter and pulse until the mixture is thoroughly incorporated and mealy, 10 to 12 times. Add the crystallized ginger.

4. In a separate bowl, whisk the eggs and milk together and then add them to the flour mixture. Pulse several times to mix, but not until the mixture forms a ball.

5. Invert the bowl over a floured work surface and carefully remove the blade. Fold the dough over on itself several times to give it a final mixing.

6. Use a bench scraper or a knife to divide the dough into 3 equal pieces. Pat each piece into a disk 5 or 6 inches (12½ to 15 cm) in diameter. Use a floured bench scraper or a knife to cut each disk into 6 wedges.

7. Arrange the scones on the prepared pan, keeping them about 1½ inches (4 cm) apart all around.

8. To make the almond topping, combine the egg white and almonds in a small mixing bowl and use a rubber spatula to stir them together so that all the almond pieces are evenly coated with the egg white. Stir in the cinnamon and sugar. Top each scone with about 2 teaspoons of the topping by placing the topping on the scone, then using your fingertips to spread it evenly all over.

9. Bake the scones until they are well risen, firm to the touch, and the topping is a deep golden color, about 15 minutes.

10. Arrange the scones on a platter to serve. If possible, serve them immediately after they are baked.

SERVING: Serve the scones with butter, clotted cream, or nothing. I prefer mine plain, since the ginger and almonds provide plenty of richness.

STORAGE: Keep the scones loosely covered with plastic wrap on the day they are baked. Double wrap in plastic and freeze for longer storage. Defrost and reheat at 375°F (190°C) for about 5 minutes before serving, or to warm cooled freshly baked scones.

VARIATIONS

CINNAMON RAISIN SCONES: Replace the ground ginger with ground cinnamon. Replace the crystallized ginger with dark raisins, golden raisins, or a combination of the two. Use the almond topping, or brush the tops of the scones with milk and sprinkle lightly with a mixture of 2 tablespoons sugar and ¼ teaspoon ground cinnamon.

ORANGE-SCENTED DRIED CRANBERRY SCONES: Reduce the ground ginger to ¼ teaspoon and replace the crystallized ginger with dried cranberries. Add the grated zest of a large orange to the milk and egg mixture. Leave the tops of the scones plain or use the almond topping or the cinnamon-sugar variation above.

Makes 12 large scones

3 cups all-purpose flour
(spoon flour into a dry-measure cup and level off)

½ cup dark brown sugar

1 tablespoon baking powder

½ teaspoon salt

8 tablespoons (1 stick) cold salted butter,
cut into 12 pieces

2 large eggs

¾ cup heavy whipping cream, light cream, or half-and-half

1 cookie sheet or jelly-roll pan lined with parchment or foil

Butterscotch Scones

Good butterscotch flavor can be elusive. Butterscotch isn't quite the same as caramel, although they have elements in common. To my mind, good butterscotch always has a hint of saltiness, too. This butterscotch scone stands proudly alongside any butterscotch candy I've ever tasted, though it has significantly less sugar in it. Brown sugar and salted butter provide the right elements.

1. Set a rack in the middle level of the oven and preheat to 400°F (200°C).

2. Combine the dry ingredients in the bowl of a food processor. Pulse several times to mix.

3. Add the butter and pulse until the mixture is thoroughly incorporated and the mixture is mealy, 10 to 12 times.

4. Whisk the eggs and cream together and add them. Pulse several times to mix, but not until the mixture forms a ball.

5. Invert the bowl onto a floured work surface and carefully remove the blade. Fold the dough over on itself several times to give it a final mixing.

6. Use a bench scraper or a knife to divide the dough into 3 equal pieces. Pat each piece of dough into a disk about 5 inches (13 cm) in diameter. Use a floured bench scraper or a knife to cut each disk into 4 wedges.

7. Arrange the scones on the prepared pan, keeping them about 1½ inches (4 cm) apart all around. Bake the scones until they are well risen, firm to the touch, and a deep golden color, about 15 minutes.

8. Arrange the scones on a platter to serve. If possible, serve them immediately after they are baked.

SERVING: Serve the scones with butter, clotted cream, or nothing. I prefer mine plain, since the butterscotch flavor provides plenty of richness.

STORAGE: Keep the scones loosely covered with plastic wrap on the day they are baked. Double wrap in plastic and freeze for longer storage. Defrost and reheat at 375°F (190°C) for about 5 minutes before serving, or to warm cooled freshly baked scones.

VARIATIONS

BUTTERSCOTCH CHOCOLATE CHUNK SCONES: Stir 6 ounces (175 g) bittersweet or semisweet chocolate, cut into ¼- to ½-inch (¾- to 1-cm) chunks, into the flour mixture before adding the liquid.

Makes 12 large scones

....

3 ounces (75 grams) milk chocolate, cut into ¼-inch (6-mm) pieces

¼ cup alkalized (Dutch process) cocoa powder, sifted after measuring

⅓ cup sugar

2 ⅔ cups all-purpose flour
(spoon flour into a dry-measure cup and level off)

3 teaspoons baking powder

½ teaspoon salt

6 tablespoons (¾ stick) cold unsalted butter, cut into 12 pieces

6 ounces (175 grams) bittersweet chocolate, cut into ½-inch (1-cm) chunks

1 large egg

¾ cup milk

1 cookie sheet or jelly-roll pan lined with parchment or foil

Triple Chocolate Scones

I'm sure a true Scotsman would keel over at the thought of a chocolate scone. But these are quite restrained, even though they contain three forms of chocolate: milk, bittersweet, and cocoa powder. I use cut-up bittersweet chocolate for the chunks in the scones instead of chocolate chips because the latter are seldom made from high-quality chocolate.

1. Set a rack in the middle level of the oven and preheat to 400°F (200°C).

2. Combine the milk chocolate, cocoa, and sugar in the bowl of a food processor fitted with the metal blade. Pulse repeatedly until the chocolate is finely ground. Don't over-process or the chocolate will melt.

3. Add the flour, baking powder, and salt and pulse 5 to 6 times to mix thoroughly. Add the butter and pulse until it is finely mixed in and the mixture resembles cornmeal, 10 to 12 pulses. Add the bittersweet chocolate chunks to the bowl.

4. Quickly whisk the egg and milk together and add to the bowl. Pulse 3 or 4 times rapidly, until all is thoroughly incorporated but the dough does not form a ball.

5. Invert the bowl onto a floured work surface and carefully remove the blade. Fold the dough over on itself several times to give it a final mixing.

6. Use a bench scraper or a knife to divide the dough into 3 equal pieces. Pat each piece of dough into a disk about 5 inches (13 cm) in diameter. Use a floured bench scraper or a knife to cut each disk into 4 wedges.

7. Arrange the scones on the prepared pan, keeping them about 1½ inches (4 cm) apart all around. Bake the scones until they are well risen, firm to the touch, and the topping is a deep golden color, about 15 minutes.

8. Arrange the scones on a platter to serve. If possible, serve them immediately after they are baked.

....

SERVING: Serve the scones with butter, clotted cream, or nothing. I prefer mine plain, since the chocolate has plenty of richness.

STORAGE: Keep the scones loosely covered with plastic wrap on the day they are baked. Double wrap in plastic and freeze for longer storage. Defrost and reheat at 375°F (190°C) for about 5 minutes before serving, or to warm cooled freshly baked scones.

....

VARIATIONS: Finish these with the Almond Topping from the Ginger Scones, page 54.

CRUMB TOPPING

1 cup all-purpose flour
(spoon flour into a dry-measure cup and level off)

½ teaspoon baking powder

¼ teaspoon ground cinnamon

6 tablespoons (¾ stick) unsalted butter

⅓ cup light brown sugar

MUFFIN BATTER

2 ½ cups all-purpose flour
(spoon flour into a dry-measure cup and level off)

2 teaspoons baking powder

¼ teaspoon salt

¼ teaspoon freshly grated nutmeg

8 tablespoons (1 stick) unsalted butter, softened

¾ cup sugar

½ cup light brown sugar

2 large eggs

½ cup milk

1 pint blueberries, rinsed, drained, and picked over,
see *Note* below

One 12-cavity muffin pan with paper liners

Blueberry Crumb Muffins

There's nothing better than a blueberry muffin, and I've tasted hundreds of different versions in my search for the perfect one. My ideal is a sweet muffin, but one that's not overly sweet, and it must be packed with blueberries. The crumb topping adds a note of richness and a perfect contrast in texture to these moist, tender muffins.

1. Set a rack in the middle level of the oven and preheat to 375°F (190°C).

2. For the crumb topping, combine the flour, baking powder, and cinnamon in a medium mixing bowl and stir well to mix. Melt the butter in a small pan. Remove from the heat, then add the brown sugar to the pan of melted butter and use a small heatproof rubber spatula to stir them together. Scrape the butter and sugar mixture into the flour mixture, stirring it in until the flour is evenly moistened. Set aside while preparing the muffin batter.

3. Combine the flour, baking powder, salt, and nutmeg in a mixing bowl and stir well to mix.

4. Combine the butter and sugars in the bowl of an electric mixer fitted with the paddle attachment. Beat on medium speed for about 1 minute, or until well mixed and a little lightened in color. Beat in the eggs one at a time, beating smooth after each.

5. Decrease the mixer speed to low and beat in ½ the flour mixture. Stop the mixer and use a large rubber spatula to scrape down the bowl and beater.

6. On low speed, beat in the milk. After the batter has absorbed the milk, beat in the remaining flour mixture. Stop and scrape down the bowl and beater again.

7. Add the blueberries to the bowl and beat them into the batter on the lowest speed for no more than 2 to 3 seconds, to crush some of the berries slightly.

8. Remove the bowl from the mixer and use a large rubber spatula to give a final mixing to the batter.

9. Divide the batter equally among the cavities in the muffin pan. Break the crumb topping into small crumbs with your fingertips and scatter over the top of each muffin. Bake the muffins until they are well risen, feel firm to the touch, and the topping is golden, about 30 minutes. Cool the muffins in the pan on a rack.

SERVING: These are perfect for breakfast or brunch, but really they're good any time of the day or night.

STORAGE: Keep the muffins loosely covered with plastic wrap on the day they are baked. Wrap tightly and freeze for longer storage. If frozen, defrost at room temperature and reheat at 350°F (180°C) for 5 minutes, then cool before serving.

VARIATIONS

Of course you may omit the crumb topping if you wish. If you do, sprinkle the tops of the muffins with a mixture of 2 tablespoons sugar and ¼ teaspoon ground cinnamon before baking.

WHOLE WHEAT RAISIN MUFFINS: For the muffin batter, substitute whole wheat flour for 1 cup of the flour, ground cinnamon for the nutmeg, 1¼ cups dark brown sugar for the sugar and light brown sugar, and 2 cups dark raisins for the blueberries. Omit the crumb topping and leave the tops of the muffins plain.

Note: The best way to handle the blueberries is to rinse them well in a colander and pour them onto a jelly-roll pan lined with paper towels. The toweling will absorb the water clinging to the berries and it will be easy to spot any green or shriveled berries or stems, which should be removed.

Makes 12 standard muffins

2 cups all-purpose flour
(spoon flour into a dry-measure cup and level off)

1½ teaspoons baking powder

1 teaspoon baking soda

½ teaspoon salt

1 teaspoon caraway seeds, optional

8 tablespoons (1 stick) unsalted butter, melted

¼ cup sugar

1 large egg

1¼ cups buttermilk

¾ cup dark raisins or currants tossed with
1 tablespoon flour

One 12-cavity muffin pan with paper liners

Irish Soda Bread Muffins

Real Irish soda bread is made from nothing more than flour, baking soda, salt, and buttermilk. Fancier versions include a little butter and sugar for flavor and tenderness, or maybe a few raisins and/or caraway seeds, but real soda bread has nothing to do with the cakelike commercial versions. I'm using my friend and colleague Cara Tannenbaum's technique for mixing a muffin batter starting with melted butter—you just add all the ingredients one at a time and they're in the oven in no time.

1. Set a rack in the middle level of the oven and preheat to 350°F (180°C).

2. Combine the flour, baking powder, baking soda, salt, and caraway seeds, if using, in a mixing bowl and stir well to combine.

3. In a large mixing bowl, whisk together the butter and sugar. Whisk in the egg and ½ the buttermilk. Use a large rubber spatula to gently stir ½ the flour mixture into the liquid. Stir in the remaining buttermilk.

4. Stir in the raisins followed by the remaining flour mixture.

5. Divide the batter equally among the cavities in the muffin pan. Bake the muffins until they are well risen and feel firm to the touch, about 30 minutes. Cool the muffins in the pan on a rack.

SERVING: Perfect for breakfast or brunch, these muffins are best spread with a little butter and/or marmalade.

STORAGE: Keep the muffins loosely covered with plastic wrap on the day they are baked. Wrap tightly and freeze for longer storage. If frozen, defrost at room temperature and reheat at 350°F (180°C) for 5 minutes, then cool before serving.

1½ cups all-purpose flour
(spoon flour into a dry-measure cup and level off)

⅔ cup alkalized (Dutch process) cocoa powder,
sifted after measuring

1 teaspoon baking soda

½ teaspoon salt

3 medium bananas, peeled and mashed with a
fork to make 1½ cups

½ cup sour cream

12 tablespoons (1½ sticks) unsalted butter, softened

1 cup granulated sugar

½ cup light brown sugar

3 large eggs

Two 12-cavity muffin pans with 16 paper liners

Cocoa Banana Muffins

For the best banana flavor, make sure to use very ripe bananas. Their peels should be covered with dark brown, if not black, speckles. If the bananas are not ripe enough, these will taste no better than cocoa potato muffins.

1. Set a rack in the middle level of the oven and preheat to 350°F (180°C).

2. Combine the flour, cocoa, baking soda, and salt in a mixing bowl and stir well to mix.

3. In a separate bowl, stir together the mashed bananas and sour cream; set aside.

4. Combine the butter, sugar, and brown sugar in the bowl of an electric mixer fitted with the paddle attachment. Beat on medium speed until well mixed and a little lightened in color, about 1 minute. Beat in the eggs one at a time, beating smooth after each addition.

5. Decrease the mixer speed to low and beat in ½ the flour mixture. Stop the mixer and use a large rubber spatula to scrape down the bowl and beater. Beat in the banana mixture. After the batter has absorbed the banana mixture, beat in the remaining flour mixture. Stop and scrape down the bowl and beater again.

6. Remove the bowl from the mixer and use a large rubber spatula to give a final mixing to the batter.

7. Divide the batter equally among the cavities in the muffin pans. Bake the muffins until they are well risen and feel firm to the touch, about 30 minutes. Because this is such a liquid batter, test a muffin with a toothpick or the point of a thin-bladed knife—it should emerge with just a few moist crumbs clinging to it.

8. Cool the muffins in the pan on a rack.

SERVING: Perfect for breakfast or brunch, these are also good at any time of the day or night.

STORAGE: Keep the muffins loosely covered with plastic wrap on the day they are baked. Wrap tightly and freeze for longer storage. If frozen, defrost at room temperature and reheat at 350°F (180°C) for 5 minutes, and cool before serving.

BLUEBERRY CRUMB MUFFINS (*Left*), COCOA BANANA MUFFINS (*Middle*), IRISH SODA BREAD MUFFINS (*Right*).

3 cups all-purpose flour
(spoon flour into a dry-measure cup and level off)

1 cup rolled oats

⅓ cup sugar

1 tablespoon baking powder

¾ teaspoon salt

8 tablespoons (1 stick) cold unsalted butter, cold,
cut into 12 pieces

1 large egg

1 cup buttermilk

One 9 x 13 x 2-inch (23 x 33 x 5-cm) pan lined with buttered foil, plus 2 cookie sheets or jelly-roll pans lined with parchment or foil for drying the rusks

Sweet Rusks for Dunking

This type of rusk, called a *beschuit* in Dutch, is a breakfast and tea bread. It is as common in South Africa as it is in the Netherlands, a remnant of that country's original Dutch settlers. If the Dutch name sounds like biscotti, it's for good reason: Rusks of all kinds, whether yeast risen or baking powder risen as the ones here, are first baked, then cut or separated and baked again, just like the toasted Italian cookies. This recipe comes from Reina Teeger, via her sister, my friend Kyra Effren. It seems Reina was able to pry the recipe from the chef at a game reserve in South Africa that she and her husband once visited. Unlike biscotti, which are crisp and penetrable with normal teeth, rusks must be dunked in tea, coffee, or (preferably warm) milk to soften them. They are much too hard to be eaten dry.

1. Set a rack in the middle level of the oven and preheat to 350°F (180°C).

2. Combine the flour, oats, sugar, baking powder, and salt in the bowl of a food processor fitted with the metal blade. Pulse 10 to 12 times to finely grind the oatmeal.

3. Add the butter to the bowl and pulse about 12 times, or until the butter is completely worked into the dry ingredients, but the mixture remains cool and powdery.

4. Whisk the egg and buttermilk together and add to the bowl. Pulse until the dough is evenly moistened but does not necessarily form a ball.

5. Invert the bowl to a floured work surface and carefully remove the blade. Gently knead the dough a few times until it is smooth.

6. Squeeze and roll the dough into a cylinder about 12 inches (30 cm) long. Cut the dough into thirds and roll each third into a cylinder that is 12 inches (30 cm) long. Use a bench scraper or a knife to cut one of the pieces of dough at 1-inch (2½/¼-cm) intervals to make 12 equal pieces. Repeat with the remaining pieces of dough to make a total of 36 pieces.

7. Between the palms of your hands, roll a piece of dough into an even sphere. Place it in the pan starting at the top left corner. Continue rolling the dough into spheres and arranging the spheres in the pan so that you have 4 pieces of dough across the 9-inch (23-cm) side of the pan and 9 pieces of dough across the 13-inch (33-cm) side of the pan, touching each other. The pieces of dough will automatically form little rectangles as they press against one another.

8. Bake the rusks until they are well risen and deep golden, about 40 minutes. Cool the rusks on a rack in the pan until they are cool enough to handle.

9. While they are cooling, readjust the oven racks to the upper and lower thirds and decrease the heat to 250°F (120°C). Leave the oven door ajar for a minute or two to cool.

10. Lift the rusks out of the pan by using the foil lining and place them on a cutting board. Break the rusks apart where they touch each other—they should come apart easily. If not, use a small paring knife to cut them apart from one another.

11. Arrange 18 of the rusks, cut side down, on each of the prepared pans. Bake the rusks until they are very dry and crisp, about 1½ hours.

12. Cool the rusks in the pans on racks.

....

SERVING: Serve the rusks for breakfast or tea; they are not a dessert.

STORAGE: Keep the rusks between sheets of parchment or wax paper in a tin or plastic container with a tight-fitting lid. If they soften, bake them again as in steps 11 and 12.

....

VARIATIONS

Substitute Muesli cereal or another whole grain breakfast cereal, such as bran flakes, for the rolled oats.

70 Armenian "Barbary" Bread

71 Turkish Flatbread

72 Pita Bread

74 Fougasse: Pierced
French Flatbread

76 Crisp Cornmeal Flatbread

77 Instant Sandwich Bread

78 French Bread for Baguettes
& Other Loaves

80 Pain de Campagne

82 Semolina Sesame Braid

83 Pain de Seigle:
French Rye Bread

84 Seven Grain & Seed Bread

85 Prosciutto Bread

86 Elegant Dinner Rolls

88 Rosemary Olive Knots

90 Cornetti: Olive-Oil Rolls
from Bologna

2.

Breads

Baking bread at home needn't be time consuming.
In reality, most breads require very little attention aside
from the mixing and shaping process. You'll need to
be available to check the risings—both as dough and
as the formed loaf, loaves, or rolls—of course, but that's
just a matter of taking a quick look.

The breads here fall into several rough categories:

Flatbreads: As their name implies, these are thinner breads, often of Middle Eastern origin.

Pan Loaves: These are the familiar rectangular loaves that are baked in a loaf pan.

Free-Form Loaves: Everything from baguettes to *boules* (round loaves) fits into this category.

Rolls: These are individual breads, used to accompany a meal or as a base for sandwiches.

Throughout the chapter there is an emphasis on using whole grains for better flavor, texture, and appearance. And there are plenty of recipes that use plain white flour as well.

Most of the breads here are made according to a new method for mixing bread doughs. First you just stir the ingredients together or give them a spin in the food processor or mixer, and allow the dough to rest for 10 to 20 minutes. Afterward, you might mix again briefly by machine, or just fold the dough over on itself several times to make it smoother and more elastic. It was recently discovered by bread technologists that mixing a dough vigorously or for a long time can deprive it of the natural sweet flavor of wheat, a flavor found in the best breads.

Bread Ingredients
and Techniques

Yeast, a fungal leavener, is suited to elastic, gluten-forming doughs that accommodate its slow development of carbon dioxide. Bread is an example of a product where high gluten content is desirable, as opposed to cake, which would be tough if you were to develop the gluten considerably. Most recipes (in this book and elsewhere) call for active dry yeast, which is granulated yeast that comes in small jars or individual envelopes. An envelope of yeast contains ¼ ounce or 7 grams (about 2½ teaspoons) of active dry yeast. Dry yeast is also available in bulk; all the recipes in this book call for measuring-spoon amounts of dry yeast, so bulk yeast is easy to use. Yeast will have an expiration date and should be kept in the refrigerator or freezer.

Yeast is also available in small moist cakes and in instant form. Instant yeast is faster acting (although "instant" is an exaggeration), but it doesn't lend quite the same depth of flavor. Cake yeast is available in ⅔-ounce (16-gram), 2-ounce (50-gram), and 1-pound (450-gram) cakes. The first two sizes are available in different regions. One-pound blocks may sometimes be purchased from a friendly bakery. A ⅔-ounce (16-gram) cake is equivalent to 1 envelope or 2½ teaspoons dry yeast. A 2-ounce (50-gram) block is equivalent to 3 envelopes of yeast, so just cut off a third for a recipe that calls for 1 envelope or

2½ teaspoons of dry yeast. If you buy a 1-pound (450-gram) cake of yeast and don't use it all at once, divide it into eight 2-ounce (50-gram) pieces (dividing visually is okay), wrap them in plastic, and freeze. Divide further, if necessary, and chop slightly. Dissolve the yeast while it is still frozen or it will become pasty and unmanageable.

All yeast has to be dissolved in liquid before being added to a dough. Warm liquid between 100° and 110°F (37 to 43°C) is perfect. To dissolve cake yeast, crumble, then whisk into the warm liquid. For dry yeast, whisk while pouring it in slowly. Modern dry yeast dissolves almost immediately.

Current thinking about mixing bread doughs dictates mixing less in order to preserve the natural sweet wheat flavor of the flour. When flour is mixed for a long time in dough, some of the flavor-carrying substances oxidize and lose their flavor. That's why all the recipes for breads and other yeast-risen doughs in this book call for mixing just to combine, then allowing the dough to rest. After a rest, the dough mixes smooth with a minimum of kneading, preserving that elusive flavor. Lots of chemical changes occur in the dough while it's resting, including the absorption of dead yeast cells, which helps to make the dough smooth and elastic without a lot of kneading.

Proofing is the final rising before baking. Breads and rolls should be covered during proofing to avoid thickening the crust too much. Proof to a 100% increase in size unless otherwise stated in the recipe. In general, when it comes to bread and other yeast doughs, the leaner the dough, the cooler the rise. Bread doughs can rise very well, if slowly, at a cool room temperature, developing the best flavor and texture possible.

When shaping bread doughs, you will often form them into a round loaf or loaves. This stretches a smooth, even skin onto the outside of the dough that becomes an attractive crust after baking. On a flour-free work surface, form small pieces of dough into rounds under the cupped palm of your hand, moving in a circle and just touching the top of the dough with the center of your palm. For large pieces, use both hands to press the bottom of the dough toward the center of the bottom, rotating it as you do so for an even shape.

For best results when forming loaves, round the loaf-sized pieces of dough first, then cover and allow to rest for 20 minutes. For a pan loaf, invert the dough so that the smoothest part is on the bottom and press the dough into a rough rectangle. Fold the left and right sides inward an inch (2½ cm) or so, then roll it up from the top down, pinching the seam together where it meets. Invert the formed loaf into the pan, making sure the seam is on the bottom, and gently press it to fill the pan. For a baguette, form as for a pan loaf, then roll the resulting piece of dough under the palms of your hands to elongate it, slightly pointing the ends.

To slash loaves before baking, use a single-edge razor and hold it at a 20-degree angle to the top of the loaf. Slash only ⅛ inch (3 mm) or less into the loaf—you want to cut only the crust, not into the crumb below.

To apply an egg wash, whisk the egg and salt (or other ingredients as specified in the recipe) until very liquid. When brushing on the egg wash, clean off the brush on the side of the egg-wash bowl or cup to eliminate excess, just as you would when loading a paintbrush. This will avoid making puddles of egg wash. For all yeast-risen pastries, make sure to completely egg wash the sides, too, or there will be a pallid strip at the bottom of the loaf or rolls.

To test for doneness, insert the tip of a knife and inspect the crumb, or use an instant-read thermometer plunged into the center. It should read between 200°F and 210°F (90°C to 100°C).

A WORD ABOUT ORGANIC LEAVENERS: Sourdough starter (*levain* in French) is the most common organic leavener and it imparts a characteristic sour taste to breads. Although much has been written over the years about "natural yeasts in the air" being "captured" by sourdough starters, the true explanation is actually much simpler: The natural yeasts are actually present in the flour itself, having grown on the wheat as it was maturing. Some sourdoughs are prepared by adding a naturally yeast-rich ingredient, such as raisins, potatoes, or even cabbage, to flour and water. Many European starters, such as those used for making traditional German rye breads, are made from rye and/or whole wheat flour, both rich in the natural yeasts that promote the formation of a good sourdough.

fig. a

fig. b

fig. c

GENERAL MIXING GUIDE TO SOFT DOUGHS

a. Using a bench scraper on a lightly floured surface, begin folding over the rested soft dough (here we use a pain de campagne).

b. After folding over one third, fold over the second third with the bench scraper.

c. This shows the smoothness of the finished folded-up, risen dough.

Makes two 15-inch (38-cm) long and 5-inch (13-cm) wide oval flatbreads

....

4 cups unbleached all-purpose flour
(spoon flour into a dry-measure cup and level off)

1 cup whole wheat flour

2 teaspoons salt

4 teaspoons (1½ envelopes) active dry yeast

2 cups warm water, about 110°F (45°C)

2 tablespoons olive oil

2 teaspoons black sesame or nigella seeds, optional

2 cookie sheets or jelly-roll pans lined with parchment or foil

Armenian "Barbary" Bread

There's a bit of a debate as to whether this is an Afghan, Armenian, or Iranian bread. I've seen and tasted it at the Armenian bakeries in Watertown, Massachusetts. Most have a couple of different versions, one that they make, and another imported from Canada that's larger, whiter, and tastes more industrial made. Basically, berberi, or barbary, bread is a long, oval flatbread, dimpled on top and sometimes sprinkled with black sesame or nigella seeds. It's light and tender and makes a perfect bread to serve with Middle Eastern cheeses or with puréed salads such as baba ganoush or hummus. Thanks to my dear friend Sandy Leonard, who lives in Watertown, for tracking down this recipe.

....

1. Combine the white flour, whole wheat flour, and salt in a mixing bowl and stir well to combine.

2. In a separate large bowl, whisk the yeast into the water, then whisk in the olive oil. Stir about 2 cups of the flour mixture into the liquid, until it is smooth. Continue beating in the remaining flour mixture, 1 cup at a time, waiting until it is absorbed before adding more. After all the flour has been added, the dough should be medium soft.

3. Cover the bowl with a towel or plastic wrap and allow the dough to rest for 20 minutes.

4. Invert the dough from the bowl onto a floured work surface and use a bench scraper to fold it over on itself several times to make it smoother and more elastic.

5. Place the dough in a clean oiled bowl and turn it over so that the top is oiled. Cover the bowl with a towel or plastic wrap and allow the dough to rise until it doubles in bulk, 1 to 2 hours, depending on the temperature of the room.

6. Once the dough has risen, invert it onto a floured work surface and use a bench scraper or knife to divide it into 2 equal pieces.

7. Gently press and stretch one piece of dough, trying not to deflate it too much, into a long narrow oval, 12 to 15 inches (30 to 38 cm) long and 4 to 5 (10 to 13 cm) inches wide. Flour the top lightly, then fold the shaped dough into thirds and transfer it to one of the prepared pans. Unfold the dough and adjust its shape in the pan. Repeat with the other piece of dough.

8. Cover each bread with a towel or oiled plastic wrap and allow to rise until doubled in bulk, about 1 hour.

9. About 20 minutes before the breads are fully risen, set racks in the upper and lower thirds of the oven and preheat to 425°F (220°C).

10. Uncover one of the breads, and use your fingertip to dimple the top gently at 1-inch (2½-cm) intervals, without pressing too hard, or the dough will deflate. Sprinkle with the seeds, if using. Repeat with the other bread.

11. Bake the breads for 10 minutes, then switch the pan in the lower third of the oven to the upper third and vice versa, turning each pan from back to front at the same time. Continue baking the breads until they are deep golden and firm-spongy to the touch, about 10 additional minutes.

12. Slide or lift the breads from the pans onto racks to cool.

....

SERVING: These flatbreads are a perfect accompaniment to Middle Eastern meze or hors d'oeuvres. But they are excellent with any kind of food.

STORAGE: Keep the breads loosely covered at room temperature on the day they are baked. Wrap in plastic and freeze for longer storage. Defrost frozen breads and reheat them at 375°F (190°C) for 7 to 8 minutes and cool before serving.

Makes two 8- to 9-inch (20- to 23-cm) loaves,
about 1 inch (2 1/2 cm) thick

....

4 cups unbleached all-purpose flour
(spoon flour into a dry-measure cup and level off)

2½ teaspoons salt

4 teaspoons (1½ envelopes) active dry yeast

1¾ cups warm water, about 110°F (45°C)

1 tablespoon olive oil

2 cookie sheets or jelly-roll pans dusted
with cornmeal

VARIATIONS

MIXED-GRAIN TURKISH FLATBREAD:
For more deeply flavored bread, substitute
½ cup whole wheat flour and ½ cup whole grain
rye flour for 1 cup of the unbleached all-purpose
flour.

SESAME TURKISH FLATBREAD: Omit the
flour before dimpling the top of the bread.
Quickly paint the top of each bread with water
and sprinkle each with 1 tablespoon of sesame
seeds immediately before baking.

Turkish Flatbread

I tasted this bread at Alaysa, a Turkish restaurant in Melbourne, Australia, in 2002. At the back of the dining room there sits an immense wood-burning oven, and while we were having lunch we could see the bakers were all hard at work, dividing the risen dough and shaping the small disk-shaped loaves. As soon as a dozen or so were formed, they were arranged on a large wooden peel and went straight into the oven. One of the bakers told me that they normally make several thousand of these a day to supply their own restaurant and others in the neighborhood. Achieving the right texture of a light open crumb in the baked bread requires working with very soft dough. Don't hesitate to flour the work surface or your hands to make handling the dough easier, but please resist the temptation to work more flour into the dough—it will toughen it.

....

1. Combine the flour and salt in the bowl of a food processor fitted with the metal blade. Pulse several times to combine.

2. Whisk the yeast into the water and whisk in the oil. Add the liquid to the food processor and pulse to form a soft dough. Let the machine run continuously for 10 seconds.

3. Invert the food processor bowl over an oiled mixing bowl to turn out the dough. Carefully remove the blade and transfer any dough on it to the bowl. Cover the bowl with plastic wrap and allow the dough to rest for 20 minutes.

4. Invert the rested dough to a floured work surface and use a bench scraper to fold the dough over on itself several times, as in the photographs on page 69. Return the folded dough to the oiled mixing bowl (you might have to oil it again first) and turn the dough over so that the top is also oiled. Cover the bowl with plastic wrap and let the dough rise until doubled in bulk, about 1 hour, depending on the temperature of the room.

5. Invert the dough from the bowl to a floured work surface without deflating it too much. Use a bench scraper or a knife to divide the dough into 2 equal pieces. Flour a 9-inch (23-cm) diameter cake cardboard or tart pan bottom and arrange one of the pieces of dough on it. Gently tug and press the dough into an 8- or 9-inch (20- to 23-cm) disk. Slide a metal spatula or long, thin-bladed knife under the dough to make sure it hasn't stuck, then slide it from the cardboard onto one of the prepared pans. Repeat with the second piece of dough.

6. Dust the top of each bread lightly with flour, using no more than 1 teaspoon. Gently dimple the top of each with your fingertips at about 1½-inch (4-cm) intervals, without pressing beyond the center of the bread. Cover each loaf with a towel or plastic wrap and allow them to rest until the dough starts to puff a little, about 20 minutes.

7. After the breads are formed, set racks in the upper and lower thirds of the oven and preheat to 450°F (230°C).

8. Bake for 10 minutes, then switch the pan in the lower third of the oven to the upper third and vice versa, turning each pan from back to front at the same time. Bake until they are deep golden and firm-spongy to the touch, 10 to 15 additional minutes. Slide the breads from the pans onto racks to cool

....

SERVING: These flatbreads, served in wedges, are a perfect accompaniment to Middle Eastern meze or hors d'oeuvres. Split and filled they make perfect sandwiches.

STORAGE: Keep the breads loosely covered at room temperature on the day they are baked. Wrap in plastic and freeze for longer storage. Defrost the breads and reheat them at 375°F (190°C) for 7 to 8 minutes, then cool before serving.

4 cups unbleached, all-purpose flour
(spoon flour into a dry-measure cup and level off)

1½ teaspoons salt

2½ teaspoons (1 envelope) active dry yeast

1½ cups warm water, about 110°F (45°C)

2 tablespoons olive oil

Cornmeal for transferring breads

Baking stone or an oven rack covered with 2 inverted
jelly-roll pans or cookie sheets side by side

Pita Bread

I was fascinated the first time I made pita and actually saw it puff into a balloon in the oven during its short baking time. My ideal pita is served at Moustache, a Middle Eastern restaurant near where I live in Greenwich Village. It makes some of the best Middle Eastern food I have ever eaten. Their pita is large, puffy, and always baked to order—it is a real treat. Pita is fun to make for a small, casual party. If your kitchen is large enough, let the guests help bake the bread while you attend to other things.

1. Stir together the flour and salt in the bowl of an electric mixer.

2. In a separate bowl, whisk the yeast into the water, then whisk in the oil. Use a large rubber spatula to stir the liquid into the flour, continuing to stir until the dough is evenly moistened.

3. Place the bowl on the mixer fitted with the dough hook and mix on the lowest speed for 2 minutes. Stop the mixer and let the dough rest for 10 minutes.

4. Mix the dough on medium speed for 2 minutes, or until it is smooth and elastic. Scrape the dough into an oiled bowl and turn the dough over so that the top is oiled. Press plastic wrap against the surface of the dough and let the dough rise until it has doubled in bulk, about 1 hour.

5. Scrape the dough out onto a floured work surface and press it into a disk. Cut the disk into 12 wedges. Round each wedge into a ball, rolling it under your cupped hand to stretch a smooth even skin around the ball of dough (figure a).

6. Line up the balls of dough next to one another and cover them with a towel or a piece of oiled plastic wrap. Let the pieces of dough rest for 15 minutes.

7. In the meantime, set a rack in the middle level of the oven and place the baking stone or inverted cookie sheets or jelly-roll pans on it. Preheat the oven to 500°F (250°C).

8. While the oven is heating, roll out each piece of dough into a 7-inch (17½-cm) disk using a rolling pin and pressing very hard because the dough resists (figures b and c). If the dough is very uncooperative roll each disk as much as you can, then set aside, overlapping the disks in order as you go. After you reach the last disk, go back to the first one and roll it again, then repeat with the others in order—this may be the only way to get the pieces of dough thin enough.

9. Cover the pieces of dough with a cloth or plastic wrap and let rest for 15 minutes.

10. Cover a peel or stiff piece of cardboard with cornmeal. Transfer as many pieces of dough as you can fit into the oven at the same time to the peel. Use the peel to deposit the breads to the heated pan or baking stone, pulling it away with a quick sharp movement.

11. Bake for 2 to 4 minutes, or until the breads are well puffed and golden. Bake as many of the disks of dough at a time as will fit in the oven without overlapping—it is better to bake fewer at a time and have them puff successfully than to stuff them in the oven.

12. Transfer the pita to racks as they are baked—they will deflate, but will remain open on the inside. Continue until you have baked all the pieces of dough.

SERVING: Serve as bread with Middle Eastern food, or slash open the end of a pita and fill it for a sandwich. I like to slide slices of ham and Gruyère into a pita and toast it in the toaster oven until the bread is crisp and the cheese is melted.

STORAGE: Keep the leftover pita in a plastic bag in the refrigerator and reheat in a 375°F (190°C) oven or toaster oven for 5 minutes. Freeze for longer storage.

fig. a

ROLLING PITA BREAD

a. On a floured surface, roll each rounded wedge of dough under your palm to stretch a smooth even skin all around (step 5).

b. Aftet the balls of dough have rested for 15 minutes, begin to roll them out by pressing them flat onto a floured surface with the palm of your hand (step 8).

c. Then with a rolling pin, press very hard to roll each piece of dough into a 7-inch (17½-cm) disk (step 8).

fig. b

fig. c

....

5½ cups unbleached all-purpose flour
(spoon flour into a dry-measure cup and level off)

2½ teaspoons salt

4 teaspoons (1½ envelopes) active dry yeast

2 cups warm tap water, about 110°F (45°C)

4 tablespoons olive oil

Olive oil for brushing the outside of the fougasse

2 cookie sheets or jelly-roll pans lined with
parchment or foil

Fougasse:
Pierced French Flatbread

A fougasse is a unique flatbread in that is pierced through to the bottom in a series of slashes to increase the quantity of crust. There are two principal shapes associated with the fougasses of southern France, a pierced leaf, as in the recipe here, and a long rectangular shape that resembles a ladder. The ladder shape is impractical to prepare in a home oven because the largest size baking pan available still won't make the 2- to 3-foot (61- to 91-cm) long fougasses associated with that shape. Finally, there is also a sweet version, flavored with fennel and orange zest, and encrusted with sugar before baking, usually made in an individual size.

1. Combine the flour and salt in a mixing bowl and stir well to combine.

2. In another large mixing bowl, whisk the yeast into the water, then whisk in the oil.

3. Use a large rubber spatula to stir about 2 cups of the flour and salt mixture into the liquid. Beat for a few seconds until smooth. Stir in the remaining flour mixture about 1 cup at a time, beating smooth after each addition. After the last of the flour has been absorbed, cover the bowl with a towel or plastic wrap and let it rest for 20 minutes.

4. Scrape the dough out of the bowl onto a floured work surface and use a bench scraper to fold the dough over onto itself several times to make it smoother and more elastic (see page 69).

5. Place the dough in a clean oiled bowl and turn it over so that the top is oiled. Cover the bowl with a towel or plastic wrap and let the dough rise until doubled in bulk, 1 to 2 hours, depending on the room temperature.

6. After the dough has risen, invert it from the bowl onto a floured work surface. Use a bench scraper or a knife to divide the dough into 2 equal pieces.

7. Place the first piece of dough on a lightly floured work surface and gently press and stretch it into a triangle, about 8 inches (20 cm) across at the base, and about 12 inches (30 cm) long from the base to the top point. Fold the dough into thirds and transfer it to one of the prepared pans. Unfold the dough and even out the shape again (see figure a). Use a pizza wheel to cut 3 to 4 diagonal slashes on either side of the median strip that bisects the triangle from top to base (see figure b). Cover the fougasse with a towel and repeat with the remaining dough.

8. Let the fougasses rest for about 10 minutes, then gently pull in both directions to make the fougasse a couple of inches wider and longer and to open up the slashes. Brush the fougasse with olive oil and cover again. Let the fougasses rise until they have doubled in bulk, about 1 hour.

9. About 20 minutes before the fougasses are completely risen, set racks in the upper and lower thirds of the oven and preheat to 450°F (230°C).

10. Bake the fougasses for about 10 minutes, then switch the pan in the lower third of the oven to the upper third and vice versa, turning each pan from back to front at the same time. Bake the fougasses until they are

FORMING THE FOUGASSE

a. After unfolding the transferred dough onto the prepared pan, even out the triangular shape again to about 8 inches (20 cm) along the base and 12 inches (30 cm) along the sides (step 7).

b. Using a pizza wheel, cut 3 to 4 diagonal slashes on each half of the triangle (step 7).

fig. a

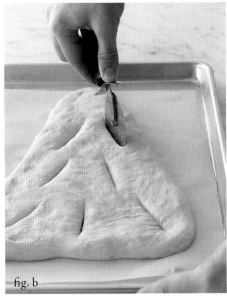

fig. b

deep golden and firm, 10 to 15 additional minutes. Slide each fougasse onto a rack to cool.

SERVING: Though this is a fine bread to serve with a meal, I wouldn't serve butter with it.

STORAGE: Keep the fougasses loosely covered at room temperature on the day they are baked. Wrap in plastic and freeze for longer storage. Defrost and reheat them at 375°F (190°C) for 7 to 8 minutes and cool before serving.

VARIATIONS

PART WHOLE-GRAIN FOUGASSE: Substitute 1 cup whole wheat flour and 1 cup whole-grain rye flour for 2 cups of the all-purpose flour. If you wish, dust the outside of the fougasses with whole wheat flour instead of painting them with olive oil.

Each of the following variations may be made with either the white flour or whole-grain dough.

BACON FOUGASSE: Slice 4 ounces (100 grams) thick-cut bacon into ½-inch (1-cm) wide strips. Cook the bacon over low heat until the fat is rendered and the bacon is crisp, 5 to 10 minutes. Remove from the fat with a slotted spoon to paper towels to drain and cool. Gently stir the cooled bacon into the dough right before adding the last cup of flowur.

ROSEMARY FOUGASSE: Stir 4 tablespoons chopped fresh rosemary leaves into the dough right before adding the last cup of flour.

OLIVE FOUGASSE: Stir ½ cup pitted Niçoise olives into the dough right before adding the last cup of flour.

CHEESE FOUGASSE: Stir 1 cup (about 3 ounces/75 grams) coarsely shredded Gruyère or Gouda into the dough before adding the last cup of flour. Sprinkle each fougasse with 2 tablespoons shredded cheese immediately before baking.

Makes 2 large flatbreads, each about 10 x 15 inches 25 x 38 cm)

....

2 cups all-purpose flour
(spoon flour into a dry-measure cup and level off)

⅔ cup stone-ground cornmeal

1½ teaspoons salt

¼ teaspoon cayenne pepper or hot paprika

2½ teaspoons (1 envelope) active dry yeast

¾ cup warm water, about 110°F (45°C)

¼ cup olive oil

Cornmeal for rolling the dough

2 cookie sheets or jelly-roll pans lined with parchment

Crisp Cornmeal Flatbread

This recipe was inspired by a cornmeal cracker that I saw San Francisco baker, author, and owner of the now-defunct Patisserie Française, Fran Gage prepare at a demonstration in New York. I love the crunch of the crisp bread coupled with the slight sweetness of corn. Be sure to use stone-ground cornmeal, whether yellow or white. The cornmeal regularly available in supermarkets doesn't have much corn flavor.

....

1. Combine the flour, cornmeal, salt, and cayenne pepper in the bowl of a food processor fitted with the metal blade. Pulse several times to mix.

2. In a medium mixing bowl, whisk the yeast into the water, then whisk in the oil. Add the liquid to the food processor and pulse to form a soft dough. Run the machine continuously for 10 seconds.

3. Invert the food processor bowl over an oiled mixing bowl to turn out the dough. Carefully remove the blade and transfer any dough on it to the bowl. Cover the bowl with plastic wrap and allow the dough to rest for 20 minutes.

4. Invert the rested dough to a floured work surface and use a bench scraper to fold the dough over on itself several times (see page 69).

5. Return the folded dough to the oiled mixing bowl (you might have to oil it again first) and turn the dough over so that the top is also oiled. Cover the bowl with plastic wrap and let the dough rise until doubled in bulk, about 1 hour, depending on the temperature of the room.

6. Set racks in the upper and lower thirds of the oven and preheat to 350°F (180°C).

7. Invert the risen dough to a surface lightly dusted with cornmeal. Without deflating the dough too much, use a bench scraper or a knife to divide the dough in half. Working with one piece of dough at a time, gently press it into a rough rectangle using the palms of your hands.

8. Lightly dust the dough with cornmeal and roll the dough as thinly as possible, keeping the dimensions of the baking pan you are going to use in mind as you go. If the dough is very resistant, slide it out of the way, cover it with a towel or plastic wrap, and work on the second piece of dough. After getting the second piece of dough as thin as possible,

return to the first one and it will cooperate much better.

9. After one of the pieces of dough is large enough, cut away any thick edges with scissors and slide it onto one of the prepared pans. Repeat with the second sheet of dough.

10. Pierce the dough all over at 1-inch (2½-cm) intervals with the tines of a fork. Bake the flatbreads for about 20 minutes, or until golden and crisp. About halfway through the baking, switch the pan in the lower third of the oven to the upper third and vice versa, turning each pan from back to front at the same time. Cool the baked flatbreads on the pans on racks.

....

SERVING: Break the breads into irregular pieces and arrange them in a napkin-lined bread basket. Use them as you would crackers—to accompany soup or salad, or with hors d'oeuvre dips or spreads.

STORAGE: Keep the flatbreads loosely covered on the day they are baked. Store them in a tin or plastic container with a tight-fitting lid. If they soften, arrange them on a cookie sheet or jelly-roll pan and bake them in a 300°F (150°C) oven for about 15 minutes. After they cool they will be crisp again.

Makes one 12 x 18-inch (30 x 45-cm) loaf, enough for twelve 4-inch (10-cm) square sandwiches

....

5½ cups unbleached all-purpose flour
(spoon flour into a dry-measure cup and level off)

2½ teaspoons salt

2 teaspoons sugar

5 tablespoons unsalted butter, cut into 8 pieces and softened

2½ teaspoons (1 envelope) active dry yeast

2½ cups warm water, about 110°F (45°C)

One 12 x 18-inch (30 x 45-cm) pan buttered and the bottom lined with a rectangle of parchment or buttered wax paper cut to fit

Instant Sandwich Bread

Here's an easy version of a tender, buttery sandwich bread that's ready in no time. It only rises once, in the pan, so that cuts out quite a bit of time. And the pan is a jelly-roll pan, instead of a loaf pan, so that the r ising, as well as the baking, are both accomplished in minimal time. Baking the bread in this type of pan will give you a large "sheet cake" shaped loaf that you can split horizontally, fill, and then cut into the shapes and sizes you wish.

1. Combine the flour, salt, and sugar in the bowl of a food processor fitted with the metal blade. Pulse several times to mix.

2. Add the butter and pulse again 8 to 10 times to completely mix it in, though the mixture should remain powdery.

3. Whisk the yeast into the water and add to the bowl. Pulse repeatedly to form a shaggy dough. Let rest in the bowl for 10 minutes.

4. Pulse again 6 to 8 times, or until the dough forms a ball. Invert the food processor bowl over a lightly oiled mixing bowl. Turn the dough to coat all sides, cover the bowl with plastic wrap, and let the dough rest for 30 minutes. It will just begin to puff.

5. Lightly flour the dough and scrape it into the prepared pan. Using the palms of your hands, evenly press the dough into the pan. If it resists, cover the pan with a towel or plastic wrap and let the dough rest for 5 minutes, then continue pressing it into the pan. Cover the pan with a towel or plastic wrap and let the dough rise until it has doubled in bulk, about 1 hour, depending on the temperature of the room.

6. About 20 minutes before the dough is completely risen, set a rack in the middle of the oven and preheat the oven to 400°F (200°C).

7. Bake the bread until it is well risen and firm to the touch, about 25 minutes. Cool the bread in the pan for 5 minutes, then slide it onto a rack to cool completely.

....

SERVING: Split horizontally and fill with your favorite sandwich filling.

STORAGE: Keep the bread loosely covered on the day it is baked. Wrap in plastic and freeze for longer storage. Defrost the bread and reheat at 375°F (190°C) for 7 to 8 minutes and cool before splitting and filling.

Makes 4 loaves of French bread, each about 18 inches long

1½ cups warm water, about 110°F (45°C)

....

2 jelly-roll pans dusted with cornmeal

FIRST DOUGH

1 cup room-temperature water

2 cups unbleached all-purpose flour
(spoon flour into a dry-measure cup and level off)

SECOND DOUGH

4 cups unbleached all-purpose flour
(spoon flour into a dry-measure cup and level off)

2 teaspoons salt

4 teaspoons (about 1½ envelopes/⅜ ounce/11 grams)
active dry yeast

French Bread for Baguettes
& Other Loaves

A simple French bread, such as a baguette, isn't difficult to prepare, but the dough needs long rests and rising time to develop flavor. The work of preparing the dough is easy and not very time consuming, but you have to plan on starting early and making it on a day when you'll be home for most of the day to monitor the risings of the dough. Shaping variations are given at the end of the recipe so you'll be able to produce a variety of different breads from this one easy-to-prepare dough.

1. To make the first dough, combine the water and flour in the bowl of an electric mixer. Use a large rubber spatula to stir them together. Place the bowl on the mixer with the paddle and beat the dough on the lowest speed, stopping and scraping down the bowl and beater a couple of times while the dough is mixing, until the dough is elastic and clings around the paddle, 3 to 4 minutes. Remove the bowl from the mixer, remove the paddle, and cover the dough with plastic wrap. Let the dough rest for 1 hour.

2. To make the second dough, place the flour and salt in a large mixing bowl and stir well to combine. In a separate bowl, whisk the yeast into the water. Use a large rubber spatula to stir the yeast liquid into the flour and salt. Continue stirring until the dough is evenly moistened, but it will not be particularly smooth—this doesn't matter at this point. Cover the bowl with plastic wrap and set aside until the first dough is finished resting. It will begin rising while it's resting.

3. An hour after setting the first dough to rest, scrape the second dough over it in the mixer bowl. Use a large rubber spatula to mix the two doughs together as well as possible.

4. Place the bowl on the mixer with the dough hook and mix on low speed just until the two doughs are thoroughly combined, about 2 minutes. Stop the mixer and let the dough rest for 15 minutes.

5. Start the mixer again on low speed and mix the dough until it becomes smooth and elastic, about 2 minutes.

6. Scrape the dough from the mixer bowl into an oiled mixing bowl and turn the dough over so that the top is oiled. Cover the bowl with a towel or plastic wrap and allow the dough to rise until it is very aerated and more than doubled in bulk, about 2 hours.

7. Scrape the dough out to a floured work surface and fold it over on itself several times. Return it to a freshly oiled bowl and turn it so that the top is oiled. Cover again and let the dough rest for 1 hour.

8. To shape the baguettes, scrape the dough onto a floured work surface and use a knife or a bench scraper to divide it into 4 equal pieces. Gently press each piece of dough, without deflating it too much, into a rectangle, approximately 9 inches (23 cm) wide and 7 to 8 inches (13 to 20 cm) long. Working with one piece of dough at a time, fold the two shorter edges inward about 1 inch (2½ cm), then roll up the dough jelly-roll style from one of the 9-inch (23-cm)

sides. Pinch the dough together to seal the seam. Place the partially formed baguette aside under a towel and repeat with the remaining pieces of dough.

9. Starting with the first baguette that you shaped, roll the dough under the palms of both hands to elongate it. Don't flour the work surface or the dough will just slide back and forth and not roll well. Press a little harder over the ends to taper them. Arrange the loaves, equidistant from each other and the sides of the pan, as they are formed, on the prepared pans. Remember to place them seam side down.

10. Cover each pan with a towel and let the loaves rise until they have doubled in bulk, 1 to 2 hours, depending on the temperature of the room.

11. About 20 minutes before the loaves are completely risen, set racks in the upper and lower thirds of the oven and preheat to 425°F (220°C).

12. Before baking the loaves, uncover them and use a single-edge razor blade to slash a series of diagonal cuts into the top of each loaf, holding the blade at about a 25-degree angle to the top of the loaf. Make 4 to 5 cuts in each loaf.

13. Bake the baguettes for about 15 minutes, then switch the pan in the lower third of the oven to the upper third and vice versa, turning each pan from back to front at the same time.

14. Continue baking until they are well risen, deep golden, and feel firm to the touch, 10 to 15 additional minutes. Slide the baked baguettes onto racks to cool.

....

SERVING: A baguette is a truly all-purpose bread. Use it as bread with a meal, split for sandwiches, or thinly slice on the diagonal and toast for dips and spreads. Any leftover bread that becomes stale makes excellent bread crumbs.

STORAGE: Keep the bread loosely covered on the day it is baked. Wrap tightly and freeze for longer storage. Defrost and reheat at 375°F (190°C), directly on the oven rack, for 7 to 8 minutes, and cool on a rack before serving.

VARIATIONS

WHEAT-SHEAF LOAF (EPI): This is a great way to increase the ratio of crust to crumb in a baguette. After the baguettes have risen, use scissors to cut through the dough at a 45-degree angle to each side, in alternating cuts. Start at the top of the loaf and make 3 to 4 cuts on each side. After cutting through the loaf, pull the points of the cut areas outward, so that they resemble branches. Needless to say, you must be very gentle with the risen dough during the cutting and shaping or it will deflate. Bake just as you would for baguettes.

Makes two 9-inch (23-cm) round loaves or three 18-inch
(45-cm) long loaves, 4 to 5 inches (10 to 13 cm) wide

....

1 batch French Bread dough, page 78, made with 1 cup
whole wheat flour replacing one of the cups of white flour
in the first dough, prepared up to the end of step 7.

2 jelly-roll pans dusted with cornmeal

80

Pain de Campagne

This "country bread" is a variation of the basic French Bread on page 78. I like to add a little whole wheat flour to the dough to approximate the "old-fashioned" taste this bread has in France. The shape of this bread is different, too, though there isn't any reason why you couldn't make a baguette or *epi* from it. I like to bake it as a large round loaf—the recipe makes two perfectly sized ones. This type of loaf is frequently risen in a cloth-lined basket called a *banneton* and inverted onto the pan before baking. You can approximate it by using a 9-inch (22-cm) round bread basket lined with a floured napkin, or bake the loaves free-form as in these instructions. Sometimes I bake this dough as a double-thick baguette, called a *bâtard*, making only two from the recipe.

1. Scrape the dough onto a lightly floured work surface. Use a bench scraper or a knife to divide the dough into 2 equal pieces.

2. Cup both hands around one of the pieces of dough, pushing inward at the bottom (figure a) and rotating the dough in your hands to make it round and to pull all the uneven edges of the dough underneath the sphere of dough you are forming (figure b). Repeat with the second piece of dough. Cover the round loaves with a towel and let them rest for 10 minutes.

3. After the dough has rested, gently repeat the rounding, making sure the loaves are perfectly even spheres.

4. Place one ball of dough (*boule*) on each of the 2 baking pans and cover them with towels. Let them rise until they have doubled in bulk, 1 to 2 hours.

5. About 20 minutes before the *boules* are fully risen, set racks in the upper and lower thirds of the oven and preheat to 400°F (200°C). Use a single-edge razor to slash 5 lines on the top of each *boule,* spacing them equidistant and holding the blade perpendicular to the loaf. Be careful to slash just the top skin of the dough. Repeat with 5 more lines diagonal to the first ones (figure c).

6. Bake the *boules* for about 15 minutes, then switch the pan in the lower third of the oven to the upper third and vice versa, turning each pan from back to front at the same time. Continue baking until they are well risen, deep golden, and feel firm to the touch, 15 to 20 minutes longer. Slide the baked *boules* to racks to cool.

....

SERVING: Use a sharp serrated knife to cut the bread into thin slices. When I want to make smaller slices to serve with a meal, I cut the loaf in half first, then I stand the loaf cut side down and slice at ½-inch (1-cm) intervals.

STORAGE: Keep the bread loosely covered on the day it is baked. Wrap tightly and freeze for longer storage. Defrost and reheat at 375°F (190°C), directly on the oven rack, for 7 to 8 minutes, and cool on a rack before serving.

....

VARIATIONS

BÂTARDS: Shape these the same way as the baguettes on page 78, but only make 2, using twice as much dough for each. Slash and bake as for the baguettes, but bake the bâtards 10 minutes longer.

fig. a

fig. b

FORMING PAIN DE CAMPAGNE

a. On a lightly floured surface, cup your hands around a piece of dough, pushing inward at the bottom (step 2).

b. Rotate the dough in your hands, making it round and pulling uneven edges underneath (step 2).

c. Using a single-edge razor, slash 5 lines across the top of the formed boule, repeating 5 more lines at a diagonal to the first ones (step 5).

fig. c

Makes 1 large braided loaf, about 16 inches (40 cm) long

....

2 cups unbleached all-purpose flour
(spoon flour into a dry-measure cup and level off)

¾ cup semolina flour

2 teaspoons salt

2½ teaspoons (1 envelope) active dry yeast

1½ cups warm water, about 110°F (45°C)

2 tablespoons sesame seeds

1 jelly-roll pan dusted with cornmeal

VARIATIONS

Shape the bread as a *bâtard* (page 80) or 2 small *boules* (pages 80–81) instead of braiding it. Add 2 teaspoons of crushed fennel seeds (see Fennel Fig & Almond Bread, page 42) and 1 cup golden raisins to the dough right before completing the machine mixing in step 4. Omit the sesame seeds and sprinkle the outside of each loaf with additional semolina flour after moistening.

Semolina Sesame Braid

The sweetness of semolina and the nutty flavor of sesame seeds combine to make this a delicious bread. To make the dough, you'll need fine-textured semolina, referred to as semolina flour. It's light yellow in color and resembles finely milled cornmeal. Semolina is made from a type of wheat, *Triticum durum*, similar to the one used for making ordinary flour, but it is a different species of the same genus. It is characteristically very high in the proteins that form gluten, so it's necessary to use only a portion of it in a bread dough to avoid making the dough excessively tough and elastic. Most semolina is used in manufacturing dry pasta such as spaghetti.

....

1. Combine the flour, semolina flour, and salt in the bowl of an electric mixer and stir well to combine.

2. Whisk the yeast into the water and add to the flour mixture. Use a large rubber spatula to mix the liquid into the flour, continuing to mix until it forms a rough dough with no dry spots.

3. Place the bowl on the mixer with the dough hook and mix on low speed for about 3 minutes. Stop the mixer and allow the dough to rest for 20 minutes.

4. Start the mixer again on low to medium speed and mix the dough until it is elastic, about 2 minutes. Remove the bowl from the mixer, cover it with a towel or plastic wrap, and allow to rest for 10 minutes.

5. Scrape the dough from the bowl onto a lightly floured work surface. Use a bench scraper to fold the dough over on itself several times to make it smoother and more elastic. Place the dough in an oiled bowl and turn the dough over so that the top is oiled. Cover with a towel or plastic wrap and allow it to rise until doubled in bulk, 1 to 2 hours, depending on the temperature of the room.

6. After the dough has risen, scrape it from the bowl onto a lightly floured work surface. Form the dough into a rough rectangle without deflating it too much. Use a bench scraper or a knife to divide the dough into 3 equal pieces.

7. Roll each piece of dough under the palms of your hands to form a cylinder about 16 inches (40 cm) long. Place the 3 cylinders of dough next to one another and, starting from the middle, alternately cross the strands of dough over each other to form a braid. Pinch the ends together and turn them under at the end. Turn the loaf around and repeat the braiding from the middle outward to the other end. Slide both hands under the loaf, one at each narrow end, and lift the braid to the prepared pan.

8. Brush water all over the outside of the loaf and evenly sprinkle the moistened areas with the sesame seeds. Cover the braid with a towel or plastic wrap and let it rise at room temperature until doubled, about 1 hour.

9. About 20 minutes before the braid is completely risen, set a rack in the middle of the oven and preheat to 400°F (200°C).

10. Bake the braid until it is well risen, deep golden, and feels firm when pressed with a fingertip, 30 to 40 minutes. Slide the braid onto a rack to cool.

....

SERVING: A perfect accompaniment to a meal, semolina bread also makes excellent toast. Or slice the bread very thinly (this is easier if the bread is a day or so old) and paint the slices with melted butter or good olive oil. Bake them on a jelly-roll pan at 300°F (150°C) until they are crisp and golden—this goes well with cheeses, pâtés, or soups.

STORAGE: Loosely cover with plastic wrap the day it is made, or wrap tightly and freeze for longer storage. Defrost the bread and reheat it at 350°F (180°C) for about 10 minutes, and cool it before serving.

Makes 2 thin baguettes, each about 12 inches (30 cm) long

....

SPONGE

1 teaspoon active dry yeast

½ cup warm water, about 110°F (45°C)

1 cup unbleached all-purpose flour
(spoon flour into a dry-measure cup and level off)

RYE DOUGH

1½ teaspoons active dry yeast
(the rest of the envelope you opened for the sponge)

1 cup warm water, about 110°F (45°C)

Sponge

1¼ cups medium or whole-grain rye flour

¾ cup unbleached all-purpose flour

1½ teaspoons salt

1 jelly-roll pan dusted with cornmeal

VARIATIONS

Add 1 teaspoon of caraway seeds or ground caraway to the dough. Or paint the outside of the unrisen loaves with water and sprinkle each one with 1½ teaspoons of caraway seeds. Form the entire quantity of dough into 1 large or 2 small *boules*, as on pages 80–81. Moisten and sprinkle with caraway seeds if you wish. A large *boule* will take 45 to 50 minutes to bake.

Pain de Seigle:
French Rye Bread

At the end of the first summer season I worked in Monte Carlo, I went to Nice with some friends to celebrate with dinner. We ordered enormous *plateaux de fruits de mer*—large platters of mostly raw shellfish. These were accompanied by thin slices of gray-looking bread served with butter. I took a bite of the bread, and then another, and then I identified the familiar taste—rye bread! The rye bread I knew back home was Jewish rye, while the French rye bread was less crusty, but equally delicious. Here's a recipe for the French rye bread. Don't be turned off by the fact that you need to prepare a sponge the day before (and don't be tempted to skip it—it's essential). It does require forethought, but the sponge takes all of 5 minutes to prepare, so it doesn't add an excessive amount of work to the process.

....

1. Make the sponge the day before you intend to bake the bread (it keeps in the refrigerator for up to 5 days as long as you watch that it doesn't dry out, and you deflate it occasionally). Whisk the yeast into the water in a small mixing bowl. Use a small rubber spatula to stir in the flour, stirring vigorously so that the sponge becomes somewhat elastic. Scrape the inside of the bowl free of any bits stuck to it, then use the spatula to press the sponge into a coherent ball. Cover the bowl tightly with plastic wrap and set it aside at room temperature to rise for 2 hours.

2. After the sponge has risen, use a small rubber spatula to deflate it and stir it back into a ball. Cover the bowl with plastic wrap again and refrigerate until you are ready to prepare the rye dough, at least overnight.

3. When you are ready to prepare the rye dough, whisk the yeast into the water in the bowl of an electric mixer. Scrape the sponge into the bowl and use a large rubber spatula to mix the liquid and sponge together until smooth. Stir in the rye flour in 3 additions, stirring the dough smooth after each. Add the all-purpose flour and salt and continue stirring until the dough is evenly moistened and there are no dry spots.

4. Place the bowl on the mixer with the dough hook and mix on low speed for 3 minutes. Scrape the sides of the bowl and the hook and allow the dough to rest for 10 minutes.

5. Mix the dough on low to medium speed until it is smooth and elastic, about 3 minutes. Scrape the dough into an oiled bowl then turn it so that the top is oiled. Cover with a towel or plastic wrap and let the dough rise until doubled, 1 to 2 hours.

6. Scrape the risen dough to a lightly floured work surface and use a bench scraper or a knife to divide it in half. Stretch ½ of the dough into a rough 6-inch (15-cm) square. Roll jelly-roll style from one side, and pinch the end to seal it. Repeat with the other piece of dough. Using the palms of your hands, roll the first piece of dough into a cylinder about 12 inches (30 cm) long. Repeat.

7. Arrange the formed loaves equidistant from each other and the sides of the pan. Cover the pan with a towel or plastic wrap and set aside to rise for about 45 minutes. The dough should only just start to puff; it does not have to rise until doubled.

8. About 20 minutes before the loaves are risen, set a rack in the middle of the oven and preheat to 375°F (190°C). Bake until the loaves are well risen and firm to the touch, about 35 minutes. Slide the loaves from the pans onto racks to cool.

....

SERVING: Slice the bread thinly and serve it with butter. It's also great toasted.

STORAGE: Keep loosely covered with plastic wrap on the day that it is baked. Wrap and freeze for longer storage. Defrost and serve at room temperature.

1 cup rolled oats

2 cups boiling water

⅓ cup sunflower seeds

⅓ cup poppy seeds

⅓ cup sesame seeds

5 teaspoons (2 envelopes) active dry yeast

1 cup warm water, about 110°F (45°C)

3 cups unbleached all-purpose flour
(spoon flour into a dry-measure cup and level off)

1 cup whole wheat flour

1 cup medium or whole grain rye flour

4 tablespoons light brown sugar

2 teaspoons salt

4 tablespoons unsalted butter,
cut into 12 pieces and softened

Two 9 x 5 x 3-inch (23 x 13 x 7-cm) loaf pans, buttered and
the bottoms lined with rectangles of parchment or buttered
wax paper cut to fit

VARIATIONS

You have the most leeway with the seeds. You may increase or decrease the quantity of any of them as long as you have 1 cup of seeds total. Sometimes I use ¼ cup each of the seeds listed and add ¼ cup of black sesame or nigella seeds. Cooked brown rice may replace up to ½ the oatmeal. Add it to the oats and water at the beginning.

Seven Grain & Seed Bread

Lots of recipes for multigrain breads simply call for adding a 5-, 7-, or 9-grain breakfast cereal to some fairly simple bread dough. This recipe goes one step further by including flavorful grains and seeds that bake into a loaf with excellent texture. The best place to shop for these ingredients is a health-food store or a supermarket that has a "bulk" foods department. Please don't be afraid to ask for a taste of the items you purchase, especially the seeds, since they can become rancid very quickly when stored at room temperature.

1. Combine the oats and boiling water in a medium mixing bowl and stir well to combine. Let the oatmeal cool, then stir in all the seeds.

2. Whisk the yeast into the water in a mixing bowl and set aside.

3. Combine the flour, whole wheat flour, rye flour, brown sugar, and salt in the bowl of an electric mixer. Use the paddle attachment to mix on low speed for 2 minutes. Add the butter and mix again until it is evenly incorporated.

4. Add the oatmeal and seed mixture and the dissolved yeast mixture to the bowl and mix again on low speed until a soft dough forms. Remove the bowl from the mixer and cover it with a towel or plastic wrap. Let the dough rest for 20 minutes.

5. Return the bowl to the mixer and, using the dough hook, mix the dough on low to medium speed until smooth, 3 to 4 minutes.

6. Scrape the dough into a buttered bowl and turn it over so that the top is buttered. Cover the bowl with a towel or plastic wrap and let the dough rise until doubled in bulk, 1 to 2 hours, depending on the room temperature.

7. Once the dough has risen, invert it onto a floured work surface and use the palms of your hands to press it into a rough rectangle. Use a bench scraper or a knife to divide the dough in half.

8. Press and stretch one of the pieces of dough into a rectangle a little longer than the loaf pan. Fold the two short ends inward to make a rectangle approximately the same length as the pan. Roll up one of the long ends, jelly-roll style, and pinch the seam together. Invert the formed loaf into one of the prepared pans, seamside down. Repeat with the remaining piece of dough.

9. Cover the pans with towels or buttered plastic wrap and allow the loaves to rise until they completely fill the pans, 1 to 2 hours, depending on the temperature of the room.

10. About 20 minutes before the loaves are completely risen, set a rack in the middle of the oven and preheat to 375°F (190°C).

11. Place the fully risen loaves in the oven and immediately decrease the temperature to 350°F (180°C). Bake the loaves until they are well risen, deep golden, and firm, about 30 minutes. Cool the loaves in the pans on racks for 5 minutes, then unmold them and cool on their sides on racks.

SERVING: Excellent at breakfast or brunch, this bread is also very good toasted. I also like it combined with ham, cheese, or a combination as a sandwich.

STORAGE: Keep the loaves loosely covered at room temperature on the day they are baked. Wrap in plastic and freeze for longer storage. Defrost the loaves and reheat them at 375°F (190°) for 7 to 8 minutes, and cool before serving.

Makes 2 loaves, each about 10 inches (25 cm) long

....

4 cups unbleached all-purpose flour
(spoon flour into a dry-measure cup and level off)

1½ teaspoons salt

1½ teaspoons sugar

1 tablespoon coarsely ground or cracked black pepper

4 teaspoons (about 1½ envelopes) active dry yeast

1½ cups warm water, about 110°F (45°C)

3 tablespoons olive oil

6 ounces (175 grams) prosciutto, sliced ⅛ inch (3 mm) thick when you purchase it, then cut into ¼-inch (½-cm) squares

1 jelly-roll pan covered with cornmeal

VARIATIONS

Prosciutto bread also makes a good braided bread. Make one large 1 (the baking time will be a little longer) or 2 small ones, as in the Semolina Sesame Braid on page 82.

Substitute bacon or salt pork (with skin removed) for the prosciutto. Dice and cook a pound (425 grams) in a wide sauté pan over low to medium heat, stirring occasionally to brown evenly. Drain on paper towels, allowing to cool before adding to the dough. You may also use the rendered fat instead of the olive oil.

Prosciutto Bread

Bread that includes something rich and fatty such as ham, bacon, or salt pork is an old tradition common to many nationalities. In the United States it is sometimes also referred to as "crackling bread," which is a key to its origin, I think. Nowadays when we no longer render animal fat to use for cooking, cracklings—those little pieces of stray meat and skin that accumulate while fat is being melted down or rendered—are but a faint memory, even in cultures that used to have them available regularly. This bread uses purchased prosciutto, but there are instructions for using bacon or salt pork as a substitute.

1. In a large mixing bowl, combine the flour, salt, sugar, and pepper and stir well.

2. In another bowl, whisk the yeast into the water, then whisk in the oil. Use a large rubber spatula to stir the liquid into the dry ingredients, continuing to stir until they are completely moistened and no dry areas remain. Mix in the prosciutto, using the spatula to fold the dough repeatedly from the bottom of the bowl over the top of the dough, until it is evenly distributed. Cover the bowl with a towel and let the dough rest for 10 minutes.

3. Scrape the dough onto a lightly floured work surface and use a bench scraper to fold the dough over onto itself several times to make it smoother and more elastic.

4. Place the dough in an oiled bowl and turn the dough over so that the top is oiled. Cover the bowl with a towel or plastic wrap and let rise until it has doubled in bulk, 1 to 2 hours, depending on the temperature of the room.

5. Scrape the risen dough out onto a lightly floured work surface. Use a bench scraper or a knife to divide the dough into 2 equal pieces. Shape each piece of dough into a *bâtard* (see page 80). Arrange the loaves on the prepared pan equidistant from each other and from the sides of the pan. Cover the pan with a towel or oiled plastic wrap and let the loaves rise until doubled.

6. About 20 minutes before the loaves are completely risen, set a rack in the middle level of the oven and preheat to 400°F (200°C).

7. Use a single-edge razor blade to make 4 to 5 diagonal slashes on the top of each loaf, holding the blade at a 20-degree angle to the top of the loaf and only slashing through the very outside of the loaf and not into the crumb within.

8. Bake the loaves until they are well risen, deep golden, and firm to the touch, about 40 minutes. Slide the loaves from the pan onto racks to cool.

....

SERVING: Serve the prosciutto bread with hors d'oeuvres, or with first courses, especially if they are Italian dishes. It's also a very good accompaniment to a simple salad.

STORAGE: Keep the loaves loosely covered with plastic wrap on the day they are baked. Wrap in plastic and freeze for longer storage. Defrost the bread and reheat it at 350°F (180°C) for 10 minutes, and cool it before serving.

3 cups unbleached all-purpose flour
(spoon flour into a dry-measure cup and level off)

2 teaspoons sugar

2 teaspoons salt

2½ teaspoons (1 envelope) active dry yeast

¾ cup warm water, about 110°F (45°C)

1 large egg

1 large egg yolk

3 tablespoons unsalted butter, melted and cooled

Egg white wash: 1 egg white well beaten with a pinch
of salt

Elegant Dinner Rolls

I always find serving guests individual rolls more festive than passing slices of a larger loaf of bread. Maybe I got that impression from a photograph I saw as a child of the dining room of an extremely fancy Parisian restaurant, where each plate was topped with a stiff-looking folded white napkin and each napkin bore an elaborately knotted individual roll. These are really easy to make and you may shape them several ways. They're also easy to make in advance and freeze in case you do want to make them for a party.

1. Combine the flour, sugar, and salt in the bowl of a food processor fitted with the metal blade. Pulse several times to mix.

2. Whisk the yeast into the water in a small bowl, and whisk in the egg, egg yolk, and butter. Pour the liquid into the food processor bowl and pulse repeatedly until the dough forms a ball. Let the dough rest in the food processor bowl for 10 minutes.

3. After the dough has rested, run the machine continuously for 15 seconds. Invert the food processor bowl onto a floured surface to turn out the dough. Carefully remove the blade and transfer any dough on it to the surface. Use a bench scraper to fold the dough over onto itself several times. Place the dough in a buttered bowl and turn it over so that the top is buttered. Cover the bowl with a towel or plastic wrap and let the dough rise until it has doubled in bulk, 1 to 2 hours, depending on the temperature of the room.

4. Scrape the dough onto a floured surface and divide it in half. Roll each half into a cylinder about 6 inches (15 cm) long. Use a bench scraper or a knife to divide each cylinder into 6 equal pieces.

5. Place all the pieces of dough on your left and sweep away any excess flour or bits of dough from the work surface directly in front of you. Make sure there is a clear area to your right. Taking one piece of dough at a time, cup your right hand over it so that the top of the dough barely touches the inside of your palm. Gently press and move your hand in a circle to round the piece of dough into a sphere and tighten the skin on the outside of it. Place the rounded piece of dough to your right and cover it with a towel or plastic wrap. If the dough is sticky, lightly flour the palm of your hand—not the dough or the work surface. If you are left-handed, put the cut pieces of dough on your right and the rounded ones on your left.

6. You can leave the rolls round, or you may roll the palm of your hand over each one to make a small cylindrical roll before arranging them on the pan. For knotted rolls, elongate the cylinders of dough to about 4 inches (10 cm), then tie them in a single knot, leaving one end of the strand protruding slightly at the top and the other end under the roll.

7. Arrange the formed rolls on the prepared pan, leaving about 2 inches (5 cm) all around each one to allow room for expansion. Cover the pan with a towel or buttered plastic wrap and let the rolls rise until they have doubled in bulk, 1 to 2 hours.

8. About 20 minutes before the rolls are fully risen, set a rack in the middle of the oven and preheat to 400°F (200°C).

9. Immediately before placing the rolls in the oven, gently and carefully brush them with the egg white wash. Bake the rolls until they are well risen, well colored, and firm, about 20 minutes. Slide the rolls on the parchment paper onto a rack to cool.

....

SERVING: Serve the rolls in a napkin-lined basket. For breakfast serve them with butter and preserves or marmalade.

STORAGE: Keep the rolls loosely covered with plastic wrap on the day they are baked. Wrap tightly and freeze for longer storage. Defrost the rolls and reheat them at 375°F (190°C) for 3 to 4 minutes, and cool them before serving.

VARIATIONS

However you choose to shape the rolls, you can sprinkle them with a pinch of poppy seeds or sesame seeds immediately after brushing with the egg wash.

For medium sandwich or hamburger rolls, divide the dough into a total of 8 pieces and form into rounds, cover, and allow them to rest for 5 minutes. Wrap a flat-weave (non-terry cloth) towel around a small heavy saucepan. Flour the cloth on the bottom of the pan. Slam the pan against one of the rounded pieces of dough 2 to 3 times to flatten it into a hamburger shape. Arrange on the pan and continue with the remaining pieces of dough, lightly flouring the cloth on the bottom of the pan as needed. After the rolls have risen, paint with the egg wash and sprinkle with either type of seeds, if you wish.

DOUGH

3½ cups unbleached all-purpose flour
(spoon flour into a dry-measure cup and level off)

2 teaspoons salt

2½ teaspoons (1 envelope) active dry yeast

1½ cups warm water, about 110°F (45°C)

3 tablespoons olive oil

FILLING

½ cup pitted Gaeta or Kalamata olives, cut into
¼-inch (6-mm) pieces

3 tablespoons chopped fresh rosemary leaves

1 tablespoon olive oil

½ teaspoon freshly ground black pepper

1 cookie sheet or jelly-roll pan lined with parchment or foil

Rosemary Olive Knots

Sometimes I jokingly refer to these as rosemary olive Danish, because the technique of filling the dough before cutting and shaping it is adapted from a method for handling Danish pastry dough. This is an easy dough to prepare. Just don't neglect to chill the filled dough or it might be too difficult to handle.

1. Combine the flour and salt in the bowl of a food processor fitted with the metal blade. Pulse several times to mix.

2. Whisk the yeast into the water in a small bowl and whisk in the oil. Pour the liquid into the processor bowl and pulse until the dough forms a ball. Let rest for 10 minutes, then let the machine run continuously for 15 seconds.

3. Invert the food processor bowl over a lightly floured surface to turn out the dough. Carefully remove the blade and transfer any dough on it to the surface. Use a bench scraper to fold the dough over on itself several times. Place the dough into an oiled bowl and turn it over so that the top is oiled. Cover the bowl with a towel or plastic wrap and let the dough rise until it has doubled in bulk, about 1 hour.

4. Scrape the dough to a floured work surface and lightly flour the top of the dough. Pat the dough into a 10-inch (25-cm) square. Fold the dough into thirds and slide both hands under it, palms up and flat, and lift it to a floured cookie sheet or small cutting board. Unfold the dough, even out the shape, and cover it with plastic wrap. Refrigerate the dough until it firms up, about 1 hour.

5. While the dough is chilling, for the filling, place the olives, rosemary, oil, and pepper in a small bowl and stir well to combine.

6. When the dough is firm, remove it from the refrigerator, leaving it on the pan or cutting board. Evenly distribute the filling on the bottom half of the dough in a 5 x 10-inch (13 x 25-cm) rectangle. Fold the top half of the dough down over the filling without pulling on it or stretching it, and press well with the palms of your hands to adhere (figure a).

7. Use a sharp pizza wheel to cut the dough into 12 equal strips, each about ¾ inch (2 cm) wide and 5 inches (13 cm) long (figure b). Set the prepared pan next to the dough. One at a time, loosely knot the strips of dough, letting one end of the strip protrude slightly at the top and arranging the other end under the roll. As the strips are knotted, transfer them to the prepared pan, leaving about 2 inches (5 cm) all around each one to allow room for expansion (see figure c).

8. Cover the pan with a towel or oiled plastic wrap and let the rolls rise until they have doubled in bulk, about 1 hour.

9. About 20 minutes before the rolls are completely risen, set a rack in the middle of the oven and preheat to 400°F (200°C).

10. Bake the rolls until they are well risen, deep golden, and feel firm to the touch, about 30 minutes. Slide the rolls on parchment paper onto a rack to cool.

SERVING: These are good split and filled with a strong cheese such as an aged Gruyère, prosciutto, soft goat cheese and roasted peppers, or even sliced summer tomatoes dressed with a little olive oil, salt, and garlic. You can also serve them with a meal, but I think they go best with stronger-flavored first courses, rather than main courses.

STORAGE: Keep the rolls loosely covered with plastic wrap on the day they are baked. Bag and freeze for longer storage. Defrost and reheat at 350°F (180°C) for 5 to 6 minutes, and cool before serving.

fig. a

fig.b

fig. c

FORMING THE KNOTS

a. After evenly distributing the filling over the bottom half of the dough, gently fold over the top half (step 6).

b. Using a pizza wheel, cut the dough into 12 equal strips (step 7).

c. After forming each knot with one end of the strip protruding from the top, and one underneath, place them on the prepared pan, leaving about 2 inches (5 cm) all around each one (step 7).

Makes 12 large individual rolls

....

5 cups unbleached, all-purpose flour
(spoon flour into a dry-measure cup and level off)

2 teaspoons salt

2 teaspoons sugar

¼ cup olive oil, plus more for brushing the dough

2½ teaspoons (1 envelope) active dry yeast

2 cups warm water, about 110°F (45°C)

2 cookie sheets or jelly-roll pans lined with parchment
or foil

Cornetti:
Olive-Oil Rolls from Bologna

I first saw Margherita Simili, the great Italian baker, demonstrate how to make these rolls at the old Peter Kump's Cooking School in the late 1980s. Margherita was in the United States to visit and teach at numerous cooking schools. Marcella Hazan, whom she helped back then with her classes in Bologna by doing all the pasta, pastry, and breads, accompanied her that day. These rolls are both beautiful and delicious, but require just a little bit of practice to get right. The shaping is not difficult, but you do need to be careful to keep the pieces of dough uniform in size and shape so that the finished rolls look attractive and appetizing.

1. Use a large rubber spatula to stir together the flour, salt, and sugar in the bowl of an electric mixer. Stir in the oil, making sure it is evenly distributed throughout the mixture.

2. Whisk the yeast into the water and stir the mixture into the flour and oil mixture.

3. Place the bowl on the mixer and mix with the paddle on the lowest speed for 2 minutes. Stop the mixer and let the dough rest for 10 minutes.

4. Mix the dough again on medium speed for 2 minutes, or until it is smooth and elastic.

5. Scrape the dough into an oiled bowl and turn it over so that the top is oiled. Press plastic wrap against the surface and let the dough rise until it has doubled in bulk, about 1 hour.

6. Scrape the dough onto a lightly floured work surface and press it into a rough square. Use a knife or a bench scraper to cut the dough in half, then in half again to make 4 pieces. Cut each of the resulting pieces of dough into 3 pieces to make 12 pieces in all. Form each piece of dough into a rough sphere and cover them with a towel or plastic wrap and allow them to rest for 5 minutes.

7. To roll the dough, take one of the pieces of dough and flour it lightly. Place the dough on a floured surface and roll it with a small rolling pin to make a thin rectangle of dough about 12 inches (30 cm) long and 3½ inches (9 cm) wide. If the dough resists, set it aside, covered, and roll another piece—after the first piece of dough has rested for a few minutes it will roll out more easily. Continue until all the pieces have been rolled out.

8. To shape a roll, place a rectangle of dough in front of you horizontally on the work surface and cut the dough diagonally into 2 triangles (figure a). Join the triangles at the points and lightly brush them with olive oil (figure b). With your hands, begin rolling up the dough from the far ends toward the center (figure c). Repeat with the remaining rectangles.

9. Turn the right hand roll at a right angle to the left one, positioning their two middles together to form a cross. Place the shaped roll on the pan. Repeat with the remaining rectangles of dough, positioning the rolls equidistant from one another on the pans.

10. Cover the pans with a towel or oiled plastic wrap and allow the rolls to rise until they are not quite doubled in bulk, about 45 minutes.

FORMING THE CORNETTI

a. Cut a rectangle of dough diagonally with a pizza wheel to make 2 triangles (step 8).

b. Join the triangles at the points and brush lightly with olive oil (step 8).

c. Using your hands, roll the dough from the far ends toward the center (step 8).

fig. a

fig. b

fig. c

11. About 15 minutes before the rolls are fully risen, set racks in the upper and lower thirds of the oven and preheat to 400°F (200°C).

12. Bake the rolls until they are well risen, about 15 minutes. Move the bottom pan to the top rack and switch the pans from back to front while you are moving them. Continue baking until the rolls are a deep golden color, about 10 minutes longer. Slide the rolls on the parchment paper onto a rack to cool.

·······································

SERVING: These are the ultimate fancy dinner rolls.

STORAGE: Keep the rolls loosely covered on the day they are baked. Bag and freeze for longer storage. For advance preparation, freeze the rolls, then defrost, reheat at 375°F (190°C) for 5 minutes, and cool them before serving.

95 Quick Brioche Braid

97 Marbled Chocolate
   Brioche Loaf

99 Cinnamon Raisin
   Breakfast Ring

100 Chocolate Babka Loaf

102 Kouing Amman: Breton
    Butter & Sugar Pastry

104 Ginger-Scented Panettone

105 Bakery Crumb Buns

108 Pecan Stickiest Buns

109 One-Step Croissants

112 Grissini: Classic Italian
    Breadsticks

113 Cornmeal Buttermilk Waffles

114 Dough for Thick-Crusted Pizza
    & for Focaccia

115 Sfincione: Palermo Focaccia

116 Focaccia alla Barese:
    Apulian Onion, Anchovy,
    & Olive Focaccia

118 Nonna's Pizza

119 Filled Ham & Cheese Focaccia

3

Yeast-Risen Specialties
Sweet & Savory

It's difficult to create a blanket definition that covers the recipes in this chapter, both because they overlap so much with bread recipes, and because yeast-risen specialties can be so different from one another. Most of the recipes here originated using a plain bread dough as a base. In the case of the sweet variations, butter, eggs, sugar, and enrichments such as dried or candied fruit, nuts, toppings, and fillings transformed them. In the savory variations, different methods of shaping, enrichments—some of which overlap with the ones for sweet variations—and savory fillings or toppings were used to create new specialties.

Like bread doughs, these specialties are made with little mixing and rest periods. Cover yeast-risen pastries when proofing them. Butter-rich doughs should be proofed at a slightly warmer temperature than bread doughs to avoid having the butter solidify and slow things down. Another factor contributes to success here, and that is having all the ingredients at room temperature when you start. Cold ingredients in this type of dough will slow down rising time considerably and delay the process. To test for doneness, plunge in a paring knife and inspect the crumb, or use an instant-read thermometer plunged into the center. It should read between 200°F and 210°F (90°C and 100°C).

Here is a list of general categories covered in this chapter:

Large and individual yeast-risen pastries without fillings or toppings: Brioche specialties such as loaves or braids; croissants; and others.

Yeast-Risen cakes: Panettone is probably the best example of this category.

Large and individual yeast-risen cakes with fillings and/or toppings: Babka, sticky buns, and crumb buns.

Savory yeast-risen specialties without fillings or toppings: Breadsticks and waffles or pancakes.

Savory yeast-risen specialties with fillings or toppings: Focaccia and pizza.

No one would identify any of these recipes as a bread, though the procedures for preparing the basic doughs have many similarities to those for preparing bread doughs.

Makes one 16-inch (40-cm) long braid, about thirty ½-inch (1-cm) slices

....

½ cup milk

2½ teaspoons (about 1 envelope/7 grams) active dry yeast

3 cups unbleached all-purpose flour (spoon flour into a dry-measure cup and level off)

8 tablespoons (1 stick) cold unsalted butter, cut into 12 pieces, see Note

¼ cup sugar

1 teaspoon salt

2 large eggs

2 large egg yolks

Egg wash: 1 large egg well beaten with a pinch of salt

1 cookie sheet or jelly-roll pan lined with parchment or foil

Note: Normally, brioche dough is prepared using softened butter. I keep the butter cooler here because food processor mixing can heat the dough. If you start out with soft butter, the dough would be almost liquid by the time it was completely mixed.

VARIATIONS

BRIOCHE LOAVES: Divide the dough in half after it is mixed. Butter two 8½ x 4½ x 2¾-inch (22 x 5 x 7-cm) loaf pans and line the bottom of each with a rectangle of parchment or buttered wax paper cut to fit. Evenly press one of the pieces of dough into each pan. Allow the dough to rise, covered, until it completely fills the pans. Bake as below. These loaves might require a few minutes more baking time since they are thicker.

Quick Brioche Braid

Brioche in any form is as elegantly rich and buttery as any pastry can be. This easy braid is made from a fast version of brioche dough immediately after it emerges from the food processor. The dough is quite soft, so don't handle it too much—braiding the loaf directly on the pan where it will bake also makes the process much easier.

....

1. Heat the milk in a small saucepan until it is just lukewarm, about 110°F (45°C). Pour the milk into a small bowl and whisk in the yeast. Use a small rubber spatula to stir in 1 cup of the flour thoroughly. Cover the bowl with plastic wrap and set aside for 20 minutes. The mixture will become bubbly and somewhat risen.

2. Combine the butter, sugar, salt, eggs, and egg yolks in the bowl of a food processor fitted with the metal blade. Pulse repeatedly until the butter is evenly distributed throughout the resulting liquid. At this point the mixture may appear separated—it will come together as soon as some of the flour is added.

3. Scrape the yeast mixture into the bowl and pulse 6 times to mix it in thoroughly. Add 1 cup of the remaining flour and pulse again until the flour is completely incorporated and the mixture is smooth. Use a thin-bladed metal spatula to scrape down the inside of the bowl. Add the remaining flour and pulse again until incorporated. Let the dough rest for 10 minutes.

4. Start the food processor and allow it to run continuously for 10 seconds. Invert the food processor bowl over a floured work surface to turn out the dough. Carefully remove the blade and transfer any dough on it to the surface. Use a bench scraper to fold the dough over on itself 5 to 6 times, adding pinches of flour if necessary, until it is slightly more elastic.

5. Use a bench scraper or a knife to divide the dough into 3 equal pieces. Roll each piece of dough under the palms of your hands until it is approximately 12 inches (30 cm) long. If the dough is too sticky to roll, slide it into a small floured pan and refrigerate it for about 20 minutes. Place the cylinders of dough lengthwise in the center of the length of the prepared pan, about ½ inch (1 cm) apart from each other.

6. Starting in the middle of the dough, braid the cylinders of dough over one another. When you reach the end, pinch the ends of the dough together and turn them under. Turn the pan around and repeat the braiding and finishing on the other side of the loaf.

7. Cover the braid with a towel or buttered plastic wrap and let it rise until doubled in bulk, 1 to 2 hours, depending on the temperature of the room.

8. Set a rack in the middle of the oven and preheat to 350°F (180°C).

9. Immediately before placing the braid in the oven, brush it with the egg wash. Be sure to clean off the brush every time you dip it in, to avoid having the egg wash puddle at the bottom of the braid. Bake the braid until it is well risen and deep golden, 35 to 40 minutes. Slide the braid on the parchment paper onto a rack to cool.

....

SERVING: Slide the braid onto a cutting board and slice it at the table. Serve it with fruit preserves but no butter for breakfast or brunch.

STORAGE: Keep the braid loosely covered with plastic wrap on the day it is baked. Wrap and freeze for longer storage. Defrost, reheat at 350°F (180°C) for 7 to 8 minutes, then cool before serving.

Makes one 9 x 5 x 3-inch (23 x 13 x 7-cm) loaf, about sixteen ½-inch (1-cm) slices

··

BRIOCHE DOUGH

½ cup milk

2½ teaspoons (1 envelope) active dry yeast

2½ cups unbleached all-purpose flour
(spoon flour into a dry-measure cup and level off)

7 tablespoons cold unsalted butter, cut into 12 pieces

¼ cup sugar

½ teaspoon salt

1 large egg

2 large egg yolks

2 teaspoons finely grated lemon zest

1 tablespoon dark rum

CHOCOLATE ENRICHMENT

1 tablespoon water

½ teaspoon baking soda

Pinch of ground cinnamon

1½ ounces (37½ grams) bittersweet (not unsweetened) chocolate, melted and cooled

3 tablespoons unbleached all-purpose flour

One 9 x 5 x 3-inch (23 x 13 x 7-cm) loaf pan buttered and the bottom lined with a rectangle of parchment or buttered wax paper cut to fit

Marbled Chocolate
Brioche Loaf

I love swirls of chocolate threading through any kind of a plain cake. This marbled brioche is fairly straightforward to prepare since you mix everything in the food processor. Marbling the plain and chocolate doughs together requires a little patience, but the reward is a beautiful loaf with an alluringly different flavor achieved by adding grated lemon zest and rum to the dough.

1. To make the brioche dough, heat the milk in a small saucepan until it is just lukewarm, about 110°F (45°C). Pour the milk into a small bowl and whisk in the yeast. Use a small rubber spatula to stir in 1 cup of the flour thoroughly. Cover the bowl with plastic wrap and set aside for 20 minutes. The mixture will become bubbly and somewhat risen.

2. Combine the butter, sugar, salt, egg, egg yolks, lemon zest, and rum in the bowl of a food processor fitted with the metal blade. Pulse repeatedly until the butter is evenly distributed throughout the resulting liquid. At this point the mixture may appear separated—it will come together as soon as some of the flour is added.

3. Scrape the yeast mixture into the bowl and pulse 6 times to mix it in thoroughly. Add the remaining flour and pulse again until the flour is completely incorporated and the mixture is smooth. Use a thin-bladed metal spatula to scrape down the inside of the bowl. Let the dough rest for 10 minutes.

4. Start the food processor and allow it to run continuously for 10 seconds. Invert the food processor bowl over a floured work surface to turn out the dough. Carefully remove the blade and transfer any dough on it to the surface. Use a bench scraper to fold the dough over on itself 5 to 6 times, adding pinches of flour if necessary, until it is slightly more elastic. Use a bench scraper or knife to divide the dough into 3 equal pieces.

5. Return one piece of the dough to the food processor. Cover the remaining pieces of dough with a towel or plastic wrap.

6. To prepare the Chocolate Enrichment, combine the water, baking soda, and cinnamon. Stir them into the melted and cooled chocolate. Scrape the chocolate mixture into the food processor bowl and pulse 3 to 4 times to incorporate. Add the flour and pulse continuously for 10 seconds, or until the dough is smooth. Invert the food processor bowl over a floured work surface to turn out the dough. Carefully remove the blade and transfer any dough on it to the surface. Use a bench scraper to fold the chocolate dough over on itself 5 to 6 times, adding pinches of flour if necessary, until it is slightly more elastic.

7. Flour a cutting board and set it aside. Press one of the pieces of plain dough into a 5-inch (13-cm) square and place it on the cutting board. Repeat with the chocolate dough, arranging it directly on top of the square of plain dough on the cutting board. Repeat

98

fig. a

fig. b

MARBLED CHOCOLATE BRIOCHE LOAF

a. Sandwich a 5-inch (13-cm) square of chocolate dough between two plain ones (step 7).

b. Using a bench scraper, cut each wide strip into 10 smaller pieces (step 8).

with the remaining piece of plain dough. The squares and the stacking don't need to be perfectly precise (figure a).

8. Use a knife or a bench scraper to cut the stacked dough into 3 strips, each one about 1¾ inches (4½ cm) wide. Then cut across one of the strips making ten ½-inch (1-cm) pieces (figure b). Slide the cut pieces of dough into a bowl. Repeat with the remaining strips of dough.

9. Slide your hands, palms upward, under the pieces of dough in the bowl and toss them gently a few times like a salad.

10. Sprinkle the pieces of dough in the bowl with 1 teaspoon of water to make them slightly sticky. Gently press and squeeze the dough together into a cohesive ball. Invert the dough to a floured work surface and press it into a thick 4 x 8-inch (10 x 20-cm) rectangle. Place the rectangle of dough in the prepared pan and gently press it to fill the pan completely.

11. Cover the pan with buttered plastic wrap and let the dough rise about 1 inch (2½ cm) over the top of the pan, for 1 to 2 hours, depending on the temperature of the room.

12. About 20 minutes before the loaf is fully risen, set a rack in the middle of the oven and preheat to 350°F (180°C).

13. Bake the loaf until it is well risen and deep golden, 35 to 40 minutes. Cool the loaf in the pan on a rack for 5 minutes, then unmold it and finish cooling it on its side to prevent it from compressing and becoming heavy.

SERVING: Place the loaf on a cutting board and slice it at the table. If you want to serve something with it, I think orange marmalade or raspberry preserves are the best choices.

STORAGE: On the day it is baked, keep the loaf loosely covered with plastic wrap. Wrap and freeze for longer storage. Defrost, reheat at 350°F (180°C) for 7 to 8 minutes, then cool before serving.

Makes one 10-inch (25-cm) diameter ring, about
12 generous servings

....

1 batch brioche dough, such as in Quick Brioche Braid,
page 95

CINNAMON RAISIN FILLING

8 tablespoons (1 stick) unsalted butter, softened

½ cup light brown sugar

1 teaspoon ground cinnamon

1 cup dark raisins or currants

1½ cups (about 6 ounces) pecan pieces, coarsely chopped

Egg wash: 1 large egg well beaten with a pinch of salt

Confectioners' sugar for dusting

1 cookie sheet or jelly-roll pan lined with
parchment or foil

Cinnamon Raisin
Breakfast Ring

This is just the type of treat to serve when you have guests for breakfast or brunch. Rather than fuss with preparing it the same day, make and bake it the day before—you'll just need to reheat and cool it right before serving. Many recipes for this type of yeast-risen coffee cake use a very sweet dough, but I find that after the addition of the sweet filling, these are entirely too sweet. I like to use brioche dough for this—its delicate buttery flavor marries perfectly with the cinnamon raisin filling. Sometimes this type of a ring is finished with an icing, but I prefer a simple dusting of confectioners' sugar.

....

1. Prepare the brioche dough up to the end of step 6 on page 95. Place the dough in a buttered bowl and turn it over so that the top is buttered. Cover the bowl with plastic wrap and refrigerate for 1 hour.

2. While the dough is chilling, prepare the filling. Use a rubber spatula to beat the butter until it is smooth and fluffy, then beat in the sugar and cinnamon.

3. Scrape the dough out onto a lightly floured work surface and press it into a rough square. Flour the dough and roll it to a rectangle approximately 10 x 15 inches (25 x 38 cm). Use a medium metal offset spatula to spread the filling evenly all over the dough. Evenly scatter the raisins and 1 cup of the chopped pecans over the filling.

4. Starting at one of the longer ends, roll up the dough jelly-roll style, without stretching it. Pinch the end of the dough in place to seal.

5. Bring the pan close to the roll of dough, and roll the dough right onto the pan. If the rim of the pan stops the roll of dough, gently lift it onto the pan without stretching it. Arrange the roll so that the seam is underneath and join the ends to make a circle about 10 inches (25 cm) in diameter. Overlap the ends where they meet and pinch them together as neatly as possible. Gently press down on the roll with the palm of your hand to flatten it slightly.

6. Use scissors to cut from the outside of the perimeter about ¾ of the way through toward the center 1½ inches (4 cm) apart all around the ring. Working right to left, one at a time, give each cut piece of the ring a twist to the right, so that the spiral of the filled dough is facing upward.

7. Cover the ring with buttered plastic wrap and allow it to rise until doubled, 1 to 2 hours, depending on the temperature of the room.

8. About 20 minutes before the ring is fully risen, set a rack in the middle of the oven and preheat to 350°F (180°C).

9. Carefully brush only the outside surfaces (not the exposed spiral parts) of the ring with the egg wash and scatter the remaining ½ cup pecans on the egg-washed surface.

10. Bake the ring until it is well risen, deep golden, and firm, 25 to 30 minutes. Cool in the pan on a rack for 10 minutes, then slide the parchment onto the rack to finish cooling the ring completely. Immediately before serving, dust with confectioners' sugar.

....

SERVING: Slide the ring onto a platter and cut it at the table. It needs no accompaniment.

STORAGE: Keep the ring loosely covered with plastic wrap on the day it is baked. Wrap and freeze for longer storage. Defrost, reheat at 350°F (180°C) for 10 minutes, and cool before serving.

BABKA DOUGH

1¼ cups milk

5 teaspoons (2 envelopes) active dry yeast

8 tablespoons (1 stick) unsalted butter, melted and cooled

½ cup sugar

½ teaspoon salt

6 large egg yolks

2 teaspoons vanilla extract

3¾ cups unbleached all-purpose flour
(spoon flour into a dry-measure cup and level off)

CHOCOLATE FILLING

8 ounces (225 grams) bittersweet (not unsweetened) chocolate, coarsely chopped

½ cup sugar

1 tablespoon alkalized (Dutch process) cocoa powder

½ teaspoon ground cinnamon

1 cup (about 4 ounces/100 grams) walnut or pecan pieces, coarsely chopped

Two 8½ x 4½ x 2¾-inch (22 x 11 x 7-cm) loaf pans, buttered and the bottoms lined with rectangles of parchment or buttered wax paper cut to fit

Chocolate Babka Loaf

Probably original to Russia, Poland, or another location in Eastern Europe, in the United States babka is primarily associated with the Jewish baking tradition. A store-bought babka has usually been baked in a loaf pan, whereas homemade versions are baked in a tube or Bundt pan—there are instructions for both shapes here. Thanks to Mildred Shapiro for sharing her family babka recipe.

1. Warm the milk in a small saucepan until it is just lukewarm, about 110°F (45°C). Pour the milk into the bowl of an electric mixer and whisk in the yeast. Whisk in the butter, sugar, salt, egg yolks, and vanilla. Use a large rubber spatula to stir in ½ the flour.

2. Place the bowl on the mixer and use the paddle attachment to beat the dough on low speed. Add the remaining flour about ½ cup at a time, beating to incorporate between additions. When all the flour has been added, beat the dough for 2 minutes. Stop the mixer and allow the dough to rest for 10 minutes. Beat the dough on low to medium speed for 2 minutes more.

3. Scrape the dough into a buttered bowl and turn it over so that the top is buttered. Cover the bowl with plastic wrap and refrigerate for 1½ hours.

4. While the dough is chilling, prepare the filling. In a food processor fitted with the metal blade, combine the chocolate with the sugar, cocoa, and cinnamon, and pulse to grind finely. Pour the filling into a bowl and set aside.

5. After the dough has chilled, scrape it onto a floured work surface and press it out to a rectangle about 10 x 15 inches (25 x 38 cm) (figure a). Evenly scatter the chocolate filling on the dough. Scatter the chopped walnuts over the filling (figure b). Roll up the dough from one long side jelly-roll style (figure c), and pinch the ends to seal. Use a knife to cut the roll into 2 equal pieces.

6. Invert one of the rolls, seam side down, into one of the prepared pans (figure d). Repeat with the second roll. Cover the pans with towels or buttered plastic wrap and let them rise until doubled in bulk, 1 to 2 hours, depending on the temperature of the room.

7. About 20 minutes before the babkas are completely risen, set a rack in the middle of the oven and preheat to 350°F (180°C).

8. Bake until the babkas are well risen and deep golden, about 45 minutes. Cool in the pans on a rack for 10 minutes, then unmold and cool on their sides to prevent collapsing.

SERVING: Slide a loaf onto a cutting board and slice it at the table. Serve babkas for breakfast, brunch, or any time with tea or coffee.

STORAGE: Keep the babkas loosely covered with plastic wrap on the day they are baked. Wrap and freeze for longer storage. Defrost, reheat at 350°F (180°C) for 10 minutes, and cool before serving.

VARIATIONS

HOME-STYLE CHOCOLATE BABKA: Bake the babka in a buttered 10-inch (12-cup/25 cm) tube or Bundt pan. Place the whole coil of dough in the pan seam side down. Join the ends together as well as possible. The baking time is the same.

BABKA WITH TRADITIONAL FILLING: Whip 3 egg whites with an electric mixer until they hold a soft peak. Add ½ cup sugar 1 tablespoon at a time, continuing to whip the egg whites until they hold a firm peak. Spread the egg-white mixture on the rectangle of dough and sprinkle with 2 teaspoons ground cinnamon, 1 cup dark raisins, and 1½ cups walnut or pecan pieces, coarsely chopped. Bake in a tube pan.

fig. a

fig. b

fig. c

STEPS

a. Press the dough out to a rectangle about 10 x 15 inches (25 x 38 cm) as described in step 5.

b. After evenly spreading out the chocolate filling, scatter the chopped nuts on top (step 5).

c. Roll up the dough, jelly-roll style, using both hands on the long end of the dough (step 5).

d. These tube pans are ready to be covered with towels or buttered plastic wrap and left to rise for 1 to 2 hours (step 6).

fig. d

Makes one 10-inch (25-cm) cake, about 12 generous servings

....

DOUGH

2½ teaspoons (1 envelope) active dry yeast

¾ cup warm water, about 110°F (45°C)

2 cups unbleached all-purpose flour
(spoon flour into a dry-measure cup and level off)

1 teaspoon salt

2 tablespoons unsalted butter, melted

ROLLING AND FOLDING

8 ounces (2 sticks/225 grams) unsalted butter, chilled

¼ cup flour (you may not need all of it)

1 cup sugar

One 10-inch (25-cm) cake pan 2 inches (5 cm) deep, buttered and the bottom lined with a disk of parchment cut to fit

STEPS

a. Fold the top portion of the dough over the middle section, then fold the bottom portion up over the middle (step 8).

b. After rolling the dough out into a 10-inch (25-cm) disk, trim the dough or push the corners in with your palms to make it round (step 12).

c. Fold the dough into the prepared 10-inch (25-cm) pan and press it into as round a shape as possible (step 13).

Kouing Amman:
Breton Butter & Sugar Pastry

This Breton specialty is like a cross between croissant dough and palmiers—rolling and folding in butter and lots of sugar at the same time. The result is flaky, buttery, and irresistible.

....

1. Whisk the yeast into the water and set aside.

2. Stir the flour and salt together with a large rubber spatula in a medium bowl.

3. Whisk the melted butter into the yeast mixture and gently stir the mixture into the flour and salt to make a soft dough. Avoid overmixing or the dough will become elastic and difficult to handle later on.

4. Cover the bowl with plastic wrap and refrigerate for 30 minutes.

5. After the dough has chilled, place the butter for rolling and folding on a floured work surface and pound it gently with a rolling pin to soften it— the object is to get the butter to be about the same consistency as the dough. Add pinches of flour to the butter, but don't use more than ¼ cup of flour for the process. Use a plastic scraper or a bench

scraper to push the butter into a cohesive mass once it is soft and malleable.

6. Scatter about ¼ cup of the sugar on the work surface and scrape the chilled dough onto it. Use your hands to press the dough into a rough rectangle, then flour it lightly. Roll the dough with gentle strokes until it is a rectangle about 8 x 12 inches (20 x 30 cm).

7. Position the dough so that one of the shorter ends is facing you. Smear tablespoon bits of the butter evenly all over the ²/₃ of the dough closer to you, leaving the top ¹/₃ unbuttered.

8. Fold the top (unbuttered) portion of the dough over the middle (buttered) section, then fold the bottom (buttered) portion up over the middle section to make a package of 3 layers of dough enclosing 2 layers of butter (figure a). Scatter about ¼ cup of the sugar on the work surface and the dough and turn the package so that one of the short ends is facing you again. Gently press the dough with the rolling pin in even strokes to make it thinner. Roll the dough back into an 8 x 12-inch (20 x 30-cm) rectangle.

9. Fold the dough as before, folding the top portion over the middle and the bottom portion up. Wrap the dough in plastic wrap and refrigerate it for 1 hour.

10. Place the dough back on a sugared work surface and sprinkle the dough again with about ¼ cup of the sugar. Position it again so that one of the short ends is facing you. Roll the dough back into an 8 x 12-inch (20 x 30-cm) rectangle and fold it again as in step 8.

11. Cover the dough with a towel and let it rest on the work surface for 15 minutes.

12. Generously sprinkle the work surface with about ¼ cup of the sugar and roll the dough out into a 10-inch (25-cm) disk. Press the corners inward as you roll so that the sides of the dough are as rounded as possible (figure b). You may trim the dough a little to help make it into a disk, but don't waste too much of it.

13. Fold the dough in half and place it in the prepared pan. Unfold the disk and press it into as round a shape as possible (figure c). Scatter any remaining sugar on top.

14. Cover the pan with plastic wrap and let the dough rise until it is well puffed but not doubled, about 2 hours.

15. About 20 minutes before you intend to bake the kouing amman, set a rack in the middle of the oven and preheat to 350°F (180°C). Bake the kouing amman until it is well

fig. a

fig. b

fig. c

puffed and the sugar is caramelized, about 1 hour. Watch it carefully during the last 20 minutes of baking to make sure the sugar doesn't start to get too dark. If it does, lower the oven temperature to 300°F (150°C) and continue baking until the pastry is firm and caramelized.

16. Cool the kouing amman in the pan on a rack for 5 minutes, then invert it from the pan onto a rack or cardboard, remove the paper, and turn it right side up again on a rack. Cool completely.

....

SERVING: Kouing amman is good at any time of the day or night, but especially as a snack with tea or coffee—it isn't really a dessert. Cut thin wedges; it is rich and sweet.

STORAGE: Keep loosely covered on the day it is baked. Double wrap and freeze for longer storage. After freezing, defrost and reheat at 350°F (180°C), and cool before serving.

Makes 1 tall 9-inch (23-cm) cake, about 16 servings

SPONGE

4 teaspoons (about 1½ envelopes) active dry yeast

½ cup warm water, about 110°F (45°C)

¾ cup unbleached all-purpose flour
(spoon flour into a dry-measure cup and level off)

DOUGH

10 tablespoons (1¼ sticks) unsalted butter, softened

⅓ cup sugar

½ teaspoon salt

2 teaspoons finely grated lemon zest

2 tablespoons finely grated or chopped ginger, see *Note*

2 teaspoons vanilla extract

3 large eggs

3¼ cups unbleached all-purpose flour

3 large egg yolks

¾ cup golden raisins

¾ cup crystallized ginger, cut into ⅜-inch (1-cm) dice

3 tablespoons unsalted butter, melted, for brushing the panettone when it comes out of the oven

Confectioners' sugar for sprinkling

One 9-inch (23-cm) springform pan, buttered and lined with a disk of parchment or buttered wax paper cut to fit

Note: Grating fresh ginger can be difficult. First peel the ginger, then grate it on a box grater that has small diagonally set holes in it—like miniature versions of the largest teardrop-shaped hole on the back of the grater. If you don't have this style grater, cut a 2-inch (5-cm) peeled length of ginger into slices, then stack the slices and chop them finely. Use a medium chef's knife to chop the ginger as you would chop parsley. Don't use a Microplane®, which I love for other uses, as you'll only get juice.

Ginger-Scented Panettone

This is a revved up version of the traditional Italian Christmas cake. Originally a Milanese specialty, panettone is now popular all over Italy and excellent versions are made by both industrial and artisanal bakeries. I make one version or another of panettone around Christmas—it reminds me of my childhood when we hardly ever ate anything that wasn't Italian. A good panettone is moist and flavorful. In Italy it is almost always made with sourdough starter—flour and water that ferments and develops organisms that produce lactic acid, among other things, thus retarding staling and preventing mold from forming. You can bake a perfectly good panettone at home, by just using an envelope or so of yeast from the supermarket. The version here is a new one I like a lot—most other people like it, too, because it omits everyone's least favorite ingredient, candied fruit. See the variation for a more traditional approach to flavoring.

VARIATION

PANETTONE ALLA MILANESE: Omit the fresh and crystallized ginger. Reduce the amount of golden raisins to ⅓ cup, and add ⅓ cup dark raisins and ½ cup diced citron or candied orange peel.

1. To make the sponge, whisk the yeast into the water in a small bowl. Thoroughly stir in the flour. Cover the bowl with plastic wrap and set aside while you prepare the other ingredients, about 20 minutes.

2. Combine the butter, sugar, salt, lemon zest, ginger, and vanilla in the bowl of an electric mixer. Place the bowl on the mixer with the paddle and beat on low to medium speed until well mixed, about 2 minutes. Beat in the eggs, one at a time, beating smooth after each addition.

3. Remove the bowl from the mixer (leave the paddle in the bowl) and scrape in the sponge. Place the bowl back on the mixer and beat on low speed until the sponge is incorporated. On lowest speed, beat in 2 cups of the flour. Beat in the egg yolks, beating smooth afterward. Beat in the remaining 1¼ cups flour and continue beating until the dough is smooth, about 2 minutes. Stop the mixer and let the dough rest for 15 minutes.

4. Add the raisins and crystallized ginger to the bowl and beat the dough again until they are evenly distributed—the dough will be very soft. Scrape the dough into a buttered bowl and cover with plastic wrap. Let the dough rise until doubled, 1 to 2 hours, depending on the temperature of the room.

5. Use a large rubber spatula inserted between the bowl and the dough to fold the dough over on itself, from the outside in, all around it. Invert the dough to a floured surface and round it slightly (see *boules*, page 80). Slide your hands under the dough and drop it into the prepared pan. Gently press the top of the dough to make it flat and even. Cover the pan with buttered plastic wrap and let the dough rise until it fills the pan, about 1½ hours.

6. About 20 minutes before the dough is fully risen, set a rack in the middle of the oven and preheat to 350°F (180°C).

7. Bake the panettone until it is well risen, deep golden, and a toothpick or the point of a small knife inserted into the center of the cake emerges clean, about 40 minutes. Cool the panettone in the pan on a rack for 5 minutes, then unmold it onto the rack, turn it right side up again, and brush it all over with melted butter. Cool the panettone completely.

SERVING: Dust the panettone lightly with confectioners' sugar just before serving. Serve the panettone around the Christmas holidays with tea or coffee.

STORAGE: After the panettone has cooled, double wrap it in plastic wrap and keep it at room temperature for a few days. Freeze for longer storage. Defrost and bring to room temperature before serving.

SWEET YEAST DOUGH FOR BUNS

⅔ cup milk

5 teaspoons (2 envelopes) active dry yeast

8 tablespoons (1 stick) unsalted butter, softened

½ cup sugar

2 teaspoons salt

¼ teaspoon ground cinnamon

⅛ teaspoon freshly grated nutmeg

2 teaspoons vanilla extract

2 large eggs

2 large egg yolks

4 cups unbleached all-purpose flour
(spoon flour into a dry-measure cup and level off)

CRUMB TOPPING

3 ounces (about 1⅓ cups/75 grams) almond paste, cut into 12 pieces

1 large egg white

½ cup granulated sugar

½ cup light brown sugar

2 teaspoons ground cinnamon

8 ounces (2 sticks/225 grams) unsalted butter, softened

4 cups unbleached all-purpose flour
(spoon flour into a dry-measure cup and level off)

Confectioners' sugar for finishing

One 12 x 18-inch (30 x 45-cm) jelly-roll pan, buttered and lined with parchment or buttered wax paper (or substitute two 9 x 13 x 2-inch (23 x 33 x 5-cm) pans)

Bakery Crumb Buns

When I was a child, these crumb buns were available in any number of local bakeries near where we lived. Born a crumb-topping addict, I always looked forward to slowly picking off large pieces of the generous topping to enjoy first. Somehow there was always enough still stuck to the cake below to provide a second course from the bun. Although I learned to make many different and delicious types of crumb toppings in the ensuing years, none of them ever had the rich, dense quality of the one I remembered. It wasn't until I came across a book about commercial baking by William J. Sultan that I discovered the secret: The fabulous crumb topping contained a small amount of almond paste—just enough to impart the dense richness I remembered. Also the weight of the topping exceeds the weight of the cake below—that's how you get buns that offer the two-course experience.

1. To make the dough, heat the milk in a small saucepan until it is just lukewarm, about 110°F (45°C). Pour the milk into a small bowl and whisk in the yeast. Set aside.

2. Combine the butter, sugar, salt, spices, and vanilla in the bowl of an electric mixer. With the paddle attachment, beat until well combined, about 2 minutes. Beat in the eggs and egg yolks one at a time, beating smooth after each addition.

3. Decrease the speed to lowest and beat in ½ the flour. Stop and use a large rubber spatula to scrape down the bowl and beater. Beat in the yeast mixture. After the liquid has been absorbed, beat in the remaining flour. Scrape down the bowl and beater, then beat the dough for 2 minutes. Stop the mixer and let the dough rest for 15 minutes.

4. Beat the dough on low to medium until it is smooth and fairly elastic, about 2 additional minutes. Scrape the dough into a buttered bowl and turn it over so that the top is buttered. Cover the bowl with a towel or plastic wrap and let the dough rise until doubled in bulk, 1 to 2 hours, depending on the temperature of the room.

5. While the dough is rising, prepare the crumb topping. Combine the almond paste and egg white in the bowl of an electric mixer. With the paddle attachment, beat on low to medium speed until smooth, about 2 minutes. Beat in the sugar, brown sugar, and cinnamon. Beat in the butter a couple of tablespoons at a time, beating smooth after each addition. Stop and scrape the bowl and beater several times while adding the butter.

6. Decrease speed to the lowest and add the flour 1 cup at a time, stopping and scraping down 2 to 3 times. Scrape the crumb topping into a large bowl and use your fingertips to break it up into ¼- to ½-inch (⅔- to 1-cm) crumbs. Set aside at room temperature.

7. After the dough has risen, scrape it out onto a floured work surface and pat it into a rough rectangle. Lightly flour the dough and gently roll it into a 10 x 16-inch (25 x 40-cm) rectangle.

8. Use a bench scraper or a knife to cut the dough into twenty 2 x 4-inch (5 x 10-cm) rectangles, cutting five 2-inch (5-cm) wide strips on the 10-inch (25-cm) side and cutting across every 4 inches (10 cm) on the 16-inch (40-cm) side.

9. Arrange the buns on the prepared pan, 5 across the 12-inch (30-cm) side of the pan and 4 down the 18-inch (45-cm) side. Leave

106

about ¹/₃ inch (³/₄ cm) all around each bun —they will grow together as they rise and bake. If you are using two 9 x 13-inch (23 x 33-cm) pans, arrange the buns in 2 rows of 5 in each pan, spacing them as in the larger pan.

10. Brush the tops of the buns with water and scatter on half the crumb topping—it doesn't matter if some falls between the buns. Cover the pan with plastic wrap and let the buns rise until doubled in bulk, about 1 hour at room temperature.

11. About 20 minutes before the buns are completely risen, set a rack in the middle of the oven and preheat to 375°F (190°C).

12. Scatter the remaining crumb topping over the buns and bake them until they are well risen and the topping is deep golden, about 30 minutes. If you are using 2 pans, put them into the oven smaller side inward, leaving a space between them. About halfway through the baking time, turn the pans back to front so that they bake evenly.

13. Slide the pan to a rack to cool for 5 minutes, then slide the buns out of the pan, still on the paper, onto a rack to cool.

14. Immediately before serving, lightly dust the buns with confectioners' sugar and gently pull them apart—they will easily separate from one another. If any resist, use a small paring knife to cut them apart.

....

SERVING: Arrange the buns in a napkin-lined basket to serve them for breakfast, brunch, or tea.

STORAGE: Keep the buns loosely covered with plastic wrap on the day they are baked. Wrap and freeze for longer storage. Defrost, reheat at 350°F (180°C) for about 10 minutes, and cool before serving.

Makes 15 buns

1 batch Sweet Yeast Dough as in Bakery Crumb Buns, page 105, omitting the spices from the dough, prepared up to the end of step 5

FILLING

8 tablespoons (1 stick) unsalted butter, very soft

1 cup light brown sugar

1½ teaspoons ground cinnamon

1 cup (about 4 ounces/100 grams) pecan pieces, coarsely chopped

STICKY BUN MIXTURE

8 tablespoons (1 stick) unsalted butter, melted

¾ cup light brown sugar

⅓ cup dark corn syrup

2 cups (about 8 ounces/225 grams) pecan halves, pieces, or a combination

One 9 x 13 x 2-inch (23 x 33 x 5-cm) pan, buttered and lined, bottom and sides, with buttered foil

VARIATIONS

CINNAMON RAISIN BUNS: Prepare the recipe up to the end of step 5. Scatter the dough with 1 cup dark raisins—or omit the pecans and use 2 cups of raisins. Cut and arrange in the pan where the foil is only buttered, omitting the Sticky Bun Mixture. Allow to rise and bake as below. Let the buns cool in the pan for 5 minutes, then lift the foil on one of the narrow ends of the pan, and slide the buns, still on the foil, onto a rack to cool completely.

Pecan Stickiest Buns

If you're making sticky buns, I think it's best to go all the way and then some—there's no such thing as a "light" sticky bun. These are loaded with pecans, brown sugar, and butter, and they are lethally addictive.

1. For the filling, use a small rubber spatula to stir together the butter, brown sugar, and cinnamon. Set aside.

2. Flour a work surface and press the dough into a rough rectangle. Even up the sides and corners with your hands and lightly flour the dough. Gently roll it into a 12 x 20-inch (30 x 50-cm) rectangle.

3. Dot the butter mixture for the filling all over the dough and use a small metal offset spatula to spread it evenly. Scatter the chopped pecans for the filling over the butter mixture.

4. Roll up the dough jelly-roll style from one of the 12-inch (30-cm) ends without stretching it, pinching the end in place to seal it. Use a sharp knife to divide the roll into 3 equal pieces, then cut each into 5 equal pieces.

5. Use a rubber spatula to mix together all the ingredients for the sticky bun mixture and scrape it into the prepared pan. Spread it evenly. Arrange the cut buns, cut side down, on the mixture, making 3 rows of 5 buns, and keeping them about ½ inch (1 cm) apart all around.

6. Cover the pan with a towel or buttered plastic wrap and let the buns rise until doubled in bulk.

7. About 20 minutes before the buns are fully risen, set a rack in the middle of the oven and preheat to 375°F (190°C).

8. Bake the buns 25 to 30 minutes, until they are firm and golden and the sugar mixture in the bottom of the pan is bubbling gently.

9. Place the pan on a rack and allow to cool for 5 minutes. Place a cutting board on the pan and invert. Lift off the pan. Carefully peel away the foil. If some of the pecans stick to the foil, just pry them off with a fork and replace them on the buns. Cool the buns completely.

SERVING: Arrange the cooled buns on a platter and serve them for breakfast or brunch.

STORAGE: Keep the buns loosely covered with plastic wrap on the day they are made. Wrap and freeze for longer storage. Defrost, reheat at 350°F (180°C) for 10 minutes, and cool before serving.

Makes 12 medium croissants

½ cup milk

4 teaspoons (1½ envelopes) active dry yeast

2 cups unbleached all-purpose flour
(spoon flour into a dry-measure cup and level off)

2 tablespoons sugar

¾ teaspoon salt

20 tablespoons (2½ sticks) cold unsalted butter

Egg wash: 1 large egg well beaten with a pinch of salt

2 jelly-roll pans lined with parchment or foil

One-Step Croissants

My standard croissant recipe calls for an 8-hour to overnight chill after the dough is mixed, then begins the process of layering the dough with the butter and rolling and folding it repeatedly. After all that, you have to chill the dough again before rolling it out to make the croissants. In this method, the mixing is accomplished in the food processor and the dough is rolled and folded once instead of several times. After a short rise, the dough is ready to be made into croissants. I've made puff pastry this way for years, so I knew the croissants would work out just as well, and they did.

1. Heat half the milk in a small saucepan until it is just lukewarm. Pour the milk into a small bowl and whisk in the yeast. Set aside.

2. Combine the flour, sugar, and salt in the bowl of a food processor fitted with the metal blade. Pulse several times to mix. Add 4 tablespoons of the butter (leave the remaining butter in the refrigerator) and pulse continuously until it is finely mixed into the dry ingredients.

3. Cut the remaining 2 sticks of butter into ½-inch (1-cm) pieces and add to the bowl. Pulse two times only.

4. Add the cold milk to the yeast mixture and add to the food processor. Pulse 3 times only—the dough will not form a ball.

5. Invert the work to a floured surface and carefully remove the blade. Quickly press the dough into a ball. Flatten it to a rough rectangle and flour under and on the dough. Roll it quickly to a 12 x 15-inch (30 x 38-cm) rectangle.

6. Fold one of the larger sides down over the middle and the bottom one over that, making a long thin 3-layered package that is 4 x 15 inches (10 x 37½ cm). Roll up the dough from one of the 4-inch (10-cm) sides, then flatten the dough to a rough square. Lightly flour the dough and slide it into a plastic bag. Let the dough rise in the bag at room temperature for 1 to 1½ hours—the dough will not fully double in size.

7. After the dough is risen, use the palm of one hand to deflate it, still inside the bag. Refrigerate the dough for an hour or up to 8 hours.

8. Remove the dough from the bag and place it on a floured work surface. Flour the dough and gently press it to deflate. Roll it to a 12 x 15-inch (30 x 38-cm) rectangle. Roll gently, and if the dough resists, let it rest for 5 minutes, then roll again. If at any point the dough becomes too soft to handle, slide a cookie sheet under it and refrigerate it for 10 to 15 minutes.

9. Once the dough is rolled to the correct size, straighten the edges and make the corners even. Use a sharp pizza wheel to cut the dough into two 7½ x 12-inch (19 x 30-cm) strips. Cut each strip into 6 triangles, each with a base of about 4 inches (10 cm) (figure a on page 110).

10. To form the croissants, face the 4-inch (10-cm) side of one of the triangles toward you. Gently pull the two corners closest to

110

you outward to make the base about 6 inches (15 cm) wide. Roll up the dough from the side facing you, gently pulling on the point of the triangle with the other hand as you do (figure b). Repeat with all the croissants.

11. Place one of the croissants on one of the prepared pans and curve the end out in front of it to make a crescent shape. Arrange 6 croissants on each pan, leaving them plenty of room all around for expansion. Cover each pan with buttered plastic wrap and let the croissants rise until they're almost double, as before.

12. About 20 minutes before the croissants are finished rising, set racks in the upper and lower thirds of the oven and preheat to 350°F (180°C). Carefully brush the risen croissants with the egg wash, making sure to dry the brush to avoid having it puddle under the croissants (figure c).

13. Bake the croissants for about 15 minutes, then switch the bottom pan to the top and vice versa, turning the pans back to front at the same time. Bake the croissants for 10 to 15 minutes longer, or until they are deep golden and springy to the touch. Slide the croissants still on the paper, from the pans to racks to cool.

SERVING: Serve the croissants with your favorite preserves or marmalade—no butter is needed.

STORAGE: Keep the croissants loosely covered with plastic wrap the day they are made. Bag and freeze for longer storage. Defrost, reheat at 375°F (190°C) for 2 minutes, then cool and serve.

fig. a

FORMING CROISSANTS

a. Use a sharp pizza wheel to cut the dough into two 7½ x 12-inch (19 x 30-cm) strips. Cut each strip into 6 triangles, each with a base of about 4 inches (10 cm), as described in step 9.

b. Roll up the dough from the side facing you, gently pulling on the point of the triangle with the other hand as you do (step 10).

c. Carefully brush the risen croissants with the egg wash, making sure to dry the brush to avoid having it puddle under the croissants (step 12).

fig. c

fig. b

Makes twenty-four 15-inch long (38-cm) breadsticks

....

2 cups unbleached all-purpose flour
(spoon flour into a dry-measure cup and level off)

1 teaspoon salt

3½ tablespoons extra virgin olive oil or lard

2½ teaspoons (1 envelope) active dry yeast

⅓ cup warm water, about 110°F (45°C)

⅓ cup cold tap water

2 jelly-roll pans lightly dusted with cornmeal

Grissini:
Classic Italian Breadsticks

If you go to a fine restaurant in the Piemonte area of Italy, you won't find bread on the table when you sit down, but you will find three or four 2½ to 3-foot (75- to 90-cm) long breadsticks. They're a specialty of Piemonte, particularly the town of Asti, and they're the perfect thing to accompany the rich and delicate food of the region. Good breadsticks are easy to make: Everything goes into the food processor and they are made in no time. You may use either olive oil or lard as the fat in the dough. The breadsticks are excellent with olive oil, but the flavor of the ones made with lard is superior in my opinion—they have a crunchier texture and a more rustic flavor. You'll notice that the dough is made with both warm and cold water. Warm water is necessary to dissolve dry yeast, but the addition of the cold water afterward prevents the dough from overheating while being mixed.

....

1. Combine the flour, salt, and oil or lard in the bowl of a food processor fitted with the metal blade. Pulse 10 to 15 times to incorporate the fat.

2. Whisk the yeast into the warm water and add the mixture to the bowl. Pulse very quickly 2 to 3 times. Add the cold water and pulse until the dough forms a ball. Pulse continuously for 10 seconds.

3. Invert the food processor bowl over an oiled bowl to turn out the dough. Carefully remove the blade and transfer any dough on it to the bowl. Turn the dough so that the top is oiled. Cover the bowl with plastic wrap and allow the dough to rise at room temperature until doubled in bulk, about 1 hour.

4. Scrape the risen dough to a lightly floured work surface and fold it over on itself several times to deflate. Replace the dough in the bowl and cover it again. Refrigerate the dough for 1 hour or up to 24 hours.

5. When you are ready to bake the grissini, set racks in the upper and lower third of the oven and preheat to 325°F (160°C).

6. Remove the dough from the refrigerator and scrape it onto a floured work surface. Press the dough to deflate it and shape it into a square. Use a bench scraper or a knife to cut the square of dough into 4 equal smaller squares. Working with 1 square of dough at a time, cut through the center to make 2 rectangles, then cut across twice to make 6 pieces. Set the cut pieces of dough to your left. Repeat with the remaining squares of dough to make 24 equal pieces.

7. Place one of the prepared pans to your right. Roll one piece of the dough under the palms of your hands, pressing fairly vigorously, to make a thin pencil-like strand about 15 inches (38 cm) long. Arrange it on the pan and continue with the remaining pieces of dough placing 12 on each pan. If the dough is sticky, flour your hands, but not the dough or the work surface.

8. Bake the breadsticks (they don't need to rise first) for 12 minutes, then switch the bottom pan to the top rack and vice versa, turning them back to front at the same time. Continue baking the breadsticks until they are evenly golden and crisp, 10 to 20 minutes longer.

9. Cool the breadsticks on the pans on racks.

....

SERVING: Serve the breadsticks along with other bread for a meal, or with hors d'oeuvres. In Parma, they wrap transparently thin slices of prosciutto around breadsticks as a little nibble with drinks before dinner.

STORAGE: Keep the breadsticks loosely covered with plastic wrap on the day they are baked. Store them between sheets of wax paper in a tin or plastic container with a tight-fitting lid. In a cool place, they'll stay fresh for a week or two.

1 cup whole milk

1 teaspoon active dry yeast

1½ cups all-purpose flour
(spoon flour into a dry-measure cup and level off)

⅓ cup stone-ground yellow cornmeal

1 tablespoon sugar

½ teaspoon salt

¼ teaspoon baking soda

1 cup buttermilk

6 tablespoons (¾ stick) unsalted butter, melted

2 large eggs

Butter and warmed maple syrup for serving

Waffle iron

Cornmeal Buttermilk Waffles

Making yeast-risen waffles isn't at all time consuming, so don't worry, you won't have to get up at 3:00 a.m. to have them ready for breakfast. In fact, most of the mixing is accomplished in about 10 minutes the night before. All you have to do in the morning is heat up the waffle iron and bake the waffles. Thanks to my dear friend Dorie Greenspan, the waffle maven, for suggesting the method here. You'll notice that there's a little bit of baking soda in the batter—it isn't there as leavening, but to slightly neutralize the acidity of the buttermilk so it doesn't slow down the yeast.

1. The night before you intend to serve the waffles, heat the milk in a small pan to just lukewarm, about 110°F (45°C). Pour it into a small bowl and whisk in the yeast.

2. Combine the flour, cornmeal, sugar, salt, and baking soda in a large mixing bowl and stir well to mix.

3. In a separate bowl, whisk the buttermilk, butter, and eggs together smoothly.

4. Add the buttermilk mixture and the milk and yeast mixture to the dry ingredients and gently whisk everything together until smooth. Tightly cover the bowl with plastic wrap and refrigerate it until the next morning.

5. When you are ready to bake the waffles, close the waffle iron and allow it to heat for about 20 minutes. Open the waffle iron and brush the surface, even if it is nonstick, with a little vegetable oil. Add enough of the batter to completely cover the bottom cavity of the waffle iron, then close the cover. Let the waffle bake for about 3 minutes, then check to see if it is done—it should appear evenly deep golden.

6. Serve the waffle immediately, or place it on a jelly-roll pan, cover it loosely with foil, and place in a 250°F (120°C) oven, adding more waffles to the pan as they are done.

7. Arrange the waffles on a warm platter to serve.

SERVING: Serve the waffles with butter and warmed maple syrup, or your favorite waffle topping.

STORAGE: While I probably wouldn't throw away any leftover waffles, they are really an in-the-moment food, like a soufflé. Wrap and refrigerate leftovers and try toasting them lightly—they have to taste better than a frozen waffle.

VARIATIONS

CORNMEAL WAFFLES WITH A HINT OF LEMON AND BLUEBERRY SAUCE: Add the finely grated zest of a small lemon to the waffle batter along with the liquids. Make a blueberry sauce by cooking a pint of rinsed and picked-over blueberries with 3 tablespoons water, ¼ cup sugar, a pinch each of ground cinnamon and freshly grated nutmeg, and 2 tablespoons of butter. Bring it to a boil, stirring occasionally, then simmer for 5 minutes. Make the sauce the night before and reheat it right before you serve the waffles.

Makes 1 crust for a 12 x 18-inch (30 x 45-cm) or 11 x 17-inch (28 x 43-cm) focaccia or pizza

....

4 cups unbleached all-purpose flour
(spoon flour into a dry-measure cup and level off)

2 teaspoons salt

2½ teaspoons (1 envelope) active dry yeast

1⅔ cups warm water, about 110°F (45°C)

3 tablespoons olive oil

Olive oil for the pan

One 12 x 18-inch (30 x 45-cm) or an 11 x 17-inch
(28 x 43-cm) jelly-roll pan, generously oiled

Dough for Thick-Crusted Pizza & for Focaccia

This dough is used in recipes for several focacce with toppings, one with a filling, and for a thick-crusted home-style pizza. New York food writer Molly O'Neill once defined the difference between pizza and focaccia very simply in an article in the *New York Times* food section about pizza: A focaccia is usually eaten at room temperature, whereas a pizza, whether thick or thin-crusted, is usually eaten right after it comes out of the oven. I would add one more point—focacce have less topping than pizzas do, and real Italian pizzas have much less topping than their American-style cousins, especially when it comes to the use of cheese. I've been served pizzas in New York that had so much melted cheese on them I thought I was eating fondue. Use this dough for the focaccia and pizza recipes in this chapter. See the variations at the end of the recipe for plainer focacce. The dough is very simple to prepare—you just stir all the ingredients together and let it rise once before pressing it into the pan, and briefly again as you prepare the toppings.

1. Combine the flour and salt in a large mixing bowl and stir well to mix.

2. In a separate bowl, whisk the yeast into the water and whisk in the oil.

3. Use a large rubber spatula to make a well in the center of the flour in the bowl. Pour in the liquid and use the spatula to begin stirring in the center of the bowl, gradually stirring in a circle toward the sides of the bowl, incorporating more flour as you stir. When all the flour has been incorporated, the dough will still be fairly soft. Use the spatula to dig down to the bottom of the bowl from the side, between the bowl and the dough, and repeatedly fold the dough over on itself, until no dry bits remain.

4. Cover the bowl with plastic wrap and allow the dough to rise at room temperature until doubled in bulk, 1 to 2 hours, depending on the temperature of the room.

5. Scrape the dough into the prepared pan without folding it over on itself. Lightly oil the palms of your hands to prevent sticking and press down on the dough so that it evenly fills the pan (see figure a, page 117). If the dough resists, cover it with a towel and let it rest for 10 minutes before continuing.

6. Cover the pan with oiled plastic wrap and allow the dough to rise until doubled, up to 1 hour. While the dough is rising prepare the toppings.

....

VARIATIONS

BARE BONES FOCACCIA: To make the simplest focaccia, use your fingertips to dimple the dough all over at 1½-inch (4-cm) intervals and drizzle the top with a couple of tablespoons of olive oil. Sprinkle with 1 teaspoon of kosher or another coarse salt. Bake as for any of the other focaccia recipes.

ROSEMARY FOCACCIA: Add 3 tablespoons chopped fresh rosemary leaves to the flour and salt. Finish as for Bare Bones Focaccia, above.

Makes one 12 x 18-inch (30 x 45-cm) or 11 x 17-inch (28 x 43-cm) focaccia, 6 to 8 generous servings

....

FOCACCIA DOUGH, page 114

TOPPING

½ cup olive oil

1 large onion, about 8 ounces (225 grams), peeled, halved, and thinly sliced from stem to root end

1 (2-ounce/50-gram) can anchovy fillets in olive oil, drained and coarsely chopped

1¼ cups tomato purée

Salt (only a little because of the anchovies and cheese) and freshly ground black pepper

1 cup (about 4 ounces/100 grams) coarsely grated caciocavallo cheese, or ½ cup (about 2 ounces/50 grams) finely grated Pecorino Romano

2 teaspoons dried oregano leaves

1 cup fine, dry bread crumbs

Sfincione: Palermo Focaccia

This focaccia is topped with some of the quintessential ingredients of Sicilian cooking: tomatoes, anchovies, and bread crumbs. In Palermo, sfincione is street food. One of the formerly great temples of casual Palermo food, the Antica Focacceria di San Francesco, also serves it, but I tasted the sfincione there on a recent trip and it had a crust like industrially made white bread and almost nonexistent topping. The experience made me happy that I know how to make my own sfincione. Caciocavallo cheese might be difficult to find. I have substituted Pecorino Romano with excellent results.

1. While the crust is rising, prepare the topping. Pour ¼ cup of the olive oil into a 10-inch sauté pan and place over low to medium heat. Add the onion, and cook it slowly until it softens and begins to color lightly. Stir in the anchovies.

2. Add the tomato purée and simmer the sauce just enough to diminish the raw tomato flavor, about 10 minutes. Season with salt and pepper, under-salting slightly. Scrape the sauce onto a plate or glass pie pan and place it in the refrigerator for a few minutes to cool.

3. When the crust is almost risen, set a rack in the lower third of the oven and preheat to 425°F (220°C).

4. Uncover the crust and use a fingertip to gently dimple it at 1½-inch (4-cm) intervals. Drop spoonfuls of the sauce all over the top of the crust and use a small metal offset spatula to evenly spread a thin layer of the sauce all over the dough.

5. Sprinkle the sauce with the cheese, and then the oregano, and the bread crumbs, one at a time. Drizzle with the remaining ¼ cup of olive oil.

6. Bake the sfincione until it is well risen and the topping is dry and beginning to color, about 30 minutes. Turn the pan back to front about halfway through the baking.

7. Let the sfincione cool in the pan on a rack for 5 minutes, then use a wide metal spatula to slide it onto a rack to finish cooling.

....

SERVING: Use a sharp serrated knife or a pizza wheel to cut the sfincione into squares. In Palermo they eat sfincione at any time of day. My favorite way to serve it is cut into 2-inch (5-cm) squares with drinks before dinner—it makes a fine and substantial hors d'oeuvre.

STORAGE: Keep the sfincione loosely covered with plastic wrap on the day it is baked—if you're preparing it early in the day for the evening, leave it right on the cooling rack. Wrap and freeze for longer storage. Defrost, reheat at 375°F (190°C) for about 10 minutes, and cool before serving.

Makes one 12 x 18-inch (30 x 45-cm) or 11 x 17-inch (28 x 43-cm) focaccia, 6 to 8 generous servings

FOCACCIA DOUGH, page 114

TOPPING

⅓ cup olive oil

1 large onion, about 8 ounces (225 grams), peeled, halved, and thinly sliced from stem to root end

1 (2-ounce/50-gram) can anchovies in olive oil, drained and coarsely chopped

Salt (only a little because of the anchovies) and freshly ground black pepper

⅓ cup Gaeta or oil-cured black olives, pitted and quartered, see Note

⅓ cup Cerignola or other flavorful green olives, pitted and quartered

A light sprinkling of kosher or other coarse salt

Focaccia alla Barese:
Apulian Onion, Anchovy, & Olive Focaccia

This is a traditional Christmas Eve antipasto in Apulia. Please don't be repelled by the presence of the anchovies—they melt into the topping and add a pleasant note of saltiness, but no strong fishy taste. My dear friend and second mother, Ann Amendolara Nurse, taught me to make this.

1. While the crust is rising, prepare the topping. Pour about half of the olive oil into a 10-inch (25-cm) sauté pan and place over low to medium heat. Add the onion slices, and cook them slowly until they soften and begin to color lightly. Stir in the anchovies and cook 1 minute longer. Taste and adjust seasoning with salt and pepper if necessary.

2. Scrape the sauce onto a plate or glass pie pan and place it in the refrigerator for a few minutes to cool. Stir in the olives.

3. When the crust is almost risen, set a rack in the lower third of the oven and preheat to 425°F (220°C).

4. Uncover the crust and use a fingertip to gently dimple it at 1½-inch intervals (figure b). Drop spoonfuls of the onion mixture all over the top of the crust (figure c) and use a small metal offset spatula to spread a thin layer of the sauce evenly all over the dough.

5. Sprinkle the topping with a few pinches of kosher salt. Drizzle with the remaining olive oil.

6. Bake the focaccia until it is well risen and the topping is dry and beginning to color, about 30 minutes. Turn the pan back to front about halfway through the baking.

7. Let the focaccia cool in the pan on a rack for 5 minutes, then use a wide metal spatula to slide it onto a rack to finish cooling.

SERVING: Use a sharp serrated knife or a pizza wheel to cut the focaccia into squares. Serve the focaccia cut into 2-inch (5-cm) squares as an hors d'oeuvre, or as part of an assortment of antipasti as a first course.

STORAGE: Keep the focaccia loosely covered with plastic wrap on the day it is baked—if you're preparing it early in the day for the evening, leave it right on the cooling rack. Wrap and freeze for longer storage. Defrost, reheat at 375°F (190°C) for about 10 minutes, and cool before serving.

Note: The best way to pit olives is to press them one at a time with the side of a knife blade—the pit pops right to the surface.

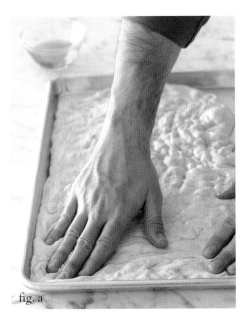
fig. a

fig. b

fig. c

STEPS

a. With lightly oiled palms, press the dough so that it evenly fills the pan (step 5, page 114).

b. Using your fingertips, gently dimple the dough at 1½-inch intervals (step 4).

c. Drop spoonfuls of the onion mixture all over the top of the crust (step 4).

TOPPING

3 cups chopped tomatoes, see *Note*

¾ cup (about 3 ounces/75 grams) coarsely grated or diced mozzarella, optional

½ cup (about 2 ounces/50 grams) finely grated Pecorino Romano cheese

1 large garlic clove, cut into paper-thin slices

1 teaspoon dried oregano leaves

3 tablespoons olive oil

Nonna's Pizza

This is the pizza that I remember my maternal grandmother, Clotilde Basile Lo Conte, making for family celebrations as long as 50 years ago. My mother once told me that when she was a child in Italy, her mother would make bread once a week and send it to the communal oven down the street to be baked. If there was some dough left over, she would press it into a baking pan and make a simple pizza like this one. When we had this pizza at home, we only had mozzarella on it if there happened to be some left over in the refrigerator, so it's not an essential ingredient. If you do use mozzarella, try to get the freshly made type, which has a sweeter, milkier flavor than the industrially made ones. But don't break the bank and use imported buffalo milk mozzarella, as it's wildly expensive and leaks out enormous puddles of water while the pizza is baking.

1. When the crust is almost risen, set a rack in the lower third of the oven and preheat to 425°F (220°C).

2. Uncover the crust and gently dimple it at 1½-inch (4-cm) intervals, using a fingertip.

3. Evenly scatter the tomatoes on the crust, followed by the mozzarella, if using, Pecorino, sliced garlic, and oregano. Drizzle with the oil.

4. Bake the pizza until it is well risen and the topping is dry and beginning to color, about 30 minutes. Turn the pan back to front about halfway through the baking.

5. Let the pizza cool in the pan on a rack for 5 minutes, then use a wide metal spatula to slide it onto a cutting board. Cut and serve immediately.

SERVING: Use a sharp serrated knife or a pizza wheel to cut the pizza into squares. Serve the pizza for lunch, or as a snack in the evening. Or cut it into 2-inch (5-cm) squares as an hors d'oeuvre.

STORAGE: For advance preparation, underbake the pizza slightly, until the dough is baked through, but the cheese has not yet colored. About 20 minutes before serving, bake it at 450°F (225°C) for about 10 minutes. Wrap and refrigerate leftovers.

Note: During the summer I like to use fresh tomatoes for this. First core, then peel about 2 pounds (900 grams) of perfectly ripe plum tomatoes or other small tomatoes (large tomatoes can be too watery) by plunging them into boiling water for about 10 seconds. Slip off the skins. Cut the tomatoes in half and squeeze out the seeds and liquid surrounding them. Cut the tomatoes into approximately ½-inch (1-cm) dice and measure out 3 cups. Failing fresh tomatoes, I use imported Italian plum tomatoes, or a wonderful California brand, Redpack. Drain two 28-ounce (800-gram) cans of tomatoes in a colander set over a bowl. Remove the colander from over the bowl and split the tomatoes open, scraping out the seeds into the bowl. Replace the tomatoes in the colander as they are seeded. Dice the tomatoes and measure the tomatoes as above. Save the tomato juices for a soup or sauce.

Makes one 12 x 18-inch (30 x 45-cm) or 11 x 17-inch (28 x 43-cm) focaccia, 6 to 8 generous servings, more as an hors d'oeuvre

....

FOCACCIA DOUGH, page 114, prepared up to the end of step 4

FILLING

12 ounces (350 grams) prosciutto, thinly sliced and cut into ½-inch (1-cm) squares

12 ounces (350 grams) fresh mozzarella, coarsely shredded or cut into thin slices, then into ½-inch (1-cm) squares

3 tablespoons grated Parmigiano-Reggiano

Freshly ground black pepper

TOPPING

2 tablespoons olive oil

1 teaspoon kosher or other coarse salt

One 12 x 18-inch (30 x 45-cm) or 11 x 17-inch (28 x 43-cm) jelly-roll pan, generously oiled

Filled Ham & Cheese
Focaccia

This is a fun and easy way to make a focaccia you can serve as part of an assortment of first courses or as an hors d'oeuvre. The filling here is prosciutto and mozzarella with a sprinkling of Parmigiano-Reggiano. You could just as easily use boiled ham and Gruyère with excellent results. Or, make up a filling of your own—the techniques of filling, shaping, and baking can be applied to lot of different combinations. Just bear in mind that whatever you use to fill the focaccia must have an assertive flavor, and be both fairly flat and low in moisture—so sliced meats and/or cheeses are perfect.

1. Scrape the dough to a lightly floured work surface without folding it over on itself. Lightly flour the top of the dough and press it into a rough rectangle, at least 10 x 15 inches (25 x 38 cm).

2. Distribute the prosciutto and mozzarella evenly on one side of the dough in a 10 x 7 ½-inch (25 x 19-cm) rectangle. Scatter the Parmigiano and pepper on the filling. Lightly brush the uncovered dough with water so that it adheres easily to the filling and the dough.

3. Fold the uncovered dough over the filling without stretching it. Flour the top of the dough and use the palms of your hands to press and seal the package of dough and filling. Slide both hands, palms up, under the dough and lift it into the prepared pan, lining up the 10-inch side of the dough with the shorter side of the pan.

4. Lightly oil the palms of your hands and press the dough to fill the pan. If it resists, cover the pan with a towel or plastic wrap and leave it for 15 minutes. You should then easily be able to finish pressing the dough into the pan.

5. Cover the pan again and let the dough rise until doubled, about 1 hour.

6. About 20 minutes before the dough is completely risen, set a rack in the lower third of the oven and preheat to 400°F (200°C).

7. Use a fingertip to dimple the dough all over at 1½-inch (4-cm) intervals. Drizzle the top with the oil and sprinkle with the salt.

8. Bake the focaccia until it is well risen and beginning to color, about 30 minutes. Turn the pan back to front about halfway through the baking.

9. Let the focaccia cool in the pan on a rack for 5 minutes, then use a wide metal spatula to slide it onto a rack to finish cooling.

....

SERVING: Use a sharp serrated knife to cut the focaccia into squares. Cut the focaccia into 2-inch (5-cm) squares as an hors d'oeuvre, or as part of an assortment of antipasti for a first course.

STORAGE: Keep the focaccia loosely covered with plastic wrap on the day it is baked—if you're preparing it early in the day for the evening, leave it right on the cooling rack. Wrap and freeze for longer storage. Defrost, reheat at 375°F (190°C) for about 10 minutes, and cool before serving.

128 Rich Pie Dough for
Savory Pies & Tarts

132 Olive-Oil Dough for
Savory Pies & Tarts

133 No-Roll Flaky Dough

135 Corn Pudding Tart

136 Ham & Egg Tart

139 Roasted Pepper &
Goat Cheese Tart

140 Swiss Onion Tart

141 Gruyère, Scallion,
& Walnut Tart

142 Tomato & Cantal Tart

145 Shrimp & Toasted
Pumpkinseed Tart

146 Curried Fish Pie

148 Ligurian Savoy Cabbage Pie

150 Zucchini & Ricotta Pie

151 Pizza Chiena: Neapolitan
Meat & Cheese Pie

152 Chicken Pie with
Biscuit Topping

4

Savory Tarts & Pies

Savory baking is one of my favorite parts of my field, since it combines both cooking and baking skills and provides tasty and elegant results. It's a practical type of baking, too: A savory pie or tart can be the star of a brunch, lunch, casual supper, or buffet. They're especially good for buffets because they can easily be made in advance, taking off pressure at the last minute. Made as individual pies or tarts, they're perfect as an appetizer or as the main course of a light meal.

I've loosely defined the categories this way:

Tarts: These are baked in removable bottom pans with straight (non-sloping) fluted sides.

Pies: These may be baked in a standard pie pan with sloping sides, with or without a top crust. Some pies are baked in rectangular pans and also have a top crust.

Tartlets: Individual tarts, usually a single portion and about 4 1/2 inches (11 cm) in diameter.

There are a few important things to bear in mind about savory pies and tarts:

Meat, fish, and shellfish need to be just cooked through, but no more, before being combined with other filling ingredients so that they don't overcook and toughen while the filling is baking. Vegetables and greens need to be completely cooked or they'll leach water into the filling and might prevent it from setting properly. Season carefully and overseason slightly when eggs are being added to the filling. I like to add the eggs last so that I can get an accurate idea of the filling's flavor first. Slight overseasoning is important because the eggs introduce liquid which will dilute the flavor of the filling. Finally, monitor the baking carefully so that the crust is well baked through, especially on the bottom, and always bake pies and tarts of this type on the lowest rack in your oven.

Additional Ingredients
for Savory Tarts & Pies

CHEESE

Valued for its flavor, which can be sweet and mild or piquant and assertive, and for its richness, cheese is often a component of fillings and pastry doughs. Use the largest holes on a box grater to shred semihard cheeses such as Gruyère or Emmentaler. For hard cheese such as Parmigiano-Reggiano, use a Microplane® or the small diagonally set holes of a box grater. Dice mozzarella as you would vegetables.

Although there are literally thousands of cheese varieties, they all begin in the same way: as milk treated with enzymes or bacteria, and sometimes heat, to separate it into curds and whey. What is curdled at this primary stage (cow's or sheep's milk, skimmed milk or milk that has been mixed with cream to increase its fat content) and how it is curdled (with rennet or starter, heated before or during inoculation or not at all) determines the type of cheese produced.

After the curd is cut or broken up, it is drained and sometimes salted. At this point, fresh cheeses such as ricotta and cream cheese are ready for use.

Cured cheeses go through more processing. The drained curds are stirred, molded, allowed to drain and become firm, unmolded, then ripened in temperature- and humidity-controlled environments for very specific amounts of time. Different curing agents, added alone or in combination into or onto the cheese, include bacteria, enzymes, molds, and yeast.

All cheeses should be refrigerated. In general, soft and fresh cheeses need to be consumed within days of purchasing, while hard cheeses will keep longer. Always directly cover cut surfaces to prevent drying out.

BASKET CHEESE: This is fresh unsalted cow's milk cheese traditionally molded in a basket.

CACIOCAVALLO: The name of this cow's milk cheese from southern Italy literally means "cheese on horseback," although no one knows exactly why. (One theory is that its distinctive shape resembles a saddlebag.) Caciocavallo is available semiaged or, more commonly, aged so that it has a sharp flavor and is hard enough to be grated. The latter is the type called for in this book. Caciocavallo melts quickly and evenly, which makes it a great ingredient in savory tarts, but it is also delicious sliced and eaten plain. Good quality aged provolone (not the deli-counter slicing variety) or Pecorino Romano make adequate substitutes when caciocavallo is not available.

CHEDDAR: When I call for cheddar cheese, I always mean the extra-sharp variety, because it has more flavor from longer aging. Cheddar cheese, which originated in England, has been made at least since the twelfth century. I favor the ones made in New York and Vermont. There is such a wide variety of cheddar available today that it can sometimes be hard to pick one, but do look beyond the orange-colored blocks available in the supermarket, and especially seek out white cheddar, which has no artificial coloring added.

COTTAGE CHEESE: This spreadable curd cheese is available almost everywhere today, but it gets its name from the fact that it was originally a homemade product. It is sold in plastic tubs in a range of curd sizes. It's mild and relatively low in calories.

CREAM CHEESE: Made from cream and milk, cream cheese is an unripened cheese with a rich, tangy, buttery flavor. It is the principal ingredient in cheesecakes and cheese fillings. Most cream cheese is stabilized with gum arabic, which makes it smoother and allows it to mix easily with other ingredients. Since cream cheese is quite perishable (and should never be frozen), only buy as much as is needed for a particular purpose. Whipped cream cheese should not be substituted in a recipe, since its higher air content would alter the final product. Where it is possible to use lower-fat cream cheese I've noted that, but never use nonfat cream cheese for baking—it doesn't have the same flavor or texture.

FETA CHEESE: Sharp, salty feta cheese is one of Greece's best-known foods (although it is also made in other countries.) It was originally made by shepherds using goat's or sheep's milk, but today's feta is often made with cow's milk. Feta is made in large white blocks. It's better to purchase feta that is sliced in the store for you than to purchase the packaged kind, which is already crumbled and therefore risks drying out. French feta is a particularly creamy and mild type that I like best for baking and eating.

GOAT CHEESE: Goat cheese is, as the name implies, made from goat's milk. It comes in a range of sharpness, from super-mild to quite tangy, and is made in many countries, although it is most closely associated with France, where it is known as *chèvre*. Goat cheese should be snowy white in color and soft in texture. There are many styles, shapes, and degrees of aging in goat cheeses. When it is called for in a recipe it means the fresh, crumbly variety, such as Montrachet.

GORGONZOLA AND OTHER BLUE CHEESES: Blue cheeses take their name from the blue (or sometimes greenish) veins of mold that run through them. At one time this mold developed naturally during aging, but today's blue cheeses are inoculated with it to ensure proper veining with the mold. If you don't recognize blue cheese by its look, you certainly will recognize its smell, which can be pungent. Gorgonzola is an Italian blue cheese from the town of Gorgonzola in Lombardy, the region around Milan. Gorgonzola dolce is a mild variety, though stronger types, which are aged longer, also exist.

GOUDA: Holland's famous gouda cheese is recognizable by its shape: It is made in a round form with gently curved sides. Gouda has a brown rind and is sometimes encased in black wax. The edible part of the cheese is pale yellow and has a mild, nutty taste. It has excellent melting qualities.

GRUYÈRE: Prepared in the cantons of Fribourg, Neuchâtel, and Vaud in Switzerland, Gruyère is a firm cheese with an ivory color. Although similar to Emmentaler cheese (the cheese with the large holes usually referred to as "Swiss cheese"), Gruyère has smaller holes, a slightly higher fat content, and a nuttier flavor, similar to that of hazelnuts. Gruyère melts smoothly—it is often the main ingredient in classic cheese fondue.

MASCARPONE: This rich Italian cheese, similar to cream cheese, is the main ingredient in *tiramisù* and many other Italian preparations. Both imported and domestic brands are available in 8- to 18-ounce (225- to 500-gram) plastic tubs.

MOZZARELLA: Soft, milky mozzarella cheese is one of Italy's great gifts to the world. Fresh domestic mozzarella is quite good, and you may *not* want to spend extra money for expensive imported *mozzarella di bufala* (water buffalo's milk mozzarella) from Italy when baking, since it can leak out a lot of whey when heated. Freshly made domestic mozzarella is increasingly easier to find and works very well in recipes. Try to avoid the packages of industrially made mozzarella that bear little resemblance to the real thing.

PARMIGIANO-REGGIANO: Only cheese made in a specific area of the Emilia Romagna region of Italy can be labeled "Parmigiano-Reggiano" in dotted letters up and down its rind. This is real Parmesan, a hard grating cheese that is part of a larger family of cheeses known as *grana*. Always buy whole pieces of Parmigiano-Reggiano, wrap them tightly in wax paper, then aluminum foil, and grate them just before using. Pre-grated cheese may have pieces of rind or other undesirable items included in the mix, and it dries out quickly once it's grated.

PECORINO ROMANO: *Pecorino* is simply the Italian word for a sheep's (ewe's) milk cheese, the most widely available of which is Pecorino Romano. This aged, somewhat sharp cheese has quite a strong flavor. In central and southern Italy, grated Pecorino Romano is often used just as grated Parmigiano-Reggiano would be, and sometimes it is used in combination with it.

Store and handle exactly the same way as Parmigiano-Reggiano.

RICOTTA: Smooth, creamy ricotta is a whey cheese, similar in appearance to cottage cheese, that is wonderful in both sweet and savory preparations. Ricotta in this book means full-fat ricotta. Ricotta does not keep indefinitely and cannot be frozen, so don't buy it too far in advance. Freshly made ricotta from a reputable cheese store will have a fresher and cleaner taste and a firmer texture than the industrially made ricotta you buy in sealed plastic tubs in the grocery store

VEGETABLES

Vegetables can add not only flavor but a splash of color. They are used in several savory preparations in this book, although not nearly as frequently as fruits. As a general rule, look for fresh, unblemished vegetables with no dark or soft spots. If you are going to be using vegetables unpeeled, it is worthwhile to seek out organic and/or locally grown varieties. Unless otherwise indicated, store in plastic bags in the refrigerator.

To cut vegetables into small or large dice, cut the vegetable into thick slices, then cut the slices into sticks. Cut through a bundle of sticks to make cubes. I usually peel and coarsely cut onions, then throw them into the food processor for chopping, pulsing it on and off until they are the right size.

BELL PEPPERS: Bell peppers, like chile peppers, are part of the Capsicum family, but they are sweet rather than spicy. They come in a variety of colors ranging from deep red to bright yellow to dark green and even to brown and purple. Red and yellow bell peppers are sweeter than green ones. Look for peppers with smooth, firm skin.

CHILE PEPPERS: Spicy chile peppers can range from mild with just a hint of bite to searingly hot, depending on which variety you choose. You can also somewhat lessen their heat by discarding the seeds and membranes before use. Never touch your eyes or nose with your fingers after handling chile peppers; if you are particularly sensitive to the power of chile peppers, you may want to wear disposable gloves when handling them.

JALAPEÑO: The small size of a green jalapeño—only about 2 inches (5 cm) long—belies its spiciness. Though I find them only mildly spicy (or not at all), they can surprise you and occasionally be very hot.

SERRANO: The Mexican serrano pepper is smaller and thinner than a jalapeño, but it is usually much hotter.

CORN: The appearance of tender and sweet fresh corn on the cob at a farmer's market or farm stand is one of the surest signs that summer has arrived. Fresh corn is usually added to recipes while still uncooked. To remove corn kernels from the cob, simply

shuck the ears and pull off any stray silk. Stand the cob upright in a shallow bowl by holding the top with one hand, and saw off the kernels, working from top to bottom, with a serrated knife. Corn is also dried and ground to make cornmeal, polenta, and other corn products.

OLIVES: Olives are actually a fruit, but since we use them in savory preparations, I've included them here. When shopping for olives, I like to go to a gourmet or grocery store that has them in bins and has a high turnover.

CERIGNOLA OLIVES: Cerignola olives are large green olives from Puglia in Italy. They are now available in black and red varieties, though the green ones are what is called for in these recipes.

GAETA OLIVES: Gaeta olives are small black Italian olives with an assertive taste.

ONIONS: Without onions, there would be no savory cooking, or none that you'd really want to eat. They are used in every culture in the world. The genus Allium includes many varieties of onions, garlic, leeks, shallots, scallions, chives, and some strikingly beautiful ornamentals.

GARLIC: Garlic is the strongest member of the onion family. When purchasing garlic, look for firm bulbs covered in papery white skin. Garlic can be stored at room temperature, although older garlic can be unpleasantly

126 harsh. If you cut into a clove of garlic and see a little green sprout in the center, dig it out with the tip of a paring knife and discard it. Store garlic at room temperature.

LEEKS: Leeks are mild and sweet and look like gigantic scallions. Usually there is a large amount of sand or grit in leeks, so it's a good idea to cut them lengthwise and soak them in a couple of changes of cold water to be sure they are perfectly clean before proceeding with a recipe.

RED ONIONS: These are large onions with a purple skin and purple and white flesh. They may be eaten either raw or cooked.

SCALLIONS: Also known as green onions or spring onions, scallions are one of the milder forms of onion and often a good choice when you will be using an onion in uncooked form. Look for firm stalks with no brown spots on the green leaves, because most recipes call for the white part of the scallions as well as some of the green portion.

SHALLOTS: Shallots are small onions covered in brown skin. They tend to be very sweet, as onions go, and their flesh is often tinged with pink or purple.

YELLOW ONIONS: These are probably the most common onions—the one to reach for when a recipe does not specify a particular type. They are sometimes labeled as "cooking onions." As the name implies, the skin of yellow onions has a yellow tint. They can be stored in a dry, cool place, unrefrigerated, for a couple of weeks. They are usually served cooked, most often cooked until translucent or caramelized in the first step of a recipe.

WHITE ONIONS: White onions are similar to yellow onions in texture, although their flavor is slightly less sweet. They are covered in white skin and may be stored at cool room temperature. I like white onions for savory fillings where I don't want to emphasize a strong sweet flavor.

PUMPKIN: Because pumpkins can be wildly inconsistent, ranging from dense and delicious to watery and flavorless, I tend to favor canned pumpkin when I'm baking. It's not only more convenient but more reliable. Look for a brand that lists pumpkin as the sole ingredient, and be sure not to buy "pumpkin pie" filling by mistake. Peeled, seeded, and cubed winter squash can be steamed or gently roasted, cooled, and puréed, and substituted for pumpkin, as can roasted, cooled, peeled, and puréed sweet potatoes.

PEAS: Freshly shelled green peas are a fleeting late spring/early summer treat. Frozen peas are a completely acceptable year-round substitute. Because peas are so small, frozen ones thaw very quickly and can then be used the same as freshly shelled peas.

SAVOY CABBAGE: Curly Savoy cabbage is my favorite type of cabbage—it has a more delicate taste than standard green cabbage and a more tender texture as well. Look for heads of cabbage without brown spots.

MEAT & FISH

Meat and fish may be either fresh—in which case they should be used within a day or so of purchase—or cured for longer storage. Cured products usually develop a strong taste, which means they can be used sparingly to add a little punch to a recipe.

Meat and meat products: Italy and other European countries have a dizzying array of pork products—salami; hams, both raw and cooked; sausages, both fresh and dried; and almost every other part of the pig, cured and smoked or dried. Valued for their flavor, richness, and texture, most pork products are highly salted, which is a consideration when using them as an ingredient in pastry fillings.

BACON: Bacon is pork belly that has been cured and smoked. The salty, smoky taste and crisp yet chewy texture of bacon knows no substitute. Bacon is usually sold in thin strips, although you may also find artisanal bacon that is hand-cut at the time of purchase. Store bacon in the refrigerator.

CAPICOLA: Capicola is a cured Italian cold cut made from the head and neck of a pig. It is sold thinly sliced on a deli slicer. Store tightly wrapped in the refrigerator.

HAM: When I call for ham, I mean boiled ham—the kind that has been boned, cured, and cooked in water. It is pale pink in color and has a soft texture and a milder taste than smoked products. Some boiled hams are smoked, but those are labeled "smoked ham."

LARD: The best lard for baking is called "leaf lard" and is rendered from the hard pork fat that encases the kidneys. Lard available in the supermarket is a slightly deodorized version rendered from pork fat in general. Outside the United States, lard is used extensively for deep-frying (as is beef fat, or suet) because of its ability to withstand high temperatures for a long time without breaking down, as well as for pastry dough preparation and cooking in general. Used in moderation, good quality lard imparts a fine flavor to baked foods, and is a lot more healthful and natural than chemically rendered oils and shortenings.

PROSCIUTTO: Prosciutto is a raw ham that has been seasoned, salt-cured, and air-dried, but not smoked or cooked. What we call prosciutto in the United States is called *prosciutto crudo* (raw) in Italy in order to differentiate it from *prosciutto cotto*, which is a boiled ham. Prosciutto is usually sold in thin slices, but since it is sliced on the spot, you may ask for a thicker slice if you intend to cut it into cubes. It may be either imported or domestic; Italian prosciutto will be labeled by its place of origin (Parma and San Daniele are a couple). Serrano raw hams from Spain are also now available in the United States.

SALT PORK: Salt pork is a salt-cured layer of pork fat that is similar to bacon. It adds a wonderful and distinctive flavor to many preparations. Salt pork is often blanched briefly in order to remove some of the salt. Store salt pork tightly wrapped in the refrigerator or freezer.

SOPPRESSATA: Soppressata, originally from the Italian region of Calabria, is a pork salami flavored with chile pepper and red wine.

Fish and fish products: Freshness is the most important quality when choosing fish, which should smell sweet and of the sea. Any fish that smells "fishy" is past its prime and won't impart anything but a foul taste to anything you prepare with it.

ANCHOVIES: Anchovies are small fish in the sardine family that have been preserved either in oil or in salt. They add a sharp, pungent flavor to many savory foods. Salted anchovies tend to be meatier and tastier, but before using they need to be skinned, rinsed, and boned (just slice down the belly of the anchovy with the tip of a paring knife and the two halves should lift away easily from the spine). Anchovies in oil are more commonly available and simply need to be rinsed. Anchovies are often sautéed in a pan along with onions and/or garlic, and they quickly dissolve into a pulp, imparting a salty flavor, much the same way that fish sauce does in Southeast Asian cooking.

SMOKED SALMON: Pink and delicious smoked salmon is just what its name implies. It may be either hot-smoked or cold-smoked. Keep smoked salmon in the refrigerator, but bring it to room temperature before serving. I love Scottish and Irish salmon, as well as Nova, that very New York–style smoked salmon often called "lox."

OCEAN FISH: Firm-fleshed white fish, called for in the recipe for Curried Fish Pie (page 146), includes any number of varieties of fish, such as cod or halibut. In this case you want a fish that offers a thick fillet rather than a thin one. Though it's not traditional, a thick slice of salmon could also be substituted.

127

Makes dough for the crust of a 10- or 11-inch (25- or 28-cm) tart, a 9-inch (23-cm) single-crust pie, or 6 to 8 individual tarts, depending on the size of the pans

....

1½ cups all-purpose flour
(spoon flour into a dry-measure cup and level off)

½ teaspoon salt

1 teaspoon baking powder

10 tablespoons (1¼ sticks) cold unsalted butter,
cut into 12 pieces

1 large egg

1 large egg yolk

Rich Pie Dough
for Savory Pies & Tarts

This is as good and as delicate as it is easy to prepare. It's fine for a pie or tart and may also be used for a double-crust pie. Any dough that has a high butter content benefits from low temperatures: have all the ingredients cold when you begin to mix; refrigerate the dough after mixing; and refrigerate the dough again after it has been rolled out and fitted into the pan. The cool temperature makes the dough easier to handle because the butter isn't melting, and the resting period helps to relax the gluten strands formed while mixing and rolling.

1. Combine the flour, salt, and baking powder in the bowl of a food processor fitted with the metal blade. Add the butter and pulse about 20 times to finely mix in the butter.

2. Add the egg and egg yolk and pulse until the dough just begins to form a ball.

3. Invert the food processor bowl over a floured work surface to turn out the dough. Carefully remove the blade and transfer any dough on it to the work surface. Use your hands to press the dough into a disk about ½ inch (1 cm) thick.

4. Follow instructions on the opposite page for rolling dough to fit a pan.

   Note: Double the recipe if you need it for a double-crust pie.

....

STORAGE: Wrap dough disk in plastic wrap and refrigerate for at least an hour or up to 2 days.

Rolling Dough
and Forming Pie & Tart Crusts

Here are some general instructions for the mechanics of handling simple pastry doughs. Following a simple system, rather than rolling at random, makes the process easier and results in a perfectly round piece of dough, reducing waste when you line the pan.

ROLLING

Start by flouring the work surface and the dough with pinches of flour—then you can renew the flour as often as you need to without adding much extra flour to the dough. Press the dough to shape it into a rough disk. Holding the rolling pin with one hand at each end, press the dough in strokes close to each other, starting at the edge of the dough closest to you and continuing to the far edge. Turn the dough 45 degrees to the right and repeat. Turn again and repeat. Pressing the dough this way will soften a flaky dough slightly so that it rolls easily; if you try to roll a dough that's hard from the refrigerator it will just break apart.

After pressing, start rolling the dough by rolling away from you to the far end and back again (see figure a). Use a firm but gentle pressure—pressing too hard might cut right through the dough. Turn the dough 45 degrees as before and roll again. Continue

fig. a

fig. b

turning and rolling until the dough is the desired size. Don't forget to renew pinches of flour as needed, as you roll (see figure b). For a 1-inch (2½-cm) deep tart pan, the right size is about 3 inches (7½ cm) larger in diameter than the pan. For a standard 9-inch (23-cm) pie pan, called for in all pie recipes here, the dough should be rolled to 13 inches (33 cm) in diameter to allow enough to cover the rim of the pan and fold some under for a fluted edge. For a double-crust pie, it can be 12 inches (30 cm) in diameter, since the dough is trimmed even with the outer rim.

ROLLING DOUGH

a. Start by rolling the dough away from you from 6 to 12 o'clock.

b. Remember to occasionally lift the dough and toss some flour underneath so that the dough does not stick to the surface.

FORMING TART CRUST

a. Using a rolling pin, sever the dough at the rim of the tart pan.

b. Using your thumb inside the pan and your forefinger on the rim, press in and down at the same time to make the top edge of the crust.

fig. a

fig. b

FORMING TART CRUST

Fold the dough in half and slide both hands, palms up, under it. Transfer it to the pan, lining up the fold with the diameter of the pan. With the uncovered part of the pan closer to you, slide both hands underneath the dough and unfold it toward you. Press the dough flat against the bottom of the pan and use your fingertips to gently push it into the angle formed by the bottom and side of the pan. With both hands perpendicular to the bottom of the pan, press the dough into the side of the pan. Use a bench scraper, the back of a knife, or a rolling pin to trim away the excess dough at the top of the pan (see figure a). Using your thumb inside the pan and your forefinger on the rim, press in and down at the same time to make the top edge of the crust straight and even (see figure b).

FORMING PIECRUST

Transfer the dough to the pan and unfold it as for a tart crust (see figure a, opposite page). Press the dough well into the pan, letting the excess dough hang over the top rim of the pan. For a double-crust pie, use a bench scraper or the back of a knife to trim the dough even with the top rim of the pan. For a single-crust pie, use scissors to trim away all

but ½ inch (1 cm) of the dough hanging over the edge of the pan. Turn the dough under, even with the edge of the pan all around. Flute the edge of the crust by pinching your thumb and forefinger of one hand together on the outside of the dough and your forefinger of the other hand on the inside. Pinch outside and push toward the pinch from the inside, repeating the pinching and pushing all around the edge of the pie (see figure b, opposite page).

When you make a double-crust pie, moisten the edge of the bottom crust with water and put the top crust in place the same way you would place dough into a pan. Unfold it and trim away all but ½ inch (1 cm). Fold the edge of the top crust under the edge of the bottom crust and flute as above.

Note: To roll the dough for a square or rectangular pan, the procedure is almost the same. First form the dough into a square. When you are pressing and rolling the dough, turn it 90 degrees between presses or rolls. Everything else is exactly the same.

BAKING EMPTY PIE AND TART CRUSTS

This is known as baking "blind." Pierce the dough all over at ½-inch (1-cm) intervals with the tines of a fork. Line the dough with parchment paper, leaving it a little larger than the pan for easy removal, and fill the shell with dried beans. Bake until the dough looks dull and dry, then remove the paper and beans and continue baking until golden and baked through. Never use foil, which might crease and cut through the dough. I never partially bake a crust that is to be filled with a preparation that needs to be baked. Between the addition of the baking powder to the dough, which makes it press firmly against the bottom of the pan, and baking the pie or tart in the bottom of the oven, the crust always bakes through perfectly.

FORMING PIECRUST

a. Transfer the folded dough by placing your hands, palms up, underneath it and lining up the fold with the center of the pan.

b. Using the thumb and forefinger of one hand, pinch the outside of the dough around the forefinger inside the edge of the dough to form crimping.

fig. a

fig. b

SINGLE-CRUST QUANTITIES
**Makes dough for the crust of a 10- or 11-inch
(25- or 28-cm) single-crust pie or tart**

DOUBLE-CRUST QUANTITIES
**Makes dough for the crust of a 10- or 11-inch
(25- or 28-cm) double-crust pie or tart**

1½ cups all-purpose flour
(spoon flour into a dry-measure cup and level off)

½ teaspoon sugar

½ teaspoon salt

½ teaspoon baking powder

¼ cup olive oil

1 large egg

1 large egg yolk

2 tablespoons water

3 cups all-purpose flour
(spoon flour into a dry-measure cup and level off)

1 teaspoon sugar

1 teaspoon salt

1 teaspoon baking powder

½ cup olive oil

3 large eggs

2 large egg yolks

Olive-Oil Dough
for Savory Pies & Tarts

This dough has a fine tender texture and an excellent flavor that isn't assertively olive-y. Of course, it's perfect for any Mediterranean-style savory pie or tart, but it can also function well in other recipes. It only takes about 5 minutes to make and has the advantage of being very tolerant if you take a little longer to roll it out, since the oil won't melt and make the dough sticky and unmanageable, as butter sometimes does. I'm giving you two quantities here, one for a single-crust pie or tart and another for a double crust. The doughs are identical, but the liquid ratio is slightly different in each.

1. Combine the flour, sugar, salt, and baking powder in the bowl of a food processor fitted with the metal blade. Pulse several times.

2. Add the oil, egg(s), yolk(s) and the water, if making the smaller quantity. Pulse repeatedly until the dough forms a shaggy ball. Don't overmix or the oil might separate from the dough and make it impossible to handle later on.

3. Invert the food processor bowl over a floured work surface to turn out the dough. Carefully remove the blade and transfer any dough on it to the work surface. Press the dough into a roughly ½-inch (1-cm) thick disk (2 disks for the larger amount) without folding it over on itself.

4. Follow the instructions on page 129 for rolling dough to fit a pan. With olive-oil dough you can press harder, and you will need to, because this dough is much more elastic than a butter-based dough.

STORAGE: Wrap in plastic and refrigerate until needed. This dough can chill for several days.

Makes dough for the crust of a 10- or 11-inch (25- or 28-cm) tart

....

1½ cups all-purpose flour
(spoon flour into a dry-measure cup and level off)

1 teaspoon salt

1 teaspoon baking powder

10 tablespoons (1¼ sticks) cold unsalted butter,
cut into 8 to 10 pieces

2 tablespoons cold water

No-Roll Flaky Dough

This dough makes a fine tart or pie crust. My preference is to use it for the former, because a pie pan is deeper and it's more difficult to push the crumbly mixture up the side of a 2-inch (5-cm) deep pan. I also prefer using a rolled dough for a pie because it affords the advantage of making an attractive fluted edge on the pie. Be absolutely sure to keep the ingredients separate looking, like a crumb topping. If you go too far and they form a ball, you'll have no recourse but to roll out the dough. Use this in any recipe in this chapter that calls for a tart crust made from flaky dough.

1. Combine the flour, salt, and baking powder in the bowl of a food processor fitted with the metal blade. Add the butter and pulse until the ingredients are coming together but some small pieces of butter remain visible, 8 to 10 pulses.

2. Add the water and pulse a couple of times. At this point the dough will look like separate clumps of dough, somewhat like a crumb topping.

3. Invert the processor bowl over a tart pan to turn out the dough. Carefully remove the blade and transfer any dough to the pan.

4. Use a fork to distribute the dough in the pan: Make an even layer of the crumbly mixture, then go back and push some away from the center outward to make ½ inch (1 cm) around the inside of the pan about twice as tall to cover the side of the pan.

5. Using floured fingertips, begin to press down gently on the crumbly mixture so it adheres together as a coherent dough. Use your thumbs, held perpendicular to the pan, to press the dough against the side of the pan. Make sure the dough on the side of the pan is even in thickness—if it is thinner at the top where the heat is strongest, the edges will burn while it's baking.

6. Finally, using your thumb inside the pan and your forefinger on the rim, press in and down at the same time to make the top edge of the crust straight and even (see figure b, page 130).

....

STORAGE: Slide the pan into a plastic bag or cover it with plastic wrap and refrigerate it until needed. This also freezes well, especially if you need to make several and want to get them out of the way in advance. The unbaked crust is fine for 2 days in the refrigerator and 1 month in the freezer.

Makes one 10- or 11-inch (25- or 28-cm) tart, about 8 generous servings

....

5 ears of fresh sweet corn, yellow, white, or mixed

4 tablespoons unsalted butter, melted

1 bunch scallions (green onions), white part and about half the green, finely sliced

1 small bunch chives, finely sliced

1 small hot chile pepper, such as a jalapeño or a serrano, stemmed, halved, seeded, and finely sliced

or ¼ teaspoon crushed red pepper

1½ cups heavy whipping cream

Salt and freshly ground black pepper

3 large eggs

One 10- or 11-inch (25- or 28-cm) tart crust, unbaked, made from Rich Pie Dough, page 128, or No-Roll Flaky Dough, page 133

Corn Pudding Tart

Vicky Zeph, chef-owner, along with her brother Mike, of Zephs' Restaurant in Peekskill, New York, makes the best corn pudding I have ever tasted. I like it because it isn't overly sweet as some corn puddings can be. The only difference between Vicky's pudding and the tart filling here is that she uses 15 ears of corn (9 grated and 6 with the kernels cut off). The resulting pudding holds its shape well enough to be spooned onto a plate without running. When I spoke with Vicky about this recipe, she agreed that less corn would make a creamier tart filling.

1. Set a rack in the lowest level of the oven and preheat to 350°F (180°C).

2. Set a box grater over a shallow bowl and grate the kernels from 3 of the ears of corn, using the large teardrop-shaped holes. After grating the corn, use the back of a knife to scrape any remaining juices from the cobs into the bowl. Use a knife to cut the whole kernels from the remaining 2 ears of corn.

3. Stir in the butter, and then the scallions, chives, chile, cream, and salt and pepper, one at a time. Taste for seasoning and add more salt to taste, keeping the filling a little overseasoned to make up for the addition of the eggs. Whisk the eggs in a bowl, then stir them into the filling.

4. Pour the filling into the tart crust. Bake the tart until the crust is baked through and well colored on the bottom and the filling is set and puffed, about 30 minutes.

5. Cool the tart on a rack until it is no longer red-hot and serve it warm. After the tart has cooled slightly, unmold it by removing the sides of the pan.

SERVING: This is a perfect accompaniment to baked ham or roast chicken. Or serve it for brunch with bacon or sausages.

STORAGE: Wrap and refrigerate leftovers and reheat them briefly at 375°F (190°C) before serving.

Makes one 10- or 11-inch (25- or 28-cm) tart, about 8 generous servings

....

6 ounces (175 grams) best quality thinly sliced boiled ham, cut into ¼-inch (6-mm) shreds

⅔ cup milk

⅔ cup heavy whipping cream

Salt, freshly ground black pepper, and freshly grated nutmeg

4 large eggs

One 10- or 11-inch (25- or 28-cm) tart crust, unbaked, made from Rich Pie Dough, page 128, or No-Roll Flaky Dough, page 133

Ham & Egg Tart

Ham and eggs go well together no matter how you combine them. I like small dices of ham in scrambled eggs, and a slice of ham cooked with fried eggs. This pie combines them in a new way and is perfect for breakfast, brunch, or lunch. The good news is that you can have the crust chilling (from the day before, if need be) and the ham and completed filling ready to go, so you'll just need to fill the crust and bake it in time to serve a beautifully puffed tart hot from the oven. By the way, this is equally good when cooled to room temperature, and also makes a great hors d'oeuvre.

1. Set a rack in the lowest level of the oven and preheat to 375°F (190°C).

2. Put the ham in a bowl and toss through it with your fingertips to separate the shreds. Arrange them over the prepared crust.

3. Whisk together the milk, cream, salt, pepper, and nutmeg in a medium bowl. Taste for seasoning—the filling should be slightly overseasoned before the eggs are added. Whisk in the eggs 2 at a time, then pour into the crust.

4. Bake the tart until the crust is baked through, well colored on the bottom, and the filling is set and puffed, about 30 minutes.

5. Cool the tart for a few minutes on a rack before unmolding.

....

SERVING: Serve the tart on its own for breakfast or brunch. For lunch, add a salad.

STORAGE: Loosely cover the cooled tart with plastic wrap if you are going to serve it at room temperature. Wrap and refrigerate leftovers and reheat them briefly at 375°F (190°C) before serving.

VARIATIONS

QUICHE LORRAINE: Replace the ham with 8 ounces (225 grams) thick-cut bacon, cut into ½-inch (1-cm) pieces. Cover the bacon with cold water in a saucepan and bring it to a boil to decrease its smoky flavor. Drain the bacon and cook it in a sauté pan over low heat until it has rendered most of its fat, but not until it is crisp. Remove the bacon with a slotted spoon and drain it on paper towels. Scatter the bacon over the crust instead of ham and continue with the recipe, at step 3. By the way, a real Quiche Lorraine contains no cheese.

HAM & CHEESE TART: Reduce the ham to 4 ounces (100 grams) and scatter 1 cup coarsely grated Gruyère, cheddar, or Gouda over the top. Continue with the recipe at step 3, taking the saltiness of the cheese into consideration when you season the liquid.

Makes one 10- or 11-inch (25- or 28-cm) tart, about 8 generous servings

....

ROASTED PEPPERS

4 medium bell peppers, about 2 pounds (900 grams)

Salt

2 tablespoons olive oil

1 garlic clove, peeled and thinly sliced

CRUST AND FILLING

One 10- or 11-inch (25- or 28-cm) tart crust, unbaked, made from Olive-Oil Dough, page 132

10 ounces (250 grams) mild goat cheese such as Montrachet, crumbled

6 large eggs

Salt and freshly ground black pepper

¼ cup chopped flat leaf (Italian) parsley

1 jelly-roll pan lined with foil for roasting the peppers

Roasted Pepper &
Goat Cheese Tart

The slightly bittersweet flavor of a freshly roasted sweet pepper pairs so well with a mild goat cheese such as Montrachet, that I decided to combine them in a delicately perfumed tart. My instinct was to pour a custard over the ingredients, but then I realized that this tart would taste better at room temperature (after the custard had lost its puff). Except in a few narrow circumstances, I don't usually like heated goat cheese. So I decided on an egg mixture like that for a frittata with plenty of chopped parsley in it to emphasize the freshness of the flavors. Next, I decided to hide the goat cheese between two layers of peppers so there was no risk it would be exposed and perhaps become dry and chalky in the oven. Any color pepper is fine for this, but remember that the red and yellow ones are sweeter than the green ones. It's best to roast the peppers in advance if you can. They really benefit from marinating in the oil and garlic for a day before you bake the tart.

1. To roast the peppers, place an oven rack about 6 inches (15 cm) from the heating element and preheat the broiler. Place the peppers on the prepared pan and slide them under the broiler. Let the skins of the peppers char on one side, then use tongs to turn each pepper 90 degrees. Repeat until the peppers are evenly charred on all sides and have collapsed. Alternatively, use an outdoor gas or charcoal grill set on medium (use uniform white ash for charcoal) and char the peppers right on the grill.

2. Transfer the peppers to a bowl and cover it with plastic wrap. The peppers will steam as they begin to cool and the skins will loosen on their own. When the peppers are cool enough to handle, place them in a colander and stem, peel, and seed them. The peppers will pretty much separate into smaller pieces as you peel them. Place the cleaned peppers back in the bowl and continue until all the peppers have been cleaned and seeded. (Do not peel the peppers under running water or much of their flavor will be lost.)

3. Place a layer of peppers in a shallow bowl. Sprinkle with a pinch or two of salt and drizzle on very little olive oil. Scatter a few of the garlic slices over the peppers. Repeat until you have layered all the peppers with the seasonings. Cover the bowl and

refrigerate it for up to 3 days. If you make the peppers more than a day before baking the tart, remove the garlic no more than 24 hours after adding it.

4. When you are ready to bake the tart, set a rack in the lowest level of the oven and preheat to 375°F (190°C).

5. Sprinkle the tart crust with half of the cheese. Cover the cheese with a layer of the marinated peppers, overlapping slightly. Repeat with the remaining cheese and remaining peppers, ending with peppers on top.

6. Whisk the eggs with the salt, pepper, and parsley and pour the mixture into the crust.

7. Bake the tart until the filling is set and well colored and the crust is baked through, about 30 minutes. Cool the tart on a rack.

....

SERVING: Serve the tart in wedges for brunch, as an appetizer, or as the main course for lunch. It's also good as an hors d'oeuvre when cut into thin wedges.

STORAGE: Keep the tart at room temperature until you intend to serve it on the day it is baked. Wrap and refrigerate leftovers and bring to room temperature before serving again.

½ cup (about 3 ounces/75 grams) diced thick-cut bacon

3 tablespoons unsalted butter

1½ pounds (675 g) white onions

Salt

1 tablespoon all-purpose flour

½ cup milk

½ cup heavy whipping cream

Freshly ground black pepper and freshly grated nutmeg

3 large eggs

One 10- or 11-inch (25- or 28-cm) tart crust, unbaked, made from Rich Pie Dough, page 128, or No-Roll Flaky Dough, page 133

Swiss Onion Tart

This onion tart, a cheese-custard filled tart, and a thin onion soup are the main elements of the breakfast eaten at dawn in Basel for the first day of Fastnacht, their annual Carnival celebration. We would certainly think of it more as an appetizer or a brunch dish. The secret of a good onion tart is cooking the onions for a long time to fully develop their sweetness. The method here is geared toward first releasing, then evaporating, the high water content of the onions, so that you are left with a vividly flavorful base for the tart filling.

1. Cook the bacon, uncovered, over medium heat in a large pan, such as an enameled cast-iron Dutch oven, which will easily hold the onions later. Stir occasionally so that the bacon colors evenly, and remove it with a slotted spoon when it is crisp. Drain the bacon on a plate covered with a paper towel.

2. Pour off the bacon fat from the pan and add the butter. Place the pan over medium heat, add the onions, salt them generously, and wait until the onions begin to sizzle. Decrease the heat to low, cover the pan, and cook the onions until they have exuded a lot of water, about 20 minutes. While they are cooking, uncover the pan occasionally and stir the onions. Uncover the pan and let the onions continue to cook slowly until they are very reduced and golden, another 20 minutes or so.

3. When the onions are almost cooked, set a rack in the lowest level of the oven and preheat to 350° (180°C).

4. Put the flour in a medium mixing bowl and whisk in the milk a little at a time. After all the milk has been added, whisk in the cream. Stir in the onions and taste for seasoning. Add more salt if necessary, and grind in some pepper and very little nutmeg —the filling should be slightly overseasoned to make up for the addition of the eggs. Whisk in the eggs.

5. Pour the filling into the tart crust and scatter the drained bacon over it.

6. Bake the tart until the crust is baked through and well colored on the bottom and the filling is set and puffed, about 30 minutes.

7. Cool the tart on a rack before unmolding.

SERVING: If you want to serve the tart as soon as it is baked, get everything ready early in the day or the day before so you'll only have to scatter and pour everything into the crust before baking. Just be very careful when unmolding the tart from a hot pan. This makes a great lunch with a green salad and a fruit dessert.

STORAGE: Loosely cover the cooled tart with plastic wrap if you are going to serve it at room temperature. Wrap and refrigerate leftovers and reheat them briefly at 375°F (190°) before serving.

VARIATIONS

SWISS ONION & CHEESE TART: Add ¾ cup (about 3 ounces/75 grams) coarsely grated Gruyère, sprinkling the cheese over the crust before pouring in the custard.

Makes one 10- or 11-inch (25- or 28-cm) tart, about 8 generous servings

....

2 tablespoons unsalted butter

1 bunch scallions (green onions), white part and about half the green, thinly sliced

One 10- or 11-inch (25- or 28-cm) tart crust, unbaked, made from Rich Pie Dough, page 128, or No-Roll Flaky Dough, page 133

1½ cups (about 5 ounces/150 grams) coarsely shredded Gruyère cheese

1 cup (about 4 ounces/100 grams) walnut pieces, toasted, cooled, and coarsely chopped

½ cup milk

½ cup heavy whipping cream

3 large eggs

Salt, freshly ground black pepper, and freshly grated nutmeg

Gruyère, Scallion, *&* Walnut Tart

I could bake and eat this tart once a week since I am totally addicted to Gruyère. Make sure to get real Swiss Gruyère, or the tart just won't have the right flavor. Sharp cheddar makes a good substitute.

1. Set a rack in the lowest level of the oven and preheat to 350°F (180°C).

2. Melt the butter in a small sauté pan over medium heat and add the scallions. Cook, stirring occasionally, until wilted, 3 to 4 minutes. Scrape the scallions into a small bowl and set aside to cool for a few minutes.

3. Distribute the cooked scallions evenly over the tart crust, then scatter the cheese and walnuts on top.

4. Whisk together the milk, cream, eggs, salt, pepper, and nutmeg in a medium bowl and pour into the crust.

5. Bake the tart until the crust is baked through and well colored on the bottom and the filling is set and puffed, about 30 minutes. Cool the tart on a rack before unmolding.

SERVING: If you want to serve the tart as soon as it is baked, get everything ready early in the day or the day before so you'll only have to scatter and pour everything into the crust before baking. Just be very careful when unmolding the tart from a hot pan. This makes a great lunch with a green salad and a non-custardy, non-pastry dessert.

STORAGE: Loosely cover the cooled tart with plastic wrap if you are going to serve it at room temperature. Wrap and refrigerate leftovers and reheat them briefly at 375°F (190°C) before serving.

Makes one 10- or 11-inch (25- or 28-cm) tart, about 8 generous servings

....

2 tablespoons Dijon mustard

One 10- or 11-inch tart crust, unbaked, made from Rich Pie Dough, page 128, or No-Roll Flaky Dough, page 133

8 ounces (225 grams) Cantal cheese, coarsely shredded, about 2 cups

2 perfectly ripe tomatoes, about 12 ounces (350 grams), sliced ¼ inch (⅔ cm) thick

Freshly ground black pepper

1 teaspoon extra virgin olive oil

6 or 8 leaves fresh basil, rinsed, dried, and torn into small pieces

Tomato & Cantal Tart

This recipe comes from my late friend, cooking-school owner Peter Kump. Peter always made this tart for summer parties at his house in East Hampton on Long Island. The secret of its success lies in having perfectly ripe tomatoes, which you can only get during the summer from your own garden or at a farmer's market. I was so eager to prepare this once during the winter that I experimented with baking sliced plum (Roma) tomatoes with a little salt and sugar and it worked perfectly. See the variation at the end of the recipe for instructions on how to do this. Cantal is a French cheese very similar to Gruyère, which makes an acceptable substitute. Another good substitute is Italian Fontina.

1. Set a rack in the lowest level of the oven and preheat to 350°F (180°C).

2. Spread the mustard in the bottom of the tart crust and top with about half the cheese.

3. Arrange the tomato slices, slightly overlapping, on top of the cheese. Grind some pepper on the tomatoes, but don't salt them or they will get very watery while baking. Top the tomatoes with the remaining cheese.

4. Bake the tart until the crust is baked through and well colored on the bottom and the cheese is bubbling, about 25 minutes.

5. Unmold the tart while it is warm and slide it to a platter. Drizzle the oil over the surface and scatter with the basil. Serve immediately.

SERVING: This is a perfect lunch dish or hors d'oeuvre. Serve with a green salad for lunch.

STORAGE: This doesn't make particularly good leftovers because the cheese congeals. Wrap and refrigerate any leftovers and reheat in a toaster oven.

....

VARIATIONS

ROASTED TOMATO & CANTAL TART: Slice 8 plum tomatoes, as ripe as possible, and arrange them in a single layer on a couple of pans lined with buttered parchment or foil. Sprinkle very sparingly with salt and sugar and bake them at 350°F (180°C) until they are slightly shriveled and the excess moisture has evaporated, 30 to 40 minutes. Cool on the pans before continuing with the tart recipe, substituting these for the fresh ripe tomatoes.

Makes one 10- or 11-inch (25- or 28-cm) tart, about 8 servings

CORNMEAL PASTRY DOUGH

¾ cup all-purpose flour
(spoon flour into a dry-measure cup and level off)

¾ cup stone-ground yellow cornmeal

1 teaspoon salt

1 teaspoon baking powder

8 tablespoons (1 stick) cold unsalted butter, cut into 10 pieces

1 large egg

FILLING

¾ pound (350 grams) medium shrimp, shelled, deveined, and each cut into 4 to 5 pieces, shells reserved

2 cups water

1 teaspoon salt

1 cup hulled raw pumpkinseeds

3 tablespoons unsalted butter

½ teaspoon ground cumin

½ teaspoon dried oregano

¼ teaspoon ground cloves

1 cup cilantro leaves, rinsed and dried

2 to 4 fresh serrano chiles, stemmed, halved, and seeded

⅓ cup coarsely chopped white onion

½ cup sour cream

3 large eggs

One 10-inch (25-cm) tart pan with removable bottom

VARIATION

You may also use a crust made from No-Roll Flaky Dough (page 133) in place of the cornmeal crust provided here.

Shrimp &
Toasted Pumpkinseed Tart

This recipe is based on the famous Mexican sauce *pipian verde*, made from toasted pumpkinseeds, chiles, and sour cream. I learned about it from my friend chef Roberto Santibañez, former culinary director of the Rosa Mexicano restaurant group. *Pipianes* (the plural) are a fascinating category of Mexican sauces, used frequently in Mexico, but not as well known in the United States, as mole sauces. This one uses fairly hot serrano chiles to flavor it. If you seed them as in this recipe, you'll get flavor and very mild heat. If you want the filling more spicy, leave half the chiles whole after removing their stems.

1. For the dough, place the dry ingredients in a food processor fitted with the metal blade. Pulse to mix. Add the butter and pulse to mix in finely. Add the egg and pulse repeatedly until the dough forms a ball, about ten 1-second pulses. Form the dough into a disk and flour the dough and the work surface.

2. Roll the dough out to fit the pan, following the instructions for Rich Pie Dough on page 128. Refrigerate the crust while preparing the filling.

3. Set the shrimp aside in the refrigerator. Combine the shrimp shells, water, and salt in a nonreactive saucepan. Bring to a simmer and continue to cook until the liquid is reduced to about 1 cup. Strain away and discard the shells. Reserve the liquid.

4. Set a rack in the lowest level of the oven and preheat to 375°F (190°C).

5. Lightly toast the pumpkinseeds in a sauté pan until they are just slightly golden. Do not let them turn brown. Pour the pumpkinseeds into the blender jar and set aside. Add 2 tablespoons of the butter to the same pan. When it is melted and foamy, add the shrimp. Toss or stir once, then sprinkle the cumin all over the shrimp. Sauté the shrimp

until they firm up and turn pink, no more than 1 minute. Scrape the shrimp onto a plate or bowl.

6. Add the reduced shrimp liquid, oregano, cloves, cilantro, chiles, and onion to the pumpkinseeds in the blender jar. Purée until smooth.

7. Melt the remaining 1 tablespoon of butter in a saucepan and stir in the pumpkinseed mixture. Cook, stirring, until heated through, then whisk in the sour cream. Remove the saucepan from the heat and stir in the shrimp. In a large bowl, whisk the eggs, then stir the shrimp mixture into the beaten eggs. Pour the filling into the tart shell.

8. Bake the tart until the dough is baked through and the filling is set, about 25 minutes. Serve immediately.

SERVING: If you don't serve the tart straight out of the oven, serve it within an hour or two of baking. It's perfect served as wedges with drinks before dinner. Or add a salad and a fruit dessert for a light meal.

STORAGE: Keep at room temperature for no more than one or two hours. Cover leftovers with plastic wrap and refrigerate.

Makes one large oval or one 9 x 13 x 2-inch
(23 x 33 x 5-cm) pie, about 12 generous servings

....

One double-batch Rich Pie Dough, page 128

CURRIED FISH FILLING

1¼ cups fresh white bread crumbs (crustless fresh French or Italian bread, diced and ground in the food processor)

1 cup warm milk

¼ cup vegetable oil, such as canola

1 large onion, 10 to 12 ounces (257 to 350 grams), peeled and chopped

3 large garlic cloves, peeled and grated on a Microplane®

1½ pounds (700 grams) firm-fleshed fish, such as cod or halibut, cut into ½-inch (1-cm) dice

2 teaspoons salt

2½ tablespoons best-quality curry powder (more if you like a strong curry flavor)

1 tablespoon ground turmeric

½ teaspoon ground cloves

1 cup milk

1 tablespoon sugar

1 tablespoon cider vinegar

⅔ cup golden raisins

⅔ cup mango chutney, chopped if chunky

⅔ cup (about 3 ounces/75 grams) slivered almonds, toasted and coarsely chopped

5 large eggs

CUSTARD TOPPING

1½ cups milk, heated to about 120°F (50°C)

3 large eggs

8 to 10 fresh lemon, lime, or bay leaves, rinsed well to remove any sprays

One 3- to 3½-quart oval enameled cast-iron gratin dish or a 9 x 13 x 2-inch (23 x 33 x 5-cm) glass baking dish, buttered

Curried Fish Pie

A great supper or buffet dish, this South African pie is derived from a popular dish called *bobotie*—a mixture of ground beef and seasonings, with sweet and sour elements. *Bobotie* is a mainstay of the Cape Malay cooking of Cape Town and may be made with beef, lamb, or fish. This version comes from my friend Kyra Effren, who grew up in Stellenbosh, outside Cape Town, and made this once for a party at her home in Dallas. The pastry crust is my addition. I like to bake the pie in an oval enameled cast-iron gratin, but a rectangular glass baking dish works just as well. And if you're not preparing this for a party, you can halve the recipe and use a 12-inch (30-cm) tart pan instead. If you have leftover grilled or baked fish, by all means use it for this, just decrease the cooking time after adding the milk to 1 minute. You'll need at least 2 and up to 3 cups of flaked, cooked fish.

1. Place the dough on a floured work surface and shape it into a square. Flour the dough and press it out, then roll it, according to the instructions on page 129. If you're using a gratin dish, measure the width and depth of the pan. The width of the dough should be the same width as the pan, plus 2 times its depth, plus 1½ inches (4 cm); calculate the length the same way. For a 9 x 13-inch (23 x 33-cm) pan, the dough should be about 15 x 19 inches (38 x 48 cm).

2. Fold the dough in half lengthwise and transfer it to the pan, lining up the fold with the middle of the pan. Unfold the dough into the pan and press it well into the bottom and sides. Trim away all but ½ inch (1 cm) of the excess dough at the rim of the pan and let it hang over the edge for the time being.

3. For the filling, soak the bread crumbs in the warm milk and set aside.

4. Combine the oil, onion, and garlic in a wide sauté pan and place over medium heat. When the onion starts to sizzle, reduce the heat and let the onion and garlic cook until soft and just beginning to color slightly, about 15 minutes.

5. While the onion is cooking, set a rack in the lowest level of the oven and preheat to 375°F (190°C).

6. Add the fish to the pan in an even layer and sprinkle with the salt, curry powder, turmeric, and cloves. Toss or stir the fish and seasonings with the onion and garlic just until the fish is evenly coated. Add the milk and increase the heat to medium. When the liquid starts to simmer, regulate the heat until it just simmers gently and cook until the fish may be flaked easily with a fork, about 15 minutes.

7. Remove the pan from the heat and use 2 forks to shred the fish into large flakes. Stir in the sugar, vinegar, raisins, chutney, almonds, and the soaked bread crumbs. Taste for seasoning and adjust with salt, sugar, and vinegar. The filling should be slightly over-salted, with a subtle sweetness and a strong hint of acidity from the vinegar.

8. Whisk the eggs in a bowl until very liquid and use a large rubber spatula to stir them into the fish mixture. Scrape the filling into the crust and trim away the excess dough even with the rim of the pan.

9. Bake the pie until the filling is set and the dough is baked through and golden, 35 to 40 minutes.

10. While the pie is baking, whisk together the milk and eggs for the custard and have it ready on the stove.

11. When the pie is done, remove it from the oven and evenly pour the custard over it. Scatter the leaves over the custard and return the pie to the oven to bake until the custard is set, about 10 minutes. Cool the pie on a rack.

SERVING: Remove the leaves from the top of the pie before serving. Cut and serve the pie right from the baking dish. The pie is best just cooled to room temperature, so you should be removing it from the oven about 1 hour before you intend to serve it. For advance preparation, prepare the crust and cover and refrigerate it up to 24 hours before you intend to bake the pie. The filling may also be covered and refrigerated in a glass or stainless-steel bowl for up to 24 hours—then bring it to room temperature for a couple of hours before baking. You'll only need to prepare the custard topping while the pie is baking.

STORAGE: Wrap and refrigerate leftovers and bring them to room temperature before serving again.

Makes one 10- or 11-inch (25- or 28-cm) tart, 8 to 10 servings

....

1 batch of Olive-Oil Dough for a double-crust pie, page 132

1 medium head (3 pounds/1.36 kg) Savoy cabbage

Boiling salted water

3 tablespoons olive oil

1 medium (about 8 ounces/225 grams) white onion, halved, and thinly sliced from root to stem end

2 garlic cloves, peeled and grated on a Microplane®

Salt and freshly ground black pepper

12 ounces (350 grams/about 1½ cups) whole-milk ricotta

4 large eggs, lightly beaten

½ cup chopped flat-leaf (Italian) parsley

½ cup grated Parmigiano-Reggiano cheese

One 10- or 11-inch (25- or 28-cm) fluted tart pan with removable bottom

---

Ligurian Savoy
Cabbage Pie

If cabbage pie doesn't sound appealing, remember that cabbage is one of those vegetables that easily absorbs the flavors of the other ingredients cooked with it, adding it to its already sweet and earthy taste. The model of this pie is one I tasted many years ago in Ventimiglia, the first town over the French border on the Mediterranean coast in Italy. I remember tasting it for the first time and loving it, but I couldn't figure out what the filling was made from. I asked Mme Frolla, my chef's wife. She said, "Eet's da shoo [cabbage in French is chou], darrrrrling, like da choucroute [sauerkraut in French]." Well at first I thought she meant it was sauerkraut, but then I realized it was cabbage. There is a strong tradition of making pies like this one from greens and vegetables of all kinds in Liguria, the Italian region that includes the Riviera area we were visiting. Savoy cabbage is the first choice for this, but plain green cabbage can be just as good, as long as you cook it slowly to develop its full sweetness.

1. Roll half the dough and line the tart pan, as in the instructions on page 129. Roll the remaining dough into a disk about 1 inch (2½cm) larger in diameter than your tart pan. Slide it onto a floured cookie sheet, cover it with plastic wrap, and set it aside while preparing the filling.

2. Halve and core the cabbage. Pull off the outer leaves and cut away any thick ribs. Separate the remaining cabbage into leaves. Add the cabbage to the boiling salted water and return to a boil. Cook at a steady boil for about 3 minutes. Drain and cool the cabbage. When it is cool enough to handle, stack piles of leaves on a cutting board and shred them about ¼ inch (6 mm) wide.

3. Combine the oil, onion, and garlic in a wide sauté pan. Place over medium heat and cook until the onion starts to sizzle. Reduce the heat to low and cook until the onion and garlic are translucent and wilted, about 10 minutes. Stir in the cabbage. Increase the heat to high and cook until the oil starts to sizzle again. Reduce the heat to low and cook the cabbage, stirring occasionally, until it is wilted and reduced in volume, about 20 minutes. Pour the cabbage into a bowl and season it with salt and pepper. It should be slightly overseasoned to make up for the addition of the ricotta and eggs.

4. While the cabbage is cooking, set a rack in the lowest level of the oven and preheat to 375°F (190°C).

5. One at a time, add the ricotta, eggs, parsley, and Parmigiano-Reggiano into the cabbage, stirring after each addition until smooth.

6. Scrape the filling into the prepared bottom crust and smooth the top. Slide the top crust over the filling and sever the edge of the top crust, pressing it firmly into the edge of the bottom crust with a fingertip protected by a folded towel. Use the point of a knife to cut several vent holes in the top crust.

7. Bake the pie until the crust is deep golden and the filling is set, about 30 minutes. Cool the pie on a rack.

....

SERVING: Serve the pie at room temperature as part of an assortment of antipasti, or as an hors d'oeuvre with drinks.

STORAGE: It's best to serve the pie on the day it is baked, but if you have to prepare it a day in advance, wrap and refrigerate it. Reheat the pie at 350°F (180°C) for about 20 minutes, cool, and serve. Wrap and refrigerate leftovers and bring them to room temperature before serving again.

Makes one 10- or 11-inch (25- or 28-cm) tart,
8 to 10 servings

....

2½ pounds (1.1 kg) small, firm zucchini, shredded on
the largest grating blade of a food processor

1½ teaspoons salt

1 batch Olive-Oil Dough for a double-crust pie,
page 132

3 tablespoons olive oil

1 medium (about 8 ounces/225 grams) white onion,
halved, and thinly sliced from root to stem end

Salt and freshly ground black pepper

12 ounces (about 1½ cups/ 350 grams) whole-milk ricotta

4 large eggs

1 tablespoon chopped fresh marjoram, fresh oregano, or
flat-leaf (Italian) parsley

¾ cup grated Parmigiano-Reggiano cheese

One 10- or 11-inch (25- or 28-cm) fluted tart pan with
removable bottom

Zucchini & Ricotta Pie

This pie filling is based on a chicken stuffing devised by the late Richard Olney for his 1974 book, *Simple French Food*. One of the times I visited Richard at his hilltop farmhouse near Toulon just prior to the publication of that book, he prepared a grilled butterflied guinea hen with this stuffing slipped under the skin. I remember thinking at the time that the stuffing would make a good filling for a savory pie—it has taken over thirty years for me to get around to doing it. If you use larger zucchini that are 2 inches (5 cm) or more in diameter, use 3 pounds (1.36 kg). The extra weight is all water, which will drain out in Step 1.

1. In a bowl, toss the zucchini with the salt and scrape it into a colander. Set the colander over the bowl and let the zucchini drain for 1 to 2 hours. Rinse the zucchini, then firmly squeeze out any excess water, a handful at a time.

2. While the zucchini is draining, roll half the dough and line the tart pan, as in the instructions on page 129. Roll the remaining dough into a disk about an inch (2½ cm) larger in diameter than your tart pan. Slide it onto a floured cookie sheet, cover it with plastic wrap, and set it aside while preparing the filling.

3. After the zucchini is squeezed dry and you are ready to start cooking the filling, set a rack in the lowest level of the oven and preheat to 375°F (190°C).

4. Combine the oil and onion in a wide sauté pan. Place over medium heat and cook until the onion starts to sizzle. Reduce the heat to low and cook until the onion is translucent and wilted, about 10 minutes. Add the zucchini and stir everything together. Increase the heat to high and cook until the oil starts to sizzle again. Reduce the heat to low and cook the zucchini, stirring occasionally, until it is wilted and reduced in volume, about 20 minutes. Pour the cooked

zucchini into a bowl and season it with salt and pepper. It should be slightly over-seasoned to make up for the addition of the ricotta and eggs.

5. Add the ricotta, then the eggs, marjoram, and Parmigiano-Reggiano one at a time, stirring after each addition until smooth.

6. Scrape the filling into the prepared bottom crust and smooth the top. Slide the top crust onto the filling and sever the edge of the top crust, pressing it firmly into the edge of the bottom crust with a fingertip protected by a folded towel. Use the point of a knife to cut several vent holes in the top crust.

7. Bake the pie until the crust is a deep golden color and the filling is set, about 30 minutes. Cool the pie on a rack.

....

SERVING: Serve the pie at room temperature as an appetizer, as an hors d'oeuvre with drinks, or as the main course of a light meal.

STORAGE: It's best to serve the pie on the day it is baked, but if you have to prepare it a day in advance, wrap and refrigerate it. Reheat the pie at 350° (180°C) for about 20 minutes, cool, and serve it. Wrap and refrigerate leftovers and bring them to room temperature before serving again.

Makes one 9 x 13 x 2-inch (23 x 33 x 5-cm) pie, about 24 2-inch square servings

PASTRY DOUGH

4 cups all-purpose flour
(spoon flour into a dry-measure cup and level off)

1 teaspoon salt

1 teaspoon baking powder

4 large eggs

⅓ cup olive oil

½ cup water

FILLING

2 pounds (900 grams) whole-milk ricotta

6 large eggs

1 teaspoon freshly ground black pepper

½ cup finely grated Pecorino Romano

½ cup chopped flat-leaf parsley

8 ounces (225 grams) thinly sliced prosciutto

1 pound (450 grams) fresh Italian basket cheese, cut into ¼-inch (6-mm) slices

8 ounces (225 grams) soppressata or other peeled, dried sausage, thinly sliced

1 pound (450 grams) fresh mozzarella, cut into ¼-inch (6-mm) slices

8 ounces (225 grams) capicola, thinly sliced

Egg wash: 1 egg well beaten with a pinch of salt

One 9 x 13 x 2-inch (23 x 33 x 5-cm) pan, brushed with oil

Pizza Chiena: Neapolitan Meat & Cheese Pie

"Pizza chiena" is Neapolitan dialect for what would be called "pizza ripiena" or filled pizza in Italian. Originally this pastry was made like a giant turnover with a raw pizza crust—the type used for a standard large individual pizza in Naples—and filled with ricotta and cured meats before being folded over and baked. It is the ancestor of what pizzerias now call a calzone. By and by, the pizza crust was transformed into a pastry dough, though there are some versions of pizza chiena that use a yeast-risen crust that recalls the original pizza crust. The assortment of cured meats and cheeses here is a fairly standard one, though it varies from town to town, and even family by family, so don't be afraid to experiment with your own combinations—it's thoroughly Italian to do that. This recipe is based on information from two dear friends, Ann Amendolara Nurse and Anna Teresa Callen, who is the author of numerous books on Italian cooking. Please note that there is no salt in the filling—the meats and cheeses, especially the Pecorino Romano, are salty enough.

STORAGE: Keep the pie at room temperature between baking and serving the day it is baked. Wrap and refrigerate leftovers. Bring them to room temperature before serving again.

1. For the dough, combine the flour, salt, and baking powder in the bowl of a food processor fitted with the metal blade. Pulse several times to mix. Whisk together the eggs, oil, and water in a bowl, and then add to the dry ingredients. Pulse to mix the dough and continue pulsing until the dough forms a ball. Invert the food processor bowl over a floured work surface to turn out the dough. Carefully remove the blade and transfer any dough on it to the work surface. Press the dough into a rough rectangle and wrap it in plastic. Refrigerate the dough for 1 hour or as long as 2 days.

2. When you are ready to assemble and bake the pie, set a rack in the lower third of the oven and preheat to 350°F (180°C).

3. For the filling, put the ricotta in a large bowl and beat it smooth with a large rubber spatula. Add the eggs, one at a time, beating smooth after each. Beat in the pepper, grated cheese, and parsley. Set aside briefly.

4. Remove the dough from the refrigerator and use a bench scraper or a knife to cut off ⅔ of it. Roll the larger piece of dough to a rectangle about 14 x 18 inches (35 x 45 cm). Fold it in thirds lengthwise and center it in the pan. Unfold the dough to cover the inside of the pan. Press the dough well into the bottom and sides of the pan and leave any excess dough hanging over the rim.

5. Spread ⅓ of the filling in the dough-lined pan and top with ½ the prosciutto slices. Top with ½ the slices of basket cheese, followed by ½ the slices of soppressata. Top with ½ the mozzarella slices, then top the mozzarella with ½ the slices of capicola. Spread the capicola with another ⅓ of the ricotta filling.

6. Top the middle layer of filling with the remaining meats and cheeses, layering them as in step 5. Spread the top with the remaining ricotta filling.

7. For the top crust, roll the remaining piece of dough to a 9 x 13-inch (23 x 33-cm) rectangle and arrange it over the filling. Brush the top crust with the egg wash. Trim the edge of the bottom crust to an even ½-inch (1-cm) overhang and fold it over the top crust. Cut four 2-inch (5-cm) vent holes in the top crust with the point of a knife. Bake the pie until the crust is baked through and the filling is set and firm, about 1 hour. Cool on a rack.

SERVING: Cut the pie into 2-inch (5-cm) squares right in the pan. Use an offset spatula or pie server to lift the squares from the pan. Serve the pie as a first

Makes one 9 x 13 x 2-inch (23 x 33 x 5-cm) pie, 4 to 6 servings

CHICKEN AND VEGETABLES

1½ pounds (700 grams) skinless, boneless chicken thighs, trimmed of fat, cut into 1½-inch (4-cm) pieces

1 quart (1 liter) water

1 teaspoon salt

2 large sprigs flat-leaf parsley

1 small bay leaf

1 sprig fresh thyme, or - teaspoon dried thyme leaves tied in a small cheesecloth bag

1 medium onion (about 6 ounces/175 grams) peeled, halved, and cut into 1-inch (2½-cm) dice

4 large carrots (about 6 ounces/175 grams) peeled and cut into ½-inch (1-cm) slices

½ cup heavy whipping cream

Salt and freshly ground black pepper

1 cup frozen peas

BISCUIT TOPPING

3 cups all-purpose flour (spoon flour into a dry-measure cup and level off)

3 teaspoons baking powder

1½ teaspoons salt

10 tablespoons (1¼ sticks) cold unsalted butter, cut into 12 pieces

1¼ cups milk or buttermilk

One 9 x 13 x 2-inch (23 x 33 x 5-cm) glass baking dish or an oval gratin dish of similar capacity

VARIATIONS

Add other vegetables to the filling, such as peeled and cubed boiling potatoes covered with salted water and brought to a boil, and removed from the heat right after you set the chicken to cook. When the chicken is cooked the potatoes will be ready. You may also add ½ pound (225 grams) mushrooms, sliced ¼ inch (6 mm) thick, and cooked in 2 tablespoons butter until the liquid evaporates.

Chicken Pie
with Biscuit Topping

I love chicken pie but never seem to make it as often as I would like. This new method of preparing it greatly reduces the preparation time and lets you have the pie in the oven in less than an hour. And if you cook the chicken the day before, it will go even more quickly. You can add any assortment of vegetables you like—I always throw in a handful of frozen peas since they don't need to be cooked before going into the filling. I like using onion and carrots as the other vegetables, since they can cook right along with the chicken. If you prefer white meat, rather than the all-dark-meat version here, just substitute skinless, boneless chicken breasts for the thighs. The initial cooking time will be about 10 minutes shorter.

1. To cook the chicken, combine the chicken, water, salt, parsley, bay leaf, and thyme in a large saucepan or medium enameled iron Dutch oven. Place over medium heat and bring to a simmer, occasionally skimming off any foam that rises to the top. Lower the heat and cook the chicken until it is tender, about 30 minutes. Add the onion and carrots during the last 10 minutes. (You may need to increase the heat for a few minutes to get the liquid simmering again after adding the vegetables.)

2. When the chicken and vegetables are cooked, set a strainer or colander over a bowl and pour in the contents of the pan, reserving the broth. Invert the solid contents into the baking dish and let the chicken and vegetables cool for a few minutes.

3. Return the broth to the pan, and place it over medium heat. Bring to a boil, reduce to a simmer, and then simmer until reduced to about 3 cups. Add the cream and continue reducing to 2½ to 3 cups. Taste and correct the seasoning with salt and pepper.

4. After you add the cream to the broth, set a rack in the middle level of the oven and preheat to 375°(190°C).

5. Remove the parsley, bay leaf, and thyme from the chicken and vegetables and scatter the peas on top. Pour on the sauce and even out with a rubber spatula.

6. For the biscuit topping, combine the flour, baking powder, and salt in the bowl of a food processor fitted with the metal blade. Add the butter and pulse until it is mixed in finely. Add the milk and pulse until the dough just starts to come together. Invert the food processor bowl over a floured work surface to turn out the dough. Carefully remove the blade and transfer any dough on it to the work surface. Press the dough together and fold it over onto itself 2 or 3 times to make it smoother. Press the dough into an approximately 9 x 13-inch (23 x 33-cm) rectangle. Cut it into 12 equal pieces. Gently pat each piece into an approximately 3-inch (7½-cm) disk. Place the disks over the chicken filling. You may cover and refrigerate the pie for up to one day before baking it. If you do, remember to preheat the oven about 1 hour before you intend to serve the pie.

7. Bake the pie until the dough is baked through and well colored and the filling is bubbling, about 25 minutes. Set the pie on a rack for a few minutes to cool slightly, then serve immediately.

SERVING: Spoon out one of the biscuits onto a warm plate, then serve several large spoonfuls of the chicken, vegetables, and sauce next to it.

STORAGE: Wrap and refrigerate leftovers. Reheat gently at 350°F (180°C) to serve again.

160 Sweet Tart Dough

164 Chocolate Nut Dough

165 Press-In Cookie Dough

166 Parisian Fruit Tarts

169 Bittersweet Chocolate Tart

170 Mango & Rice Tart

171 Banana Walnut Tart

173 Lemony Cheese Tart
     with Sour-Cream Glaze

174 Pumpkin Pecan Buttermilk Tart
     with Cinnamon Whipped Cream

175 Bourbon-Scented Pecan Tart

176 Roman Almond &
     Pine Nut Tart

179 Chocolate Orange
     Hazelnut Tart

180 Breton Apple Pie

182 Maida's Big Apple Pie

183 Sour-Cream Apple Pie

184 Blueberry Crumble Pie

187 Neapolitan Easter Pie

188 Raspberry Almond Tartlets

189 Lemon Lime Tartlets

190 Chocolate Caramel Pecan
     Tartlets

5.

Sweet Tarts & Pies

Pies and tarts are the mainstays of the baking repertoire, yet so many people are afflicted with fear of pastry and fear of rolling that they're either unwilling to try baking pies or, worse, they resort to prepared refrigerated crusts from the supermarket. Making pastry dough and rolling it out are both easy tasks, as you'll see in the instructions that follow. There are also several options for doughs that are pressed into the pan instead of being rolled out, which are simple alternatives if you're trying pie or tart baking for the first time.

Flaky doughs require leaving some small pieces of butter intact during mixing—these create irregular layers throughout the dough, and cause flakiness when they melt during baking and steam inflates the spaces they left behind. A flaky dough needs to have a gentle gluten development. Too much mixing results in a strong gluten, causing the dough to shrink when the gluten strands retract during baking and making a dough tough in texture. In cold weather, a flaky dough will absorb a little more water than what is specified in the recipe. Just be careful not to add too much water, or the dough will become damp and heavy and lose its flakiness.

In sweet doughs, the butter is worked in completely, stopping before the dry ingredients and butter become pasty. Sweet doughs are tender and have a much weaker gluten content than flaky doughs. The presence of sugar dilutes the flour's gluten-forming capabilities, and also allows the dough to be handled less gently without developing an excessively strong gluten.

Some recipes call for letting the dough rest after mixing. This allows the gluten strands formed during mixing to relax, and makes the dough easier to roll and more tender after baking. Resting overnight is best; four hours is the minimum. Chilling buttery doughs after mixing also allows the butter to solidify again so the dough is easier to handle. Other recipes call for resting after rolling or shaping: This cuts down on shrinkage and results in a more tender crust.

The fillings and presentations of the pies and tarts here are simple to do, but extravagant in both flavor and appearance. There are a few standards, but since I've covered so many of those in other books, many of the recipes here are new twists on old favorites.

In general, a tart is baked in a straight-sided fluted pan with a removable bottom. All the tart recipes in this chapter call for a pan that is 1 inch (2½ cm) high.

The pies, with one exception, are baked in a 9-inch (23-cm) glass pie pan—the glass lets you see whether the bottom crust is sufficiently baked before removing the pie from the oven.

Tartlets are baked in individual 2½-inch (6-cm) round pans, widely available in cookware shops or from various Web sites. If you don't have time to purchase them before you want to bake some tartlets, mini-muffin pans are adequate.

To test fruit pies and tarts for doneness, a visual check is important. The crust should be lightly browned and the fruit filling should be bubbling gently before you remove the pan from the oven. Custard fillings should appear set, except for the narrowest circle, less than ¾ inch (2 cm), right in the center. I like to open the oven and give the side of the pan a gentle shake to see how much of the filling still jiggles.

Fruit tarts in particular look very pretty when finished with decoratively arranged fruit. I often use berries for fruit pie and tart toppings, since they hold up well and don't need much more than a coat of glaze or a dusting of confectioners' sugar for finishing. Pineapple and mango slices work well, too.

The best glaze is the simplest—apricot or raspberry preserves, depending on the color of the fruit to be glazed. Combine the preserves with a few tablespoons of water and strain into a small saucepan. When you are ready to glaze the fruit, bring the mixture to a boil and then let it reduce over low heat for about 5 minutes, or until thickened but still pourable. Cool it slightly before brushing it onto the fruit.

If you've never tried baking a pie or tart before, you'll be amazed at how easy it is. If you're experienced, then you'll find plenty of new flavor combinations to expand your repertoire.

Additional Ingredients
for Sweet Tarts & Pies

FRUITS

The range of fruits used in dessert-making is almost limitless. This bounty is made possible by an increased production of American fruit and by a widened availability of imported fruit, including many exotic tropical fruits seldom before seen in our country.

As a general rule, look for fresh, unblemished fruits with no dark or soft spots. If you are going to be using fruits unpeeled, it is worthwhile to seek out organic and/or locally grown varieties. Unless otherwise indicated, store fruits in plastic bags in the refrigerator.

APPLES: Fall and winter apple varieties are in season from September through March, peaking in October. Fresh apples of any variety should be firm, crisp, and well colored, with no sign of decay, infestation, or dehydration. The flesh should not yield to gentle pressure.

Keep apples loosely covered at a cool room temperature. If your kitchen is on the warm side, however, it is better to store apples in a plastic bag in the refrigerator.

Golden Delicious are good all-purpose apples, and I use them when more interesting varieties are not available. Granny Smiths, also widely available, are tart and crisp, and

sometimes remain too firm after being baked in a pie. They are better suited for cooked fillings, where you can cook them gently for a long time. McIntosh apples are best suited for making a sauce or purée, since they disintegrate completely when exposed to even the lowest heat. Northern Spies are the ultimate pie apple with a well-balanced flavor, juicy, but not watery flesh, and a slight firmness that keeps them from either disintegrating or remaining too hard. They are primarily available in the northern states from Minnesota eastward.

When peeling apples I like to use a paring knife, first removing the stem and blossom end with the point of the knife as you would remove the stem of a tomato. Start at one end and remove the peel in a continuous ribbon, turning the apple against the knife. Halve the apple and use the smaller end of a melon baller to scoop out the core and any remnants of the blossom inside the apple. If you peel apples in advance, put them in a plastic bag and expel as much air as possible from the bag. Seal the bag and refrigerate the apples. They might darken very slightly, but not much. Never soak apples in water and lemon juice, because their porous flesh will absorb a lot of the water.

APRICOTS: Apricots are a small stone fruit available in early summer. Because the apricot season is not particularly long, and because some apricots can be terribly mealy and lacking in flavor, I often recommend the use of canned apricot halves as an alternative. The canned fruit can be quite good, so don't hesitate to use it because you think it second best. (See Dried Fruit on the opposite page for information about dried apricots.)

Fresh apricots usually do not need to be peeled, as their skin is very tender. To peel other stone fruits, such as peaches, bring a pan half-filled with water to a boil. Have a bowl of ice water near the stove. Cut an X in the blossom end of each piece of fruit and carefully add several at a time to the boiling water. Cook for about 20 seconds, then use a slotted spoon to lift them out and immediately transfer them to the ice water. Slip off the skin starting at the X. If the fruit is perfectly ripe, it will peel easily; if not, remove any stubborn bits of skin with a paring knife.

BERRIES: Strawberries, raspberries, blackberries, and blueberries are all late spring and summer fruits, although they are available year-round in modern supermarkets. (Given the quality of strawberries imported long distances in the winter, I'm not sure I can call this progress.) All berries are soft and perishable and should be handled gently and used quickly—ideally the same day you buy them. Look for firm berries with a bright color. Wash berries only right before using them, and rinse them quickly; do not soak berries or they will become waterlogged. (I never wash raspberries.) Store berries at room temperature, uncovered, if you will be using them the same day. If not, refrigerate, covered, and use them as soon as possible.

PINEAPPLE: Truly ripe fresh pineapples can be hard to come by. Because pineapples are very perishable when ripe, they are usually picked before reaching maturity so they can survive shipping. Unfortunately, pineapple does not appreciably ripen once picked. This is a roundabout way of saying that air-shipped pineapples, which reach the market in a shorter period of time, are worth seeking out.

Contrary to popular belief, pulling a leaf out of a pineapple's crown does not necessarily indicate ripeness. As with most fruits, a pleasant smell is the best indication of a pineapple's ripeness. Also look for fresh green leaves, a base free of mold and stickiness, plump eyes that protrude from the skin, heaviness, and flesh that yields gently when squeezed. An unripe pineapple can be left loosely wrapped in a perforated paper bag at cool room temperature for a day or two.

To peel a pineapple, use a sharp serrated knife to remove the stem end (bottom) and the crown. Stand the pineapple upright and cut away the skin, following the curve of the fruit to the base. Use the point of a small paring knife or a small melon baller to scoop out any remaining "eyes."

CANDIED FRUIT: Fruit and fruit peels (such as orange peel) are cooked in sugar and then drained and slightly dried to create candied fruit. Candied fruit is most commonly chopped into small dice and used sparingly.

CRYSTALLIZED GINGER: Crystallized ginger, available in chunks, chips, and slices, adds a sharp, slightly spicy note to many sweets. It may also be eaten like candy. Store crystallized ginger in a tightly sealed container in the refrigerator.

CITRUS FRUIT: Citrus fruits—such as lemons, limes, and oranges—can be used in several forms. Their zest, the colored part of the peel, contains a large quantity of citrus oil and can be cut into wide strips and infused in liquids or grated and added directly to batters or other mixtures. Freshly squeezed juice is used as a flavoring, as well as to prevent low-acid fruit from darkening. Look for citrus fruit that is heavy for its size (indicating a high juice content), with vibrant-looking skin that is neither dried out nor moldy and with no mushy spots. Citrus may be kept at room temperature for a day or two, but in hot weather or for longer storage refrigerate in a plastic bag. Citrus fruits will yield more juice if you bring them to room temperature before juicing them. The recipes in this book use a couple of special varieties of citrus fruit.

When making citrus zest, nothing works better than a Microplane® grater. Remember to pass each section of the skin over the grater only once so that you only remove the zest, or colored part of the skin, and none of the bitter white pith beneath. Some recipes call for strips of citrus zest (usually steeped in liquid for flavoring). Use a sharp peeler to remove ½-inch (1-cm) wide strips of the zest without taking any of the white pith beneath.

To peel citrus entirely, use a sharp serrated knife to cut away the top and bottom of the fruit. Stand it upright on one of the flat-cut ends and use the knife to remove both the skin and all the white pith beneath, following the curve of the fruit.

MEYER LEMONS: Meyer lemons have a sweeter, less acidic flavor than common lemons, so recipes calling for them incorporate less sugar.

PERSIAN LIMES: Persian limes are less bitter than the smaller key limes. Fruit simply labeled as "limes" in your grocery store are most likely Persian limes.

DRIED FRUIT: The most common dried fruits are raisins, currants, prunes, and apricots, though dried figs, cranberries, and cherries are also available. Sometimes dried fruits are added to fresh fruit preparations, such as raisins to an apple filling, to add a touch of sweetness and a different texture. Other dried fruits, such as prunes and apricots, are used in cooked fruit compotes and purées.

Store dried fruit, once out of the package, in tightly sealed plastic bags or glass jars. For long periods of time, especially in warm weather, store in the refrigerator. When a recipe calls for plumping dried fruit—or when your dried fruit is no longer fresh and moist—simply place the fruit in a saucepan, cover with cold water, bring to a boil, and then drain.

TROPICAL FRUIT: Tropical fruit—also known as "exotic fruit"—includes kiwi, mango, papaya, guava, passion fruit, and even the mundane banana.

PASSION-FRUIT PURÉE: I usually recommend using fresh fruit as often as possible, but in some cases, frozen products are more reliable. Passion-fruit purée is one example. This concentrated juice of the passion fruit is increasingly available in a pouch or a bottle. Do not try to substitute bottled passion-fruit juice or nectar, which is diluted for use as a beverage and has much less flavor.

FRUIT PRESERVES: Preserves are sweet, spreadable preparations of fruit, with some form of sugar, and probably pectin (the natural jelling agent in some fruits, such as apples and oranges) to provide body. Unlike jam, which is a thick fruit purée, preserves contain chunks of fruit.

159

1½ cups all-purpose flour
(spoon flour into a dry-measure cup and level off)

¼ cup sugar

1 teaspoon baking powder

½ teaspoon salt

6 tablespoons (¾ stick) cold unsalted butter,
cut into 8 pieces

1 large egg

1 large egg yolk

1 tablespoon water

Sweet Tart Dough

This is a variation on a dough I have been making for years. It's quick to prepare, easy to roll out (though it can also be pressed into a pan instead), and always bakes up tender and flavorful—who could ask for anything more? The recipe doubles easily, but don't try to make more than a double batch in the food processor at one time—most food processors will not handle larger amounts of dough.

Note: If you do use a 10-inch (25-cm) tart pan instead of an 11-inch (28-cm) tart pan, only use about ¾ of the dough to line the pan. Otherwise you might not have room for all the filling.

1. Combine the flour, sugar, baking powder, and salt in the bowl of a food processor fitted with the metal blade. Pulse several times to mix.

2. Add the butter and pulse repeatedly until the butter is finely mixed into the dry ingredients—you do not want any visible pieces of butter.

3. Add the egg, egg yolk, and water. Pulse repeatedly until the dough forms a ball.

4. Invert the food processor bowl over a floured work surface to turn out the dough. Carefully remove the blade and transfer any dough on it to the work surface. Form the dough into a disk about ½ inch (1 cm) thick. Wrap the dough in plastic and refrigerate it.

....

STORAGE: Keep the dough refrigerated for up to 3 days before using it.

VARIATION

NUT TART DOUGH: Begin by placing only the sugar in the food processor and then adding ½ cup coarsely chopped nuts, such as almonds or hazelnuts. Pulse until the nuts are finely ground. Add the remaining dry ingredients and pulse to mix. Continue from step 2.

Rolling & Forming Tart
and Piecrusts from Sweet Tart Dough

A sweet dough differs from one that contains no sugar in one important way: The presence of the sugar makes the dough much less elastic, since sugar naturally inhibits the formation of a strong gluten. The resulting dough is easier to handle and also won't toughen from excess handling the way a flaky or other sugar-free dough might. In fact, before beginning to roll a sweet dough, I always like to give it a gentle kneading to soften it slightly so it won't break apart when I start rolling. See pages 129–131 of Chapter 4 for photographic instruction of rolling dough, as well as instructions for forming tart and piecrusts. See Note on page 160 regarding the quantity of dough to use, whether you roll it or press it into the pan.

Place the dough on a floured work surface, dust it lightly with flour, and knead for about 15 seconds, squeezing and folding it over on itself so that it becomes malleable but remains cool. Shape the dough into a disk.

Start rolling the dough by rolling away from you to the far end and back again without rolling over the ends. Use a firm but gentle pressure—pressing too hard might cut right through the dough. Turn the dough 45 degrees as before and roll again. Continue turning and rolling until the dough is the desired size. As you roll, don't forget to add

pinches of flour as needed. For a 1-inch (2½-cm) deep tart pan, the dough should be rolled about 3 inches (7 cm) larger than the diameter of the pan. For a standard 9-inch (23-cm) pie pan called for in all the pie recipes in this chapter, the dough should be 13 inches (33 cm) in diameter to allow enough to cover the rim of the pan and to fold some under for a fluted edge. For a double-crust pie, it can be 12 inches (30 cm), since the dough is trimmed even with the outer rim.

··

PRESSING DOUGH INTO THE PAN
Because of the presence of sugar and egg, this dough sticks to itself easily, so some recipes call for the dough to be pressed into a pan rather than rolled out and then transferred to the pan. To press the dough into the pan, cut off about ⅓ of the dough and reserve it. Using the floured palm of your hand, press the larger piece of dough to cover the bottom of the pan. Divide the remaining dough into 3 pieces and roll each into a cylinder about 10 inches (25 cm) long. Arrange the 3 cylinders of dough against the inside of the pan, slightly overlapping where they meet, to form the rim of the tart. Using floured fingertips, press the dough against the side of the pan, making sure it is well joined to the dough in the bottom of the pan. Use your thumbs, held

fig. a

PRESSING DOUGH INTO THE PAN

a. Arrange the 3 cylinders of remaining dough against the inside of the pan, overlapping where they meet, to form the rim of the tart.

perpendicular to the pan, to press the dough against the side of the pan (see figure a). Make sure the dough on the side of the pan is even in thickness—if it is thinner at the top where the heat is strongest, the edges will burn while it's baking. Finally, using your thumb inside the pan and your forefinger on the rim, press in and down at the same time to make the top edge of the crust straight and even.

162 For a piecrust, divide the dough into 5 more-or-less equal pieces. Use 2 for the bottom of the pan and 2 for the sides, rolling them into fat cylinders, as for the tart crust. Use the last piece of dough to make the cylinder that will form the fluted top rim of the piecrust.

....

ROLLING TARTLET CRUSTS

Use either Sweet Tart Dough (page 160), Nut Tart Dough (page 160), or Chocolate Nut Dough (page 164) for tartlet shells, whether they are prebaked before being filled or baked with the filling inside. The sweet tartlet recipes call for 24 individual tartlet pans, each about 2½ inches (6 cm) in diameter. (These are easily available in specialty cookware stores.) You'll also need a plain or fluted round cutter slightly larger in diameter than the top of one of the tartlet pans. Before you start, set the tartlet pans side by side on a jelly-roll pan.

Flour the work surface and dough and gently knead it until softened slightly and malleable. Divide the dough into 3 pieces. Press and shape one of the pieces of dough into a rough square. Lightly flour it and press it with the rolling pin to flatten. Turn the square 90 degrees and repeat. Roll the dough from the edge nearest you to the far edge and back again without rolling over the ends. Turn the dough 90 degrees and repeat. Continue rolling and turning the dough until it is about ⅛ inch (3 mm) thick.

Use the cutter to cut rounds from the square piece of dough, cutting them close together to get as many as possible. Arrange a circle of dough in one of the tartlet pans, centering it on the pan and gently pressing with a fingertip to push the dough into the bottom and sides of the pan (see figure a). Repeat with the remaining circles of dough.

Working one at a time, repeat with the remaining 2 pieces of dough, first rolling into a rough square and then cutting out circles of dough. If you need a few more crusts after rolling out the dough, press the scraps together, knead briefly, and start again with the rolling. Thoroughly chill the tartlet crusts before baking or filling.

If the crusts are to be baked before being filled, position the oven rack in the middle level of the oven and preheat to 350°F (180°C) for about 20 minutes before you intend to bake them. Use a fork to pierce the dough in several places to prevent it from losing its shape while it is baking. Bake the tartlet shells until they are set and golden, 12 to 15 minutes. Cool in the pans on a rack, and carefully remove the baked crusts from the pans before they have cooled completely.

Use baked tartlet shells on the same day they are baked. Fill and bake unbaked tartlet shells on the same day you line the pans with dough. (Leaving them longer in the refrigerator might cause the pans to develop rust that the crusts may absorb.)

fig. a

fig. b

ROLLING TARTLET CRUSTS

a. Center a cut round of dough in one of the tartlet pans and gently press with a fingertip to push the dough into the bottom and sides of the pan.

b. Tartlet crusts can be prepared in (clockwise from top) 4½-inch (11-cm) tart pans, mini-muffin pans, and 2½-inch (6-cm) tartlet pans.

**Makes one 10- or 11-inch (25- or 28-cm) tart crust
or one 9-inch (23-cm) piecrust**

....

⅓ cup (about 1½ ounces/40 grams)
whole or slivered almonds

⅓ cup sugar

1 cup all-purpose flour
(spoon flour into a dry-measure cup and level off)

⅓ cup alkalized (Dutch process) cocoa,
sifted after measuring

1 teaspoon baking powder

½ teaspoon salt

6 tablespoons (¾ stick) cold unsalted butter,
cut into 8 pieces

1 large egg

1 large egg yolk

1 tablespoon cold water

Chocolate Nut Dough

This is a fun recipe to use for any tart or pie with a chocolate filling. Although it's very similar to the nut variation for Sweet Tart Dough, the proportions are slightly different. I use almonds in this version, but you can substitute walnuts, hazelnuts, or pecans.

1. Combine the almonds and sugar in the bowl of a food processor fitted with the metal blade. Pulse repeatedly until the almonds are finely ground.

2. Scrape down the inside of the bowl with a spatula and pulse 2 to 3 times more.

3. Add the flour, cocoa, baking powder, and salt and pulse again to mix.

4. Add the butter and pulse repeatedly until it is finely mixed into the dry ingredients—you don't want any visible pieces of butter.

5. Add the egg, egg yolk, and water. Pulse repeatedly until the dough forms a ball.

6. Invert the food processor bowl over a floured work surface to turn out the dough. Carefully remove the blade and transfer any dough on it to the work surface. Form the dough into a disk about ½ inch (1 cm) thick. Wrap the dough in plastic and refrigerate it.

....

STORAGE: Keep the dough refrigerated for up to 3 days before using it.

Makes one 10- or 11-inch (25- or 28-cm) tart crust, eight 4½-inch (11¼-cm) tart crusts, or twenty-four 2-inch (5-cm) tart crusts

....

10 tablespoons (1¼ sticks) unsalted butter, softened

⅓ cup sugar

1 teaspoon vanilla extract

1 large egg yolk

1⅓ cups all-purpose flour
(spoon flour into a dry-measure cup and level off)

One 10- or 11-inch (25- or 28-cm) tart pan with removable bottom, eight 4½-inch (11¼-cm) fluted tart pans with removable bottoms, or twenty-four 2-inch (5-cm) tartlet pans, buttered

Press-In Cookie Dough

This makes a fine tart crust, especially if you want one that's baked first, then filled with something that doesn't require baking such as in the Parisian Fruit Tarts, page 166. The dough is fast to prepare and to press into the pan, but leave yourself some time to chill the formed tart crust to minimize shrinkage when it bakes. The dough is very soft after mixing, so be sure to handle it gently and always with floured hands.

1. Combine the butter, sugar, and vanilla in the bowl of an electric mixer. Beat with the paddle on medium speed until whitened, about 5 minutes. Beating the butter and sugar aerates the mixture, and the air helps the dough bake to a light texture.

2. Add the egg yolk and continue beating until it is absorbed and the mixture is smooth. Use a large rubber spatula to incorporate the flour.

3. Scrape the dough from the bowl onto a floured work surface and shape the dough into a rough cylinder. See Pressing Sweet Dough into the Pan Instead of Rolling It on page 161 for further instruction.

4. Cover the pan with plastic wrap or slide it into a plastic bag and seal securely. Refrigerate the formed crust for at least 1 hour or up to 2 days.

5. About 20 minutes before baking, set an oven rack in the middle of the oven and preheat to 350°F (180°C). Use a fork to pierce the chilled tart crust(s) at 1-inch (2½-cm) intervals to keep it from puffing up and distorting while it's baking.

6. For the large or medium tart crusts, bake the tart shell until it is evenly golden, 20 to 25 minutes. Check occasionally after it has been baking for about 5 minutes. If large bubbles appear on the bottom of the crust, slide out the pan on the oven rack and quickly pierce the bubbles with a fork to flatten them. The tartlets take 5 to 10 minutes less. Cool the tart crust(s) on a rack.

....

STORAGE: Use the crust on the same day it is baked. After it has cooled, cover loosely with plastic wrap until you are ready to fill it.

PASTRY CREAM

1 cup milk

½ cup heavy whipping cream

⅓ cup sugar

3 tablespoons all-purpose flour

4 large egg yolks

2 teaspoons vanilla extract

About 5 cups of assorted fruits and berries, such as rinsed and dried blueberries; picked over but unwashed raspberries; rinsed, drained, hulled, and halved small strawberries; peeled, halved, and sliced kiwis; peeled and cored pineapple, cut into ¾-inch (2-cm) dice; peeled and diced mango

TOPPING GLAZE

¾ cup apricot preserves

2 tablespoons water

Six 4½-inch (10-cm) Press-In Cookie Dough tart crusts, page 165, baked and still in the pan

Parisian Fruit Tarts

This type of tart—a cookie dough crust, covered with a thin layer of pastry cream and topped with an assortment of glazed fruit—has been the mainstay of pastry shops in Paris and many other cities for the better part of a century. In the past, the fruit was carefully arranged in concentric rows in the crust and then painted with a simple glaze. Nowadays the fruit is mixed together with the glaze fruit-salad style, resulting in a tart that is more casual, and manages to pack in a lot more fruit. Use berries, kiwi (more for color than anything else), diced pineapple, and maybe some mango. Avoid fruits that would discolor, such as apples, pears, or peaches, and anything that would be excessively juicy, such as melon. Aside from these restrictions, feel free to make your own assortment of fruit. This is essentially a summer tart, best when all the seasonal fruits and berries are at their peak of flavor. I prefer to do this as individual 4½-inch (11-cm) tarts, though they lack the dramatic punch of one large one, which is not easy to cut into neat wedges.

1. For the pastry cream, bring the milk, cream, and half of the sugar to a simmer. In a bowl, whisk the remaining sugar with the flour, then whisk in the egg yolks. Whisk ⅓ of the simmering milk into the yolk mixture. Return the milk to a simmer and add the yolk mixture, whisking constantly until the cream thickens and comes to a boil. Allow to boil, whisking constantly, until slightly thickened, about 30 seconds. Remove from the heat and whisk in the vanilla. Scrape the pastry cream into a glass bowl and press plastic wrap directly against the surface. Chill until cold.

2. After the pastry cream is completely cold and you are ready to assemble the tart, layer a little of each fruit in a large bowl, repeating the layers until you have used all the fruit—this method will cut down on mixing and bruising the fruit too much later on.

3. To make the topping glaze, put the preserves and water in a small bowl and stir well to mix. Strain into a small saucepan and bring to a boil over low heat, stirring occasionally. Let the glaze reduce to about ⅔ its original volume, then pour into a shallow bowl and let cool for 10 minutes.

4. Carefully spread ⅙ of the chilled pastry cream in each tart crust. Don't whisk it first or it might liquefy. Just scrape it into the crusts and use a small offset metal spatula to spread it evenly.

5. Drizzle the cooled glaze over the fruit. Use a large rubber spatula to gently toss the fruit and coat with glaze. Scrape the glazed fruit over the pastry cream neatly, making sure it comes all the way to the edge of the crust and mounds evenly in the center.

6. Unmold the tarts and slide them from the pan base onto a platter.

SERVING: This dessert doesn't need anything else to embellish it.

STORAGE: Try to assemble the tarts as close as possible to the time you intend to serve them, though they can certainly wait a few hours at a cool room temperature. If you do want to assemble these at the last minute, keep the fruit separate so the berries won't stain the other fruit. Leave the glaze in the pan and just reheat it gently. Then all you'll have to do just before serving is spread the pastry cream in the crusts, mix the fruit with the glaze, and arrange the fruit in the tart shells.

Makes one 10- or 11-inch (25- or 28-cm) tart, about 10 servings

1¾ cups heavy whipping cream

¼ cup light corn syrup

1 pound (450 grams) bittersweet (not unsweetened) chocolate, melted and cooled

6 tablespoons (¾ stick) unsalted butter, softened

One 10- or 11-inch (25- or 28-cm) Press-In Cookie Dough crust, page 165, baked

1 tablespoon chocolate shavings for finishing

Confectioners' sugar for sprinkling

Bittersweet Chocolate Tart

Nothing could be simpler—or better—than this tart. The flavor of the filling is of course entirely dependent on the quality of the chocolate you use, so hang the budget and get the best available—you only need a single pound. We're fortunate that chocolate is now labeled with its cocoa content—the actual percentage of ground-up roasted cocoa beans used in the mixture. For this tart, I use chocolate in the 65 to 70 percent range. More than that might be just a little too bitter.

1. Combine the cream and corn syrup in a medium saucepan and whisk well. Place over medium heat and bring to just a slight simmer—about 140°F (60°C). Pour the cream into a bowl and let it cool to 110°F (45°C)—you'll be able to insert a fingertip in the cream and leave it there without any burning sensation.

2. Pour the cooled cream mixture over the chocolate and use a small whisk to mix it in, just to combine smoothly, without whisking air into the mixture.

3. Let the ganache stand at room temperature until it is cool to the touch, about 85°F (30°C).

4. Whisk in the butter, a couple of tablespoons at a time. The butter has to be very soft—the consistency of stiff mayonnaise—or it will form lumps.

5. Once all the butter has been incorporated, scrape the filling into the prepared tart shell and smooth the top. Refrigerate for 1 hour to set the filling.

6. After the filling has set, bring the tart to room temperature for 1 to 2 hours before serving. Just before serving, scatter the chocolate shavings in the center of the filling and dust them very lightly with confectioners' sugar.

SERVING: Unmold the tart and slide it onto a platter. Serve it with a few raspberries if you like, but it is best unadorned.

STORAGE: Keep the tart at a cool room temperature for up to half a day before serving. Wrap leftovers and keep at a cool room temperature for 24 hours.

VARIATIONS

CHOCOLATE RASPBERRY TART: Defrost a 10-ounce (275-gram) package of frozen raspberries in syrup. Strain away the seeds, pressing the pulp through the strainer with a rubber spatula into a medium saucepan. Bring the purée to a boil over medium heat, reduce the heat so that the purée simmers, and let it reduce to about ½ cup. Reduce the cream in the recipe to 1¼ cups and add the raspberry purée to the chocolate along with the cooled cream. Continue with the recipe at step 3.

CHOCOLATE PASSION-FRUIT TART: Replace the frozen raspberries in the variation above with 1 cup frozen or bottled passion-fruit purée and ¾ cup granulated sugar. Bring to a boil over medium heat, reduce the heat so that the purée just simmers, and let it reduce to about ½ cup. Reduce the cream in the recipe to 1¼ cups and add the passion-fruit purée to the chocolate along with the cooled cream. Continue with the recipe at step 3.

Makes one 10- or 11-inch (25- or 28-cm) tart, about 10 servings

....

1½ cups water

1 cup Thai jasmine rice

¾ cup sugar

⅓ cup water

1½ cups Thai coconut cream

¼ teaspoon salt

One 10- or 11-inch (25- or 28-cm) Press-In Cookie Dough crust, baked, page 165

3 ripe medium mangoes, peeled, cut away from the seed, and neatly sliced

Mango & Rice Tart

During my first trip to Thailand in June 2006, I became absolutely crazy about every kind of Thai food and have since even bought the many ingredients necessary to prepare it at home. Mango and sticky rice is the quintessential Thai sweet, meant to be eaten between meals, though, and not necessarily as a dessert. I've used it as a model for this tart filling, but I'm using quicker cooling Thai jasmine rice, a fragrant variety of long-grain rice easily available in Asian stores. I've also lightened it a little without sacrificing any of the essential flavor of the original. Please note that the coconut cream referred to here is a thicker variety of unsweetened coconut milk, available in Asian grocery stores, not the sweetened kind used for making cocktails. Coconut cream differs from coconut milk in that it is skimmed off the first mixing of ground fresh coconut and water and has a higher fat content. Coconut milk comes from the second moistening of the coconut with more water.

1. Bring the water to a simmer in a heavy medium saucepan that has a tight-fitting lid. Add the rice and stir once. Reduce the heat to medium-low (not the lowest setting), and cover the pan. Let the rice cook for 20 minutes.

2. While the rice is cooking, make a syrup from the sugar and water. Combine them in a small saucepan and set over low heat. Stir occasionally so that all the sugar dissolves. When the syrup comes to a boil, let it boil for 3 minutes, then scrape the syrup into a heat-proof bowl (if there are a few undissolved sugar crystals in the syrup it's okay). Gently stir the coconut cream and salt into the hot syrup until smooth.

3. Scrape the hot rice into the sweetened coconut cream and use a large rubber spatula to gently mix them together. At this point, the mixture is very liquid. Leave the rice in the bowl, uncovered, until it is completely cooled and has absorbed most of the coconut cream, about 3 hours. Cover the bowl and let it sit at a cool room temperature.

4. When you are almost ready to serve the tart, scrape the coconut rice into the tart crust and spread it evenly with a small offset metal spatula. Arrange the mango slices over the rice in an overlapping concentric pattern, reserving a few of the smallest ones for the center of the tart.

....

SERVING: This is an excellent dessert for a light meal— a composed salad such as a salad Niçoise would be perfect before it. Use a sharp, thin-bladed knife to cut the tart into wedges. In Thailand it would be common to serve some freshly made coconut cream, available everywhere, with the sticky rice with mango. An easy alternative here is some very lightly sweetened whipped cream made with 1 cup of cream and 1 tablespoon of sugar.

**Makes one 10- or 11-inch (25- or 28-cm) tart,
8 to 10 servings**

....

FILLING

⅔ cup (about 2½ ounces/70 grams) walnut pieces

½ cup light brown sugar, firmly packed

6 tablespoons (¾ stick) unsalted butter, softened

1 large egg

1 large egg yolk

¼ teaspoon ground cinnamon

1 teaspoon vanilla extract

¼ cup all-purpose flour
(spoon flour into a dry-measure cup and level off)

½ teaspoon baking powder

BANANAS AND FINISHING

3 large bananas, about 1½ pounds (600 grams)

½ cup walnut pieces (about 2 ounces/50 grams), coarsely
chopped

1 tablespoon dark rum

One 10- or 11-inch (25- or 28-cm) tart crust, unbaked,
made from Sweet Tart Dough or Nut Tart Dough, page 160

Banana Walnut Tart

Walnuts and bananas are a good combination in any presentation, but work especially well in this tart, where the walnut filling covers the bananas, which bake to a sweet, jam-like consistency.

1. Set a rack in the lowest level of the oven and preheat to 350°F (180°C).

2. For the filling, pulse the walnut pieces and brown sugar in a food processor fitted with the metal blade until the nuts are finely ground. Add the butter, egg, egg yolk, cinnamon, vanilla, flour, and baking powder. Pulse to make a thin batter.

3. Cut the bananas into ¾-inch (2-cm) slices. Arrange the slices evenly over the crust. Pour the filling over the bananas and spread evenly with the back of a spoon or a small offset spatula. Scatter the chopped walnuts over the filling.

4. Bake the tart until the crust is baked through and the filling is set and nicely golden.

5. Remove the tart from the oven, place on a rack, and immediately sprinkle with the rum. Cool the tart completely before filling.

....

SERVING: Serve the tart at room temperature with a little sweetened whipped cream.

STORAGE: Keep the tart at room temperature the day it is baked. Wrap and refrigerate leftovers. Bring to room temperature before serving again.

Makes one 11-inch (28-cm) tart, about 10 servings

FILLING

16 ounces (450 grams) cream cheese, softened to room temperature

½ cup sugar

1 teaspoon vanilla extract

2 teaspoons finely grated lemon zest

2 large eggs

2 large egg yolks

1 cup sour cream

One 11-inch (28-cm) tart crust, unbaked, made from Sweet Tart Dough, page 160

SOUR-CREAM GLAZE

1 cup sour cream

3 tablespoons sugar

1 teaspoon vanilla extract

Lemony Cheese Tart
with Sour-Cream Glaze

I remember a pineapple cheese pie recipe that circulated in the 1950s, and it had a filling and glaze similar to this one. Somehow I don't miss the canned pineapple from the old recipe, but it would be fun to serve some lightly sugared mixed berries with this.

1. Set a rack on the lowest level of the oven and preheat to 325° (160°C).

2. Beat the cream cheese and sugar in the bowl of an electric mixer set on low speed, using the paddle attachment. Beat for 1 minute, or until the mixture is smooth. Stop the mixer and scrape down the bowl and paddle.

3. Add the vanilla, lemon zest, and one of the eggs. Beat on low speed until smooth. Scrape down again and add the second egg. Beat and scrape again. Follow the same procedure for adding the egg yolks, one at a time. Beat in the sour cream until smooth.

4. Use a large rubber spatula to give a final mixing to the filling and scrape it into the prepared pastry crust, smoothing the top.

5. Bake the tart until the crust is baked through and the filling is set and no longer wobbly in the center, about 30 minutes.

6. While the tart is baking, prepare the glaze. Whisk together the sour cream, sugar, and vanilla until just combined. Remove the tart from the oven and immediately scrape the sour-cream mixture over the top. Use a small offset metal spatula to spread the glaze evenly all over the tart.

7. Return the tart to the oven and bake 10 minutes longer, just to set the glaze—it will firm as it cools. Cool the tart on a rack.

SERVING: Unmold the tart and slide it from the metal tart pan base onto a platter. Serve wedges of the tart alone or with some lightly sugared berries.

STORAGE: Keep the tart at a cool room temperature on the day it is baked. Wrap loosely in plastic and refrigerate leftovers. Bring to room temperature before serving again.

VARIATION

CHOCOLATE CHEESE TART: Omit the lemon zest. Add 5 ounces (150 grams) bittersweet (not unsweetened) chocolate, melted and cooled, to the cream-cheese mixture along with the first egg. Bake and finish as instructed here.

Makes one 10- or 11-inch (25- or 28-cm) tart, about 10 servings

··

FILLING

1½ cups canned unsweetened pumpkin puree

3 large eggs

⅔ cup sugar, plus extra for sprinkling

½ teaspoon salt

1 teaspoon ground cinnamon

½ teaspoon ground ginger

¼ teaspoon freshly grated nutmeg

¾ cup buttermilk

¾ cup pecan pieces, coarsely chopped

One 10- or 11-inch (25- or 28-cm) tart crust, unbaked, made from Sweet Tart Dough, page 160

CINNAMON WHIPPED CREAM

1 cup heavy whipping cream

2 tablespoons sugar

1 teaspoon ground cinnamon

Pumpkin-Pecan Buttermilk
Tart with Cinnamon Whipped Cream

This is a great showstopper for holiday meals—lighter and more festive than plain pumpkin pie. I like to use canned, prepared pumpkin for this. I find that it's not much different from making the pumpkin purée yourself. It's also not always easy to find the right variety of pumpkin for pie filling— meaning the squat, orange-fleshed type, not the pumpkin we use for jack-o'-lanterns.

1. Set a rack on the lowest level of the oven and preheat to 350°F (180°C).

2. For the filling, place the pumpkin in a bowl and whisk in the eggs. Whisk in the ⅔ cup sugar, then the salt, cinnamon, ginger, nutmeg, and buttermilk. Pour the filling into the crust and sprinkle the top with pecans and sugar.

3. Bake the tart until the dough is baked through and the filling is set, 30 to 35 minutes. Cool the tart on a rack.

4. For the whipped cream, just before serving, combine the cream, sugar, and cinnamon. Whip until a soft peak forms.

··

SERVING: Slide the tart onto a platter and serve in wedges with the cinnamon whipped cream on the side.

STORAGE: Keep the tart at a cool room temperature, loosely covered with plastic wrap, on the day it is baked. Wrap and refrigerate leftovers and bring them to room temperature before serving again.

**Makes one 11-inch (28-cm) tart,
about 10 servings**

....

1¼ cups dark corn syrup

½ cup sugar

4 tablespoons unsalted butter, cut into 6 pieces

3 large eggs

Pinch of salt

1½ tablespoons best-quality bourbon

2½ cups (about 9 ounces/250 grams) pecan pieces

One 11-inch (28-cm) tart crust, unbaked,
made from Sweet Tart Dough, page 160

Bourbon-Scented Pecan Tart

I much prefer using this buttery and very sweet pecan filling in a tart rather than a pie, and I find the thinner layer of filling is less rich and yet perfectly satisfying. A Southerner would be horrified, but I like this just as much when it's made with walnuts.

1. Set a rack in the lowest level of the oven and preheat to 350°F (180°C).

2. Stir the corn syrup and sugar together in a medium saucepan and place over low heat. Allow the syrup to come to a full boil without stirring, which could cause the mixture to crystallize and harden. When the syrup boils, remove it from the heat and add the butter without stirring it in, just allow it to melt.

3. In a medium bowl, whisk the eggs with the salt and bourbon, just until they are blended.

4. Use a rubber spatula to stir the melted butter into the syrup. Whisking constantly but slowly, pour the syrup into the egg mixture in a slow, steady stream. Don't overmix or the filling will be cloudy instead of clear.

5. Let the bowl of filling rest for a few minutes, then use a large metal spoon to skim off the foam from the surface. Stir in the pecans, then pour the filling into the prepared crust. Use a fork to distribute the pecans evenly in the crust.

6. Bake the tart until the crust is baked through, the filling is set and slightly puffed, and tiny bubbles are breaking on the surface (the infallible sign of doneness), 35 to 40 minutes. Cool the pie on a rack and serve at room temperature.

....

SERVING: Serve the pie with some slightly sweetened whipped cream.

STORAGE: Keep the pie at room temperature on the day it is baked. Cover and refrigerate leftovers and bring back to room temperature before serving again. Pecan tart freezes very well: Double-wrap it in plastic and freeze for up to a month. Unwrap, defrost, and reheat at 350°F (180°C) for about 10 minutes, and cool before serving.

....

VARIATION

WALNUT TART: Omit the bourbon and instead add 2 teaspoons of vanilla extract and ¼ teaspoon of ground cinnamon to the eggs. Substitute walnut pieces for the pecans.

Makes one 10- or 11-inch (25- or 28-cm) tart, about 10 servings

....

8 ounces (about 1 cup/225 grams) canned almond paste, cut into ½-inch (1-cm) cubes

⅓ cup granulated sugar

2 large eggs

8 tablespoons (1 stick) unsalted butter, softened

2 large egg yolks

2 teaspoons vanilla extract

2 teaspoons finely grated lemon zest

⅓ cup all-purpose flour
(spoon flour into a dry-measure cup and level off)

One 10- or 11-inch (25- or 28-cm) tart crust, unbaked, made from Sweet Tart Dough, page 160

½ cup pine nuts (pignoli)

Confectioners' sugar for finishing

Roman Almond &
Pine Nut Tart

Tarts like this are available in one form or another in many pastry shops in southern Italy. This one was inspired by a tart I tasted in the late 1980s at Giolitti, an elegant Roman pastry shop mostly known for its exquisite gelati. Though the Roman version is baked in a deeper pan, I like to use a tart pan with a removable bottom. That way the tart is only 1 inch (2½ cm) high, about half the size of a typical Roman one, but it conveys the flavor and texture of the filling perfectly without being cloying.

1. Set a rack on the lowest level of the oven and preheat to 350°F (180°C).

2. Combine the almond paste and sugar in the bowl of an electric mixer. Beat on medium speed with the paddle until the mixture is reduced to fine crumbs, about 2 minutes. Add one of the eggs and continue beating until the mixture turns into a heavy paste.

3. Beat in the butter until it is completely incorporated. Stop and scrape down the bowl and paddles. Beat in the second egg, then the egg yolks, beating until smooth after each addition. Stop and scrape down the bowl and paddles.

4. Beat in the vanilla and lemon zest, followed by the flour, only beating until it is incorporated.

5. Use a large rubber spatula to give a final mixing to the filling and scrape it into the prepared pastry crust. Use a small offset metal spatula to spread the filling evenly in the crust.

6. Scatter the pine nuts all over the almond filling, gently pressing them with the palm of your hand to make them adhere.

7. Bake the tart until the crust is baked through and the filling is set and well colored, 30 to 35 minutes. Cool the tart on a rack.

....

SERVING: Unmold the tart and slide it onto a platter. Dust lightly with confectioners' sugar immediately before serving. This is better served as a tea pastry rather than a dessert.

STORAGE: Keep the tart at room temperature wrapped in plastic. It will start to become dry after a couple of days.

Makes one 10- or 11-inch (25- or 28-cm) tart, about 10 servings

....

¾ cup heavy whipping cream

¼ cup sugar

6 tablespoons (¾ stick) unsalted butter, cut into 6 pieces

6 ounces (175 grams) bittersweet (not unsweetened) chocolate, cut into ¼-inch (6-mm) pieces

3 large eggs

1 tablespoon finely grated orange zest

1 tablespoon dark rum

One 10- or 11-inch (25- or 28-cm) tart crust, unbaked, made from Nut Tart Dough, page 160

½ cup (about 2 ounces/50 grams) hazelnuts, toasted, skins rubbed off, and coarsely chopped or crushed with the bottom of a heavy pan

2 ounces bittersweet, not unsweetened, chocolate melted with 1 tablespoon of butter, for finishing

Chocolate Orange Hazelnut Tart

Christine Ferber is one of France's most talented pastry chefs. She grew up in Alsace, a place where baking is taken very seriously, and has written prolifically on the subject. I have four of her books, one on jams and preserves, one on pickling and patés, another on cooking with fruit, and the one from which I very loosely adapted this recipe, *Mes Tartes Sucrées et Salées (My Sweet and Savory Tarts)*. My recipe is actually a combination of several of Ferber's. The tart is a baked ganache, scented with orange zest and rum, topped with chopped hazelnuts, in a sweet hazelnut pastry crust. A final drizzle of chocolate makes a simple decoration. Although they aren't very French, I think pecans also work well here.

1. Set a rack in the lowest level of the oven and preheat to 350°F (180°C).

2. For the filling, combine the cream and sugar in a large saucepan and bring to a boil over medium heat, whisking occasionally to make sure the sugar dissolves. Decrease the heat to low, add the butter, and let it melt. Remove the pan from the heat and add the chocolate. Gently shake the pan to submerge all the chocolate and wait 1 minute before whisking smooth.

3. In a medium bowl, whisk the eggs with the orange zest and rum. Whisk in the chocolate mixture in a steady stream, scraping out the pan with a rubber spatula.

4. Pour the chocolate filling into the tart crust and scatter the chopped hazelnuts on top.

5. Bake the tart until the crust is baked through and the filling is set and slightly puffed, 25 to 30 minutes. Cool the tart completely on a rack.

6. Pour the chocolate and butter mixture into a paper cone or a non-pleated plastic bag. Snip off the tip of the cone or bag and decorate the top of the tart with a series of random parallel lines.

SERVING: Remove the side of the pan and slide the tart from the metal pan base to a platter. Cut the tart into wedges. Serve sweetened whipped cream flavored with grated orange zest, or some sugared, peeled orange slices along with the tart.

STORAGE: Keep the tart at room temperature on the day it is baked. Wrap and refrigerate leftovers. Bring to room temperature before serving again.

Makes one 10-inch (25-cm) pie, about 12 servings

....

APPLE FILLING

3 tablespoons unsalted butter

2½ pounds (1⅛ kg) Golden Delicious apples, peeled, halved, cored, and each half cut into 6 wedges

½ cup sugar

1 tablespoon lemon juice

½ teaspoon ground cinnamon

BRETON DOUGH

8 ounces (2 sticks/225 grams) unsalted butter, softened

1 cup sugar

1 teaspoon vanilla extract

4 large egg yolks

2¾ cups all-purpose flour
(spoon flour into a dry-measure cup and level off)

Egg wash: 1 large egg well beaten with a pinch of salt

One 10-inch (25-cm) wide and 2-inch (5-cm) deep round layer pan, buttered and the bottom lined with a disk of parchment or buttered wax paper

Breton Apple Pie

A gâteau Breton is a wonderful French cake, very much like a dense pound cake, and a specialty of Brittany. This nontraditional version adds a cooked apple filling between the two layers of dough. The crust is easy to prepare—you just press it into the pan. For the top crust you'll need a couple of cake cardboards or tart pan bottoms the same diameter as the pan. My dear friend Stephanie Weaver gave me this recipe close to 30 years ago and I have made it countless times, always to rave reviews. Because the baked dough has a cakelike rather than crisp texture, it freezes beautifully—I keep a couple in the freezer around the holidays.

1. For the apple filling, melt the butter over medium heat in a pan that has a tight-fitting cover, such as an enameled cast-iron Dutch oven. Add the apples and sprinkle them with the sugar, lemon juice, and cinnamon. Cook the apples covered, checking them and stirring occasionally, until they are swimming in liquid, about 10 minutes. Uncover the pan and let the liquid evaporate, about 10 more minutes. Keep a n eye on the apples while the liquid is evaporating, and stir occasionally to prevent the apples from scorching. Most of the apples will disintegrate while the filling is cooking, making it like a chunky applesauce.

2. Meanwhile, set a rack on the lowest level of the oven and preheat to 350°F (180°C).

3. For the dough, combine the butter, sugar, and vanilla in the bowl of an electric mixer. Beat with the paddle on medium speed until very light, about 5 minutes. Beating the butter and sugar for a long time incorporates air and makes the baked dough light and delicate. Add the egg yolks, one at a time, beating until smooth after each addition. Remove the bowl from the mixer and use a large rubber spatula to incorporate the flour.

4. Place half the dough in the bottom of the prepared pan. Using your fingertips, press the dough evenly over the bottom of the pan and about 1 inch (2½ cm) up the sides. Spread the cooled filling over the dough.

5. Flour the remaining dough and press it into a 10-inch (25 cm) disk on a cardboard or tart pan bottom. Use a long-bladed knife or spatula to make sure the dough isn't stuck to the cardboard. Invert the dough to another floured cardboard and slide it onto the filling.

6. Brush the top of the Breton with the egg wash and trace a lattice pattern on it with the tines of a fork.

7. Bake the Breton until the dough is well colored and baked through, 50 to 55 minutes.

8. Cool on a rack in the pan for 10 minutes, then unmold and turn right side up again. Cool completely on a rack.

....

SERVING: Slide the Breton onto a platter and cut it into wedges at the table. Serve with sweetened whipped cream.

STORAGE: Keep the Breton loosely covered with plastic wrap at room temperature on the day it is baked. Wrap and freeze for longer storage. Defrost and bring to room temperature before serving.

BRETON APPLE PIE (*Top*), SOUR-CREAM APPLE PIE (*Middle*), MAIDA'S BIG APPLE PIE (*Bottom*).

Makes one 12-inch (30-cm) pie, about 16 servings

....

APPLE FILLING

4 tablespoons (½ stick) unsalted butter

2½ pounds (1⅛ kg) Granny Smith or other tart apples, peeled, halved, cored, and each half cut into 6 wedges

2½ pounds (1⅛ kg) Golden Delicious apples, peeled, halved, cored, and each half cut into 6 wedges

1 cup sugar

⅓ cup light brown sugar, firmly packed

1 teaspoon ground cinnamon

One double batch Rich Pie Dough, page 128

Egg wash: 1 large egg well beaten with a pinch of salt

Sugar for sprinkling on the pie before baking

1 round pizza pan, 12 to 14 inches (30 to 35 cm) in diameter, buttered

Maida's Big Apple Pie

Years ago, my friend and mentor Maida Heatter told me about making an apple pie like this. I think the first time I prepared it was for an episode of *Cooking Live* on the Food Network, back when I used to do a baking segment every Friday on Sarah Moulton's popular show. It's a fast, easy way to make a large pie for a crowd—it's perfect for Thanksgiving or just about any time you want a good, old-fashioned apple pie. The filling uses two different apples: Granny Smiths are firm and hold their shape, while the Golden Delicious will disintegrate somewhat, binding the apple slices in a chunky applesauce.

1. For the filling, melt the butter in an enameled cast-iron Dutch oven or other large pan with a cover. Add the apples and sprinkle with the sugars and cinnamon. Cover the pan and cook over medium heat for 5 minutes, until the apples have exuded their juices. Uncover and continue cooking, stirring occasionally, until the apples are tender. About ⅓ will have disintegrated, and the rest of the apple slices should remain intact. Cool the filling. The filling may be made several days in advance and stored, covered, in the refrigerator.

2. Set a rack on the lowest level and preheat the oven to 375°F (190°C).

3. Roll the Rich Pie Dough into a circle about 16 inches (40 cm) in diameter and center it on the pan. Spoon the filling into the middle, leaving a 2½-inch (6-cm) border of dough uncovered. Fold in the uncovered dough toward the center of the pie, leaving an uncovered space in the center. Brush the top of the folded-over dough with the egg wash and sprinkle with the sugar.

4. Bake the pie until the dough is a golden color and the filling is bubbling, about 40 minutes. Cool on a rack.

SERVING: Slide the pie to a large platter or cutting board to serve it. This is fine on its own, but is also very good with a little sweetened whipped cream.

STORAGE: Keep the pie loosely covered with plastic wrap on the day it is baked. Wrap leftovers and keep at room temperature. Reheat at 375°F (190°C) for 5 minutes and cool slightly before serving again.

Makes one 9-inch (23-cm) pie, about 8 servings

···

APPLE FILLING

2 pounds (900 g) Golden Delicious apples, peeled, cored, and sliced

4 tablespoons unsalted butter

½ cup sugar

SOUR-CREAM CUSTARD

2 tablespoons flour

¼ cup sugar

3 large eggs

1 teaspoon vanilla extract

¾ cup sour cream

CRUMB TOPPING

1¼ cups all-purpose flour
(spoon flour into a dry-measure cup and level off)

½ cup sugar

1 teaspoon baking powder

½ teaspoon ground cinnamon

8 tablespoons (1 stick) unsalted butter, melted

One 9-inch (23-cm) piecrust, unbaked, made from
Sweet Tart Dough, page 160

Sour-Cream Apple Pie

This is a classic: sweet pastry with apples, a creamy sour-cream custard, and a crunchy crumb topping. Cooking the apples before combining them with the custard prevents them from seeping water into the custard while the pie is baking.

1. Set a rack on the lowest level of the oven and preheat to 350°F (180°C).

2. For the filling, place the apples in a large sauté pan with the butter and sugar. Cook over high heat, stirring and tossing, until about half the apples have dissolved, 5 to 7 minutes. Transfer the apple mixture to a bowl to cool.

3. For the custard, whisk together the flour and sugar in a bowl, then whisk in the eggs, vanilla, and sour cream in order.

4. To make the crumb topping, mix together the flour, sugar, baking powder, and cinnamon in a medium bowl. Pour in the melted butter and stir until the mixture forms a crumbly mass.

5. Stir the cooled apples into the sour-cream custard filling and pour into the dough-lined pan. Sprinkle the crumbs over the filling.

6. Bake the pie until the dough is baked through, the filling is set, and the crumbs are a deep golden color, 50 to 55 minutes. Cool the pie on a rack.

SERVING: This rich pie needs no accompaniment. Make sure the pie is completely cooled or the flavors will be obscured by the heat.

STORAGE: Keep the pie loosely covered with plastic wrap at a cool room temperature on the day it is baked. Wrap and refrigerate leftovers and bring them to room temperature before serving again.

CRUMBLE TOPPING

1¼ cups all-purpose flour
(spoon flour into a dry-measure cup and level off)

1 teaspoon baking powder

½ teaspoon ground cinnamon

½ cup light brown sugar, firmly packed

8 tablespoons (1 stick) unsalted butter, melted

BLUEBERRY FILLING

6 cups blueberries, rinsed, drained, and picked over

¾ cup granulated sugar

4 tablespoons cornstarch

2 tablespoons water

¼ teaspoon freshly grated nutmeg

3 tablespoons cold butter, cut into 10 pieces

One 9-inch (23-cm) single piecrust, unbaked, made from Sweet Tart Dough, page 160

Blueberry Crumble Pie

It will come as no surprise to anyone who knows me that I like to use a sweet dough for fruit pies. There's something homey and comforting about that tender dough wrapped around a juicy fruit filling that a flaky dough just can't match. And it's especially good when complemented with the slightly spicy flavor of fresh blueberries. I've used the following method for blueberry, cherry, and rhubarb pies for about 20 years now, and I think it results in a nicely thickened filling that doesn't go to either extreme—it's neither so juicy that it's impossible to cut a wedge of pie without it falling apart nor so firm that the filling doesn't budge when you cut into it. I achieve this by cooking some of the berries with the sugar until they release their juices, then thickening those juices with a little cornstarch. I fold those thickened juices into the rest of the berries along with the seasonings. While the pie is baking, the raw berries release more juices that mingle with those already thickened and result in a perfectly textured filling, and the cornstarch gets a second cooking in the oven so there is no starchy taste in the finished pie.

1. Set a rack on the lowest level of the oven and preheat to 350°F (180°C).

2. First, prepare the crumble topping. Combine the flour, baking powder, and cinnamon in a bowl and stir well to mix. Stir the brown sugar into the melted butter and then scrape it into the flour mixture. Use a rubber spatula to fold in the butter so that all the flour is evenly moistened. Set aside while preparing the filling.

3. For the filling, put 1 cup of the blueberries and all the sugar in a medium saucepan. Set the pan over low heat and stir often to bruise the berries so they release their juices as the mixture heats up, and their juices dissolve the sugar. Continue to cook, stirring occasionally, until the berry mixture is boiling.

4. While the berry mixture is coming to a boil, whisk the cornstarch and water together in a small bowl. Stir in about ½ cup of the blueberry juices, then pour the cornstarch mixture into the boiling berry juices, stirring vigorously with a wooden spoon or heatproof spatula. Cook, stirring constantly, until the juices thicken, return to a boil, and become clear.

5. Put the remaining berries in a large bowl with the nutmeg. Use a large rubber spatula

to fold in the thickened juices. Fold in the butter and scrape the filling into the prepared piecrust.

6. Use your fingertips to break the crumble into ¼- to ½-inch (6-mm to 1-cm) crumbs. Scatter the crumbs evenly over the filling.

7. Bake the pie until the crust and crumbs are well colored and baked through and the filling is gently bubbling, about 40 minutes. Cool the pie on a rack and serve it at room temperature.

SERVING: Make sure the pie has cooled completely or it will be impossible to serve intact wedges. Cut the pie at the table and use a triangular pie spatula to lift out the wedges. If you have some vanilla ice cream lying around, this is the time to use it.

STORAGE: Keep the pie at room temperature on the day it is baked. Cover it with foil to keep beyond the first day.

VARIATION

SOUR CHERRY CRUMBLE PIE: Substitute 2¼ pounds (1 kg) sour cherries, rinsed, dried, stemmed, and pitted, for the blueberries. Substitute ¼ teaspoon ground cinnamon for the nutmeg.

Makes one 9-inch (23-cm) pie, 8 to 10 servings

WHEAT BERRIES

½ cup hulled white wheat berries

1½ quarts (6 cups) cold water

¼ teaspoon salt

PASTRY CREAM

1 large egg

1 large egg yolk

¼ cup sugar

2 tablespoons all-purpose flour

½ cup milk

FILLING

Pastry Cream

1 cup (about 8 ounces/225 grams) whole-milk ricotta

¼ cup sugar

2 large eggs

1 teaspoon orange flower water

⅓ cup candied orange peel, cut into ¼-inch (6-mm) dice

Wheat Berries

1 double batch Sweet Tart Dough, page 160, half lining a 9-inch (23-cm) pie pan, unbaked, the other half rolled into a 9-inch (23-cm) square and chilled

Ground cinnamon for sprinkling

Neapolitan Easter Pie

The official Italian name of this pie is Pastiera Napoletana, though many Italian Americans also refer to it as *Pizza di Grano*, or grain pie. It's a sweet crust filled with ricotta, pastry cream, and cooked wheat berries, and scented with orange flower water. If you live near an Italian grocery store, they will always have wheat berries around Easter—you just need to ask for wheat or grain. Or you can buy it in a health food store. Take care when you purchase the wheat: The wheat berries you need to buy are white, not brown or red. White wheat berries cook relatively quickly, whereas the unhulled darker ones take forever to cook. If no wheat berries are available, substitute an equal amount of long-grain rice or pearl barley, either of which work equally well.

1. Early in the day you intend to bake the pie, combine the wheat berries with the cold water and salt. Bring to a boil over medium heat, then reduce the heat to low and allow the wheat to simmer gently until it is tender and cooked through, about 1 hour. Drain the cooked wheat berries and transfer them to a bowl to cool.

2. Set a rack on the lowest level of the oven and preheat to 350°F (180°C).

3. For the pastry cream, whisk the egg and egg yolk in a bowl and whisk in the sugar and flour. Whisk in the milk and scrape the mixture into a small saucepan. Place over low heat and stir constantly until the mixture thickens and comes to a gentle boil. Continue cooking, stirring constantly, for a few seconds after the cream reaches the boil.

4. Scrape the pastry cream into a bowl. Immediately whisk in the ricotta until smooth. Whisk in the sugar, then the eggs one at a time. Stir in the orange flower water, candied orange peel, and the wheat.

5. Scrape the filling into the prepared crust and sprinkle some cinnamon over the filling. Paint the edge of the crust with water.

6. Remove the chilled square of dough from the refrigerator and use a serrated cutting wheel to cut it into ¾-inch (2-cm) wide strips. Arrange 5 of the strips parallel to and equidistant from one another on the filling, letting the excess dough hang over the edge of the pie. Arrange the 5 remaining strips in exactly the same manner, but at a 45-degree angle to the first ones.

7. Gently press the ends of the strips to adhere to the edge of the bottom crust, then use a bench scraper or the back of a knife to cut off the excess dough at the rim of the pan.

8. Bake the pie until the filling is set and slightly puffed and the crust is baked through, about 40 minutes. Cool on a rack.

SERVING: Serve wedges of the pie; it needs no accompaniment.

STORAGE: Keep the pastiera at a cool room temperature on the day it is baked. Wrap and refrigerate leftovers, then bring to room temperature before serving again.

**Makes 24 individual tartlets,
about 2-inches (6 cm) in diameter**

....

24 tartlet crusts, unbaked, made from Sweet Tart Dough or Nut Tart Dough with almonds, page 160, in tartlet pans set on a jelly-roll pan

ALMOND FILLING

4 ounces (100 grams/about ½ cup) canned almond paste, cut into ½-inch (1-cm) cubes

¼ cup granulated sugar

1 large egg yolk

1 teaspoon vanilla extract

4 tablespoons unsalted butter, softened

1 large egg

3 tablespoons all-purpose flour

RASPBERRIES

2 tablespoons seedless raspberry preserves

24 to 48 fresh raspberries, depending on their size

½ cup (about 2 ounces/50 grams) sliced almonds

Confectioners' sugar for finishing

Raspberry Almond Tartlets

Hiding a couple of raspberries under the almond filling prevents them from shriveling while these tartlets are baking, and provides a pleasant surprise when you bite into one. You can adapt this to other types of fruit, such as blueberries, sour cherries, or finely diced plums or mango (use preserves of the same flavor as the fruit—for mango, use apricot). Just be sure to use only a small amount of fruit or else the juices will boil out from under the almond filling while the tartlets are baking.

1. Set a rack in the middle level of the oven and preheat to 350°F (180°C).

2. For the almond filling, combine the almond paste, sugar, and egg yolk in the bowl of a food processor fitted with the metal blade. Pulse to mix until smooth. Scrape down the bowl with a spatula. Add the vanilla, butter, and the egg and pulse again to mix—you might have to stop and scrape again to get everything to mix together smoothly. Once the mixture is smooth, add the flour, pulse, scrape, and pulse several times more until the filling is perfectly smooth.

3. Remove the bowl from the food processor and lift out the blade. Use a spatula to clean off any filling stuck to it, and let the filling fall back into the bowl.

4. Put a dab of the preserves (about ¼ teaspoon) in the bottom of each tartlet crust. Follow with a raspberry or two, depending on their size—the berries should not protrude near the top of the crust or there won't be enough room for the almond filling.

5. Using a small offset metal spatula, evenly spread 1 scant teaspoon of filling per tartlet (a bit of the berry might poke through).

6. Top the filling in each tartlet with a pinch or two of the sliced almonds, covering the filling entirely.

7. Bake the tartlets until the dough is baked through and the filling is set and golden, 15 to 20 minutes. Cool the tartlets in the pans on a rack. Remove them from the pans while they are still slightly warm, inverting the pans one at a time onto the palm of your hand—they unmold more easily when slightly warm than when completely cooled.

8. Immediately before serving, dust the tartlets with confectioners' sugar.

....

SERVING: These are a good after-dinner pastry to serve with coffee, or are excellent at teatime.

STORAGE: Keep the tartlets loosely covered with plastic wrap at room temperature on the day they are baked. Wrap and freeze for longer storage. Defrost, reheat at 350°F (180°C) for 5 minutes, and cool before serving.

**Makes 24 individual tartlets,
about 2¼ inches (6 cm) in diameter**

....

2 to 3 large lemons

2 to 3 large limes

¾ cup sugar

10 tablespoons (1¼ sticks) unsalted butter,
cut into 10 pieces

8 large egg yolks

24 tartlet crusts, baked, made from Sweet Tart Dough
or Nut Tart Dough with almonds, page 160, unmolded,
set on a jelly-roll pan

Toasted sweetened coconut or sliced almonds for finishing

VARIATIONS

MEYER LEMON TARTLETS: Substitute the juice and zest of Meyer lemons for the lemon and lime juice—their mild acidity makes perfect lemon curd.

LEMON GINGER TARTLETS: Use all lemon juice and zest in the master recipe. Peel a 1-inch (2½-cm) length of fresh ginger and cut it into fine slices, then chop coarsely. Add to the lemon juice and zest to steep. Use a slotted spoon to remove and discard the zest and ginger, as in step 3. Garnish each tartlet with a strip or small cube of crystallized ginger.

ORANGE OR TANGERINE TARTLETS: Use ½ cup orange or tangerine juice and ¼ cup lemon juice in the curd recipe. Use the zest of half an orange and half a lemon for orange curd. For tangerine curd, grate the zest from a tangerine and use it with the zest of half a lemon. Use a slotted spoon to remove and discard the zest as described in step 3.

Lemon Lime Tartlets

Tart lemon lime curd and a crumbly sweet crust don't require anything else to make a perfect little tartlet. Of course, you could always add a dollop of lightly sweetened whipped cream right before serving and sprinkle it with a pinch or two of toasted sweetened coconut. The method I use for cooking the curd works well if you use a heavy enameled cast-iron pan—in a thinner pan the curd might scorch or scramble from the uneven heat. By the way, you can prepare the lemon lime curd a week or two in advance. Just pour it into a glass or stainless-steel bowl, press plastic wrap against the surface, then wrap the whole bowl and refrigerate.

1. Use a sharp vegetable peeler to strip the zest from each of the lemons and limes, avoiding any of the white pith under the colored part of the zest. Place it in an enameled cast-iron medium saucepan.

2. Squeeze and strain the juice from the lemons and limes, keeping the juices separate. Measure a generous ⅓ cup of each into a measuring cup to make a total of ¾ cup juice. Add the juice to the pan along with the sugar.

3. Bring the mixture to a simmer over medium heat, stirring occasionally to dissolve the sugar. Remove from the heat and allow the zests to steep in the juices for 5 minutes. Use a slotted spoon to discard the zest.

4. Add the butter to the pan and bring the mixture to a simmer over low heat.

5. Meanwhile, whisk the egg yolks in a bowl just to break them up. Whisk about ¼ of the hot liquid into the yolks.

6. Return the remaining liquid to low heat and let it come to a full boil. Beginning to whisk beforehand, pour the yolk mixture into the boiling liquid in a stream, but not too slowly—it should take only a few seconds to pour it in.

7. Switch to a heatproof spatula and stir the curd constantly, scraping the bottom of the pan, until it thickens, about 5 minutes. It will thicken visibly, but will not become extremely thick—most of the thickening occurs while it's cooling.

8. Scrape the curd into a glass or stainless-steel bowl and press plastic wrap against the surface. Refrigerate the curd until it is completely cooled and thickened.

9. When you are ready to serve the tartlets, spoon a generous teaspoon of the curd into each baked crust. Don't stir or agitate the curd before you fill the crusts, or it might liquefy. Sprinkle the curd with a pinch of coconut or almonds.

....

SERVING: These are a classic tea pastry, but are also welcome as a dessert.

STORAGE: The tartlet shells are best on the day they are baked, but you can prepare the curd up to 2 weeks in advance. Fill only as many shells as you need at one time. The curd will keep refrigerated for up to a month, if you have leftovers.

Makes 24 individual tartlets, about 2½ inches (6 cm) in diameter

....

¼ cup sugar

1 teaspoon water

½ cup heavy whipping cream

½ cup milk

⅛ teaspoon salt

8 ounces (225 grams) bittersweet (not unsweetened) chocolate, melted and cooled

2 tablespoons unsalted butter, softened

⅓ cup (about 1 ounce/25 grams) toasted pecan pieces, coarsely chopped

24 tartlet crusts, baked, made from Chocolate Nut Dough with pecans, page 160, unmolded, set on a jelly-roll pan

24 pecan halves, toasted, for finishing

190

Chocolate Caramel
Pecan Tartlets

Like a rich candy bar in a tartlet crust, these are a perfect little treat with coffee after dinner, when you want a little something but don't quite know what. I like these made with pecans, but you could omit them for a pure chocolate filling—just finish the tops of the tartlets with some chocolate shavings. The caramel emphasizes the flavor of both the chocolate and the pecans perfectly.

....

1. For the filling, combine the sugar and water in a large saucepan (to accommodate the caramel boiling up later when the liquid is added) and stir well so that the sugar resembles wet sand. Place the pan over medium heat until the sugar starts to melt.

2. Bring the cream to a simmer in a small pan while the sugar is beginning to cook. Once the cream is hot, remove it from the heat and set aside near the stove, covered to keep warm.

3. As the sugar begins to melt and caramelize, use a metal spoon to stir it occasionally. Decrease the heat to low and continue cooking the caramel until it is a very light golden color. Slide the pan off the burner and let the caramel continue to cook for 1 minute, utilizing the heat retained by the pan—this will prevent the caramel from darkening too much and becoming bitter.

4. Check the color of the caramel by taking a spoonful and pouring it back into the pan. Looking at the stream of caramel coming off the spoon will give you a more accurate idea of the color—the caramel always appears darker when it is in the pan. It should be a deep amber color.

5. If the caramel is too light, return it to the heat for 30 seconds, remove it, let it stand for 1 minute, then test the color again.

6. When the caramel is a deep amber color, return it to the heat and carefully and gradually add the hot cream a little at a time. Do this at arm's length, averting your face, in case some of the caramel splatters out of the pan. Bring the diluted caramel to a boil, remove from the heat, and immediately pour it into a heatproof medium bowl.

7. Stir in the milk and salt and allow the caramel to cool to about 100°F (40°C)—the bottom of the bowl will feel warm, but you'll be able to hold it comfortably in the palm of your hand.

8. Scrape the cooled chocolate into the caramel and whisk it to blend. Whisk in the butter. Taste the ganache and add a pinch of salt if it needs it—salt heightens the caramel flavor.

9. Fold the toasted pecan pieces into the ganache and spoon some of the mixture into each tartlet crust. Spread the top even with a small offset metal spatula. Top each tartlet with a pecan half.

....

SERVING: I can't think of a single time of day that these wouldn't be good, but they are the perfect little after-dinner treat.

STORAGE: Keep the tartlets loosely covered with plastic wrap at a cool room temperature on the day they are made. Wrap and store at room temperature for up to 3 days.

....

VARIATIONS

Almost any lightly toasted chopped nuts—almonds, walnuts, and hazelnuts—pair well with this filling. Sometimes I decorate the top of each tartlet with a shred of gold leaf instead of a nut meat.

From right: RASPBERRY ALMOND TARTLETS, CHOCOLATE CARAMEL PECAN TARTLETS, LEMON LIME TARTLETS.

195   Instant Puff Pastry

197   Baked Puff Pastry Layer

198   Molded Chocolate-Filled
       Napoleons

200   Raspberry Mille-Feuille

201   Feuillettés with Berries
       & Cream

202   Deep-Dish Peach Pie with
       Woven Lattice Crust

205   Pineapple Tarte Tatin

207   Apricot & Almond Strudel

208   Swiss Walnut Crescents

209   Danish Cheese Pockets

210   Perfect Elephant Ears

212   Caramelized Onion Tart
       with Gorgonzola

213   Spinach & Feta Turnovers

215   Smoked Salmon Mille-Feuilles

216   Salt & Pepper Straws

6.

Puff Pastries

Shatteringly crisp and intensely buttery, puff pastry occupies a unique place among pastry doughs. No other dough can replicate its delicate texture and flavor. Puff pastry preparation used to be time consuming, with long rests between multiple rollings and foldings of the dough, but no more. The recipe for puff pastry in this chapter needs to be rolled out only once—then it's shaped and chilled and ready for use in an hour or so. I jokingly refer to it as "instant," but it's not far from it.

Puff pastry needs to have a fairly strong gluten development or the layers of dough and butter won't have the necessary strength to puff away from one another during baking. In well-made puff pastry, the initial dough is kept very slack, developing only a weak gluten. All the elasticity of puff pastry is developed during the rolling and folding, resulting in a dough that rises well, shrinks minimally, and is tender when baked. Developing the gluten in the dough too much before folding and rolling in the butter will result in a dough that is difficult to roll, both during the folding process, and afterward when it is rolled to make a finished pastry.

Puff pastry is used two ways in the recipes that follow. Sometimes a thin, fragile baked sheet of dough is covered by or stacked with a sweet or savory filling, often forming a kind of pastry similar to what some would call a Napoleon. Here, the crisp, fragile nature of the dough is emphasized, and it is deliberately kept quite thin to achieve that texture. In other recipes where the dough is stacked with (or covers) a filling before being baked, we're looking for the dramatic rising and separation of the layers, so we can actually see the flakiness of the dough

after it's baked. And there are also a few recipes for small, unfilled pastries, where the dough is covered with sugar, grated cheese, or other seasonings and formed into a shape that puffs to a light and crisp texture during baking.

When cutting puff pastry, always make sure it is thoroughly chilled, and use a sharp knife to cut it. If the dough is soft, the top and bottom layers will fuse together and you'll lose the characteristic "leafing," or visible separation, of the layers on the side of the pastry. When forming pastries, place one rolled-out layer of puff pastry on top of another, then press them together 1/4 inch (6 mm) in from the edge to avoid losing the leafing.

I've given equivalents for using store-bought puff pastry. If you do decide to save time by purchasing ready-made dough, read the ingredients on the package carefully—the only fat in the dough should be butter. Avoid any brands that substitute margarine or other vegetable fats for all or some of the butter. The inferior flavor of a dough made with fats other than butter far outweighs the convenience it promises.

Makes about 3 pounds (1 ⅓ kg) of dough

4 cups all-purpose flour
(spoon flour into a dry-measure cup and level off)

2 teaspoons salt

18 ounces (4½ sticks) cold unsalted butter

1 cup cold water

Instant Puff Pastry

What makes this puff pastry faster is the elimination of multiple rollings and foldings as it requires only one round. Plus, there are no separate butter and dough mixtures—everything goes into the food processor and the finished dough emerges minutes later. As with any butter-rich dough, make sure everything is cool, especially the kitchen, or you'll wind up with a dough that has the consistency of mashed potatoes and will be about as easy to roll out. This recipe makes an ample batch of dough so that you can freeze some for later use.

1. Combine the flour and salt in the bowl of a food processor fitted with the metal blade. Pulse several times to mix.

2. Cut each stick of butter into about 10 pieces and add to the bowl. Pulse twice.

3. Remove the cover and use a thin-bladed metal spatula to stir the flour and butter mixture up from the bottom of the bowl. Cover and pulse twice more.

4. Add the water and pulse twice. Repeat step 3.

5. Invert the food processor bowl over a floured work surface to turn out the dough. Carefully remove the blade and transfer any dough on it to the work surface. Press the dough into a rough rectangle.

6. Flour the dough and press (don't roll) it with a rolling pin to flatten. Move the dough, making sure there is still flour under it to prevent it from sticking, and give the dough a 90-degree turn. Press again.

7. Again making sure that the surface and the dough are adequately floured, roll the dough into an 18-inch (45-cm) square.

8. Cut the square in half to make two 9 x 18-inch (23 x 45-cm) rectangles. Roll one to make it 12 x 18 inches (30 x 45 cm). From the 18-inch (45-cm) edge closest to you, fold the bottom third of the dough over the middle third and the top third down over that. Roll the dough into a tight package from one of the short ends and press down on it with the palm of your hand to make a rough square. Repeat with the other piece of dough. (See figures a–c on page 196.)

9. Wrap and refrigerate the 2 packages of dough (or you may cut them in half again and store them in ¼ batches). Chill for at least 1½ hours, before using.

STORAGE: You may keep the dough refrigerated for 2 or 3 days. If you intend to make the dough in advance, freeze it and defrost it in the refrigerator overnight before using.

fig. a

fig. b

a. Fold the bottom third of the dough over the middle third and the top third down over that (step 8, page 195).

b. Roll up the folded package of dough from one of the short ends (step 8, page 195)

c. This cross-section shows the layers in the finished dough (step 8, page 195).

fig. c

Makes one 10 x 15-inch (25 x 38-cm) baked puff pastry layer

....

¼ batch of Instant Puff Pastry, page 195, or about 12 ounces (350 grams) of prepared all-butter puff pastry

Two 10 x 15-inch (25 x 38-cm) jelly-roll pans, lined with parchment

VARIATION

If you need 2 layers, use twice the amount of dough. Use 4 pans and bake them in the upper and lower thirds of the oven. At the point where you turn the layers over, switch the bottom pan to the upper rack and vice versa. If you only have 3 pans, bake as below, and the second layer can remain refrigerated until the first one is baked. Remember to let the pans cool completely before using them again.

Baked Puff Pastry Layer

Several of the recipes in this chapter call for a baked puff pastry layer to be cut and stacked with a sweet or savory filling. These are the general instructions for rolling and baking that layer.

1. Lightly flour the work surface and place the dough on it. Flour the dough and use a rolling pin to press the dough in even strokes, close together and in the same direction (not back and forth). Turn the piece of dough 90 degrees and repeat.

2. While you are rolling out the dough, move it often and make sure there is always a light coating of flour on the work surface. Continue adding pinches of flour as needed under and on top of the dough.

3. Roll the dough starting from the edge closest to you, and roll away to the far end, without rolling over the edge. Roll back toward the beginning the same way. Turn the dough 90 degrees and repeat.

4. While you are rolling, keep the corners straight and even and keep the sides of the dough straight as well. Continue rolling and turning the dough until it is a little larger than 10 x 15 inches (25 x 38 cm).

5. Fold the dough in thirds and transfer it to one of the prepared pans. Cover the dough loosely with plastic wrap and refrigerate it for 1 hour or up to 24 hours.

6. When you are ready to bake the layer, set a rack on the middle level of the oven and preheat to 350°F (180°C).

7. Remove the dough from the refrigerator and discard the plastic wrap. Use a fork to pierce all the way through the entire rectangle of dough at 1-inch intervals. Cover the dough with the piece of parchment paper from the other pan and place the other pan, right side up, on top of the paper.

8. Bake the layer for 15 minutes. Then, using oven mitts, grasp the stack of pans firmly and turn the entire stack upside down and return it to the oven. Bake for 10 minutes.

9. Turn the stack of pans right side up again and check the color of the layer. If it is an even deep golden color, remove and cool on a rack, leaving the layer between the pans to prevent it from warping as it cools. If it is not done, continue baking, checking the layer every 5 minutes to make sure it doesn't burn.

10. Use the layer for a finished pastry on the same day it is baked.

....

STORAGE: Keep the baked puff pastry layer between the 2 pans until you are ready to use it.

Makes twenty-four 3 x 1½-inch (7 x 4-cm) rectangles
or twenty-four 2-inch (5-cm) squares

....

2 Baked Puff Pastry Layers, page 197

2 cups heavy whipping cream

2 tablespoons orange liqueur, such as Grand Marnier
or Cointreau

2½ teaspoons (1 envelope) unflavored gelatin

¼ cup cold water

1 cup egg whites (about 7 large egg whites)

1 cup sugar

12 ounces (350 grams) bittersweet (not unsweetened)
chocolate, melted and cooled

Confectioners' sugar and cocoa powder for finishing

One 9 x 13 x 2-inch (23 x 33 x 5-cm) pan, lined
with aluminum foil

Molded
Chocolate-Filled Napoleons

This was a specialty of my teacher chef Albert Kumin, who made it with a Grand Marnier mousse at the Four Seasons in New York when he was the head pastry chef, about 50 years ago. I like to use this light chocolate mousse to fill it, and I've retained the orange liqueur as a flavoring.

....

1. First prepare the layers: Slide one of the baked puff pastry layers onto a cutting board and use a sharp serrated knife to trim it to the size of the inside of the 9 x 13-inch (23 x 33-cm) pan. (The easiest way to do this is to make a pattern with a piece of parchment paper.) Use a wide spatula to transfer one of the trimmed layers to the bottom of the prepared pan. Trim the other layer in the same manner and set it aside in a safe place.

2. To start the mousse, whip the cream in a small bowl with the liqueur until it holds a soft peak. Cover and refrigerate.

3. Sprinkle the gelatin in the water and set it aside to soften.

4. Half-fill a medium saucepan with water and bring it to a full boil over medium heat. Combine the egg whites and sugar in the bowl of an electric mixer and whisk by hand, just until smooth. Set the bowl over the pan of water and whisk gently, keeping the egg whites from setting in the bottom of the bowl, until the egg whites are hot (about 140°F/60°C) and the sugar has dissolved. Remove the bowl from the heat and whisk in the softened gelatin.

5. Place the bowl on the mixer with the whip attachment and whip on medium speed until the meringue has cooled to room temperature. Don't overwhip or it will become grainy and ruin the mousse's texture.

6. While the meringue is whipping, remove the whipped cream from the refrigerator and whip again briefly if it has become watery. Once the meringue is cool (don't cheat—warm meringue will melt the whipped cream and transform your mousse into a soup), quickly fold about ⅓ of the meringue into the chocolate, then quickly fold in the rest. Fold in the whipped cream.

7. Scrape the mousse over the pastry layer in the prepared pan. Smooth the top and use a wide spatula to carefully transfer the second layer to the pan. Gently press with your fingertips to make the layer adhere to the mousse. Cover the pan with plastic wrap and refrigerate it for about 8 hours, or overnight, to set the mousse. Keep the filled Napoleon chilled no longer than 4 hours before you intend to serve it.

8. To unmold the pastry, grasp opposite ends of the foil lining the pan and lift it to a cutting board. This is best done by two people, with each one lifting a corner of the foil in each hand. Fold the foil down, away from the sides of the mousse, and run a long knife or a spatula underneath, between the pastry and the foil, to loosen it. Carefully peel away the foil so that the pastry is on the cutting board.

9. Use a long, sharp serrated knife to trim the sides even. Then gently saw through the top layer straight through the filling and the bottom layer—cutting the pastry into 2- or 3-inch (5- or 7½-cm) squares. Remember to wipe the knife clean between each cut.

10. Sprinkle the tops of the pastries with confectioners' sugar and then a tiny bit of cocoa powder.

....

SERVING: Line up the finished pastries on a platter. Keep them at a cool room temperature for several hours before serving. You could serve some berries on the side, but this dessert doesn't need accompaniment.

STORAGE: Wrap and chill leftovers and bring them to room temperature before serving again.

2 Baked Puff Pastry Layers, page 197

PASTRY CREAM

1 cup milk

⅓ cup sugar

2 tablespoons cornstarch

3 large egg yolks

2 tablespoons unsalted butter, softened

2 teaspoons vanilla extract

FILLING AND FINISHING

2 cups heavy whipping cream

3 tablespoons sugar

2 teaspoons kirsch or framboise (raspberry eau-de-vie)

Two ½-pint baskets (2 cups total) fresh raspberries

Confectioners' sugar for sprinkling

VARIATIONS

STRAWBERRY MILLE-FEUILLE: Replace the raspberries with 1 pint of strawberries, rinsed, hulled, and sliced

PLAIN MILLE-FEUILLE: Omit the berries. Reduce the heavy cream to ½ cup and fold all of it into the pastry cream, so there is only pastry cream between the layers.

Raspberry Mille-Feuille

This is one of the most spectacular desserts you can possible serve: layers of fragile, buttery puff pastry filled with pastry cream, raspberries, and whipped cream. Even though it has several components, it isn't particularly difficult to make. Advance preparation is the key here: Prepare the dough several days ahead (or cheat and use prepared dough). The pastry cream may be prepared two days before, and the layers themselves may be rolled out and placed on the pans the day before—they'll actually be more crisp and delicate for having had an overnight rest in the refrigerator. On the day you intend to serve the mille-feuille, simply bake the layers, whip some cream, and assemble it. If kept in a cool place, the assembled mille-feuille will remain in excellent condition for several hours.

1. To make the pastry cream, combine 3/4 cup milk and the sugar in a small saucepan and place over low heat. In a small bowl, whisk the remaining 1/4 cup milk with the cornstarch. Whisk in the egg yolks.

2. When the milk boils, whisk about 1/3 of it into the cornstarch mixture. Return the milk to a boil, and, beginning to whisk beforehand, pour the cornstarch mixture into the pan, whisking constantly. Continue whisking until the cream thickens and comes to a full boil, 10 to 15 seconds. Off the heat, whisk in the butter and vanilla. Scrape the cream into a glass or stainless-steel bowl and press plastic wrap against the surface. Refrigerate the pastry cream until it is completely cold or up to 24 hours before using.

3. When you are ready to assemble the mille-feuille, trim the layers first. Slide one of the baked puff pastry layers onto a cutting board and use a 9-inch (23-cm) round cake cardboard to cut a 9-inch (23-cm) disk from one side of the layer, gently holding the cardboard against the dough so as not to shatter it, and cutting with the point of a small, sharp paring knife. Move the cardboard to the far end of the puff pastry and position it so that the end of the layer lines up with the diameter of the cardboard; cut a semicircle from that side of the layer. Repeat with the second puff pastry so that you have 2 round 9-inch (23-cm) layers and 2 semicircles that will make one more 9-inch (23-cm) layer (it's used as the middle layer). Crush the scraps and save them.

4. For the filling, whip the cream with the sugar and kirsch and fold about 1/4 of it into the cooled pastry cream. Place a dab of the pastry cream on a 9-inch (23-cm) cake cardboard and press one of the round layers against it. Spread with half the pastry cream, using a medium offset metal spatula. Evenly scatter half of the berries over the cream. Top with half the whipped cream, spreading it smooth and evenly. Top the cream with the 2 semicircles of puff pastry, reassembled to form a whole circle, and repeat layering the pastry cream, berries, and whipped cream. Put the top layer in place and use a cardboard to gently press the layers together.

5. Use the spatula to smooth the sides of the mille-feuille with oozing filling. Use the palm of your hand to press the crushed scraps all around the sides. Before serving, dust the top with confectioners' sugar.

STORAGE: Keep the mille-feuille at a cool room temperature on the day it is assembled. Wrap and refrigerate leftovers and bring them to room temperature before serving.

SERVING: Cut the mille-feuille into wedges. Use a sharp serrated knife and hold it perpendicular to the top. Saw back and forth to cut through the top layer only. Continue until you have cut the top into 12 wedges. Then, holding the knife at a 45-degree angle, cut through from one side to the other—this method helps prevent the filling from squishing out.

Makes 12 individual desserts, or slightly fewer if you use a smaller pan to bake the layer

....

CRÈME ANGLAISE

1 cup heavy whipping cream

1 cup milk

⅓ cup granulated sugar

½ vanilla bean, split lengthwise

5 large egg yolks

BERRY FILLING

3 to 4 cups fresh berries (such as a combination of rinsed, hulled, and sliced strawberries; raspberries; and rinsed, picked over, and slightly crushed blueberries)

3 tablespoons granulated sugar

1 teaspoon kirsch or white rum

WHIPPED CREAM

1 cup heavy whipping cream

1 tablespoon granulated sugar

1 teaspoon vanilla extract

Confectioners' sugar for finishing

1 Baked Puff Pastry Layer, page 197, baked in a 12 x 18-inch (25 x 45-cm) pan

Feuillettés
with Berries & Cream

Like very delicate berry shortcakes, these are a perfect dessert for a dinner party—everything is ready in advance and they take only a few minutes to assemble right before serving. The crème anglaise is a nice refinement, but a lightly sweetened berry purée makes an equally good sauce.

1. For the crème anglaise, combine the cream, milk, sugar, and vanilla bean in a medium saucepan and whisk to mix. Place over low heat and bring to a full rolling boil. Meanwhile, set a fine strainer over a clean glass or stainless-steel bowl and place them near the burner where you are heating the liquids.

2. Whisk the egg yolks in a small bowl to break them up. When the liquid boils, whisk about ⅓ of it into the yolks. Return the liquid to a boil and, beginning to whisk before pouring, pour the yolk mixture into the boiling liquid. Whisk constantly until the cream thickens slightly, 10 to 15 seconds after adding the yolks. It won't be very thick—most of the thickening occurs while it's cooling. Remove the pan from the heat, never ceasing to whisk. Quickly strain the sauce into the prepared bowl. Remove the strainer and set it over the saucepan. Whisk the sauce continuously for about 30 seconds to cool it down so the yolks won't scramble. Cover the bowl and refrigerate the crème anglaise.

3. For the filling, gently toss the berries with the sugar and kirsch. Cover with plastic wrap and refrigerate until assembly.

4. For the whipped cream, whip the cream with the sugar and vanilla until it holds a soft peak. Cover and refrigerate.

5. Use a 3-inch (7-cm) plain round cutter to cut the baked layer into 24 disks. Don't worry if some shatter a little—just use those as the bottom layers.

6. When you are ready to assemble the desserts, place a puff pastry disk on each of 12 dessert plates. Rewhip the cream if necessary and put a small spoonful on each puff pastry disk. Using a slotted spoon, divide the berry mixture among the 12 desserts, placing the berries on the cream. Top each with a spoonful of the cream and place the remaining disks on the cream. Pour a large spoonful or two of the crème anglaise around each of the stacked feuillettés. Lightly dust the top of each one with confectioners' sugar.

....

SERVING: Serve the feuillettés immediately.

STORAGE: You can prepare the crème anglaise and roll out the puff pastry the day before, but the layer should be baked and the cream and berries prepared on the day you intend to serve the dessert. I certainly wouldn't throw away any leftovers, but they won't taste as fresh the following day.

Makes one 9 x 13 x 2-inch (23 x 33 x 5-cm) pie, about 8 generous servings

One 9 x 13 x 2-inch (23 x 33 x 5-cm) glass or porcelain pan

....

¼ batch of Instant Puff Pastry, page 195, or about 12 ounces (350 grams) of prepared all-butter puff pastry

5 pounds (16 to 20 medium/2⅔ kg) perfectly ripe freestone peaches

¾ cup sugar

3 tablespoons all-purpose flour

Pinch of freshly grated nutmeg

3 tablespoons cold unsalted butter, cut into 12 pieces

Egg wash: 1 large egg well beaten with a pinch of salt

Sugar for sprinkling the top of the pie

Deep-Dish Peach Pie
with Woven Lattice Crust

This is a great way to show off the best qualities of both the peach filling and the puff pastry crust. With no bottom crust to become soggy from peach juices, the top crust takes center stage in both flavor and appearance. Weaving a lattice for a pie like this is pretty easy—you just need to make sure everything is cool. Since it's woven on a cookie sheet, the partially completed lattice can be refrigerated if the dough starts to soften too much. It's much better to wait around for a few minutes than to risk ruining the appearance and texture of the crust. If you can't find perfectly ripe peaches, make the apple or plum variation.

1. To make the lattice, roll the Instant Puff Pastry dough to a 10 x 15-inch (25 x 38-cm) rectangle. Slide the dough onto a cookie sheet or the back of a jelly-roll pan and refrigerate for 10 minutes.

2. Cut a piece of parchment paper about 3 inches (7½ cm) longer and wider than the pan in which you will bake the pie. Invert the pan onto the paper and use a dark pencil to trace the outline. Turn the paper over, onto a cookie sheet or a piece of cardboard.

3. Remove the dough from the refrigerator and center it over the outline visible on the paper. Use a sharp pizza wheel to cut the dough into ten 1-inch (2½-cm) wide strips. Remove every other strip, leaving 5 covering the length of the outline. Fold back strips 1, 3, and 5 and insert one of the reserved strips perpendicular to them. Unfold the 3 strips back into place.

4. Fold back strips 2 and 4 to about 1¼ inches (3 cm) from the first added strip and insert another strip, then unfold them back into place. Repeat with strips 1, 3, and 5.

5. Turn the lattice around so that the unwoven side is facing you and repeat step 4.

6. Trim away the ends of the strips about 1 inch (2½ cm) larger than the outline all around. Chill the lattice while preparing the filling.

7. Set a rack in the middle of the oven and preheat to 375°F (190°C).

8. Bring a large pot of water to a boil. Meanwhile, cut a shallow X in the blossom end of each peach. Prepare a bowl of ice water large enough to hold all of the peaches.

9. Carefully lower 3 to 4 peaches at a time into the boiling water and leave them for about 10 seconds. Use a slotted spoon or skimmer to transfer them to the ice water. Repeat until you have blanched all of the peaches.

10. Slip the skins off the peaches and drain them on a pan lined with paper towels.

11. Use a small sharp paring knife to cut the peaches in half, cutting along their natural indentation. Twist gently to remove one of the halves, then remove the pit. Slice each peach half into 6 wedges, letting the juices and the peach slices accumulate into a mixing bowl.

12. Set a rack in the middle level of the oven and preheat to 375°F (190°C).

13. Sprinkle the peaches with the sugar, flour, and nutmeg, and use a large rubber spatula to fold the mixture together gently. Scrape the filling into the baking pan and evenly distribute the pieces of butter over the top.

14. Remove the lattice from the refrigerator and run a long spatula or a knife under it to make sure it hasn't stuck to the paper. Quickly brush it with the egg wash. Sprinkle generously with sugar.

15. Place the lattice pan or cardboard on the baking pan. Push the lattice away from you so that an inch or two is hanging off. Line up that bit of the lattice with the far edge of the baking pan. Holding the lattice in place against the baking pan with one hand, grasp the cardboard or lattice pan with the other and pull it away, letting the lattice fall into place on top of the filling.

16. Use the flat side of a knife blade to press the lattice gently to adhere it to the edge of the baking pan. Trim away all but 1/2 inch (1 cm) of the excess ends of the strips all around the edges of the baking pan.

17. Bake until the lattice is cooked through and deep golden and the filling is gently bubbling, about 35 minutes. Transfer the baking pan to a rack and cool it to room temperature.

SERVING: Use a large spoon to serve the pie. First sever and lift off a portion of the crust and place it off center on a dessert plate. Spoon some of the filling next to it. Vanilla ice cream is excellent with peach pie.

STORAGE: Serve the pie on the same day it is baked. Wrap and store leftovers at room temperature. Reheat briefly at 350°F (180°C) and cool before serving again.

....

VARIATIONS

DEEP-DISH PEACH AND RASPBERRY PIE: Add 1/2 pint (1 cup) fresh raspberries to the peach filling, sprinkling them over the filling just before adding the butter.

DEEP-DISH PLUM PIE: Substitute unpeeled plums, halved, pitted, and sliced, for the peaches.

DEEP-DISH APPLE PIE: Substitute 3½ pounds (1⅔ kg) Golden Delicious or Northern Spy apples, peeled, halved, cored, and cut into wedges, for the peaches. Omit the nutmeg and add 1/2 teaspoon ground cinnamon. After the filling is in the pan, sprinkle it with 1 tablespoon lemon juice, then dot with the butter. Continue with the recipe from step 14.

PINEAPPLE TARTE TATIN (*Top*), APRICOT & ALMOND STRUDEL (*bottom*).

Makes one 10-inch (25-cm) tart, about 8 servings

....

1 large ripe pineapple, about 3 pounds (1⅓ kg),
or 2 smaller ones, about 2 pounds (900 grams) each

⅔ cup sugar

1 tablespoon light corn syrup

1 tablespoon water

2 tablespoons (½ stick) unsalted butter, cold

¼ batch of Instant Puff Pastry, page 195,
or about 12 ounces (350 grams) of prepared
all-butter puff pastry

One 10-inch (25-cm) nonstick sauté pan with
sloping sides

Pineapple Tarte Tatin

Caramel and pineapple are a perfect combination of flavors, especially when they rest on a buttery puff pastry crust. There are dozens of ways to make a tarte tatin, but this is one I've used for years with good results: First you caramelize some sugar and butter in a nonstick sauté pan. Then the fruit goes in and it's topped with a disk of puff pastry. The tart is baked at a high temperature, just long enough so that the dough bakes through. A few minutes after it emerges from the oven, it's inverted to a platter revealing a beautifully arranged pattern of caramelized fruit on the baked puff pastry base. Tarte tatin is usually made with apples, and I've included that variation on page 206.

1. To pare the pineapple, use a sharp serrated knife to cut off the leaves and base. Stand the pineapple right side up and peel away the skin from top to bottom. Remove any remaining bits of skin with the point of a paring knife.

2. Cut the pineapple in half from top to bottom. Place ½ on a cutting board and cut it into ¾-inch (12-mm) thick slices. Repeat with the other half. Use a small round cutter to remove the core from each slice. Drain the pineapple in a colander.

3. Set a rack in the middle level of the oven and preheat to 400°F (200°C). Arrange the pineapple slices in one layer on a glass or a stainless-steel pan and bake them until the pineapple has cooked slightly and is somewhat dry, about 45 minutes.

4. Once the pineapple has cooled, combine the sugar, corn syrup, water, and butter in the sauté pan and use a wooden spoon or heat-proof silicon spatula to stir them together. Place over medium heat and bring to a boil, stirring occasionally. Decrease the heat so that the syrup simmers and let it cook until it is a deep caramel color, about 10 minutes.

5. Overlap 3 slices of pineapple in the center of the pan. Arrange the remaining slices, curved side outward, around the first 3 slices, overlapping the slices by about ⅓ as you go. Remember to place the pineapple slices so that you see the less attractive portion of the semicircular slices—so that the hole left in each slice when you cut away the core is visible to you. That means that when the tart is baked and you unmold it, the more attractive sides will be visible.

6. Set a rack in the middle of the oven and preheat to 400°F (200°C).

7. Place the dough on a floured surface and flour it. Press, then roll the dough to a rough circle about 1 inch (2½ cm) wider than the pan. Fold the dough in quarters and arrange it on the filling so that the point is at the center of the pan. Unfold the dough to cover the filling. Use scissors to trim away all but ¼ inch (6 mm) of the excess dough at the rim of the pan. Pierce the dough in 10 to 12 places with a fork.

8. Bake the tart until the dough is baked through and well colored, about 20 minutes. Cool the pan on a rack for 10 minutes.

9. Invert a platter over the dough and, tightly grasping the handle of the pan with an oven mitt, and supporting the bottom of the platter with the other hand, invert the pan

over the platter. Leave it in place for 5 minutes, then carefully lift off the pan. If any of the pineapple has remained stuck to the pan, use a fork to move it to the correct place on top of the tart.

SERVING: Tarte Tatin is best within a few hours of being baked. You can cook the fruit to the end of step 7 and keep it ready to bake as long as you wish on the day you're going to serve the tart. Roll out the dough and slide onto a cookie sheet and refrigerate it. A couple of hours before you intend to serve the tart, put the dough on, and bake the tart. The longer the tart sits around unmolded, the longer the juices have to seep into the dough and soften it. Serve the tart with some lightly sweetened whipped cream.

STORAGE: See Serving above. Wrap leftovers and keep them at room temperature.

....

VARIATION

CLASSIC TARTE TATIN WITH APPLES: Substitute 8 large Golden Delicious apples for the pineapple. Peel, halve, core, and quarter the apples but do not bake them. Arrange the apple quarters, rounded side down in the caramel, in concentric rows perpendicular to the side of the pan. Scatter any remaining apple quarters on top of the first layer. Bake the tart at 350°F (180°C) until the dough is baked through and the apples are tender, about an hour.

½ batch Instant Puff Pastry, page 195, or about
1½ pounds (1 kg) prepared all-butter puff pastry

3 ounces (75 grams/about ⅓ cup) canned almond paste

3 tablespoons sugar

2 large egg yolks

1 teaspoon finely grated lemon zest

3 tablespoons unsalted butter, softened

3 tablespoons all-purpose flour

3 pounds (1.35 kg) fresh apricots, halved, pitted, and
each half cut in half again, or about 24 well-drained
canned apricot halves

2 tablespoons sugar for sprinkling on the apricots

Egg wash: 1 large egg well beaten with a pinch of salt

2 teaspoons sugar for sprinkling on top of the pastry

1 cookie sheet or jelly-roll pan lined with
parchment or foil

SERVING: Cut the strudel crosswise into 1½-inch (3¾-cm)
long pieces. A little whipped cream is good with this.

STORAGE: Keep at room temperature on the day it is
baked. Cover and keep at room temperature for
longer storage. After about 24 hours, the pastry
begins to lose its fresh, buttery flavor.

VARIATIONS: Substitute pitted Italian prune plums
or sweet cherries, or even a couple of thinly sliced
Golden Delicious apples for the apricots. Add a
few pinches of ground cinnamon to the sugar for
sprinkling on cherries or apples.

Apricot & Almond Strudel

The Viennese/Hungarian tradition offers
many ways to prepare a strudel, using
doughs as diverse as yeast doughs, cookie
doughs, and even puff pastry. The strudel
here is made from puff pastry, but instead
of the dough being rolled around the filling,
the filling is stacked between two layers of
dough. The top layer of dough is slashed
to let steam escape. I have provided lots of
possibilities for variations. If you decide to
use canned apricots for this, try to find the
type packed in apricot juice instead of syrup
or water as they have the best flavor.

1. Place the Instant Puff Pastry dough
   on a floured work surface and dust the
   dough with flour. With a rolling pin,
   use close parallel strokes to soften the
   dough. Turn it 90 degrees and press
   again. Repeat until the dough is slightly
   softened and easy to roll, about 4 times.
   Being careful to keep both the work
   surface and the dough lightly floured at
   all times, roll the dough into a rectangle
   about 12 x 16 inches (30 x 40 cm). Slide
   the dough onto a cookie sheet and
   refrigerate it while preparing the filling.

2. Combine the almond paste and sugar
   in the bowl of an electric mixer. Beat on
   low to medium speed with the paddle
   until the paste and sugar are reduced to fine
   crumbs. Add the egg yolks one at a time,
   beating well after each. Use a large rubber
   spatula to scrape down the bowl and paddle.
   Add the lemon zest and butter and beat
   until completely incorporated. Beat in the
   flour. Use the spatula to give a final mix.

3. Set a rack in the lower third of the oven and
   preheat to 400°F (200°C).

4. Slide the chilled dough onto the floured work
   surface and use a sharp pastry wheel to trim it
   to exactly 11 x 15 inches (28 x 38 cm). Then
   cut the dough into 2 rectangles, one 5 x 15
   inches (13 x 38 cm), the other 6 x 15 inches
   (15 x 38 cm). (The larger piece becomes the
   top and is wider to accommodate the filling.)
   Slide the larger rectangle onto the cookie
   sheet and refrigerate. Fold the smaller
   rectangle in thirds lengthwise and place it on
   the prepared pan. Pierce the dough with a
   fork all over at 1-inch (2½-cm) intervals.

5. Spoon the filling lengthwise down the
   middle of the dough. Use a small metal
   offset spatula to spread evenly, leaving a ½-
   inch (1-cm) margin all around. Arrange the
   apricots evenly on top. Sprinkle the sugar.

6. Remove the other layer of dough from the
   refrigerator and keep it on the cookie sheet.

Gently fold the dough, making the two 15-
inch (38-cm) sides meet, without pressing
down at the fold. Use the pastry wheel or a
sharp thin-bladed knife to slash the fold at
about ¾-inch (2-cm) intervals the whole
length of the dough, to within 1 inch (2½ cm)
of the edges. Unfold the dough. Quickly
brush the exposed margin of the bottom crust
with egg wash, being careful to avoid
puddles. Slide the slashed layer of pastry on
top, aligning the edges. The slashes should be
straight; you may need to adjust them.

7. Use a fingertip to press the 2 layers of pastry
   together, a little in from the edge. Pierce
   through the border of dough, at ½-inch
   (1-cm) intervals, the point of a paring knife
   held perpendicular to the dough. Use the
   back of the knife to indent the 2 layers of
   pastry all around. Brush the top pastry with
   egg wash, taking care not to drip any down
   the sides. Sprinkle with sugar.

8. Bake the strudel for 15 minutes, then
   decrease the heat to 350°F (180°C). Continue
   baking the strudel until the dough is well
   colored and firm and the apricots are
   bubbling slightly, about 20 additional
   minutes. Cool on the pan on a rack for 15
   minutes, then slide the paper off the pan and
   cool completely on a rack. Slide the strudel
   off the paper onto a platter to serve.

Makes 12 filled crescents

½ cup milk

¼ cup sugar

1 tablespoon unsalted butter

1⅓ cups (5 to 6 ounces/150 to 175 grams) walnut pieces, finely ground in the food processor

⅓ cup dry bread, cake, or cookie crumbs

2 teaspoons kirsch or vanilla extract

½ teaspoon ground cinnamon

¼ batch Instant Puff Pastry, page 195, or about 12 ounces (350 grams) prepared all-butter puff pastry

Egg wash: 1 large egg well beaten with a pinch of salt

2 cookie sheets or jelly-roll pans lined with parchment or foil

Swiss Walnut Crescents

These walnut crescents, called *nussgipfeli* in Swiss German dialect, quickly became favorites of mine when I worked at a hotel outside Zurich in the early 1970s. Leftover pastries from the previous day always appeared with our staff lunch, and if you were quick enough to be in the front of the line, you had a good selection to choose from. For me, it was either one of these or a wedge of a typically Swiss version of a Linzertorte with a layer of kirsch-scented almond paste under the raspberry preserves. These crescents are a lightened Swiss version of a wonderful old Viennese pastry called a *Nussbeugel,* in which the same walnut filling is wrapped inside a tender yeast dough. Instant puff pastry is perfect for these, or use any good brand of all-butter prepared puff pastry.

1. Combine the milk, sugar, and butter in a heavy saucepan and place over medium heat and bring to a simmer. Stir in the walnuts and crumbs, and cook, stirring frequently, until the mixture thickens. Off the heat, stir in the kirsch and cinnamon. Scrape the filling onto a plate, cover it with plastic wrap, and chill it while you are rolling the dough.

2. Press the Instant Puff Pastry dough into a rough square, then roll it into a 12 x 15-inch (30 x 38-cm) rectangle. Roll gently, and if the dough resists, let it rest for 5 minutes, then roll again. If at any point the dough becomes too soft to handle, slide a cookie sheet under it and refrigerate for 10 to 15 minutes.

3. Once the dough is rolled to the correct size, straighten the edges and make the corners even. Use a sharp pizza wheel to cut the dough into two 6 x 15-inch (15 x 38-cm) strips. Cut each strip into 6 to 8 triangles, each with a base of just under 4 inches (10 cm).

4. To form the pastries, place one of the triangles on a work surface, with the 4-inch side toward you. Gently pull the 2 corners closest to you outward to make the base about 6 inches (15 cm) wide. Place about 2 tablespoons of the chilled walnut filling on the dough, leaving about a ½-inch (1 cm) border from the 6-inch (15-cm) edge. Fold the dough up over the filling and press it into place. Roll up the dough from the side nearest to you, gently pulling on the point of the triangle with the other hand as you roll. Form all the crescents this way.

5. Place a pastry on one of the prepared pans and curve the ends in front of it to form a crescent shape. Arrange 6 to 8 crescents on each pan. Chill the formed crescents for at least 1 hour, covered loosely with plastic wrap.

6. About 20 minutes before you are ready to bake the crescents, set racks in the upper and lower thirds of the oven and preheat to 375°F (190°C).

7. Carefully brush the crescents with the egg wash, making sure to dry the brush on the side of the container to avoid having the egg wash puddle under them.

8. Bake the crescents for about 15 minutes, then switch the bottom pan to the top and vice versa, turning the pans back to front at the same time. Bake them for 10 to 15 minutes longer, or until they are deep golden.

9. Slide the crescents, still on the paper, from the pans to racks to cool.

SERVING: These aren't really a dessert—you can serve them for breakfast, brunch, or tea.

STORAGE: Keep the pastries loosely covered on the day they are baked. Wrap and freeze for longer storage. Defrost, reheat at 350°F (180°C) for 10 minutes, then cool before serving again.

¼ cup sugar for rolling the dough

¼ batch Instant Puff Pastry, page 195, or about 12 ounces (350 grams) prepared all-butter puff pastry

CHEESE FILLING

12 ounces (350 grams) cream cheese, softened

⅓ cup sugar

1 teaspoon vanilla extract

2 teaspoons finely grated lemon zest

2 large egg yolks

⅓ cup golden raisins, optional

One 12-cavity muffin pan, very thickly buttered

Danish Cheese Pockets

These aren't made from Danish pastry dough, but sugaring the puff pastry dough as you roll it makes it taste very similar. I don't know if you've tried forming a pastry in which two opposite corners of a square are folded toward each other to meet over a filling—they usually open up while they're baking and the result is anything but neat looking. These cheese pockets are baked in muffin pans, an idea that comes from my dear friend Flo Braker, author of the monumental baking book *The Simple Art of Perfect Baking*. Flo developed the idea of baking a small version of a pastry like this in mini-muffin pans, and the result is just perfect.

1. Scatter about ¼ cup sugar on the work surface and place the Instant Puff Pastry dough on it. Sprinkle the dough with sugar and press it to soften, turning it 90 degrees and continuing to press, until the dough is soft enough to roll. Keeping the work surface and the dough lightly covered with sugar, roll the dough into an 11 x 15-inch (28 x 38-cm) rectangle. Slide the dough onto a cookie sheet or the back of a jelly-roll pan and chill it for about 15 minutes.

2. Set a rack in the middle of the oven and preheat to 375°F (190°C).

3. To make the filling, beat the cream cheese with the paddle in an electric mixer on medium speed until smooth. Add the remaining ingredients, one at a time, beating the filling smooth after each addition.

4. Remove the dough from the refrigerator and use a sharp pastry wheel to cut it into twelve 3½-inch (9-cm) squares. Ease a square of dough into one of the cavities in the muffin pan, pressing it well into the bottom and allowing the corners to remain open at the top. Fill the cup-shaped dough with about 2 tablespoons of the filling. Fold the corners of the dough into the center over the filling. Repeat with the remaining pieces of dough and filling.

5. Bake the pastries until they are deep golden (the sugar will caramelize beautifully) and the filling is set, about 20 minutes.

6. Place the pan on a rack and carefully slide a small thin metal spatula under each pastry and remove it from the pan. If you let them cool in the pan, the caramelized sugar might make them stick. Cool the pastries on a rack.

SERVING: These are perfect for brunch or tea.

STORAGE: Keep the pastries loosely covered at a cool room temperature on the day they are baked. They don't freeze well.

Makes about twenty-four 2½-inch (6-cm) pastries

¼ batch Instant Puff Pastry, page 195, or about 12 ounces (350 grams) prepared all-butter puff pastry

¾ cup sugar for rolling the dough

2 jelly-roll pans lined with parchment or foil

Perfect Elephant Ears

VARIATION

SAVORY CHEESE ELEPHANT EARS: Roll the dough out using flour in place of the sugar. Egg wash the whole surface of the dough and sprinkle it with cheese and paprika, as in the cheese variation of Salt & Pepper Straws, page 216.

This little pastry has a different name in every country where it is made. Palm leaves, butterflies, pig's ears, and elephant ears are the names I know, but there are doubtless many others. Really simplicity itself, they are made by rolling the puff pastry in sugar, causing it to absorb as much sugar as possible during the process. When the "ears" bake, the sugar caramelizes, and that delicate caramel flavor mingles with the butter in the dough. The caramel also provides a beautiful shiny glaze on the outside. These are always best on the day they are baked, but you can refrigerate or freeze the formed length of dough—some of the sugar will melt, but I have never noticed that this made any difference in the baked pastries. Please resist the temptation to add cinnamon, cocoa, or anything else to the sugar—it would ruin the delicacy of the buttery caramel.

1. Sprinkle the Instant Puff Pastry dough and the work surface with about half the sugar and press the dough to soften it, turning it 90 degrees and continuing to press, until the dough is soft enough to roll. Keeping the work surface and the dough generously covered with sugar, roll the dough into an 8 x 12-inch (20 x 30-cm) rectangle.

2. Trim the edges of the dough to be even, if necessary. Fold in each of the 12-inch (30-cm) sides of the dough a little less than halfway toward the middle, a little more than 1½ inches (4 cm). Repeat folding each edge in toward the middle—there should now be about a ½-inch (1-cm) gap between the 2 folded pieces of dough. Fold over again so that the ends meet in the middle, without stretching the dough in the gap, which would cause the ears to open up while they're baking.

3. Use the palm of your hand to slightly flatten the formed piece of dough. Cut it in half, wrap each half in plastic, and refrigerate them for at least 1 hour. Scrape any sugar remaining on the work surface into a bowl to use after the ears are cut.

4. Set a rack in the middle of the oven and preheat to 375°F (190°C).

5. Remove one of the pieces of dough from the refrigerator and place it on a cutting board. Use a sharp thin-bladed knife to cut the ears crosswise into ½-inch (1-cm) thick slices. Dip the cut sides in the reserved sugar and place them cutside down on the prepared pan. If you want to bake all of the elephant ears on the same day, cut the second piece of dough and arrange it on another pan, but bake only one pan at a time.

6. Bake the elephant ears until they have expanded and puffed and the sugar has caramelized, 10 to 15 minutes. Remove individual elephant ears as they are finished, as some may burn before others are baked through. Cool the elephant ears on a rack—the "public side" is the one that was baked against the pan.

SERVING: I can't think of a time in the day that I wouldn't want one of these. They're also a perfect accompaniment to a custard or fruit dessert.

STORAGE: These are best on the day they are baked, but you may store leftovers between sheets of wax paper in a tin or plastic container with a tight-fitting cover.

Makes one 10 x 15-inch (25 x 38-cm) tart, enough for about 3 dozen 2-inch (5-cm) hors d'oeuvres, or about 6 first-course servings

....

¼ batch Instant Puff Pastry, page 195, or about 12 ounces (350 grams) prepared all-butter puff pastry

4 large onions, about 2 pounds (900 grams), chopped

3 tablespoons olive oil

1 tablespoon light brown sugar

2 tablespoons balsamic vinegar

½ teaspoon salt

½ teaspoon freshly ground black pepper

8 ounces (350 grams) Gorgonzola or other blue cheese, crumbled

3 tablespoons chopped fresh tarragon

1 jelly-roll pan lined with parchment or foil

Caramelized Onion Tart
with Gorgonzola

This delicious hors d'oeuvre or first course was devised by my friend Bonnie Stern, Canada's foremost authority on food and cooking. I've taught many times at Bonnie's cooking school in Toronto, though I first tasted this tart in New York at an event promoting Canada. It's a little like a focaccia, but here puff pastry substitutes for the yeast dough.

1. Press the Instant Puff Pastry dough into a rough square, then roll it into a 12 x 15-inch (30 x 38-cm) rectangle. Roll gently, and if the dough resists, let it rest for 5 minutes, then roll again. If at any point the dough becomes too soft to handle, slide a cookie sheet under it and refrigerate for 10 to 15 minutes.

2. Once the dough is rolled to the correct size, straighten the edges and make the corners even and slide it into the prepared pan. Chill the dough while preparing the topping.

3. For the topping, combine the onions and oil in a wide sauté pan with a lid. Cook, covered, over medium heat until the onions start to sizzle. Lower the heat and cook until the onions become tender and translucent, about 15 minutes. Uncover the onions, increase the heat slightly, and add the sugar, vinegar, salt, and pepper. Continue to cook the onions, stirring occasionally, until they are richly caramelized, 20 to 25 minutes longer.

4. Scrape the onions into a shallow bowl and refrigerate briefly to cool.

5. Remove the dough from the refrigerator and pierce it with the tines of a fork at 1-inch (2½-cm) intervals. Spread the cooled onion mixture evenly over the dough. Scatter the cheese on top, then sprinkle with the tarragon. Cover with plastic wrap and refrigerate it until about 1 hour before you want to serve it. You may assemble the tart up to 24 hours before baking it.

6. About 1 hour before you want to serve the tart, set a rack in the middle of the oven and preheat to 400°F (200°C).

7. Bake the tart until the pastry is baked and crisp and the cheese is melted, about 20 minutes.

8. Cool in the pan on a rack for 5 minutes, then cut into portions. Serve immediately.

....

SERVING: As an hors d'oeuvre, serve slices along with some salted almonds and a few stalks of fresh fennel. As a first course, garnish the plate with a small frisée salad simply dressed with a little oil and lemon juice whisked together with a pinch of salt.

STORAGE: You may roll out the dough and cook the onions the day before, but assemble and bake the tart on the same day. There won't be any leftovers.

Makes twelve 4-inch (10-cm) triangular turnovers

....

⅓ batch Instant Puff Pastry, page 195, or about 16 ounces (450 grams) prepared all-butter puff pastry

2 tablespoons olive oil

1 pound (450 grams) baby spinach leaves, coarsely chopped

½ cup chopped fresh dill

2 bunches scallions (green onions), white part and an equal length of the green, thinly sliced

12 ounces (350 grams) feta cheese, crumbled

Freshly ground black pepper

Salt, if necessary after tasting

2 large eggs

Egg wash: 1 large egg well beaten with a pinch of salt

2 jelly-roll pans lined with parchment or foil

Spinach & Feta Turnovers

These are an easy and quite portable version of a typical Greek-style spinach pie. Though those are usually made from filo dough, I think puff pastry is an easier alternative—though you could also roll up portions of this filling in a couple of layers of buttered, stacked filo dough if you prefer.

....

1. Press the Instant Puff Pastry dough into a rough square, then roll it into a 12 x 16-inch (30 x 40-cm) rectangle. Roll gently, and if the dough resists, let it rest for 5 minutes, then roll again. If at any point the dough becomes too soft to handle, slide a cookie sheet under it and refrigerate for 10 to 15 minutes.

2. Once the dough is rolled to the correct size, straighten the edges and make the corners even and then slide it into a prepared pan. Chill the dough while preparing the filling.

3. Heat the oil in a wide sauté pan and add the spinach. Cook over high heat until the spinach begins to sizzle, then lower the heat to medium and cook, stirring occasionally, until the spinach has reduced to about 1 cup. Pour the spinach into a medium bowl and stir in the dill, scallions, cheese, and pepper. Taste carefully for seasoning—feta can be so salty that it might not be necessary to add any salt, but remember that the filling should be slightly overseasoned to make up for the addition of the eggs. Stir in the eggs.

4. Set racks in the upper and lower thirds of the oven and preheat to 375°F (190°C).

5. Remove the dough from the refrigerator and use a sharp pastry wheel to cut it into twelve 4-inch (10-cm) squares. Carefully brush the perimeter of one of the squares with the egg wash and place about 3 tablespoons of the filling in one corner, about ¼ inch (6 mm) from the edge. Fold the unfilled half of the dough over the filling to make a triangle. Use a fingertip to seal the two layers of dough together, pressing in about ¼ inch (6 mm) from the edge. Arrange the turnover on one of the prepared pans. Repeat with the remaining squares of dough and filling.

6. After all the turnovers are on the pans, use the point of a small sharp paring knife to slash a ½-inch (1-cm) vent in the top of each. Brush the tops of the turnovers with the egg wash, being careful not to let any drip down the sides.

7. Bake the turnovers for about 15 minutes, then move the pan on the top rack to the bottom one, and vice versa, turning the pans back to front at the same time. Continue baking the turnovers until they are well risen and deep golden, 10 to 15 additional minutes. Place the pans on racks to cool the turnovers.

....

SERVING: Serve the turnovers warm or at room temperature as a snack or a first course. As a first course, I would serve them with a little tomato salad simply dressed with olive oil, salt, and a few torn leaves of basil.

STORAGE: Keep the turnovers at room temperature until you intend to serve them. For advance preparation, refrigerate the turnovers after they are formed, then egg wash and bake them an hour or two before you intend to serve them. Refrigerate leftovers and reheat at 350°F (180°C) for 10 minutes, then cool slightly before serving again.

CARAMELIZED ONION TART (*Top*), SPINACH & FETA TURNOVERS (*Bottom Left*), SMOKED SALMON MILLE-FEUILLES (*Bottom Right*).

**Makes about 35 small rectangular pastries,
each 1½ x 2 inches (4 x 5 cm)**

....

8 ounces (225 grams) cream cheese, softened

8 tablespoons (1 stick) unsalted butter, softened

1 teaspoon finely grated lemon zest

¼ teaspoon salt

½ teaspoon freshly ground black pepper

1 small bunch fresh chives, finely snipped, about ½ cup
(or substitute a couple of thinly sliced scallions)

One 10 x 15-inch (25 x 38-cm) Baked Puff Pastry Layer,
page 197

8 ounces (225 grams) thinly sliced smoked salmon

Smoked Salmon Mille-Feuilles

These delicate sandwiches are perfect as an hors d'oeuvre or as a tea pastry. They're made from two layers of baked puff pastry with a delicate cream cheese and chive filling and thinly sliced smoked salmon sandwiched between them. If you need enough for a crowd, just use two baked puff pastry layers and double the amount of filling.

1. For the filling, combine the cream cheese and butter in the bowl of an electric mixer. Beat with the paddle on medium speed until very light, 3 to 4 minutes. Remove from the mixer and use a rubber spatula to stir in the lemon zest, salt, and pepper. Taste for seasoning, remembering that the salmon is quite salty. Gently stir in the chives.

2. Slide the Baked Puff Pastry Layer onto a cutting board and cut it in half to make two 10 x 7½-inch (25 x 19-cm) rectangles. Slide one of them onto a small cutting board or a cookie sheet for assembly.

3. Use a small metal offset spatula to spread half of the filling over the puff pastry layer. Top with the sliced salmon, completely covering the filling. Spread the remaining filling over the salmon.

4. Top with the second pastry layer. Place a pan or a cookie sheet on the assembled pastry and gently press to make the layers and filling adhere. Refrigerate the pastry for 1 hour before attempting to cut it.

5. Use a sharp serrated knife to cut the pastry into 4 strips, each about 1½ inches (4 cm) wide. Cut the strips crosswise every 2 inches (5 cm) to make small rectangles (or make diagonal cuts to make diamonds). Wipe the knife with a damp cloth after every cut to keep the top layer of pastry free of filling.

6. Bring the pastries to room temperature for 1 hour before serving.

....

SERVING: Line up the pastries on a platter to serve. If you make these as an hors d'oeuvre, serve something less rich and salty with them, such as chilled raw vegetables with a light sauce for dipping.

STORAGE: Keep the pastries at a cool room temperature before serving, or refrigerate and bring to room temperature for 1 hour. Wrap and refrigerate leftovers and bring to room temperature before serving again.

¼ batch Instant Puff Pastry, page 195, or about 12 ounces (350 grams) prepared all-butter puff pastry

Egg wash: 1 large egg well beaten with a pinch of salt

2 teaspoons kosher or other coarse salt

2 teaspoons coarsely ground black pepper

Two jelly-roll pans lined with parchment or foil

CARAWAY SALT STRAWS: Substitute caraway seeds for the pepper.

CHEESE STRAWS: Substitute 1 cup grated Parmigiano-Reggiano sprinkled with 1 teaspoon salt and 2 teaspoons sweet Hungarian or Spanish paprika for the salt and pepper. (Adding the salt emphasizes the cheese flavor, which can be overly delicate.)

Salt & Pepper Straws

These and the variations provided are one of the best possible uses for puff pastry. They're light, rich, flavorful, and a small amount of effort yields a large amount of tasty results. These are a perfect hors d'oeuvre pastry, and they freeze beautifully if you want to prepare them in advance.

1. Prepare a lightly floured work surface. Press the Instant Puff Pastry dough into a rough square, then roll it into a 12 x 18-inch (30 x 45-cm) rectangle. Roll gently, and if the dough resists, let it rest for 5 minutes, then roll again. If at any point the dough becomes too soft to handle, slide a cookie sheet under it and refrigerate for 10 to 15 minutes. After the dough is rolled, cover loosely with plastic wrap and refrigerate for 1 hour.

2. Set racks in the upper and lower thirds of the oven and preheat to 350°F (180°C).

3. Remove the dough from the refrigerator and brush with the egg wash. Scatter the salt and pepper over half the surface of the dough, in a 12 x 9-inch (30 x 23-cm) rectangle (figure a).

4. Fold the dough over to enclose the salt and pepper, so that the dough itself is now a 12 x 9-inch (30 x 23-cm) rectangle. Flour the work surface and the dough lightly and roll the dough back to a 12 x 18-inch (30 x 45-cm) rectangle. If the dough is beginning to soften, slide it onto a cookie sheet and refrigerate it for 15 minutes.

5. Use a sharp pastry wheel to cut the dough into ½ inch x 12-inch (1 x 30-cm) strips, making approximately 36.

6. Twist each strip into a corkscrew shape by positioning it at a 45-degree angle from the edge of the work surface. Roll the edge furthest from the surface toward it to make it parallel with the edge of the surface (figure b). Transfer the strips to the prepared pans, pressing the edges of the dough to the edges of the pans to prevent them from unraveling as they are baking. Chill until they are cold and firm, about 1 hour.

7. Bake the straws for about 10 minutes, then switch the bottom pan to the top rack and vice versa, turning the pans back to front at the same time. Continue baking the straws until they are puffed, dry, and golden, 10 to 15 additional minutes.

8. Immediately after taking the pans out of the oven, use a long sharp knife to trim the ends from the straws and to cut them in half crosswise. Cool in the pans on racks.

SERVING: Serve as an hors d'oeuvre with drinks.

STORAGE: Keep the straws at room temperature the day they are baked. For longer storage, pack them between sheets of wax paper in a tin or plastic container with a tight-fitting cover and freeze for a month or so. Defrost in a single layer and reheat at 350°F (180°C) for 5 minutes. Cool before serving.

a. After brushing the dough with egg wash, scatter
    the salt and pepper over half the Instant Puff Pastry
    dough, then fold over the dough to enclose the
    salt and pepper (steps 3 and 4).

b. Twist each ½-inch strip of dough into a corkscrew
    and then transfer to the prepared pan, making sure
    the edges of the strip are pressed against the edge
    of the pan to prevent unraveling (steps 6 and 7).

fig. b

fig. a

226 Perfect Pound Cake

227 Lemon Ginger Pound Cake

228 Rum-Scented Marble Cake

231 Viennese Raisin Coffee Cake

232 Sour Cream Coffee Cake

233 Blackberry Jam Cake

235 Orange-Scented
Olive Oil Cake

237 Blueberry Crumb Cake

238 Real Strawberry Shortcake

240 Classic Génoise

242 Yellow Cake Layers

243 Perfect Birthday Cake

244 Raspberry Cream Cake

247 Whipped Cream Layer Cake

248 Banana Rum Coconut
Layer Cake

250 Triple Chocolate Cake

253 Devil's Food Cake
with Fluffy White Icing

254 Milk Chocolate Mousse Cake

256 Heirloom Chocolate Cake

257 Cinnamon-Scented Baked
Chocolate Mousse Cake

258 Molten Center Chocolate
Cakes

260 Individual French
Hazelnut Cakes

261 Golden Cupcakes

263 Incredibly Moist
Chocolate Cupcakes

264 Individual New York
Cheesecakes

7.

Cakes

Cake is everyone's idea of a good time—that's why the major celebrations of life such as birthdays, christenings, Bar Mitzvahs, weddings, and anniversaries are always celebrated with special cakes. I can still remember some of my childhood birthday cakes, but I guess I was already obsessed with baking at an early age. And some of the very first things I tried my hand at were baking cakes. Most cakes are really easy to make, especially the type that only need to be unmolded and cooled before serving. If you're a little more ambitious, you can certainly make a layer cake with a minimum of effort.

Most of the cakes in this chapter emphasize wonderful flavor and texture over complexity of preparation. In fact, I've adapted several commercial methods for mixing cake batters for small-scale home use—they make the process even easier and more foolproof.

Here are the types of cakes in this chapter:

Pound Cakes and Other "Plain Cakes": These are rich cake batters that usually don't have or need any adornment, aside from a shake of confectioners' sugar or maybe a simple glaze. They're quickly mixed and don't require any special skills to prepare.

Cakes with Fruit: Other simple cakes, some made like the ones above, enriched by and flavored with fresh fruit or berries. They're also easy to prepare in advance and are usually better the day after they're baked.

Chocolate Cakes: Of course chocolate has to have a category of its own, even though chocolate cakes overlap with all the other categories here. To me, a good chocolate cake has a moist, rich quality that no other ingredient can provide—and that's why I think they should be in a category by themselves.

Layer Cakes: All of the layer cakes here are baked in two separate pans before being filled, stacked, and finished, eliminating the need to slice one large layer horizontally into two thinner ones. Fillings are either light or rich, and can be used interchangeably in different recipes.

Individual Cakes: From homey cupcakes to one of the greatest showstoppers of the cake world, the liquid-center chocolate cake, individual cakes are always well received—Who wouldn't be happy getting his or her own cake and not having to share?

I've deliberately kept the pan situation under control here, so with very few exceptions you'll be able to make all the cakes in this chapter with just a loaf pan, Bundt or other tube pan, round cake pans, and muffin pans. Cakes are about good times, and baking them should be, too.

Cake Techniques

SOFTENING INGREDIENTS

SOFTENING BUTTER: Soften butter at cool room temperature for several hours. Unwrap butter while it is cold and place it directly into the mixing bowl or on a small plate. If the room is hot, leave it out only long enough that it offers no resistance when you press on it.

SOFTENING CREAM CHEESE: Soften as for butter, above.

If you forget to remove butter or cream cheese from the refrigerator to soften, unwrap it and cut it into ½-inch (1-cm) dice. Arrange in a single layer on a microwave-safe plate and microwave on high for 3 seconds at a time until it is as soft as described above. Do not let the butter melt, especially if it is for a cake batter.

BATTERS

BUTTER CAKES, STANDARD (CREAMING) METHOD: This entails beating butter and sugar together (creaming), then alternating dry and liquid ingredients into the creamed mixture. Always start off with very soft butter and be sure to have eggs and other liquids at room temperature, as the batter might "break," or separate, if the butter has too much difficulty absorbing the liquid. This could also result in a baked cake that has a greasy, uneven crumb. When alter-nating the dry and liquid ingredients into the creamed mixture, always begin and end with the flour to avoid separation. Finally, always beat butter cake batters for 2 to 3 minutes at medium speed with an electric mixer to increase aeration and create lightness in the baked cake.

BUTTER CAKES, HIGH-RATIO METHOD: The ratio that's high here is that of sugar to flour. When the weight of the sugar equals or exceeds the weight of the flour (not the number of cups), this method works well. After all the dry ingredients are combined, the butter is fully incorporated. Liquids are added afterward, in three stages, beating a couple of minutes after each addition. If you don't have a scale, use the conversion tables at the back of this book to determine whether you can mix your cake batter in this manner.

WHOLE EGG FOAM CAKES: French génoise is the model for this type of cake. Whole eggs and sugar are whisked together by hand, then briefly heated while being gently whisked over a pan of simmering water until they are just warm, about 110°F (45°C). The mixture is then whipped to a dense foam before the dry ingredients are folded in. Be careful not to overheat the eggs and sugar or they won't absorb the requisite amount of air during whipping, resulting in a dense baked cake.

SEPARATED EGG FOAM CAKES: Composed of whites and yolks whipped separately with sugar before being combined and then having the dry ingredients folded in, these have many applications in cake baking. For this type of cake layer, always whip the egg whites to a firm peak. This results in a batter that holds its shape well after the mixing is completed, a characteristic that contributes a proper degree of lightness to the baked cake.

WHIPPING EGG WHITES: When separating eggs, make sure your hands and all utensils that come in contact with the egg whites are dry and free of any traces of fat. Begin whipping the whites on medium speed and wait until they are able to hold their shape before adding any sugar. Increase the speed to medium high, and then add the sugar in a stream, whipping only until the sugar is fully incorporated. Most prep-arations using whipped egg whites require them to be beaten to a soft peak—one that bends over when you withdraw the whisk. If you're unsure, stop the mixer and remove the whisk to check the texture. For a firm peak, whip a few seconds longer so that the egg whites form a single straight point when the whip is withdrawn. Never whip egg whites beyond a firm peak unless you are making a meringue intended to be baked hard (see below).

FOLDING IN EGG WHITES: There are several ways of accomplishing this. In a separated egg sponge cake, the yolks are folded into the whites, then the dry ingredients are folded in. In some other cases, some of the whipped egg whites is stirred into the batter to lighten it before folding in the bulk of the egg whites. Occasionally all the whites are folded into a batter at once. A good general rule: When the material to be combined with the egg whites is more liquid than the whipped whites, fold it into the whites. If the material is more dense than the whites, fold the whites into it. Fold by using a large rubber spatula to cut through the center of the bowl and scraping down to the bottom, emerging at the side and letting the mixture gently fall back upon itself. Turn the bowl and repeat until no streaks of white appear.

MERINGUES: Most meringues have an elevated sugar content that equals twice the weight of the egg whites. Egg whites whipped with a small amount of sugar and then folded into a batter for leavening are not meringue, they are whipped egg whites. There are three kinds of meringue: ordinary, or French; Swiss; and Italian. French meringue is egg whites whipped with sugar and formed into layers, decorations (mushrooms), or hollow cases and baked until crisp. I like to whip half the sugar into the whites, then fold in the rest. Sometimes the second half of the sugar is confectioners' sugar, making for a more fragile baked meringue. Cocoa or ground nuts may be added to the second half of the sugar for chocolate or nut meringue.

Swiss meringue has the egg whites and sugar combined, whisked to mix, then heated over a pan of gently boiling water until the egg whites are hot and the sugar is dissolved, 130 to 140°F (55 to 60°C). Then the meringue is whipped until risen in volume and cool. The most common use for this type of meringue is a base for buttercream. I also use it for topping a pie or cake, but with a reduced amount of sugar. Because of this, be careful not to overwhip or the meringue will be dry and grainy. *Italian meringue* requires whipping hot sugar syrup into egg whites that are already quite firm. I never use this method except when making large quantities, because the potential for failure with a small quantity is so great: It's difficult to get an accurate temperature reading for a small amount of sugar syrup, and an overcooked syrup will lump up when poured into the egg whites.

....

PREPARING AND FILLING PANS AND SPECIAL BAKING TECHNIQUES

DECORATIVE MOLDS/BUNDT PANS: Grease them with soft butter, cover with a coat of dry bread crumbs, then apply a coat of nonstick vegetable oil cooking spray for a perfect nonstick finish. Do this even with nonstick pans, especially the ones that have a black nonstick coating, which makes cakes stick like crazy.

LAYER PANS AND JELLY-ROLL PANS: Butter the inside of the pan all over with soft, not melted,

butter. If you're going to be doing a lot of baking, soften 3 to 4 tablespoons of butter in a bowl near the stove before you start. If you're greasing only one pan, cut off a few pats of butter and put them in the pan. In about 5 minutes the butter will be soft enough to spread with a brush or a crumpled piece of plastic wrap, which won't absorb butter as a paper towel would.

LINING MOLDS WITH PARCHMENT PAPER: Grease the molds with soft butter as already described. Round layer pans require a disk of parchment paper on the bottom. It's okay for the paper to be slightly smaller than the bottom of the pan, but if it is larger it may tear the side of the cake. This happens if you use a knife to loosen the cake after baking, as the point of the knife can pull on the excess paper and drag it into the bottom of the cake. I like to line jelly-roll pans so the paper covers the sides, making removal easier after baking. To do this, line up a sheet of parchment paper so that two sides of it also line the sides of the pan, then use scissors to cut away the excess paper from the other two sides. Use the same procedure for a 9 x 13 x 2-inch (23 x 33 x 5-cm) pan.

TUBE PANS: A two-piece tube pan used for angel food cakes doesn't need to be buttered. However, I prefer not to use two-piece tube pans for general baking and prefer a one-piece pan as the batter might leak if baking a batter-based cake. Butter and line the bottom of a one-piece pan with a donut-shaped piece of paper, or prepare as for Bundt pans.

PANNING BATTERS: Spread firm batters into a pan, smoothing the top with a small metal spatula. Liquid batters will seek their own level in a pan and not need to be spread. Génoise batter should be smoothed up to the top of the pan all around, a trick that helps them bake flat and straight on top. For jelly-roll pans, pour or distribute the batter over as much of the surface of the pan as possible to minimize the amount of spreading you'll need to do, then use a large offset spatula to finish the job.

BAKING IN A WATER BATH: Place the pan containing the batter in a small roasting pan. Place a quart of warm tap water on the stove. Open the oven, place the roasting pan on the rack, then pull out the pan a few inches and pour in the water so it comes halfway up the side of the pan containing the batter. When the cake is baked, use a wide spatula to remove the cake pan from the water bath and leave the pan of water in the turned-off oven to cool. If you spill the water after it has cooled, at least you won't get burned.

TESTING FOR DONENESS: Insert a thin-bladed paring knife into the center of the cake, or midway between the side of the pan and central tube for a tube cake. It should emerge dry or with only a few moist crumbs clinging to it, as specified in recipes.

....

MAKING FILLINGS/FROSTINGS

WHIPPED CREAM: Always have the cream and all the utensils cold, especially if you are going to try to whip cream in a warm room. Sometimes I pour the cream into the bowl I plan to use, and then place the bowl in the freezer for 10 minutes before whipping. Always underwhip cream if you are preparing it in advance to fold into a mousse or to cover a cake. Then right before you use it, rewhip the cream for a few seconds by hand to get it to the desired consistency. Always use granulated sugar, not confectioners' sugar, which contains cornstarch, to sweeten whipped cream, and add it at the beginning of whipping. When whipping by machine, use medium speed, which makes it easier to control the process and avoid over-whipping the cream. Whip cream to be folded into a mousse until it is still very soft and holds just the softest peak. Whip cream for covering a cake just a little more firm. All the problems associated with whipped cream, from having sheets of whipped cream fall off the side of a cake to having cream that weeps whey, originate from overwhipping cream.

FOLDING IN WHIPPED CREAM: Fold whipped cream into a preparation that is firmer than the cream; fold any preparation that is more liquid into the cream. In the latter case, you may gently whisk the elements together.

EGG-WHITE ICING: This follows the same general rules for Swiss meringue, on the opposite page. Because of the very high sugar content, the icing doesn't become firm until it cools completely, so don't try to rush this one: It won't work, and your icing will be pourable instead of holding its shape.

BUTTERCREAM: Successfully made buttercream is an emulsion of fat and water molecules, much like mayonnaise. For best results, make sure the meringue or any other base used for the buttercream is at the same temperature as the butter, which should be at room temperature and very soft. If the butter is too cold it will lump and separate to such a degree that the buttercream may never beat smooth. If the meringue is too warm, the butter will melt and never emulsify. To cool meringue efficiently, I like to switch to the paddle after the meringue is fully risen in volume and continue beating on lowest speed. Touch the bowl as a test—keep mixing until the bowl no longer feels warm. After the butter is added, the buttercream goes through three stages. At first it becomes very fluffy and soft but, beware, since the buttercream is not emulsified—you can't use it yet because it will never become firm. During the next stage the buttercream separates completely and looks like soft scrambled eggs. Don't throw it away! Just keep beating on medium speed and in no time the buttercream will become quite firm, signifying that it is fully emulsified. It seems contradictory: Soft and fluffy first, then firmer after more mixing. Let the buttercream beat for a minute or two to make it smoother, then add any flavoring at this point, beating again until it is very smooth before using it. Add liquids a little at a time or the buttercream will separate.

GANACHE: Nowadays I like to make ganache, that rich and delicious mixture of chocolate and cream, by combining cooled melted

223

fig. a

fig. b

fig. c

FROSTING THE OUTSIDE OF A CAKE

a. After placing spoonfuls of chocolate buttercream on the top of one layer of white cake, use a large offset spatula to spread them evenly.

b. Place the second layer on top of the first. Use dabs of buttercream on the back of the spatula to cover the sides of the layers.

c. Use the same method to cover the top.

d. Use the back of the spatula to sweep once around the sides of the cake to smooth the buttercream.

e. To smooth the top, spread from the outside edge to the center.

fig. d

fig. e

chocolate with cream that has been brought to a simmer and cooled to room temperature. This results in a perfectly smooth ganache, though I also like to add some corn syrup for added smoothness. Chocolate with a higher cocoa content can sometimes result in a separated ganache if it gets too hot.

FROSTING CAKES

DRIZZLING GLAZE: Use a large spoon that has a bowl that comes to a point. Dip the spoon into the glaze, then hold it straight vertically over the cake and wave it back and forth to distribute streaks of the glaze from the pointed tip. Or let the glaze cool slightly and pour it into a nonpleated heavy plastic bag. Force the glaze into one corner and twist the bag behind the glaze. Snip a tiny hole in the corner of the bag and hold it perpendicular to the work surface, gently squeezing it while waving it back and forth over the cake.

POURING GLAZE TO COVER A WHOLE CAKE: Place the cake on a rack over a pan. Starting in the center of the cake, pour the glaze in a slow spiral, reserving at least one third of it to cover the sides when you reach the edge of the cake. Immediately use a medium metal offset spatula to sweep some glaze from the top of the cake over and onto the sides, and also to spread the sides evenly. Use any glaze that has accumulated in the pan beneath to touch up the sides, if necessary.

SPLITTING CAKE LAYERS: Use a sharp, serrated knife. Hold the knife parallel to the work surface and cut a line just ½ inch (1¼ cm) deep into the side of the cake all around where you would like to cut through, rotating the cake against the knife. When you reach the starting point of the cut, continue rotating the cake against the knife, sawing with the blade, and pressing the cake more firmly against the knife. By the time you reach the center, the layer will be sliced.

FILLING CAKES: Most important is that your buttercream or any other filling you use be very soft and spreadable—if it is too firm it will tear the delicate cake layer apart. Place spoonfuls of the filling all over the cake layer, rather than placing a single quantity in the center. Use a large offset spatula to spread the filling. Having multiple spoonfuls of filling on the layer prevents having the spatula wander onto the bare cake and track crumbs into the filling.

FROSTING THE OUTSIDE OF A CAKE: Spread the sides first, using a dab of frosting on the back end of the spatula, and adding more dabs to the end of the spatula as needed. Spread to cover, not to smooth. Cover the top in the same way. Use the back of the spatula to sweep once against the side of the cake to smooth it. Then spread from the outside edge to the center to smooth the top of the cake. This is a 5-minute job, and not something to spend an hour doing. If the cake is not perfectly spread, no one but you will notice.

ADHERING NUTS OR CHOCOLATE SHAVINGS ONTO A CAKE: Press chopped or sliced nuts against the side of a cake with the palm of your hand. For the top, scatter them evenly, then use an offset spatula to spread them perfectly straight and to sweep away the excess. Use a metal spatula to press chocolate shavings against the side of a cake—if you use your hand they will melt. Follow the same procedure for covering the top as for nuts.

225

ADHERING NUTS OR CHOCOLATE SHAVINGS ONTO THE SIDE OF A CAKE

TOP: Use the palm of your hand to press sliced almonds to the side of a Chocolate and Vanilla Cake (page 245).

BOTTOM: Use a metal spatula to press chocolate shavings against the side of a Perfect Birthday Cake (page 243)—so they don't melt on your hands.

Makes one 9 x 5 x 3-inch (23 x 13 x 7-cm) pound cake, about sixteen ½-inch (1-cm) slices

··

5 large eggs, separated

1 cup sugar

1 teaspoon vanilla extract

1 teaspoon lemon extract

2 cups cake flour
(spoon flour into a dry-measure cup and level off)

1 teaspoon baking powder

16 tablespoons (2 sticks/8 ounces/225 grams) unsalted butter, softened, see *Note*

¼ teaspoon salt

One 9 x 5 x 3-inch (23 x 13 x 7-cm) loaf pan, buttered and the bottom lined with a rectangle of parchment or buttered wax paper cut to fit

Note: Don't attempt to mix this cake unless the butter is very soft, almost the consistency of mayonnaise, or the flour and butter mixture will be stiff and will not combine easily with the other elements of the batter.

PECAN OR WALNUT POUND CAKE: After you take the batter off the mixer (step 6), fold in 1 cup pecan or walnut pieces, coarsely chopped, tossed with 1 tablespoon of all-purpose flour.

Perfect Pound Cake

My aunt Rachel Malgieri Rocco was a great home baker (see her Date Walnut Bread on page 47), and I watched her prepare this pound cake countless times as a child. I was fascinated by the odd mixing method—the yolks and sugar are whipped, then the flour and butter are beaten together, the egg whites are whipped, and after everything is combined the batter goes back on the mixer for a thorough beating. Several years ago I ran into Mary Lou McGrath, my aunt's niece through marriage, and we fell to talking about all the great things we remembered our mutual aunt baking. She mentioned the pound cake and mailed me the recipe the following week. I am thrilled to have it. This is a little trouble to make because of all the different bowls you need—if you only have one mixer bowl, you can beat the butter and flour together in the same bowl as the yolks and sugar without washing it in between. Then you'll have to wash the bowl and whisk before whipping the egg whites—not much trouble compared to the exquisite result. *Note:* Don't attempt to mix this cake unless the butter is very soft, almost the consistency of mayonnaise, or the flour and butter mixture will be stiff and will not combine easily with the other elements of the batter.

1. Set a rack in the middle of the oven and preheat to 325°F (160°C).

2. In the bowl of an electric mixer, whisk the yolks by hand to break them up, then gradually whisk in the sugar in a stream. Whisk in the vanilla and lemon extracts. Place the bowl on the mixer with the paddle attachment and whip on medium speed until the mixture is pale colored and aerated, 3 to 4 minutes. Scrape the yolk mixture into a large mixing bowl.

3. Mix the cake flour with the baking powder and set aside.

4. Without washing the mixer bowl, beat the butter with the paddle on medium speed for 1 minute. Add the flour mixture, decrease the speed to lowest, and beat until the mixture forms a smooth paste. Scrape the flour and butter paste over the yolk mixture and use a large rubber spatula to stir them together.

5. If you only have one mixer bowl, wash the bowl and whisk with hot, soapy water, rinse and dry well. Combine the egg whites and salt in the bowl and place on the mixer with the whisk. Whip on medium speed until the egg whites hold a firm peak—for this recipe it doesn't matter much if the egg whites are a little overwhipped. Stir the egg whites into the flour, butter, and yolk mixture.

6. Scrape the batter back into the mixer bowl and use the paddle to beat it on medium-low speed for 5 minutes.

7. Scrape the batter into the prepared pan and smooth the top.

8. Bake the pound cake for about 1 hour, until it is well risen and beautifully cracked in the center, and a toothpick or the point of a thin knife inserted in the center emerges clean.

9. Cool the cake in the pan on a rack for 5 minutes, then unmold it onto the rack to cool rightside up.

··

SERVING: Pound cake is a perfect tea or coffee cake. If you have any left after a couple of days, it also toasts well.

STORAGE: Keep the cooled cake wrapped in plastic at room temperature, or under a cake dome. Wrap and freeze for longer storage. Defrost the cake and let it come to room temperature before serving.

2⅔ cups all-purpose flour
(spoon flour into a dry-measure cup and level off)

2 cups sugar

2 teaspoons baking powder

¼ teaspoon salt

16 tablespoons (2 sticks/8 ounces/225 grams)
unsalted butter, softened

3 large eggs

3 large egg yolks

¾ cup milk

1 tablespoon finely grated lemon zest

2 tablespoons strained lemon juice

3 tablespoons finely grated fresh ginger

1 (12-cup) tube or Bundt pan, buttered, coated with f
ine, dry bread crumbs, and sprayed with vegetable oil
cooking spray

Lemon Ginger Pound Cake

One of my favorite combinations, lemon and ginger emphasize each other so well that each flavor is more vivid because of the presence of the other. Grating ginger can be a problem, especially if you don't have a grater with small teardrop-shaped holes set at a diagonal to the metal. I love Microplane® graters, but they just reduce fresh ginger to liquid. So, failing the right grater, just slice and finely chop the peeled ginger with a sharp stainless-steel knife. The mixing method here is adapted from large-scale bakery methods, meant to produce a perfectly smooth batter with a minimum of effort, thus giving the baked cake a tender, moist crumb.

1. Set a rack in the lower third of the oven and preheat to 325°F (160°C).

2. In the bowl of an electric mixer, combine the flour, sugar, baking powder, and salt. Stir well by hand to mix. Add the butter. Beat the mixture on low speed with the paddle until the mixture is a smooth, heavy paste, 1 to 2 minutes.

3. In a separate bowl, whisk together the eggs, egg yolks, milk, lemon zest, lemon juice, and ginger. On medium speed, beat about ⅓ of the egg mixture into the flour and butter mixture. Beat for 1 minute.

4. Stop and scrape the bowl and beater. Add half of the egg mixture and beat for 2 minutes. Repeat with the other half.

5. Remove the bowl from the mixer and use a large rubber spatula to give the batter a final mixing. Scrape the batter into the prepared pan and smooth the top.

6. Bake the cake until it is well risen and firm and a toothpick or a small thin knife inserted midway between the side of the pan and the central tube emerges dry, about 1 hour.

7. Cool the cake in the pan for 5 minutes, then invert a rack over it. Invert and lift off the pan. Cool the cake completely on the rack.

SERVING: This doesn't really need any accompaniment, but some whipped cream or sliced fruit would dress it up.

STORAGE: Wrap the cooled cake in plastic wrap and keep it at room temperature. Freeze for longer storage. Defrost the cake and bring it to room temperature before serving.

Makes one 10-inch (25-cm) tube or Bundt cake, about 24 slices

....

BASE BATTER

2⅔ cups all-purpose flour (spoon flour into a dry-measure cup and level off)

1⅔ cups sugar

2 teaspoons baking powder

¼ teaspoon salt

12 ounces/350 grams (3 sticks) unsalted butter, softened

7 large eggs

3 tablespoons dark rum

CHOCOLATE BATTER

2 tablespoons dark rum

2 tablespoons milk

½ teaspoon baking soda

6 ounces (175 grams) bittersweet (not unsweetened) chocolate, melted and cooled

2 cups Base Batter, at left

1 (12-cup) tube or Bundt pan, buttered, coated with fine, dry bread crumbs, and sprayed with vegetable oil cooking spray

Rum-Scented Marble Cake

Marble cakes are both homey and festive. A marble cake looks slick when you slice into it and reveal the delicate pattern created when the two batters are swirled together. My first experience working with this type of mixture came about as the result of a marbled chocolate terrine that appeared first in the pages of the old *Cook's Magazine*, and then in my chocolate book. Everything about it was right—the texture, the flavor, the quantity of mixture in relation to the mold—everything, that is, except the marbling. Even when I barely mixed the white and dark chocolate mixtures, what I got was a few streaks of dark and white, and mostly a muddy combined color. After several frustrating attempts, I realized that I had too much dark chocolate mixture and I recast the recipe so there was twice as much white chocolate mixture as dark and the terrine marbled perfectly. So this marble cake is proportioned in the same way: Rather than dividing the base batter in half, I like to remove about one third of it and add the chocolate. Thanks to my old friend Ceri Hadda, who shared her mother's recipe years ago.

1. Set a rack in the lower third of the oven and preheat to 325°F (160°C).

2. In the bowl of an electric mixer, combine the flour, sugar, baking powder, and salt. Stir well by hand to mix. Add the butter. Beat the mixture on low speed with the paddle until the mixture is a smooth, heavy paste, 1 to 2 minutes.

3. Whisk the eggs and rum together. On medium speed, beat ⅓ of the egg mixture into the flour and butter mixture. Beat for 1 minute.

4. Stop and scrape down the bowl and beater. Add half of the egg mixture and beat for 2 minutes. Repeat with the other half.

5. Remove the bowl from the mixer and using a large rubber spatula give the batter a final mix.

6. For the chocolate batter, combine the rum, milk, and baking soda in a medium mixing bowl. Whisk well to dissolve the baking soda. Scrape in the chocolate and whisk it well. Add the 2 cups of base batter to the chocolate mixture and whisk well to combine.

7. Scrape half the remaining base batter into the prepared pan and smooth the top. Cover with the chocolate batter, making it as even a layer as possible. Finally top with the remaining base batter and smooth the top. Use a wide-bladed table knife or a thin metal spatula to marble the batter: Insert the knife into the batter at the central tube, with the flat side of the blade facing you. Draw the blade through the batter to the bottom of the pan and up and out the side of the pan closest to you, repeating the motion every inch or so around the pan, making a spiral in the batter, almost as though you were folding egg whites into it. Stop when you get back to the point where you started. Don't bother to smooth the top of the batter—it might disturb the marbling.

8. Bake the cake until it is well risen and firm, and a toothpick or a small thin knife inserted midway between the side of the pan and the central tube emerges dry, about 1 hour.

9. Cool the cake in the pan for 5 minutes, then invert a rack over it. Invert and lift off the pan. Cool the cake completely on the rack.

....

SERVING: This doesn't need any accompaniment.

STORAGE: Wrap the cooled cake in plastic wrap and keep it at room temperature. Freeze for longer storage. Defrost the cake and bring it to room temperature before serving.

1⅔ cups all-purpose flour (spoon flour into a dry-measure cup and level off)

2 teaspoons baking powder

16 tablespoons (2 sticks/8 ounces/225 grams) unsalted butter, softened

1¼ cups sugar

2 teaspoons finely grated lemon zest

1 teaspoon vanilla extract

6 large eggs, separated

1 cup (about 5½ ounces/160 grams) dark or golden raisins, tossed with 1 tablespoon flour

One 10-inch/25-cm (10- or 12-cup) Gugelhupf or Bundt pan, buttered, sprinkled with fine, dry bread crumbs, and sprayed with vegetable oil cooking spray

Viennese Raisin Coffee Cake

Vienna is the undisputed world capital of cake. There are layer cakes, mousse cakes, historical cakes (the Sachertorte of the Hotel Sacher has been a closely guarded secret recipe for over 200 years), and even plain cakes. I recently asked my friend Erika Lieben for her favorite. She wrote back a 4-word response: *Gehruerter Gugelhupf mit Rosinen* (beaten coffee cake with raisins). "Beaten" refers to the fact that this is mixed like a cake batter and is not the yeast-risen coffee cake closely associated with Vienna and made in all German-speaking countries. Though you may use any type of a tube pan for this cake, a real Gugelhupf mold has a specific shape: The top is a series of diagonal ridges and the sides may be covered with ridges in the opposite direction from the first ones, or with two bands of diagonal ridges, separated by a straight beltlike band around the circumference of the pan. They are usually smaller than typical Bundt or tube pans. Either a Bundt or tube pan will substitute perfectly well, but the resulting cake will not be quite as tall as a cake made in a Gugelhupf mold.

1. Set a rack in the lower third of the oven and preheat to 350°F (180°C).

2. Stir the flour and baking powder together and set aside.

3. Combine the butter and ¾ cup of the sugar in the bowl of an electric mixer. Beat the mixture with the paddle on medium speed until it is soft and light, 3 to 4 minutes.

4. Beat in the lemon zest and vanilla, followed by 2 of the egg yolks.

5. Beat in ⅓ of the flour mixture. Stop and scrape down the bowl and beater.

6. Beat in 2 more of the egg yolks, followed by another half of the remaining flour. Stop and scrape. Repeat using the remaining egg yolks and flour mixture.

7. Pour the egg whites into a clean, dry mixer bowl. Place on the mixer with the whisk attachment and whip the egg whites until they are very white, opaque, and beginning to hold a very soft peak. Increase the speed to medium-high and whip in the remaining ½ cup sugar in a slow stream, continuing to whip the egg whites until they hold a soft, glossy peak.

8. Fold ⅓ of the egg whites into the batter to lighten it, then fold in the floured raisins. Fold in the remaining egg whites.

9. Scrape the batter into the prepared pan and smooth the top.

10. Bake the cake until it is well risen and deep golden, and a toothpick or the point of a paring knife inserted midway between the side of the pan and the central tube emerges dry, 45 to 50 minutes. If the cake is baked in a Bundt pan it will be ready 5 to 10 minutes sooner.

11. Cool the cake in the pan on a rack for 10 minutes, then invert the cake onto the rack to cool completely.

SERVING: Serve this cake with breakfast, brunch, or tea.

STORAGE: Wrap the cake in plastic and keep it at room temperature—it will stay fresh for several days. Freeze for longer storage.

Makes one 10-inch (25-cm) tube cake, about 24 slices

....

CINNAMON SUGAR NUT FILLING

⅓ cup granulated or light brown sugar

2 teaspoons ground cinnamon

1 cup (about 4 ounces/100 grams) pecan or walnut pieces, coarsely chopped

SOUR CREAM CAKE BATTER

2 cups all-purpose flour
(spoon flour into a dry-measure cup and level off)

1 cup sugar

1 teaspoon baking powder

1 teaspoon baking soda

10 tablespoons (1¼ sticks) unsalted butter, softened

2 large eggs, at room temperature

2 large egg yolks

1 (8-ounce/225-gram) container sour cream

One 10-inch/25-cm (12-cup) tube or Bundt pan, buttered

VARIATIONS

To vary the fillimg, divide it in half and add 3 tablespoons of currants or raisins to the half that you'll use inside the cake batter—they would burn on top of the cake. You may also add ¼ cup bittersweet (not unsweetened) chocolate, cut into ¼-inch (6-mm) pieces, or chocolate chips, in addition to or instead of the currants or raisins. You can bake the cake in a 9 x 13 x 2-inch (23 x 33 x 5-cm) pan if you prefer to cut it into squares instead of slices. If you do, sprinkle all the filling on top of the cake. It will take only 35 to 40 minutes to bake.

Sour Cream Coffee Cake

This is as easy to prepare as it is good to eat. Basically a pound cake batter enriched with sour cream, it's layered with a mixture of cinnamon sugar and nuts—a mixture to which you can add cocoa, currants, raisins, or even a little melted butter. It's really essential to have the butter, eggs, and sour cream at room temperature for easy mixing, or the final texture of the cake will be heavy and grainy rather than light and delicate.

1. Set a rack in the lower third of the oven and preheat to 325°F (160°C).

2. For the filling, mix the sugar, cinnamon, and nuts in a small bowl and set aside.

3. For the batter, combine the flour, sugar, baking powder, and baking soda in the bowl of an electric mixer. Stir well by hand to mix. Add the butter. Beat the mixture on low speed with the paddle until the mixture is a smooth, heavy paste, 1 to 2 minutes.

4. Whisk the eggs, egg yolks, and sour cream together. On medium speed, beat ⅓ of the egg mixture into the flour and butter mixture. Beat for 1 minute.

5. Stop and scrape the bowl and beater, beat in another half of the remaining egg mixture and beat for 2 minutes. Repeat with the last of the egg mixture.

6. Remove the bowl from the mixer and using a rubber spatula give the batter a final mixing.

7. Scrape half the batter into the prepared pan and smooth the top. Scatter half the sugar and nut filling on the batter.

8. Scrape the remaining batter over the sugar and nut mixture and smooth the top. Scatter on the remaining sugar and nut mixture.

9. Bake the cake until it is well risen and firm, and a toothpick or a small thin knife inserted midway between the side of the pan and the central tube emerges dry, about 1 hour.

10. Cool the cake in the pan for 5 minutes, then invert a rack over it. Invert and lift off the pan, then cover the cake with another rack or a cake cardboard and turn it right side up again. Cool the cake completely.

....

SERVING: This doesn't need any accompaniment since it's so rich and flavorful.

STORAGE: Wrap the cooled cake in plastic wrap and keep it at room temperature. Freeze for longer storage. Defrost the cake and bring it to room temperature before serving.

3 cups all-purpose flour
(spoon flour into a dry-measure cup and level off)

2 tablespoons alkalized (Dutch process) cocoa

2 teaspoons ground allspice

2 teaspoons ground cinnamon

1 teaspoon baking soda

16 tablespoons (2 sticks/8 ounces/225 grams) unsalted butter, softened

2 cups sugar

4 large eggs

1 cup dark raisins

1 cup chopped walnuts or pecans

1 cup buttermilk

1 cup seedless blackberry jam

One 12-cup tube or Bundt pan, buttered, coated with fine, dry bread crumbs, and sprayed with vegetable oil cooking spray

Blackberry Jam Cake

233

This was a standard of the 19th-century American baking repertoire and deserves to be better known again. I came across the recipe so many times during a several month period—mostly in 19th- and early 20th-century handwritten manuscript cookbooks—that my curiosity got the better of me and I sat down with as many versions of the recipe as I could find and compared them. Only the more recent versions called for the cocoa, which imparts a very subtle flavor and a bit of color to the batter. Aside from that, most of the recipes were quite similar. The seedless jam is my innovation—I think it's a little better than chomping down on those enormous blackberry seeds.

1. Set a rack in the lower third of the oven and preheat to 350°F (180°C).

2. For the cake batter, stir together the flour, cocoa, spices, and baking soda; set aside.

3. Beat the butter and sugar with the paddle on medium speed until light, about 5 minutes. Beat in the eggs, one at a time, beating smooth after each addition.

4. Remove 2 tablespoons of the flour mixture and toss it with the raisins and walnuts to coat. Beat in ⅓ of the flour mixture on lowest speed. Stop and scrape down the bowl and beat, then beat in half of the buttermilk. Beat in half of the remaining flour mixture, then stop and scrape. Beat in the remaining buttermilk, followed by the remaining flour mixture. Beat in the jam, then the raisins and walnuts.

5. Use a large rubber spatula to give a final stir to the batter, then scrape it into the prepared pan. Bake the cake until it is well risen and firm, and a toothpick inserted between the side of the pan and the central tube emerges dry, about 1 hour.

6. Cool the cake in the pan for 5 minutes, then unmold onto a rack to cool.

SERVING: If you bake this cake during blackberry season, serve it with some sugared blackberries on the side.

STORAGE: Wrap the cooled cake in plastic wrap and keep it at room temperature. Freeze for longer storage. Defrost the cake and bring it to room temperature before serving.

Makes two 9-inch (22½-cm) round cakes

3 large navel oranges

3 large eggs

2½ cups sugar

1½ cups pure olive oil

1½ cups milk

2½ cups all-purpose flour
(spoon flour into a dry-measure cup and level off)

½ teaspoon baking powder

½ teaspoon baking soda

½ teaspoon salt

Two 9-inch (22½-cm) round pans, 2 inches (5 cm) deep, well oiled, and the bottoms lined with disks of parchment paper cut to fit

Orange-Scented
Olive Oil Cake

This intriguing recipe comes from my friend Fritz Blank, chef-owner of Deux Cheminées, one of Philadelphia's loveliest restaurants. I like to use pure, rather than extra virgin, olive oil to prepare it.

1. Set a rack in the middle level of the oven and preheat to 350°F (180°C).

2. Grate the zest from the oranges and place in a large mixing bowl. Use a knife to completely remove the remaining skin and bitter white pith from the oranges. Cut the oranges into ³/₈-inch (1-cm) thick slices and refrigerate, covered, for serving.

3. Add the eggs to the orange zest and whisk well to mix. Whisk in 1 cup of the sugar and continue whisking until the mixture lightens, about 1 minute. Whisk in the oil, followed by the milk.

4. In another bowl, stir together the remaining 1½ cups of sugar with the flour, baking powder, baking soda, and salt. Whisk the dry mixture into the egg mixture in 3 separate additions, whisking smooth after each addition.

5. Divide the batter equally between the 2 prepared pans.

6. Bake the cakes until they are well risen, deep golden, and firm in the center when pressed with a fingertip, 50 to 55 minutes.

7. Cool the cakes on racks for 5 minutes, then unmold, turn right side up again, and cool completely on racks.

SERVING: Serve a wedge of the cake with some of the sliced oranges. Fritz suggests a scoop of vanilla ice cream or orange sherbet as a good accompaniment.

STORAGE: Double wrap the cakes in plastic wrap, keep them at room temperature, and use them within 24 hours. Or freeze them for up to a month. Defrost and bring them to room temperature before serving.

Makes one 9 x 13 x 2-inch (23 x 33 x 5-cm) cake, about twenty-four 2-inch (5-cm) squares

CRUMB TOPPING

2 cups all-purpose flour
(spoon flour into a dry-measure cup and level off)

1 teaspoon baking powder

⅓ cup granulated sugar

⅓ cup firmly packed light brown sugar

½ teaspoon ground cinnamon

¼ teaspoon freshly grated nutmeg

12 tablespoons (1½ sticks) unsalted butter, melted

CAKE BATTER

16 tablespoons (2 sticks/8 ounces/225 grams) unsalted butter, softened

1½ cups sugar

3 large eggs

2 teaspoons vanilla extract

2½ cups all-purpose flour
(spoon flour into dry-measure cup and level off)

2 teaspoons baking powder

3 egg yolks

¼ cup milk or buttermilk

4 cups blueberries, picked over and patted dry

One 9 x 13 x 2-inch (23 x 33 x 5-cm) pan, buttered and lined fully (bottom and sides) with parchment or foil

Blueberry Crumb Cake

In New York City where I live, blueberry season is fairly long since we have blueberries from the South, then New Jersey, then finally from Maine and Michigan, consecutively throughout several months. I love this type of cake and blueberries are the perfect fruit for it—they melt to a jamlike consistency between the cake batter and crumb topping while the cake is baking.

1. Set a rack in the middle of the oven and preheat to 350°F (180°C).

2. For the crumb topping, mix the flour, baking powder, sugars, cinnamon, and nutmeg in a bowl. Stir in the melted butter. Rub the mixture between your fingers to form coarse crumbs. Scatter the crumbs over the berries as evenly as possible. Set aside.

3. In a large mixer bowl, beat the butter and sugar until soft and light. Add the eggs one at a time, beating smooth after each addition. Beat in the vanilla.

4. Stir together the flour and baking powder and add the dry mixture to the batter in 3 additions, alternating with the yolks and milk, beginning and ending with the flour. Spread the batter evenly in the prepared pan.

5. Scatter the blueberries and crumb mixture evenly over the batter, pressing in gently.

6. Bake the cake until the batter is firm and the crumbs are well colored, about 40 minutes. Cool the cake in the pan on a rack. Cut the cooled cake into twenty-four 3-inch (7-cm) squares. Remove the squares from the pan to a platter.

SERVING: This a great breakfast cake and also transports well, right in the pan, to a picnic.

STORAGE: Wrap the cooled cake in plastic wrap and keep it at room temperature. Freeze for longer storage. Defrost the cake and bring it to room temperature before serving.

VARIATIONS

SOUR CHERRY CRUMB CAKE: Substitute 3 cups pitted sour cherries for the blueberries.

PLUM CRUMB CAKE: Substitute 2 pounds (900 grams) Italian prune plums, pitted and quartered, for the blueberries. Place the plum quarters on the batter cutside down, forming neat rows.

SHORTCAKE BISCUIT

2 cups all-purpose flour
(spoon flour into a dry-measure cup and level off)

3 tablespoons sugar

1 tablespoon baking powder

½ teaspoon salt

4 tablespoons cold unsalted butter, cut into 6 pieces

1 large egg

⅔ cup buttermilk, light cream, or half-and-half

WHIPPED CREAM

1 cup heavy whipping cream

2 tablespoons sugar

1 teaspoon vanilla extract

BERRIES

4 cups strawberries, hulled and sliced

3 tablespoons sugar

2 tablespoons unsalted butter, softened,
for buttering the split biscuit

One 8-inch (20-cm) round pan, 2 inches (5 cm) deep,
buttered and the bottom lined with a disk of parchment
or buttered wax paper cut to fit

Real Strawberry Shortcake

Here's a recipe you can literally have on the table less than an hour after you start making it. I love to use really sweet, height-of-the-season strawberries for this, but don't hesitate to try it with other fruit or berries such as peaches, mixed berries, or even fresh figs.

1. Set a rack in the middle of the oven and preheat to 450°F (230°C).

2. Combine the flour, 2 tablespoons sugar, the baking powder, and salt in the bowl of a food processor fitted with the metal blade. Pulse several times to mix. Add the butter and pulse 10 to 12 times, or until the butter is finely mixed into the dry ingredients.

3. Whisk the egg and buttermilk together and add to the food processor. Pulse repeatedly until a very soft dough forms.

4. Carefully remove the blade from the bowl and use a metal spatula to scrape away any dough stuck to it. Scrape the dough into the prepared pan and use a small metal offset spatula to spread it evenly. For individual shortcakes, place eight 3- to 4-inch (7- to 10-cm) mounds

of dough on a parchment paper–lined, jelly-roll pan. Sprinkle the top of the dough(s) with the remaining tablespoon of sugar.

5. Bake the shortcake until it is well risen, deep golden, and firm in the center when pressed with a fingertip, 15 to 20 minutes, 10 to 15 minutes for individual ones.

6. While the biscuit is baking, whip the cream with the sugar and vanilla by hand or by machine on medium speed with the whip attachment. Set aside in the refrigerator.

7. Gently stir the berries and sugar together and keep at room temperature.

8. When the shortcake is ready, unmold it onto a rack and let it cool for a few minutes. Use a sharp serrated knife to cut through it horizontally to make 2 layers. Place the first layer on a platter and spread with the softened butter. Top with half of the berries and their juices, and half of the whipped cream. Add the other layer, cut side down, and top with the remaining berries and juices and cream. For individual shortcakes, split the biscuits in half horizontally and place the bottom halves on dessert plates. Top each half with ⅛ of the berry mixture and ⅛ of the whipped cream. Place the remaining halves on top. Serve immediately.

SERVING: Cut the shortcake into wedges at the table. Use a spoon to put a little of the stray berries and cream next to each portion.

STORAGE: For advance preparation, whip the cream and macerate the berries earlier the same day and keep them refrigerated. You can also prepare the biscuit up to adding the butter, just leaving the liquid to be added. But the biscuit must be baked immediately after mixing and served warm from the oven. While I wouldn't throw away leftovers, they certainly aren't as good after they have cooled off. Wrap and refrigerate leftovers and eat at midnight or later while standing in front of the refrigerator.

Makes one tall 9-inch (23-cm) layer

3 large eggs

3 large egg yolks

2 teaspoons vanilla extract

Pinch of salt

½ cup sugar

½ cup all-purpose flour
(spoon flour into a dry-measure cup and level off)

¼ cup cornstarch

One 9-inch (23-cm) springform pan, 3 inches (7 cm) deep, buttered and the bottom lined with a disk of parchment or buttered wax paper cut to fit

VARIATIONS

COCOA GÉNOISE: Substitute 1 cup all-purpose flour, ⅓ cup cornstarch, and ¼ cup alkalized (Dutch process) cocoa powder for the flour and cornstarch.

GÉNOISE TRÈS VANILLÉE: Split a vanilla bean and use the point of a paring knife to scrape out the tiny seeds. Add the seeds to the egg, egg yolk, and sugar mixture for the plain génoise.

Classic Génoise

The aristocrat of the sponge and foam cake world, génoise has been a popular cake layer for about 300 years. When it's well made, it is delicate and delicious in both texture and flavor. I have strong opinions about the right way to prepare it and am not in favor of adding melted butter to the batter—it sometimes causes the batter to fall, especially when the cake is being made by an inexperienced baker. So I've added some extra yolks, which contribute all the tenderness and moisture that the butter would and also more stability to the foam, making it easier to produce a successful layer. Génoise is almost always used with a flavored syrup brushed on the cake to provide extra flavor and moisture. Recipes that use the génoise layer later in this chapter all have the syrup as a component.

1. Set a rack in the middle level of the oven and preheat to 350°F (180°C).

2. Half-fill a saucepan with water and bring it to a boil over medium heat. Lower the heat so the water is simmering.

3. Combine the eggs, egg yolks, vanilla, and salt in the bowl of an electric mixer. Whisk by hand to break up the eggs, then gradually whisk in the sugar in a stream. Place the bowl over the simmering water and gently whisk until the mixture is lukewarm, about 115°F (45°C).

4. Place the bowl on the mixer with the whisk attachment and whip on medium to high speed until the foam is more than tripled in volume and very much lightened in color, 3 to 4 minutes (figure a). The outside of the mixer bowl will feel cool to the touch.

5. While the egg mixture is whipping, stir the flour and cornstarch together and place a strainer or sifter near them.

6. Remove the bowl from the mixer and sift ⅓ of the flour mixture over the egg foam. Use a large rubber spatula to fold in the flour mixture, making sure you dig down to the bottom of the bowl every time you pass through, so that no lumps of flour

accumulate there (figure b). Add half of the remaining flour mixture, folding until it is absorbed, then end with the remaining flour, folding in as directed.

7. Pour the batter into the prepared pan (figure c) and smooth the top.

8. Tilt the pan so that the batter runs all the way to the top of the pan all around the inside—this helps the layer to bake straight and flat instead of doming in the center.

9. Bake the génoise until it is well risen and deep golden and feels firm when pressed in the center with a fingertip, 25 to 30 minutes.

10. Immediately unmold the cake onto a rack to cool. Cover the cake with another rack and invert so it cools rightside up.

STORAGE: Double wrap the layer in plastic wrap, keep at room temperature, and use within 24 hours. Or freeze the layer for up to a month. Defrost the layer before assembling the finished cake. Don't be concerned if some of the crust from the outside of the layer pulls away with the plastic wrap—it won't affect the outcome of the finished cake.

fig. b

fig. a

fig. c

a. The consistency of the egg foam in step 4 should be tripled in volume and light in color.

b. Use a large rubber spatula to fold in the flour mixture, reaching the bottom of the bowl in the process to avoid lumps (step 6).

c. Slowly pour the batter into your prepared pan (step 7).

Makes two 9-inch (23-cm) round layers

....

1¾ cups all-purpose flour
(spoon flour into a dry-measure cup and level off)

2 teaspoons baking powder

¼ teaspoon salt

12 tablespoons (1½ sticks) unsalted butter, softened

1 cup sugar

2 teaspoons vanilla extract

3 large eggs

⅓ cup milk or buttermilk

Two 9-inch (23-cm) round cake pans, 2 inches (5 cm) deep,
buttered and the bottoms lined with disks of
parchment or buttered wax paper cut to fit

Yellow Cake Layers

Here's a great new way to make a moist cake layer that's perfect for a birthday cake or just filling with whipped cream and a few berries. It's used in several recipes for finished cakes later in this chapter. In the past it was common to whip the egg whites and fold them into the batter for this type of cake. After experimenting with a few combinations of ingredients, I realized that it isn't at all necessary, but do remember to let the batter beat on the mixer for a few minutes after it's assembled—that part is critical.

1. Set a rack in the middle level of the oven and preheat to 350°F (180°C).

2. Combine the flour, baking powder, and salt. Stir well to mix.

3. Combine the butter, sugar, and vanilla in the bowl of an electric mixer. Beat with the paddle on medium speed until lightened in color and texture, 3 to 4 minutes.

4. Beat in the eggs, one at a time, mixing well after each addition.

5. Decrease the mixer speed to the lowest and add half of the flour mixture. Stop and scrape down the bowl and beater.

6. Beat in the milk and after it is absorbed, beat in the remaining flour mixture.

7. Stop and scrape the bowl and beater. Increase the speed to medium and beat the batter continuously for 3 minutes.

8. Divide the batter equally between the 2 prepared pans and smooth the tops. Bake the layers until they are well risen and deep golden, and feel firm when pressed in the center with a fingertip, 25 to 30 minutes.

9. Cool in the pans on racks for 5 minutes, then unmold, turn right side up again, and cool completely on racks.

....

STORAGE: Double wrap the layers in plastic wrap, keep them at room temperature, and use them within 24 hours. Or freeze the layers for up to a month. Defrost before assembling the finished cake. Don't be concerned if some of the crust from the outside of the layer pulls away with the plastic wrap—it won't affect the outcome of the finished cake.

Makes one 9-inch (23-cm) 2-layer cake, about 12 servings

....

1⅓ cups heavy whipping cream

¼ cup light corn syrup

1 pound (450 grams) semisweet chocolate,
melted and cooled

4 tablespoons unsalted butter, very soft

Two 9-inch (23-cm) Yellow Cake Layers,
baked and cooled (see opposite page)

Chocolate shavings for finishing

Perfect Birthday Cake

I've always loved the combination of yellow cake layers with a chocolate filing and frosting, and so this is my dream birthday cake. You can make the ganache filling while the layers are baking and assemble the cake as soon as they both cool off. If you prefer an all-chocolate cake, use the devil's food layers on page 253 instead.

1. For the filling, combine the cream and corn syrup in a medium saucepan and whisk well to mix. Place over low heat and bring to a gentle simmer—there will just be some bubbles around the inside edge of the pan. Pour the cream into a bowl and cool it to lukewarm, about 110°F (45°C).

2. Add the cooled cream to the melted chocolate and whisk until smooth. Distribute pieces of the butter all over the chocolate cream and whisk it in—make sure the butter is very soft or it won't incorporate smoothly.

3. Refrigerate the ganache until it thickens to a spreading consistency.

4. Put a dab of the cooled ganache on a cardboard or platter and place one of the cake layers on it. Spread the layer with half of the ganache. Invert the second layer onto the filling so the cake's smooth bottom is on top. Spread the outside of the cake smoothly with the remaining ganache.

5. Use a spatula to adhere some chocolate shavings to the side of the cake.

SERVING: Cut the cake at the table, and serve the first slice to the birthday boy or girl.

STORAGE: Keep under a cake dome at a cool room temperature.

Makes one 9-inch (23-cm) round cake, about 12 servings

MOISTENING SYRUP

½ cup water

⅓ cup sugar

¼ cup sweet raspberry liqueur, such as Chambord, or 1½ tablespoons clear framboise, raspberry eau-de-vie

RASPBERRY BUTTERCREAM

1 (10-ounce/275-gram) package frozen raspberries in syrup, thawed

4 large egg whites

1 cup sugar

12 ounces/350 grams (3 sticks) unsalted butter, very soft

2 tablespoons sweet raspberry liqueur, such as Chambord, or 1 tablespoon clear framboise, raspberry eau-de-vie

FILLING AND FINISHING

⅓ cup seedless raspberry preserves

1 cup sliced blanched almonds, lightly toasted

1 cup fresh raspberries, optional

1 Classic Génoise, page 240, baked and cooled

Raspberry Cream Cake

The delicate raspberry flavor of this cake is hard to beat, except perhaps by the incredible hot-pink color of the buttercream. It's a classic cake, based on a génoise, and requires a little time to prepare, but it's worth it for a special occasion, especially for a real raspberry lover. Normally framboise (French for raspberry) refers to clear brandy or eau-de-vie distilled from fermented raspberries. It's clear because it isn't aged like "brown" brandies such as Cognac, which derive their color from the wooden casks used for aging. Unfortunately, some manufacturers of raspberry liqueurs (alcohol, sugar, and raspberry juice) are now also calling their products framboise. All you need to know is that if it's clear it's the very strong brandy, and you use the lesser amount. If it's red or purple colored, it's the liqueur, and you use the larger amount in the recipe.

1. For the syrup, combine the water and sugar in a small saucepan and place over low heat. Bring to a boil, stirring occasionally. Pour the syrup into a bowl (or a container with a cover, if you are preparing it in advance) and let it cool. Stir in the liqueur or eau-de-vie. You may prepare the syrup up to 1 week in advance and keep it refrigerated.

2. For the buttercream, first cook the raspberry purée. Force the thawed raspberries through a strainer into a saucepan. Place over medium heat and bring to a boil. Reduce the heat to low and let the raspberries simmer gently until reduced to about ½ cup, about 20 minutes. Cool the purée to room temperature. You may also prepare it in advance and refrigerate it, covered, for several days. Return the purée to room temperature before using it.

3. Half-fill a saucepan with water and place it over medium heat. Bring the water to a boil, then reduce the heat so the water just bubbles gently. Combine the egg whites and sugar in the bowl of an electric mixer and stir them together with a whisk. Rest the bowl over the pan of water without touching the water and whisk gently until the egg whites are hot, about 140°F (60°C), and the sugar is dissolved. Place the bowl on the mixer with the whisk attachment and whip

on medium speed until the meringue has cooled to room temperature, about 5 minutes. This is a critical point—if the meringue is still warm when you add the butter, the butter will melt and you'll have a mess on your hands.

4. Once the meringue has cooled, switch to the paddle attachment. On low to medium speed, beat in the butter in 6 to 8 additions. The butter has to be very soft or else it will separate into lumps and make the buttercream grainy and not smooth. After you have beaten in the last of the butter, increase the speed to medium and beat the buttercream for 5 minutes. During this time it might separate—this is a normal stage in making buttercream. Just ignore it and continue beating until it is perfectly smooth. Beat in the raspberry purée and liqueur.

5. To assemble the cake, use a long serrated knife to split the cake horizontally into 3 equal layers. Put a dab of buttercream on a cake cardboard or a tart pan bottom the same size or slightly smaller than the cake and invert the top layer of the cake onto it. (The cake will be assembled so that the top of the cake layer is the very bottom, and what was the smooth flat bottom of the layer will be the top.)

6. Use a brush to moisten the layer with about ⅓ of the syrup. Spread half the preserves on the layer. They won't cover the entire layer evenly—just spread it around so that there is some in each wedge of cake. Spread a little less than ⅓ of the buttercream on the layer.

7. Place the second layer on top of the first and repeat with half of the syrup, the remaining preserves, and half of the buttercream.

8. Place the last layer on the cake so that what was the bottom of the cake is now on top. Moisten with the last of the syrup. Spread the remaining buttercream over the entire outside of the cake. Use the palm of one hand to press the sliced almonds against the side of the cake. Decorate the top with the optional raspberries.

....

SERVING: Place the cake on a platter. Cut wedges of the cake at the table, using a long, thin-bladed knife. The icing is sticky, so wipe the knife with a wet cloth every time you cut through the cake to avoid tracking crumbs into it.

STORAGE: Keep the cake at a cool room temperature, uncovered or under a cake dome. Cover and refrigerate leftovers, but bring them to room temperature before serving again.

VARIATIONS

Use a cocoa génoise layer instead of a plain one. You could also pour the glaze from the Triple Chocolate Cake, page 250, over the buttercream surface of the cake if you chill it first as in the chocolate cake recipe—cutting into the cake to reveal the brightly colored buttercream would make quite an impression.

LEMON CREAM CAKE: Omit the raspberry purée and raspberry liqueur and flavor the buttercream with ½ cup strained fresh lemon juice and 2 teaspoons vanilla extract. Add the lemon juice slowly in 4 to 6 additions to the buttercream, or it might separate. Keep the raspberry preserves on the layers with the lemon buttercream, or not, as you wish. Flavor the syrup with 2 tablespoons white rum or 2 teaspoons vanilla extract.

CHOCOLATE CREAM CAKE: Substitute 6 ounces (175 grams) bittersweet (not unsweetened) chocolate melted with 4 tablespoons milk or water and cooled. Add to the buttercream slowly, as described immediately above for the lemon juice.

CHOCOLATE AND VANILLA CAKE: Omit the raspberry purée and raspberry liqueur and flavor the buttercream with 1 tablespoon vanilla extract. Use a chocolate génoise layer (page 240) and flavor the syrup with 2 teaspoons vanilla extract. Streak the top of the cake with chocolate (see page 267) and press toasted sliced almonds against the sides of the cake.

Makes one 9-inch (23-cm) 2-layer cake, about 12 servings

....

WHIPPED CREAM CAKE BATTER

2 cups all-purpose flour (spoon flour into
a dry-measure cup and level off)

1½ cups sugar

3 teaspoons baking powder

½ teaspoon salt

1½ cups heavy whipping cream

2 teaspoons vanilla extract

3 large eggs

CARAMEL WHIPPED CREAM
FOR FILLING AND FINISHING

½ cup sugar

1 teaspoon water

3 cups heavy whipping cream

2 teaspoons vanilla extract

Two 9-inch (23-cm) round cake pans, 2 inches (5 cm)
deep, buttered, and the bottoms lined with disks of
parchment or buttered wax paper cut to fit

Whipped Cream Layer Cake

247

I've always been fascinated by this cake recipe, which derives some of its tenderness and lightness from the butterfat and air in whipped cream. One of the times I was fortunate to visit James Beard in the mid-1970s, he recounted that someone had just submitted a recipe to a cake contest he was judging that was "little more than some sweetened whipped cream, a couple of eggs, and some flour." He had loved the cake, but felt it lacked complexity (of preparation) and therefore could not be a prize-winning recipe. Well, I'm crazy about simplicity of preparation and I think this cake is a winner, hands down. It's often finished with plain sweetened whipped cream, which you can certainly do, but the caramel whipped cream here is a perfect counterpoint to the sweet tenderness of the cake.

1. Set a rack in the middle of the oven and preheat to 350°F (180°C).

2. For the cake batter, combine the flour, ¾ cup of the sugar, the baking powder, and salt in a bowl and stir well to mix.

3. Put the cream and vanilla in a large bowl and whisk by hand until thickened and stiff. Whisk in the eggs, one at a time. Whisk in the remaining ¾ cup sugar. Whisk in the flour mixture in 3 separate additions, whisking smooth after each addition.

4. Divide the batter between the 2 prepared pans and smooth the tops. Bake the layers until they are well risen, deep golden, and firm in the center when pressed with a fingertip, 30 to 35 minutes.

5. Cool the layers in the pans on racks for 5 minutes, unmold them, and cool them right side up on the racks.

6. While the layers are baking, prepare the caramel whipped cream. Combine the sugar and water in a heavy saucepan and stir well to mix. Put ½ cup of the cream in a second small saucepan. Place the first pan on medium heat and cook undisturbed until the sugar begins to melt and caramelize—you'll see a few wisps of smoke coming out of the sugar. Reduce the heat to low and stir occasionally so that the sugar melts and caramelizes evenly. Remove it from the heat when the caramel is still very pale (the sugar will continue to darken off the heat). Slide the pan with the cream onto the burner. As soon as the cream has some bubbles around the edge, add it to the caramel at arm's length, averting your face—the caramel will boil up and may splatter out of the pan. Pour the diluted caramel into a medium bowl and cool it to room temperature. Stir in the remaining 2½ cups cream and the vanilla and chill until you are ready to finish the cake (this can be made the day before).

7. To finish the cake, whip the cream mixture by hand or with an electric mixer until it holds a firm peak. Place one of the cake layers on a cake cardboard or platter and spread it with a little less than half the whipped cream. Invert the second layer onto the cream and spread the outside of the cake with the remaining whipped cream, swirling it with the point of the spatula.

....

SERVING: Serve the cake at the table, wiping the knife with a damp cloth between cuts to keep from tracking crumbs onto the outside of the cake.

STORAGE: Cover leftovers with plastic wrap and refrigerate or the whipped cream will melt.

Makes one 9-inch (23-cm) 2-layer cake, about 12 servings

··········

BANANA CAKE

2⅓ cups all-purpose flour
(spoon flour into a dry-measure cup and level off)

1 teaspoon baking powder

½ teaspoon baking soda

¼ teaspoon salt

12 tablespoons (1½ sticks) unsalted butter, softened

⅔ cup granulated sugar

⅓ cup dark brown sugar, firmly packed

1 teaspoon vanilla extract

3 large eggs

1 cup mashed bananas
(about 2 large or 3 smaller bananas)

⅔ cup milk

1 tablespoon dark rum

WHIPPED CREAM

2½ cups heavy whipping cream

¼ cup granulated sugar

1 tablespoon dark rum

2⅔ cups (one 7-ounce/200-gram package) sweetened shredded coconut

Two 9-inch (23-cm) round cake pans, 2 inches (5 cm) deep, buttered and the bottoms lined with disks of parchment or buttered wax paper cut to fit

VARIATIONS

Use the chocolate ganache from the Perfect Birthday Cake, page 243, the caramel whipped cream from the Whipped Cream Layer Cake, page 247, or the fluffy white icing from the Devil's Food Cake, page 253, to fill and cover the cake. I would only use the coconut with the last of these—the chocolate and caramel fillings are best alone on the banana cake.

248

Banana Rum Coconut
Layer Cake

Bananas make great cakes (and muffins, quick breads, tarts, and pie fillings). One thing about bananas, though, is they have to be ripe. Never use a banana for baking if it is not at least dotted with brown spots—or even darker—or your cake won't have any banana flavor. And always mash bananas with a fork or potato masher—don't throw them in the food processor—hand-mashed bananas impart a more vivid flavor to any batter or filling. I like whipped cream with this cake, but chocolate is also a natural with it, as well as fluffy egg-white icing. See the variations at the top of the recipe. If you like, sprinkle the layers with another tablespoon of rum when assembling the cake.

1. Set a rack in the middle of the oven and preheat to 350°F (180°C).

2. For the cake, combine the flour, baking powder, baking soda, and salt and mix well.

3. Combine the butter, granulated sugar, brown sugar, and vanilla in the bowl of an electric mixer. Beat with the paddle on medium speed until lightened in color and texture, 3 to 4 minutes.

4. Beat in the eggs, one at a time, beating well after each addition.

5. In another bowl, stir the bananas, milk, and rum together until blended.

6. Decrease the mixer speed to lowest and add ⅓ of the flour mixture. Stop and scrape down the bowl and beater. Beat in half of the banana mixture.

7. Repeat step 6, adding half the flour and the remaining banana mixture, then stop and scrape again. Beat in the remaining flour mixture.

8. Stop and scrape the bowl and paddle. Increase the speed to medium and beat the batter continuously for 3 minutes.

9. Divide the batter equally between the 2 prepared pans and smooth the tops. Bake the layers until they are well risen and deep golden, and feel firm when pressed in the center with a fingertip, 25 to 30 minutes.

10. Cool the layers in the pans on racks for 5 minutes, then unmold, turn right side up again, and cool completely on the racks.

11. When you are ready to assemble the cake, whip the cream with the sugar and rum. Place one of the cake layers on a platter or cardboard and spread it with a little less than half the whipped cream. Invert the second layer onto the cream so that the smooth bottom of the layer is on top.

12. Spread the remaining cream all over the outside of the cake and press the coconut against the side of the cake to adhere. Scatter more coconut over the top of the cake and use a spatula to gently sweep across the coconut to make it even.

··········

SERVING: Slide the cake to a platter and cut wedges at the table, using a sharp, thin-bladed knife.

STORAGE: Keep the cake refrigerated or the whipped cream might melt. Wrap with plastic wrap and refrigerate leftovers.

Makes one 9-inch (23-cm) 3-layer cake, about 16 servings

....

MOISTENING SYRUP

½ cup water

⅓ cup sugar

¼ cup dark rum or a sweet liqueur, such as an
orange- or raspberry- flavored one

RICH GANACHE FOR FILLING AND SPREADING

1¼ cups heavy whipping cream

¼ cup light corn syrup

18 ounces (500 grams) semisweet or bittersweet
(not unsweetened) chocolate (55% to 65%
cocoa solids), melted and cooled

4 tablespoons unsalted butter, very soft

1 Cocoa Génoise, page 240, baked and cooled

GANACHE GLAZE

¾ cup heavy whipping cream

2 tablespoons light corn syrup

6 ounces (175 grams) semisweet or bittersweet
(not unsweetened) chocolate (55% to 65%
cocoa solids), cut into ¼-inch (6-mm) pieces

Chocolate shavings for finishing the side of the cake

Triple Chocolate Cake

This combination of chocolate cake, chocolate filling, and chocolate glaze is a classic. And the best thing about it is that you can assemble it over a period of several days, or even bake and freeze the cake layers several weeks in advance. The cake is filled and glazed with two different forms of ganache, a chocolate cream made principally from chocolate and heavy cream. The ganache used for filling the cake and spreading over the outside contains more chocolate than the glaze. The former has to be able to hold its shape to fill and cover the cake, while the latter has to be liquid so it can be poured over the cake. This is a cake for a milestone birthday or other very special occasion. By the way, if you don't want to use alcohol to flavor the sugar syrup, use ⅓ cup of orange juice or 2 teaspoons of vanilla extract.

1. For the syrup, combine the water and sugar in a small saucepan and place over low heat. Bring to a boil, stirring occasionally. Pour the syrup into a heatproof bowl (or a container with a cover if you are preparing it in advance) and let it cool. Stir in the rum. You may prepare the syrup up to a week in advance and keep it refrigerated.

2. For the rich ganache filling, combine the cream and corn syrup in a saucepan and whisk well to mix. Place over medium heat and bring to a simmer, about 160°F (70°C). Remove the pan from the heat and allow the cream to cool to lukewarm, about 110°F (45°C). Pour the cream mixture over the melted chocolate and thoroughly whisk it in. Distribute dabs of the butter all over the surface of the ganache (the butter has to be very soft, roughly the consistency of mayonnaise, or it won't incorporate smoothly) and whisk them in. Cover the bowl with plastic wrap and let it stand in a cool place, not the refrigerator, until it is of spreading consistency. You may prepare the ganache up to 1 day in advance, but leave it at a cool room temperature—if you refrigerate it, it will be too stiff to spread.

3. To assemble the cake, use a long serrated knife to split the Cocoa Génoise into 3 horizontal layers. Put a dab of ganache on a cake cardboard or a tart pan bottom the same size or slightly smaller than the cake and invert the top layer of the cake onto it. (The cake will be assembled so that the top of the cake layer is the very bottom, and what was the smooth flat bottom of the layer will be the top.)

4. Use a brush to moisten the layer with about ⅓ of the syrup. Use a large rubber spatula to beat the rich ganache for a few seconds to loosen it. Spread about ⅓ of it on the layer, using a medium offset metal spatula. Place the middle layer on the ganache and moisten with half of the remaining syrup. Spread with half of the remaining ganache. Invert the last layer onto the ganache, so that its smooth bottom is on top. Moisten the cake layer with the remaining syrup. Smoothly spread the entire outside of the cake with the remaining ganache. Slide the cake to a cookie sheet or the back of a jelly-roll pan and refrigerate it, uncovered, while preparing the glaze.

5. For the glaze, combine the cream and corn syrup in a saucepan and whisk well to mix. Place over medium heat and bring to a simmer, about 160°F (70°C). Remove the pan from the heat and add the chocolate. Let the mixture stand for 2 minutes to melt the chocolate, then whisk smooth. Don't whisk

any more than necessary or the glaze will be riddled with bubbles. Pour the glaze into a small bowl and allow it to cool to about 90°F (30°C).

6. As soon as the glaze has cooled, remove the cake from the refrigerator and place it on a rack over a jelly-roll pan. Pour the glaze onto the top of the cake, in a spiral pattern beginning in the center and ending at the edge so that the last of the glaze drips down the side of the cake. Quickly use a medium offset metal spatula to smooth the top and side of the cake, picking up more glaze from the portion that dripped onto the pan if you need to patch the side. Let the cake stand until the glaze has set, which will be fairly quickly as the cake was chilled. Use a metal spatula to press the chocolate shavings against the side of the cake.

SERVING: Remove the cake from the rack to a platter. Cut wedges of the cake at the table, using a long, thin-bladed knife. The icing is sticky, so wipe the knife with a wet cloth every time you cut through the cake to avoid tracking crumbs into it.

STORAGE: Keep the cake at a cool room temperature, uncovered or under a cake dome. Attempting to cover the cake with plastic wrap or foil will mar the glaze.

VARIATIONS

Spread 3 tablespoons of seedless raspberry preserves or orange marmalade on each of the interior layers of the cake before spreading on the ganache. (It won't seem like enough, but adding too much preserves or marmalade to the cake will make it overly sweet.) Flavor the syrup with a similar flavored liqueur.

Makes one 9-inch (23-cm) 2-layer cake, about 12 servings

CAKE BATTER

1¾ cups all-purpose flour (spoon flour into a dry-measure cup and level off)

1 teaspoon baking soda

¼ teaspoon salt

8 tablespoons (1 stick) unsalted butter, softened

1¼ cups dark brown sugar, firmly packed

2 teaspoons vanilla extract

3 large eggs

3 ounces (75 grams) unsweetened chocolate, melted and cooled

¾ cup milk or buttermilk

FLUFFY WHITE ICING

4 large egg whites

Large pinch of salt

1. cups granulated sugar

½ cup light corn syrup

Two 9-inch (23-cm) round cake pans, 2 inches (5 cm) deep, buttered and the bottoms lined with disks of parchment or buttered wax paper cut to fit

VARIATIONS

Substitute 3 cups of heavy cream whipped with ⅓ cup sugar and 2 teaspoons vanilla extract for the icing. Sometimes I add a layer of raspberries or sliced banana to the filling. To do this, spread the bottom layer with about ¼ of the whipped cream, then top with 1 cup fresh raspberries or 1 large banana, sliced. Spread another quarter of the whipped cream over the fruit, and finish the cake as directed below.

Devil's Food Cake
with Fluffy White Icing

This is an American classic, and this is about the best recipe I've ever come up with for it. A devil's food cake should be very chocolatey and also very moist, two qualities that don't often coincide in this type of cake. Using brown sugar here makes all the difference—it makes the cake super moist and also boosts the chocolate flavor. The icing is easy to make as I've simplified the method. In the past, it was prepared like a cooked meringue, in which the egg whites are whipped and a hot sugar syrup is poured over them. The method here combines all the ingredients and heats them over boiling water—it's faster and more reliable.

1. Set a rack in the middle of the oven and preheat to 350°F (180°C).

2. Combine the flour, baking soda, and salt and stir well to mix.

3. Combine the butter, brown sugar, and vanilla in the bowl of an electric mixer. Beat with the paddle on medium speed until lightened in color and texture, 3 to 4 minutes.

4. Beat in the eggs, one at a time, beating well after each. Beat in the cooled chocolate.

5. Decrease the mixer speed to lowest and add ⅓ of the flour mixture. Stop and scrape down the bowl and paddle.

6. Beat in half the milk and stop and scrape the bowl and beater.

7. Repeat steps 5 and 6 adding half of the flour and the remaining milk. Stop and scrape. Beat in the remaining flour mixture.

8. Increase the speed to medium and beat the batter continuously for 3 minutes.

9. Divide the batter equally between the prepared pans and smooth the tops. Bake the layers until they are well risen and feel firm when pressed in the center with a fingertip, 25 to 30 minutes.

10. Cool in the pans on racks for 5 minutes, then unmold, turn right side up again. and cool completely on racks.

11. For the icing, half-fill a saucepan with water and bring to a boil over medium heat. Combine the egg whites, salt, sugar, and corn syrup in the bowl of an electric mixer and whisk by hand, just to mix together.

12. Regulate the heat under the pan of water so that it boils gently and place the bowl on the pan. Whisk gently just to keep the mixture moving until it is hot (about 130°F/55°C) and all the sugar is dissolved. Place the bowl on the mixer with the whisk and whip the icing until it has cooled and become white and fluffy.

13. Put one of the cake layers rightside up on a cake cardboard or platter. Spoon a little less than half the icing on the layer, using a medium offset metal spatula to spread it evenly and to the edge all around. Invert the second layer on the icing (the smooth bottom of the layer is now on top) and gently press the layer into the icing. Spread the entire outside of the cake with the remaining icing, using the point of the spatula to swirl it all over as opposed to spreading it straight and flat.

SERVING: Cut wedges of the cake at the table, using a long, thin-bladed knife. The icing is sticky, so wipe the knife with a wet cloth every time you cut through the cake to avoid tracking crumbs into it.

STORAGE: Keep the cake under a cake dome at room temperature—plastic wrap or foil will stick to the icing and pull it off the cake.

Makes one 9-inch (23-cm) cake, about 12 servings

1 Cocoa Génoise, page 240, baked, cooled, and cut horizontally into 3 layers (only 2 layers will be used to assemble the cake; wrap and freeze the extra layer for another use)

MOISTENING SYRUP

⅓ cup water

¼ cup sugar

2 teaspoons vanilla extract

MILK CHOCOLATE MOUSSE

3 cups heavy whipping cream

⅓ cup sugar

6 large egg yolks

12 ounces (345 grams) best-quality milk chocolate, cut into ¼-inch (6-mm) pieces

4 ounces (115 g) bittersweet (not unsweetened) chocolate, cut into ¼-inch pieces

FINISHING

1 cup heavy whipping cream

2 cups milk chocolate shavings (about 8 ounces/225 g)

One 9-inch (23-cm) springform pan

Milk Chocolate Mousse Cake

For this type of chocolate mousse cake, baked cake layers are filled with chocolate mousse. (For another kind of cake that is basically a baked mousse, see the Cinnamon-Scented Baked Chocolate Mousse Cake on page 257.) This recipe is adapted from one by my friend Loretta Sartori, who runs a baking education program in Melbourne, Australia. I love the fact that the mousse sets only from the addition of the chocolate, without the use of gelatin, making it so much more delicate. Sometimes Loretta adds some prunes that have been soaked in Armagnac to the bottom layer of mousse filling. Make sure to prepare this the day before you intend to serve it to give the mousse filling plenty of time to chill and set.

1. For the syrup, bring the water and sugar to a boil in a small saucepan. Pour the syrup into a small heatproof bowl. Let cool and then stir in the vanilla.

2. For the mousse, combine 1 cup of the cream and the sugar in a medium saucepan and whisk to blend. Place over low heat and bring to a full rolling boil. Meanwhile, set a fine strainer over a clean glass or stainless-steel bowl and place them near the burner where you

are heating the liquids. Whisk the egg yolks in a small bowl to break them up. When the liquid boils, whisk about ⅓ of it into the yolks. Return the liquid to a boil and, beginning to whisk before pouring, pour the yolk mixture into the boiling liquid. Whisk constantly until the cream thickens slightly— it won't be very thick—10 to 15 seconds after adding the yolks. Remove the pan from the heat, never ceasing to whisk. Quickly strain the sauce into the prepared bowl. Remove the strainer and set it over the saucepan. Whisk the sauce continuously for about 30 seconds to cool it down so the yolks don't scramble.

3. Combine the chocolates in a large bowl and pour the hot custard cream over them. Shake the bowl to make sure all the chocolate is submerged, then let it stand for 2 minutes. Whisk until smooth and set aside to cool to room temperature.

4. Whip the remaining 2 cups cream until it holds a soft peak. Set aside in the refrigerator.

5. After the chocolate cream has cooled, place one of the cake layers in the bottom of the prepared pan. Use a brush to sprinkle the layer with half of the syrup.

6. Remove the whipped cream from the refrigerator and rewhip by hand if it has

become liquid on the bottom. Quickly fold the cream into the cooled chocolate cream. Pour half the mousse on the cake layer in the pan and use a small offset spatula to spread it evenly. Top with the other cake layer without pressing it into the mousse, and sprinkle it with the remaining syrup. Top with the remaining mousse, and spread it evenly and smoothly. Refrigerate the cake overnight, covered, to set the mousse.

7. To unmold the cake, run a small knife between the dessert and the inside of the pan. Unbuckle the side of the pan and lift it off.

8. For finishing, whip the cream and spread it smoothly all over the outside of the cake. Use a metal spatula to press the chocolate shavings against the side of the cake. Sprinkle the remaining shavings all over the top and use the spatula to sweep them into an even layer.

9. If your springform pan has a flat base, use a large spatula to loosen the cake from the pan base and move it to a platter.

SERVING: Cut wedges of the cake at the table, using a long, thin-bladed knife. Wipe the knife with a wet cloth every time you cut through the cake to avoid tracking crumbs into it.

STORAGE: Keep the cake refrigerated until serving.

Makes one 9-inch (23-cm) cake, about 12 servings

....

8 ounces (225 grams/2 sticks) unsalted butter,
cut into 12 pieces

8 ounces (225 grams) bittersweet (60% to 70% cocoa
solids) chocolate, cut into ¼-inch (6-mm) pieces

1 cup sugar

5 large eggs

½ cup all-purpose flour
(spoon flour into a dry-measure cup and level off)

Pinch of salt

One 8-inch (20-cm) round cake pan, 2 inches (5 cm) deep,
buttered

Heirloom Chocolate Cake

My friend Loretta Keller, chef/owner of the popular San Francisco restaurant Coco 500, recently shared this recipe for an over-the-top rich chocolate cake. Loretta serves the cake with a little whipped cream.

1. Set a rack in the upper third of the oven and preheat to 400°F (200°C).

2. Bring a saucepan of water to a boil. Place the butter in a heatproof mixing bowl and place over the simmering water. Stir occasionally until melted. Remove from the heat, add the chocolate, and whisk smooth.

3. Whisk the sugar into the chocolate mixture. Add the eggs all at once and whisk until combined. Do not overmix. Whisk in the flour and salt.

4. Pour the batter into the prepared pan and smooth the top. Bake the cake for 25 minutes.

5. Cool the cake on a rack, then wrap and refrigerate it in the pan. (The cooled cake is too soft to serve without refrigeration.)

6. Remove the cake from the refrigerator about 2 hours before serving to allow it to come to room temperature. Invert the cake onto a cardboard or rack. Invert a platter onto the bottom of the cake and invert the whole stack of cardboard or rack, cake, and platter. Lift off the cardboard or rack.

SERVING: Serve slices of the cake with whipped cream.

STORAGE: Keep the cake or leftovers refrigerated for up to 3 days. Freeze for longer storage, defrost, and bring to room temperature before serving.

Makes one 8-inch (20-cm) cake, about 12 generous servings

¾ cup water

⅓ cup sugar

8 tablespoons (1 stick) unsalted butter, cut into 12 pieces

14 ounces (400 grams) bittersweet (not unsweetened) chocolate, cut into ¼-inch (6-mm) pieces

7 large eggs

1 teaspoon ground cinnamon

One 8-inch (20-cm) round cake pan, 2 inches (5 cm) deep, buttered, the bottom lined with a disk of parchment or buttered wax paper cut to fit, plus another larger pan, such as a small roasting pan, to hold the cake pan during baking

Cinnamon-Scented Baked
Chocolate Mousse Cake

When I have a bare minimum of time to make a dessert, I always make this, especially since I always have all the ingredients available. You can omit the cinnamon if you like, or add a couple of tablespoons of dark rum or orange liqueur to the batter along with the eggs. This type of cake is baked much like a cheesecake, in a pan of water to insulate the bottom of the cake from strong heat while it's baking. Lessening the bottom heat will result in a just-set custardy texture, rather than a risen, porous one. The pan you position under the cake pan should be at least as deep as the cake pan.

1. Set a rack in the middle level of the oven and preheat to 325°F (160°C).

2. Combine the water and sugar in a medium saucepan and place over medium heat. Bring to a boil, stirring occasionally to dissolve the sugar. At the boil, add the butter and stir occasionally until the butter is completely melted.

3. Remove the pan from the heat and add the cut-up chocolate. Swirl the pan to submerge all the chocolate in the hot liquid and let the mixture stand for 2 minutes, then whisk until smooth.

4. In a medium mixing bowl, whisk the eggs and cinnamon to break them up. Whisk in the chocolate mixture in a stream, taking care not to overmix, or the batter will be riddled with bubbles and not bake to a smooth texture.

5. Scrape the batter into the prepared cake pan and smooth the top. Place the cake pan in another larger pan and place it on the oven rack. Pour in warm water to come halfway up the side of the cake pan.

6. Bake the cake until it is set, slightly firm, and no longer liquid in the center, 55 to 60 minutes.

7. Remove the large pan from the oven, being careful not to tilt it, which would cause hot water to slosh out of it. Place it on the work surface and use oven mitts and a wide spatula to remove the cake pan from the hot water. Cool the cake in the pan on a rack.

SERVING: Unmold the cake onto a platter. If the cake has cooled for a long time it might be necessary to heat the bottom of the pan slightly to loosen it. Cut the cake into wedges and serve it with some sweetened whipped cream.

STORAGE: This cake is best just cooled to room temperature and not refrigerated before it is served. If you must prepare it prior to the day you intend to serve it, refrigerate it, wrapped in plastic, for up to 3 days, or freeze for up to a month. Unmold the cake and bring it to room temperature for several hours before serving.

Makes 7 individual cakes

....

5 ounces (150 grams) 70% bittersweet (not unsweetened) chocolate, cut into ¼-inch (6-mm) pieces

10 tablespoons (1¼ sticks) unsalted butter, cut into 10 pieces

3 large eggs

3 large egg yolks

⅔ cup sugar

½ cup all-purpose flour
(spoon flour into a dry-measure cup and level off)

1 batch Crème Anglaise, page 201

Seven 4-ounce aluminum foil molds or porcelain ramekins, buttered and floured

Molten Center Chocolate Cakes

This is a wonderful make-ahead dessert. As long as everything is ready in advance, you can make the cake batter and fill the molds hours ahead of time—just bake them immediately before you intend to serve them. Most people agree that these were invented by the 3-star French chef Michel Bras. But Bras's version calls for the cake batter to have a frozen chocolate truffle baked in the center, unlike these cakes, where the batter itself provides the flow of warm, semiliquid chocolate. These are easier to prepare and taste better, so maybe they're the 4-star version, which, by the way, come from my friend and Hong Kong restaurateur Jennifer Morris.

1. Set a rack in the middle of the oven and preheat to 400°F (200°C).

2. Half-fill a saucepan with water and bring it to a boil. Turn off the heat. Combine the chocolate and butter in a heatproof bowl and place over the hot water. Stir occasionally until melted.

3. Whisk the eggs and egg yolks together by hand in the bowl of an electric mixer. Whisk in the sugar, then the butter and chocolate mixture. Place the bowl on the mixer and mix on medium speed with the paddle for 1 minute. Remove the bowl and whisk in the flour by hand.

4. Fill the molds to within ¼ inch (6 mm) of the top. Bake for 10 to 12 minutes (unmold one to see how liquid it is), then unmold onto warm dessert plates.

....

SERVING: Serve with the sauce.

STORAGE: These are like soufflés—you have only one chance to enjoy them. You may prepare the batter and put it in the molds several hours before you intend to serve the cakes—keep them at a cool room temperature until it's time to bake them.

Makes about twenty-four 2- to 2½-inch (5- to 6-cm) cakes,
depending on the size of the molds used

....

1 cup (about 4 ounces/100 grams) hazelnuts, with skins,
finely ground in the food processor

1 cup sugar

½ cup flour
(spoon flour into a dry-measure cup and level off)

4 large egg whites

8 tablespoons (1 stick) unsalted butter,
melted and slightly cooled

Twenty-four 2- to 2½-inch (5- to 6-cm) square or oval pans
set on a jelly-roll pan, or one 24-cavity mini muffin pan,
buttered and floured

260

Individual French
Hazelnut Cakes

Sometimes these are called *financiers* or *friands*, and they're always very popular, especially with a cup of tea or coffee. They look really impressive when made in the traditional rectangular French molds, but mini muffin pans will work just as well.

1. Set a rack in the middle level of the oven and preheat to 375°F (190°C).

2. In a medium mixing bowl, combine the hazelnuts, sugar, and flour. Use a large rubber spatula to stir in the egg whites. Then fold in the butter.

3. Spoon the batter into the prepared pans, filling them about ⅔ full.

4. Bake the cakes until they are well risen, deep golden, and firm when pressed with a fingertip, about 15 minutes. Invert them to a rack to cool, then immediately turn them rightside up to cool completely.

SERVING: Serve these after dessert with coffee, or as part of an assortment of desserts.

STORAGE: Keep the cakes loosely covered with plastic wrap on the day they are made. Arrange them in a single layer in a tin or plastic container with a tight-fitting cover and refrigerate for longer storage. Bring to room temperature before serving.

....

VARIATION: Substitute blanched almonds for all or half of the hazelnuts.

Makes 18 cupcakes

GOLDEN CAKE BATTER

2¾ cups all-purpose flour
(spoon flour into a dry-measure cup and level off)

2½ teaspoons baking powder

¼ teaspoon salt

12 tablespoons (1½ sticks) unsalted butter, softened

1½ cups sugar

2 teaspoons vanilla extract

1 teaspoon finely grated lemon zest

6 large egg yolks

1 (8-ounce/225-gram) container sour cream

CONFECTIONERS' SUGAR ICING

8 tablespoons (1 stick) unsalted butter, softened

4 cups confectioners' sugar, sifted after measuring

5 tablespoons milk or orange juice

1 teaspoon vanilla extract

Two 12-cavity muffin pans with paper liners

Golden Cupcakes

Cupcakes can be a little dry—since they're so small, they're often overbaked. But sometimes the problem lies with the recipe itself, which doesn't produce a particularly moist cake. This recipe solves that problem completely—the baked cake is dense and moist, the perfect combination for a successful cupcake. Here I've used a typical cupcake icing—butter and confectioners' sugar beaten together with just enough liquid to help dissolve the sugar, so the icing isn't grainy textured. If you would like a creamier icing, try the buttercream recipe from Raspberry Cream Cake on page 244 (omit the liqueur if you are making the cupcakes for children). Or you may omit the raspberry purée and flavor the buttercream with 2 teaspoons vanilla extract or with lemon juice, as in the recipe's variation. You'll need only a half-batch of that buttercream to frost these cupcakes.

1. Set a rack in the middle of the oven and preheat to 350°F (180°C).

2. Combine the flour, baking powder, and salt and stir well to mix.

3. In the bowl of an electric mixer, combine the butter, sugar, vanilla, and lemon zest. Beat with the paddle on medium speed until lightened in color and texture, 3 to 4 minutes. Beat in the yolks, one at a time, beating well after each addition.

4. Decrease the mixer speed to lowest and add about half of the flour mixture. Stop and scrape down the bowl and paddle.

5. Beat in the sour cream, and after it is incorporated, beat in the remaining flour mixture. Stop and scrape the bowl and beater. Increase the speed to medium and beat the batter continuously for 3 minutes.

6. Divide the batter equally among the cavities in the pans, spooning it in. Bake the cupcakes until they are well risen and deep golden and feel firm when pressed in the center with a fingertip, about 20 minutes.

7. Cool in the pans on racks for 5 minutes, then unmold, turn right side up again, and cool completely on racks.

8. For the frosting, combine the butter and ½ cup of the confectioners' sugar in the bowl of an electric mixer. Beat with the paddle on low speed until smooth. Continue adding more confectioners' sugar, ½ cup at a time, until it is absorbed— the mixture will be dry at the end. Add the milk 1 tablespoon at a time, waiting until it is incorporated before adding more. Beat in the vanilla. Increase the mixer speed to medium and beat the icing for 5 minutes to make it light.

9. Use a small offset spatula to spread some of the icing on each cupcake. See Decorating Cakes & Cupcakes, page 267, for some ideas if you want to finish the cupcakes further.

SERVING: These need no accompaniment.

STORAGE: For advance preparation, wrap and freeze the cupcakes for up to a month. Keep iced cupcakes at room temperature—the paper cases and icing keep their surface from becoming dry, but they are best on the day they are baked.

CHOCOLATE CUPCAKE BATTER

2 cups sugar

1½ cups all-purpose flour
(spoon flour into a dry-measure cup and level off)

¾ teaspoon baking soda

½ teaspoon salt

4 ounces (100 grams) unsweetened chocolate,
cut into ¼-inch (6-mm) pieces

1 cup boiling water

8 tablespoons (1 stick) unsalted butter, melted

2 large eggs

1½ teaspoons vanilla extract

½ cup sour cream

CHOCOLATE FUDGE ICING

1 cup heavy whipping cream

¼ cup light corn syrup

12 ounces (350 grams) semisweet chocolate,
melted and cooled

6 tablespoons (¾ stick) unsalted butter, very soft

1 teaspoon vanilla extract

Two 12-cavity muffin pans with paper liners

Incredibly Moist Chocolate Cupcakes

These are the best chocolate cupcakes I have ever tasted. They never succumb to the great cupcake fault of dryness. If you want a really intense chocolate experience, use the chocolate icing recipe here. For a more traditional approach, try the Fluffy White Icing from the Devil's Food Cake recipe on page 253, or a confectioners' sugar–based cupcake icing like the one on page 261.

1. Set a rack in the middle of the oven and preheat to 350°F (180°C).

2. For the cupcake batter, stir the sugar, flour, baking soda, and salt together in a mixing bowl. Set aside.

3. Put the cut-up chocolate in a large mixing bowl and pour the boiling water over it. Let stand for 2 minutes, then whisk until smooth. Whisk in the butter, then the eggs, one at a time, whisking after each addition until smooth. Whisk in the vanilla and sour cream.

4. Whisk in the flour and sugar mixture in 3 separate additions, whisking until smooth after each.

5. Divide the batter equally among the cavities in the pans, spooning it in. Bake the cupcakes until they are well risen and deep golden, and feel firm when pressed in the center with a fingertip, about 20 minutes.

6. Cool in the pans on racks for 5 minutes, then unmold, turn right side up again, and cool completely on racks.

7. For the frosting, combine the cream and corn syrup in a small saucepan and whisk well to mix. Place over low heat and bring to a simmer. Remove from the heat and pour into a bowl to cool to lukewarm, about 110°F (45°C).

8. Add the cooled cream mixture to the melted chocolate and whisk until smooth. Distribute the butter in small pieces all over the top of the chocolate mixture, then whisk it in smoothly. Whisk in the vanilla. Cool the icing until it is firm enough to spread.

9. Use a small offset spatula to spread some of the icing on each cupcake. See Decorating Cakes & Cupcakes, page 267, for some ideas if you want to finish the cupcakes further.

SERVING: These need no accompaniment.

STORAGE: For advance preparation, wrap and freeze the cupcakes for up to a month. Keep iced cupcakes at room temperature—the paper cases and icing keep the surface from becoming dry, but they are best on the day they are baked.

263

....

16 ounces (450 grams) cream cheese, softened

1 cup sugar

2 teaspoons vanilla extract

4 large eggs, at room temperature

1 large egg white

1 (8-ounce/225-gram) container sour cream

Fresh strawberries, halved, and/or other berries for finishing

9 (4-ounce/100-gram) aluminum foil cups or porcelain ramekins, buttered and the bottoms lined with small disks of parchment paper, arranged on a jelly-roll pan

Individual New York
Cheesecakes

The quintessential New York cheesecake is creamy and light-textured, with just a hint of an acidic bite from the sour cream. The recipe is simple, and baking them in individual molds eliminates all the potential problems of a cracked surface, especially since these are served upside down after they're unmolded. I usually like to decorate the top with a single strawberry half or even a spoonful of a simple berry sauce—strained frozen raspberries cooked down with a little sugar and then cooled.

1. Set a rack in the middle of the oven and preheat to 300°F (150°C).

2. Combine the cream cheese, sugar, and vanilla in the bowl of an electric mixer. Beat with the paddle on medium speed until well mixed, about 1 minute.

3. Decrease the speed to low and beat in one of the eggs. After the egg is incorporated, stop and scrape down the bowl and paddle. Repeat for the remaining eggs and egg white, one at a time. Beat in the sour cream.

4. Spoon the batter into the prepared molds, filling them to within ¼ inch (6 mm) of the top.

5. Place the jelly-roll pan in the oven and add about 2 cups of warm water to surround the outside of the cheesecake molds. Bake until firm and slightly puffed, 25 to 30 minutes.

6. After the cheesecakes are ready, turn off the oven and leave the door ajar. If your oven has a strong spring that snaps the door shut, place a wide metal spatula or other non-flammable object perpendicular to the door to prop it open 4 to 6 inches. Leave the cheesecakes in the partially open oven for an additional 35 to 40 minutes.

7. Remove the pan from the oven and transfer the individual ramekins to a small flat pan or tray covered with parchment paper. Cover loosely with plastic wrap and refrigerate until well chilled.

....

SERVING: Use a wide spatula to transfer the cheesecakes to dessert plates. Decorate each with a strawberry half, cut side up.

STORAGE: Keep the cheesecakes refrigerated for up to 2 days before serving. Plate and bring them to room temperature for an hour or two before serving.

....

VARIATIONS

INDIVIDUAL CHOCOLATE CHEESECAKES: Add 6 ounces (175 grams) bittersweet (not unsweetened) chocolate melted with ¼ cup milk or water. Let cool slightly before adding to the egg mixture, before beating in the sour cream.

Some Ideas for Decorating
Cakes & Cupcakes

Here are a few quick and easy ways to dress up cakes and cupcakes to make them look more appealing and professionally finished. Always remember the prime rule of decorating any food: Keep it simple. Decorations that are elaborately arranged tend to make food look handled and less appealing, the opposite of what decoration is supposed to accomplish. Whatever decoration you choose from the lists below, make sure its flavor is appropriate to the cake it is decorating. Decorate a cake filled with raspberry buttercream with raspberries, not strawberries. Use chocolate shavings on a chocolate cake, not a lemon one. Cake and cupcake decorations don't only have to be in good taste, they also have to taste good.

CAKES

TOASTED SLICED ALMONDS: These can be used pretty much universally, except on an all-chocolate cake. Almonds add a pleasant note of both flavor and texture, and their golden appearance is pretty. You can vary the presentation by crushing the sliced almonds more finely, or grinding them finely in the food processor, both of which offer a change from the more craggy appearance of sliced almonds. Try to find sliced almonds that are blanched (skinless), which look more tailored

than unblanched ones. To toast, spread the sliced almonds out on a jelly-roll or small roasting pan and bake them at 350°F (180°C), stirring every few minutes so they toast evenly, until they are light golden, about 10 minutes. Remove them from the hot pan to cool on another pan, or even just directly on the work surface. Don't toast nut meats destined to decorate cakes in an open pan over direct heat—they will color unevenly. A very light dusting of confectioners' sugar looks very tailored and nice over sliced, crushed, or ground almonds or other nuts. For any nut meats, you can use the palm of one hand to press them against the side of the cake. For the top, cover generously, then use a long metal spatula to sweep away the excess and make the top of the cake flat and even.

OTHER TOASTED NUTS: Walnuts or pecans, toasted and finely chopped, but not ground, will work just as well as sliced almonds.

CARAMEL "GOLD": Have a buttered cookie sheet ready and caramelize 1 cup of sugar according to the directions on page 247. Keep the caramel a fairly light amber color, removing it from the heat when it is very light and letting it finish coloring from the heat of the pan. The caramel will also cool and thicken a little. Pour the caramel onto the buttered pan and let it harden. When it is

fig. a

completely hard, lift it from the pan and break it into ½- to 1-inch (1- to 2½-cm) pieces. Pulse the pieces of caramel in the food processor to make tiny golden nuggets—just stop before the caramel becomes dust. These look appealing sprinkled over light- or dark-colored icing. But remember you are sprinkling pure sugar onto your cake so use restraint.

CHOCOLATE SHAVINGS: I like to use milk or white chocolate for shavings. They are softer than either semisweet or bittersweet chocolate and make larger, more appealing shavings. It's best to have some chocolate cut from a large bar, so that it's 1 to 2 inches (2½ to 5 cm) thick. Trying to shave a thin 4-ounce (100-gram) chocolate bar will cause it to break apart before you have very many shavings at all. Place the block of chocolate on a jelly-roll pan and hold the chocolate with a paper towel, shielding your hand to prevent it from melting the chocolate on contact. Use a melon ball scoop and shave toward you, with the scoop at a 45-degree angle to the chocolate. Shave all over the surface, rather than just on one spot, or you will make a deep trough in the chocolate that will eventually cause it to break apart. Don't attempt to press chocolate shavings against the side of a cake with your hands, as the chocolate will melt. Use a long spatula to press them on. For the top, proceed as for sliced almonds.

BERRIES: Raspberries or strawberries make a fine decoration for a cake flavored or filled with them. Pick over raspberries, but don't wash them, or they will leak water and juice onto the surface of the cake. My favorite way to use strawberries for decorating a cake is to rinse the berries, then cut them straight through from hull to point, leaving the hull attached, and push the 2 halves apart slightly into a V shape. Place the berries on their sides, so that you see the shiny interior of the strawberry surmounted by its little green frill.

CHOCOLATE STREAKING: Streaks or swirls of melted chocolate are pretty on a cake, especially if the chocolate you're using contrasts with the color of the cake beneath. Cut a couple of ounces of dark or white chocolate and melt it over some hot water or in the microwave. Let the chocolate cool for 5 to 10 minutes (you don't want it to melt the frosting under it) and stir in ½ teaspoon of mild vegetable oil—this will keep the chocolate from hardening too much after it sets. Spoon the chocolate into a heavy non-pleated plastic bag and force it into one corner. Twist the bag behind the chocolate so that it comes out in only one direction. Snip the corner of the bag with sharp scissors, making as tiny a hole as possible. Hold the bag perpendicular to the cake (start off of the cake, but near it) and use gentle pressure to push the chocolate through the opening. For

fig. b

streaks, move back and forth over the cake, always turning in the other direction when you're off the surface of the cake to avoid messy edges (figure a). For swirls, move the bag in large arcs over the cake to make overlapping curves.

GOLF LEAVES: Specialty stores (see Sources on page 312) sell small packages of tissue-thin sheets of edible gold leaf (sometimes torn into flakes or sprinkles). A small amount of lends a lovely touch to desserts and creates an especially nice contrast with chocolate, but don't go overboard or your efforts may look garish. To be edible, gold leaf must be 23-karat or above. Lower karat counts have too much copper added to be edible.

....

CUPCAKES

ICING VARIATIONS: Each of the cupcake recipes in this chapter has an icing recipe and suggestions for more. Any of the other icings in this chapter work well with cupcakes except the whipped-cream icing because you want to keep cupcakes at room temperature when you serve them, and whipped cream has a tendency to break down fairly quickly. The standard way to finish the top of a cupcake is to mound the icing on and swirl it from the top center outward with the point of a small metal spatula (figure b). A wide-bladed table knife works just as well.

fig. c

COLORED ICINGS: Using food coloring is entirely acceptable on cupcakes. I like to use liquid colors, because the amount of color added is so much easier to control. Pastel colors are fine, and you can mix a bit of red and yellow to get orange for Halloween, if you need to. But if you need a dark color, then paste colors, available at cake-decorating supply stores and Web sites, are the only way to achieve it. If you are planning on tinting your cupcake icing a dark color, I recommend isolating a small amount of icing for just 1 cupcake and tinting that first. Take a good hard look at what you've done and then decide if you want dozens of cupcakes all lined up in such an intense color.

CHOCOLATE SHAVINGS look good on cupcakes (figure c), as does chocolate streaking. For the latter, line the cupcakes in a row, then make the streaks perpendicular to the row. You can cover your work surface with a sheet of wax paper to make cleaning up a little easier.

NONPAREILS are small sugar balls that are available in white or a variety of colors. The term "nonpareils" is also used to indicate a kind of candy: chocolate disks dipped in nonpareils on one side. Multicolored nonpareils, chocolate, or multicolored chocolate shot (also called "sprinkles" or "jimmies"), and colored crystal sugar all look fine on cupcakes, a not-so-serious food. A few pinches are all you need.

272 Cocoa Nib Brownies

274 Sour Cream Brownies

275 Raisin Pecan Spice Bars

276 Caramel Crumb Bars

277 Coconut Pecan Chocolate Chunk Bars

279 Three-Way Gingersnaps

280 Honey Peanut Wafers

282 Espresso Walnut Meringues

285 Butterscotch Chocolate Chunk Cookies

286 Lemon Poppy Seed Drops

288 Lemon & Almond Tuiles

291 Cappuccino Thumbprint Cookies

292 Macadamia Shortbreads

293 New Orleans Praline Disks

295 Melting Moments

296 Spicy Hazelnut Biscotti

297 Cornmeal & Pine Nut Biscotti

298 Biscotti Regina

301 Sicilian Fig Bars

302 Pine Nut Macaroons

304 Tart Lime Wafers

306 Blackberry Jam Sandwiches with Lemon Icing

308 Chocolate Sandwich Cookies with Milk Chocolate Filling

309 Raspberry Linzer Disks

310 Viennese Punch Cookies

8.

Cookies, Bars, & Biscotti

Cookies are so universally loved that the word itself is used as a term of endearment. Aside from the fact that you get multiples—not easy to manage with other types of baked treats—cookies are fast and easy to prepare. Many recipes just need to have the ingredients stirred together and the resulting dough dropped from a spoon onto a cookie sheet, or spread in a pan to be cut into bars after baking. Of course, that's not the whole cookie story—some of these recipes do have more steps, such as rolling out the dough, baking the resulting cookies, and then sandwiching them with a filling, but on the whole cookie baking is a fun, fast endeavor.

ROLLING COOKIE DOUGH & INCORPORATING SCRAPS

a. Place scraps under the dough you are rolling.

b. Roll the dough as usual—remember to keep the dough pieces small.

c. Cut the cookies close together to avoid making too many scraps.

d. Use a metal spatula to carefully lift the cut rounds of dough.

fig. a

270 Cookies are easy to serve and need no accompaniments and little last-minute finishing. That's why there are no serving instructions with most of these recipes.

Minimal mixing is required for cookie doughs and batters. Cookies that rise a lot while baking and fall again have been overbeaten, especially if the initial mixture calls for beating butter and sugar together. Using a large rubber spatula to incorporate flour by hand when it is added last makes for more tender cookies. Most cookies are baked on cookie sheets, which may be lined with parchment, plain or nonstick foil, or silicone mats. In order to determine whether cookies and biscotti are finished baking, use a fingertip to test for firmness. Test an individual cookie by turning it over—if the bottom is a pale golden color, they are baked.

Here are the types of cookies you'll find in this chapter.

Bar Cookies: A dough or batter is spread or pressed into a jelly-roll or other square or rect-angular pan, sometimes covered with a topping, to make a thin cake that's cut into squares or rectangles after baking. Bar cookies are a great make-ahead choice, since you can freeze the baked cake before cutting into it. To pan batters for bar cookies, pour or distribute the batter over as much of the pan surface as possible, then use a large offset spatula to finish the job.

Drop Cookies: These are made from a dough or batter spooned or piped onto a baking pan. The cookies usually flatten out and spread during baking—making them the simplest and easiest of all cookies to prepare. Use a small ice-cream scoop if you want to form uniform drop cookies.

Piped Cookies: These are either extruded from a cookie press or piped out of a pastry bag. For a cookie press, push the dough into the cylinder and then press the handle once for each cookie. This pushes the dough down and through the die and results in a uniform quantity of dough every time. Firm doughs are the easiest to pipe with a pastry bag, because they hold their shape. Always use a nylon and plastic-coated canvas bag, and use the size and type of tube specified in the recipe. First insert the tube into the bag, then fold back about ⅓ of the top of the bag and hold it in your nonfavored hand (your left hand if you are right-handed) under the cuff you've just made. Using your favored hand, fill the bag no more than half full.

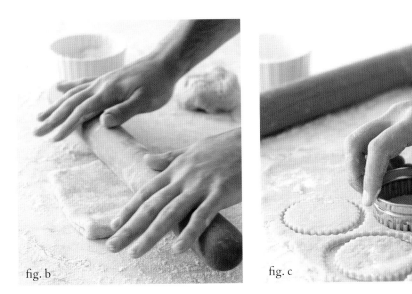

fig. b

fig. c

fig. d

To pipe, hold the bag in your favored hand, only at the top. Use the index finger of your other hand against the side of the bag to steady it. Never grip a pastry bag with both hands. For half-spheres, hold the bag perpendicular to the pan with the tip about an inch above the surface, squeeze out the desired amount of batter, then pull the bag away straight and up. To pipe fingers, hold the bag at a 45-degree angle and touch the tip to the surface, then squeeze gently as you pull the tube toward you. Lift the bag away back over the finger you just made to avoid creating a "tail." Make pipe shells or teardrops the same way.

Biscotti: Biscotti dough is shaped into logs and flattened before baking. After baking and cooling, the logs are sliced and rebaked, making the biscotti crisp. This is also the Italian word for cookies in general.

Refrigerator Cookies: These are the "icebox" cookies of the past. The dough is formed into a cylinder and chilled. Afterward, the cylinder of dough is sliced and the cookies are baked. These are another great make-ahead type of cookie.

Rolled Cookies: A dough, often chilled first, is rolled out and cut with round or patterned cutters.

A few rules make this easier: Always roll small pieces of dough, leaving the rest refrigerated until needed. (Large pieces of dough roll out easily enough, but might become too soft while you are cutting out the cookies.) Incorporate any scraps after rolling the first piece of dough under the second and you won't be left with a big pile of scraps too soft to reroll when you're finished. Cookie dough tends to be soft, so press gently with the rolling pin, moving the dough and adding pinches of flour under and on it, as in rolling pastry dough, page 197.

Molded Cookies: Molded cookies are made into a specific shape (which they retain) by hand before being baked.

Filled Cookies: Filled cookies are made from a rolled-out dough wrapped around a filling before being baked.

Sandwich Cookies: Cookie bases, usually cut from a rolled dough, are put together in pairs with a filling in between.

Whatever type of cookie you choose to prepare will be greeted with appreciation and boundless enthusiasm.

Makes one 9 x 13 x 2-inch (23 x 33 x 5-cm) pan of brownies, about twenty-four 2-inch (5-cm) squares

....

8 ounces (2 sticks/225 grams) unsalted butter, cut into 12 pieces

9 ounces (250 grams) bittersweet (not unsweetened) chocolate, cut into ¼-inch (6-mm) pieces

1¼ cups dark brown sugar, firmly packed

4 large eggs

½ teaspoon salt

¾ cup granulated sugar

1 tablespoon vanilla extract

1 ¼ cups all-purpose flour
(spoon flour into a dry-measure cup and level off)

½ cup cocoa nibs, see Sources, page 312

One 9 x 13 x 2-inch (23 x 33 x 5-cm) pan lined fully (bottom and sides) with buttered foil

Cocoa Nib Brownies

Cocoa nibs are a relatively new baking ingredient. Nibs are cocoa beans that have gone through fermenting, roasting, crushing, and skinning processes, and then are usually used to make chocolate. Pastry chefs began procuring them from chocolate manufacturers and adding them to cookie dough in the way you might add chopped nuts, except cocoa nibs, of course, have a bittersweet chocolate flavor. Now cocoa nibs are fairly easy to find under several brands. Nibs are unsweetened, so they have to be used somewhat sparingly to avoid imparting a bitter, astringent flavor. They're the perfect counterpoint to this fudgy brownie recipe, adding a little texture and a bit of balance to the batter's natural sweetness. Mixing the batter by adding the liquid to the brown sugar prevents having any lumps of brown sugar in the brownies.

1. Set a rack in the middle level of the oven and preheat to 350°F (180°C).

2. Put the cut-up butter into a medium saucepan and place over medium heat. Let the butter melt, stirring 2 to 3 times, then allow it to bubble for about 10 seconds. Remove the pan from the heat and add the chocolate. Gently shake the pan to submerge the chocolate in the hot butter and set aside for a few minutes so that the chocolate melts. Use a small whisk to mix smooth.

3. Place the brown sugar in the bowl of an electric mixer. Beat in 1 egg on lowest speed using the paddle attachment. Add the remaining eggs, one at a time, beating smooth after each. Add the salt, sugar, and vanilla and beat smooth.

4. Remove the bowl from the mixer and use a large rubber spatula to mix in the chocolate and butter mixture. Mix in the flour, followed by ¼ cup of the cocoa nibs.

5. Scrape the batter into the prepared pan and smooth the top. Scatter the remaining ¼ cup cocoa nibs on the batter.

6. Bake the brownies until they are firm, but still very moist in the center, about 30 minutes.

7. Cool the brownies in the pan on a rack.

8. Wrap the pan in plastic wrap and refrigerate the brownies for several hours or overnight before attempting to cut them—they are very moist. You might need to heat the bottom of the pan briefly over low heat to unmold the brownies, then invert them to a cutting board and peel away the foil.

....

SERVING: Use a sharp serrated knife to trim the edges and cut the brownies into 2-inch (5-cm) squares. Serve them alone or topped with ice cream.

STORAGE: The best way to keep brownies is the same as a baked cake, whole and unsliced, rather than as individual servings. Refrigerate the wrapped slab for a few days or freeze it for up to one month. If it's not practical to keep them in the pan they were baked in, wrap them with some stiff cardboard underneath. Cut the brownies then defrost them, loosely covered, before serving.

Makes one 9 x 13 x 2-inch (23 x 33 x 5-cm) pan of brownies, about twenty-four 2-inch (5-cm) squares

....

6 ounces (1½ sticks/175 grams) unsalted butter, cut into 12 pieces

7 ounces (200 grams) bittersweet (not unsweetened) chocolate, cut into ¼-inch (6-mm) pieces

1¾ cups dark brown sugar, firmly packed

4 large eggs

½ cup sour cream

½ teaspoon salt

3 teaspoons vanilla extract

1½ cups all-purpose flour
(spoon flour into a dry-measure cup and level off)

2 cups (about 8 ounces/225 grams) walnut pieces, coarsely chopped

One 9 x 13 x 2-inch (23 x 33 x 5-cm) pan lined fully (bottom and sides) with buttered foil

Sour Cream Brownies

The presence of sour cream in this brownie batter makes them extra moist and helps to cut back a little on the sweetness. I like to make these with walnuts, but pecans are just as good.

1. Set a rack in the middle of the oven and preheat to 350°F (180°C). Put the cut-up butter in a medium saucepan and place over medium heat. Let the butter melt, stirring 2 to 3 times, then allow it to bubble for about 10 seconds. Remove the pan from the heat and add the chocolate. Gently shake the pan to submerge the chocolate in the hot butter and set aside for a few minutes so that the chocolate melts. Use a small whisk to mix until smooth.

2. Place the brown sugar in the bowl of an electric mixer. Beat in 1 egg on the lowest speed using the paddle attachment. Add the remaining eggs, one at a time, beating smooth after each. Add the sour cream, salt, and vanilla and beat smooth.

3. Remove the bowl from the mixer and use a large rubber spatula to mix in the chocolate and butter mixture. Mix in the flour, followed by 1½ cups of the walnuts.

4. Scrape the batter into the prepared pan and smooth the top. Scatter the remaining walnuts on the batter.

5. Bake the brownies until they are firm, but still very moist in the center, about 30 minutes.

6. Cool the brownies in the pan on a rack.

7. Wrap the pan in plastic wrap and refrigerate the brownies for several hours or overnight before attempting to cut them—they are very moist. You might need to heat the bottom of the pan briefly over low heat to unmold the brownies, then invert them onto a cutting board and peel away the foil.

....

SERVING: Use a sharp serrated knife to trim the edges and cut the brownies into 2-inch (5-cm) squares. Serve them alone or topped with ice cream.

STORAGE: The best way to keep brownies is the same as a baked cake, unsliced, rather than as individual servings. Refrigerate the wrapped slab for a few days or freeze it for up to a month. If it's not practical to keep them in the pan they were baked in, wrap them with some stiff cardboard underneath. Cut the brownies, then defrost them, loosely covered, before serving.

Makes one 9 x 13 x 2-inch (23 x 33 x 5-cm) pan of cookies, about twenty-four 2-inch (5-cm) squares

....

1½ cups all-purpose flour
(spoon flour into a dry-measure cup and level off)

¾ teaspoon baking soda

½ teaspoon salt

1 teaspoon ground cinnamon

¼ teaspoon freshly grated nutmeg

¼ teaspoon ground cloves

6 tablespoons (¾ stick) unsalted butter, softened

1½ cups dark brown sugar, firmly packed

¼ cup granulated sugar

2 large eggs

⅓ cup mild-flavored molasses

⅓ cup sour cream

1 cup dark raisins

1 cup (about 4 ounces/100 grams) pecan pieces, coarsely chopped

One 9 x 13 x 2-inch pan, buttered and lined fully (bottom and sides) with buttered parchment or foil

Raisin Pecan Spice Bars

The best word to describe these bars is homey—they taste like someone's grandmother made them. Tender, spiced, and full of old-fashioned molasses flavor, these are perfect for the holidays and throughout the cold weather. Feel free to adjust the raisins and pecans—you could add some golden raisins as part of the amount, or use all raisins or all pecans, depending on what you like.

1. Set a rack in the lowest level of the oven and preheat to 350°F (180°C).

2. Mix the flour with the baking soda, salt, cinnamon, nutmeg, and cloves and set aside.

3. Put the butter, brown sugar, and granulated sugar in the bowl of an electric mixer. Beat with the paddle on medium speed until lightened, 2 to 3 minutes.

4. Beat in the eggs, one at a time, beating smooth after each addition.

5. Decrease the speed to low and beat in half of the flour mixture. Stop and scrape down the bowl and paddle.

6. Beat in the molasses and sour cream, then the remaining flour mixture. Remove the bowl from the mixer and use a large rubber spatula to give a final mixing to the batter. Fold in the raisins and pecans.

7. Spread the batter in the prepared pan and smooth the top. Bake until well risen and firm when pressed with a fingertip, 20 to 25 minutes.

8. Cool in the pan on a rack.

9. Invert onto a cutting board and peel away the foil. Trim the edges and use a long serrated knife to cut into 2-inch (5-cm) squares.

....

STORAGE: Keep the bars between sheets of wax paper in a tin or plastic container with a tight-fitting lid. To freeze, don't cut the bars apart, but wrap and freeze the entire baked cake, then cut it into squares after you remove it from the freezer.

Makes one 9 x 13 x 2-inch (23 x 33 x 5-cm) pan of cookies, about twenty-four 2-inch (5-cm) squares

....

DOUGH

8 ounces (2 sticks/225 grams) unsalted butter, softened

½ cup sugar

¼ teaspoon salt

1 teaspoon vanilla extract

2½ cups all-purpose flour
(spoon flour into a dry-measure cup and level off)

FILLING

4 tablespoons unsalted butter

1 tablespoon light corn syrup

¼ cup dark brown sugar, firmly packed

1 (14-ounce) can sweetened, condensed milk

One 9 x 13 x 2-inch (23 x 33 x 5-cm) pan, buttered and lined fully (bottom and sides) with buttered parchment or foil

Caramel Crumb Bars

If I had to choose one cookie above all others, it would be this one. The buttery dough and creamy caramel filling complement each other perfectly.

1. Set a rack in the lowest level of the oven and preheat to 350°F (180°C).

2. For the dough, beat the butter with the sugar and salt in an electric mixer with the paddle attachment on medium speed until soft and light, 2 to 3 minutes. Add the vanilla.

3. On the lowest speed, beat in 2¼ cups of the flour, scraping the bowl and paddle with a rubber spatula and continuing to mix just until the dough is smooth, and the flour has been absorbed.

4. Remove the bowl from the mixer and scrape ¾ of the dough into the prepared pan. Use the palm of your hand to press the dough down evenly, without compressing it too much. Chill the dough-lined pan. Work the remaining ¼ cup flour into the remaining dough with your fingertips, so that it forms ⅛- to ¼-inch (3- to 6-mm) crumbs. Set aside at room temperature.

5. For the filling, in a medium saucepan bring the butter, corn syrup, brown sugar, and condensed milk to a simmer, stirring occasionally. Allow the mixture to boil gently, stirring often, until it starts to thicken and darken slightly, about 10 minutes. Pour into a stainless-steel bowl to cool for 5 minutes.

6. Remove the dough-lined pan from the refrigerator and scrape the cooled filling onto the dough, using a small offset spatula to spread the filling evenly on the dough. Scatter the crumb mixture on the filling.

7. Bake until the filling is bubbling gently and is a deep caramel color and the dough and crumb topping are baked through, about 30 minutes.

8. Cool in the pan on a rack until lukewarm, 15 to 20 minutes. Lift the slab of baked dough out of the pan and onto a cutting board before it has cooled completely. Cut the slab into 2-inch (5-cm) squares.

....

STORAGE: Keep these at room temperature if you are serving them within a day. If not, wrap and freeze them and make sure to defrost and bring to room temperature before serving.

Makes one 9 x 13 x 2-inch (23 x 33 x 5-cm) pan of cookies, about twenty-four 2-inch (5-cm) squares

....

DOUGH

1½ cups all-purpose flour
(spoon flour into a dry-measure cup and level off)

½ teaspoon baking powder

¼ teaspoon salt

6 ounces (1½ sticks/175 grams) unsalted butter, softened

½ cup sugar

TOPPING

1¼ cups light brown sugar, firmly packed

4 large eggs

⅔ cup granulated sugar

2 teaspoons vanilla extract

2 ⅔ cups (7-ounce/200-gram package) sweetened shredded coconut

2 cups (about 8 ounces/225 grams) pecan pieces, coarsely chopped

12 ounces (350 grams) bittersweet (not unsweetened) chocolate, cut into ¼- to ½-inch (6-mm to 1-cm) pieces

One 9 x 13 x 2-inch (23 x 33 x 5-cm) pan, buttered and lined fully (bottom and sides) with buttered parchment or foil

---

Coconut Pecan Chocolate Chunk Bars

Coconut in all forms is a favorite of mine, and these bars combine it with a buttery pastry base, pecans, and bittersweet chocolate chunks. Of course you can use chocolate chips, but the chocolate chunks allow you to use a much better quality chocolate in the topping.

1. Set a rack in the lowest level of the oven and preheat to 350°F (180°C).

2. For the dough, stir together the flour, baking powder, and salt and set aside.

3. Beat the butter with the sugar in an electric mixer with the paddle attachment on medium speed until soft and light, 2 to 3 minutes.

4. On the lowest speed, beat in the flour mixture, scraping down the bowl and paddle with a rubber spatula and continuing to mix until the dough is smooth.

5. Remove the bowl from the mixer and scrape into the prepared pan. Press the dough down evenly, without compressing it too much, with the palm of your hand. Bake the dough until it is puffed and set and beginning to color, about 15 minutes.

6. Set the pan on a rack. Meanwhile, prepare the topping. Place the brown sugar in a large bowl and use a large rubber spatula to work in the eggs, one at a time, stirring until smooth after each. Stir in the granulated sugar and vanilla, then fold in the coconut and pecans.

7. Use a small strainer to sift away any dust formed by chopping the chocolate, and fold the chocolate chunks into the topping.

8. Scrape the topping onto the prebaked dough, using a small offset spatula to spread the topping evenly over the top.

9. Bake until the filling is set and nicely colored, 20 to 25 minutes.

10. Cool in the pan on a rack. Lift the slab of baked dough out of the pan and onto a cutting board before it has cooled completely. Cut the slab into 2-inch (5-cm) squares.

....

STORAGE: Keep these at room temperature if you are serving them within a day. If not, wrap and freeze them and make sure to defrost and bring to room temperature before serving.

2 or 3 cookie sheets or jelly-roll pans lined
with parchment or foil

2 cups all-purpose flour
(spoon flour into a dry-measure cup and level off)

3 teaspoons ground ginger

2 teaspoons baking soda

½ teaspoon salt

12 tablespoons (1½ sticks) unsalted butter, softened

1 cup sugar, plus more for rolling the cookies
before baking

1 large egg

1 tablespoon grated fresh ginger (see *Note* on page 104)

2 tablespoons finely chopped crystallized ginger

2 tablespoons honey

Three-Way Gingersnaps

Gingersnaps can sometimes lack a really gingery flavor, so this recipe solves the problem completely: It has ground ginger, grated fresh ginger, and finely chopped crystallized ginger in the dough. I like to bake these at a fairly low temperature so they are really crisp—it adds immeasurably to the enjoyment of this cookie. Thanks to my friend Kyra Effren, the ultimate cookie baker, for sharing her recipe upon which this is based.

1. Set racks in the upper and lower thirds of the oven and preheat to 325°F (160°C).

2. Mix the flour with the ground ginger, baking soda, and salt.

3. Combine the butter and sugar in the bowl of an electric mixer and beat with the paddle on medium speed until lightened, about 3 minutes. Beat in the egg and continue beating until smooth.

4. Decrease the mixer speed to low and beat in half of the flour mixture. Stop and scrape down the bowl and paddle.

5. Beat in the grated ginger, the crystallized ginger, and the honey. After they are incorporated, beat in the remaining flour mixture. Remove the bowl from the mixer and use a large rubber spatula to give a final mixing to the dough.

6. Roll ½ tablespoon of the dough (a tiny ice-cream scoop is perfect for measuring this) between the palms of your hands to make a little sphere, then roll it in a shallow bowl of sugar. Place it on one of the prepared pans. Continue with the remaining dough, keeping the subsequent cookies about 2 inches (5 cm) apart on all sides.

7. Bake the gingersnaps until they spread and become deep golden, 15 to 20 minutes. After the first 10 minutes, place the pan from the lower rack on the upper one and vice versa, turning the pans back to front at the same time. If you know that your oven gives strong bottom heat, stack the pan on the lower rack on top of a second one for insulation.

8. Slide the papers off the pans to cool the cookies. If you have only one more pan of gingersnaps to bake, readjust one of the racks to the middle level for baking.

STORAGE: Keep the gingersnaps between sheets of wax paper in a tin or plastic container with a tight-fitting lid.

1 cup all-purpose flour
(spoon flour into a dry-measure cup and level off)

½ teaspoon baking soda

½ cup sugar

½ cup honey

1 large egg

3 tablespoons unsalted butter, melted

1⅓ cups (about 6½ ounces/170 grams) honey-roasted peanuts, finely chopped, but not ground

2 cookie sheets or jelly-roll pans lined with silicone baking mats or buttered foil

Honey Peanut Wafers

I owe the trick of using honey-roasted peanuts in this cookie recipe to my friend and mentor Maida Heatter. They add so much to the flavor of these cookies that I can't imagine preparing them with anything else. These are a little tricky to bake because they need to spread out and come to a boil on the pan. Watch them carefully and don't bake more than 2 pans at a time, and you'll be fine. Baking these on silicone baking mats makes the process much easier.

1. Set racks in the upper and lower thirds of the oven and preheat to 350°F (180°C).

2. Stir the flour and baking soda together and set aside.

3. In a medium bowl, whisk the sugar, honey, and egg together until just mixed to avoid making a foamy mixture. Then whisk in the butter.

4. Use a large rubber spatula to stir in the flour mixture and the chopped peanuts.

5. Drop tablespoon-size pieces of the batter onto the prepared pans, keeping them about 4 inches (10 cm) apart on all sides. Moisten a fingertip with water and flatten each mound of cookie.

6. Bake the cookies for about 5 minutes, then place the pan from the lower rack on the upper one and vice versa, turning the pans back to front at the same time. If you know that your oven gives strong bottom heat, stack the pan on the lower rack on top of a second one for insulation. Continue baking for another 5 minutes, or until the cookies have spread and are evenly golden.

7. Remove the pans from the oven and slide the silicone mats onto racks to cool. As soon as you can pry the cookies off the mats, rinse the mats and bake more cookies.

STORAGE: Keep the cookies between sheets of wax paper in a tin or plastic container with a tight-fitting lid.

....

4 large egg whites

Pinch of salt

1 cup sugar

1¼ cups (about 5 ounces/150 grams) walnut pieces, finely chopped, but not ground

1 tablespoon instant espresso powder

1 ounce (25 grams) bittersweet (not unsweetened) chocolate, finely chopped

2 tablespoons cornstarch

2 cookie sheets or jelly-roll pans lined with parchment or foil

Espresso Walnut Meringues

Coffee and walnuts combine well with a sweet background, such as these meringues. The finely chopped chocolate adds an elusive flavor. Since there is so little of it, it adds to the flavor in general, but doesn't overdominate.

1. Set racks in the upper and lower thirds of the oven and preheat to 300°F (150°C).

2. Place the egg whites and salt in the bowl of an electric mixer and whip with the whisk attachment on medium speed until white, opaque, and beginning to hold their shape. Increase the speed to medium-high and whip in ½ cup of the sugar 1 tablespoon at a time, continuing to whip until the egg whites are stiff, but not dry.

3. Remove the bowl from the mixer and scatter the walnuts, and then the espresso powder, chocolate, and cornstarch on top, one at a time, in order. (Don't mix them all together beforehand.) Use a large rubber spatula to fold them in.

4. Use a soup spoon to make rough mounds of the meringue, about 2 inches (5 cm) apart on all sides, on the prepared pans.

5. Bake the meringues until they are almost dry (poke one with a fingertip to see), about 30 minutes. If you know that your oven gives strong bottom heat, bake the pan on the lower rack stacked on top of a second one for insulation. Slide the papers from the pans onto racks to cool.

STORAGE: Keep the cookies between sheets of wax paper in a tin or plastic container with a tight-fitting lid.

....

VARIATIONS

Substitute pecans or hazelnuts (with the skins still on) for the walnuts. Omit the espresso and chocolate and substitute 1 teaspoon ground cinnamon for a completely different flavor.

Makes about 48 cookies

....

1⅓ cups all-purpose flour
(spoon flour into a dry-measure cup and level off)

½ teaspoon baking soda

½ teaspoon salt

10 tablespoons (1¼ sticks) unsalted butter, softened

¾ cup light brown sugar, firmly packed

1 teaspoon vanilla extract

1 large egg

6 ounces (175 grams) bittersweet (not unsweetened) chocolate, cut into ¼-inch (6-mm) pieces

6 ounces (175 grams) milk chocolate, cut into ¼-inch (6-mm) pieces

2 cookie sheets or jelly-roll pans lined with parchment or foil

Butterscotch Chocolate Chunk Cookies

Everyone loves chocolate chip cookies of all types, and these have a strong butterscotch flavor emphasized by the brown sugar and combination of milk and dark chocolate chunks in them. After you cut up the chocolate, place it in a strainer with fairly wide mesh and sift away the dust formed by cutting it—the cookies will have a neater appearance.

1. Set racks in the upper and lower thirds of the oven and preheat to 350°F (180°C).

2. Stir the flour, baking soda, and salt together and set aside.

3. Combine the butter, brown sugar, and vanilla in the bowl of an electric mixer. Beat with the paddle on medium speed until just mixed, then beat in the egg. (Overbeating this type of cookie dough will make the cookies rise, then flatten out during baking, instead of remaining risen and moist.)

4. Remove the bowl from the mixer and use a large rubber spatula to stir in the flour mixture, then the chocolate.

5. Drop teaspoons of the dough 2 to 3 inches (5 to 7 cm) apart on the prepared pans to allow for spreading. Bake the cookies until they are spread, well risen, and golden, about 15 minutes. About halfway through the baking, place the pan from the lower rack on the upper one and vice versa, turning the pans back to front at the same time. If you know that your oven gives strong bottom heat, place the pan on the lower rack stacked on top of a second one for insulation.

6. Slide the parchment papers off the pans to cool the cookies.

....

STORAGE: Keep the cookies between sheets of wax paper in a tin or plastic container with a tight-fitting lid.

2 large eggs

⅔ cup sugar

12 tablespoons (1½ sticks) unsalted butter, melted

1 tablespoon finely grated lemon zest

1 teaspoon vanilla extract

2 cups all-purpose flour
(spoon flour into a dry-measure cup and level off)

⅓ cup poppy seeds

1⅔ cups (7 ounces/200 grams) slivered almonds, finely chopped but not ground

1½ teaspoons baking powder

¼ teaspoon salt

2 cookie sheets or jelly-roll pans lined with parchment or foil

Lemon Poppy Seed Drops

This is a simple but delicious cookie, but be careful—not everyone likes poppy seeds. They have a nutty, earthy flavor and provide a perfect bit of crunch.

1. Set racks in the upper and lower thirds of the oven and preheat to 350°F (180°C).

2. In a medium mixing bowl, whisk the eggs to break them up. Whisk in the sugar in a stream, followed by the butter, lemon zest, and vanilla.

3. In a medium bowl, mix together the flour, poppy seeds, ⅓ cup almonds, the baking powder, and salt and stir into the egg and butter mixture.

4. Spread the remaining 1⅓ cups almonds on a plate. Roll about 1 teaspoon of dough at a time in the chopped almonds, then transfer to the prepared pans, 2 to 3 inches (5 to 7 cm) apart and flatten with the bottom of a glass. Repeat until all the dough is gone.

5. Bake the cookies until they are spread, well risen, and golden, about 15 minutes. About halfway though the baking, place the pan from the lower rack on the upper one and vice versa, turning the pans back to front at the same time. If you know that your oven gives strong bottom heat, place the pan on the lower rack stacked on top of a second one for insulation.

6. Slide the parchment papers off the pans to cool the cookies.

STORAGE: Keep the cookies between sheets of wax paper in a tin or plastic container with a tight-fitting lid.

Makes about 40 cookies

....

8 tablespoons (1 stick) unsalted butter, softened

½ cup sugar

2 teaspoons finely grated lemon zest

2 teaspoons vanilla extract

2 large egg whites

¾ cup (about 3 ounces/75 grams) slivered almonds, finely ground in the food processor

⅓ cup all-purpose flour
(spoon flour into a dry-measure cup and level off)

3 cookie sheets or jelly-roll pans lined with buttered parchment or foil, see *Note*

Lemon & Almond Tuiles

You can finish these cookies in three different ways: Leave them plain and they are delicate and delicious; curve them on a rolling pin or other round form, like a classic French tuile; or sandwich strained reduced apricot or raspberry preserves between them. The word *tuile*, by the way, means "tile" in French, and refers to a curved clay roofing tile, commonly used in southern Europe.

1. Set racks in the upper and lower thirds of the oven and preheat to 350°F (180°C).

2. Combine the butter, sugar, lemon zest, and vanilla in the bowl of an electric mixer. Beat with the paddle on medium speed until smooth and well mixed. Add the egg whites, one at a time, beating after each until smooth.

3. Decrease the speed to low and beat in the ground almonds and flour, only until smoothly combined.

4. Drop small teaspoons of the dough 2 to 3 inches (5 to 7 cm) apart on the prepared pans to allow for spreading.

5. Bake the cookies until they are spread and golden, 12 to 15 minutes. About halfway through the baking, place the pan from the lower rack on the upper one and vice versa, turning the pans back to front at the same time. If you know that your oven gives strong bottom heat, stack the pan on the lower rack on top of a second one for insulation.

6. Slide the papers off the pans to cool the cookies. If you only have one more pan of cookies to bake, adjust one of the racks to the middle level before baking them.

7. If you wish to curve the cookies, bake only one pan at a time in the middle level of the oven. Have several rolling pins or other narrow cylindrical forms ready on a pan. When the cookies are baked, remove them from the paper one at a time with a spatula and place them on the rolling pin. Gently press them until they assume the curve of the cylinder. Leave them in place until they cool and they will become crisp and keep their shape.

....

STORAGE: Keep the cookies between sheets of wax paper in a tin or plastic container with a tight-fitting lid.

NOTE: For the absolute thinnest, most fragile tuile possible, use a bare buttered pan, not one lined with parchment or foil.

Makes 40 cookies

....

COOKIE DOUGH

8 ounces (2 sticks/225 grams) unsalted butter, softened

½ cup light brown sugar, firmly packed

1 teaspoon vanilla extract

2 large egg yolks

2 cups all-purpose flour
(spoon flour into a dry-measure cup and level off)

FINISHING

2 large egg whites

1½ cups (about 6 ounces/150 grams) slivered almonds, finely ground in the food processor

FILLING

1½ tablespoons very strong brewed espresso or coffee

1 teaspoon vanilla extract

6 ounces (175 grams) best quality white chocolate, melted and cooled

Cinnamon for sprinkling

2 cookie sheets or jelly-roll pans lined with parchment or foil

---

Cappuccino
Thumbprint Cookies

These are a dressed-up version of a typical thumbprint cookie, where a little sphere of dough is indented at the top and filled with reduced preserves. These are first painted with egg white and rolled in ground almonds, then filled with a white chocolate and espresso filling, just a little more sophisticated than the usual jam.

1. For the dough, combine the butter, brown sugar, and vanilla in the bowl of an electric mixer. Beat with the paddle on medium speed until well mixed and slightly lightened, about 2 minutes. Beat in the egg yolks, one at a time, beating smooth after each addition.

2. Decrease the speed to low and beat in the flour, just until it is absorbed. Use a large rubber spatula to give a final mixing to the dough. Scrape it out onto a piece of plastic wrap and shape it into an 8-inch (20-cm) square. Cover the dough with plastic wrap and slide it onto a cookie sheet. Chill the dough until it is firm, about 1 hour, or leave it for a couple of days before continuing.

3. When you are ready to bake the cookies, set racks in the upper and lower thirds of the oven and preheat to 350°F (180°C).

4. Place the egg whites and ground almonds in 2 separate shallow bowls. Use a fork to break up the egg whites and make them more liquid.

5. Remove the dough from the refrigerator and use a bench scraper or a knife to cut it into eight 1-inch (2½-cm) strips. Cut each strip into 5 equal pieces. Roll all the pieces of dough into spheres between the palms

of your hands. Use a fork to lift one and then lower it into the egg white. Using the fork again, lift it out of the egg white and drop it into the almonds and nudge it around until it is completely covered in nuts. As the cookies are coated, arrange them on the prepared pans, keeping them 1½ inches (4 cm) on all sides.

6. Use the handle of a wooden spoon or another cylindrical implement about ⅜-inch (1 cm) in diameter, or a fingertip, to press a cavity into the top of each cookie and halfway down the depth of it.

7. Bake the cookies until they are firm and the almonds are golden, 15 to 20 minutes.

8. While the cookies are baking, make the filling: whisk the coffee and vanilla into the chocolate.

9. Slide the cookies on the papers onto racks to cool. After the cookies have cooled, spoon or pipe a dab of the filling into each one. Sprinkle lightly with the cinnamon.

....

STORAGE: For advance preparation, keep these unfilled between sheets of wax paper in a tin or plastic container with a tight-fitting lid. Fill them just before serving.

Makes about twenty-four 2-inch (5-cm) square cookies

COOKIE DOUGH

½ cup sugar

1½ ounces (50 grams) unsalted macadamia nuts, crushed with the bottom of a pan

2¼ cups all-purpose flour
(spoon flour into a dry-measure cup and level off)

½ teaspoon baking powder

12 tablespoons (1½ sticks) cold unsalted butter, cut into 12 pieces

TOPPING

¾ cup (about 3 ounces/75 grams) unsalted macadamia nuts, crushed and finely chopped, but not ground

⅓ cup sugar

One 9 x 13 x 2-inch (23 x 33 x 5-cm) pan lined with buttered foil

Macadamia Shortbreads

Macadamia nuts may be expensive, but they have a delicate and elusive flavor perfect for these cookies. Everything is just mixed together and pressed into the pan—nothing could be easier.

1. Set a rack in the middle level of the oven and preheat to 325°F (160°C).

2. For the dough, combine the sugar and macadamia nuts in the bowl of a food processor fitted with the metal blade. Pulse to grind finely. Add the flour and baking powder and pulse several times to mix. Add the butter and pulse until the butter is finely mixed in. The mixture should be powdery.

3. Remove the blade of the food processor and pour the mixture into the prepared pan. Distribute it evenly all over the bottom of the pan and use the palm of one hand to press it in.

4. Use a brush to sprinkle the top of the dough generously with water. Scatter the chopped nuts and sugar evenly on the dough and use the palm of your hand to press them in.

5. Bake the cookies until they are golden and firm, about 30 minutes.

6. As soon as you remove the pan from the oven, grip the opposite ends of the foil and lift the slab of baked dough onto a cutting board. While the dough is still hot, use a long sharp knife to cut the slab into 2-inch (5-cm) squares. Let the cookies cool and they'll become crisp.

7. If you find the cookies are not crisp, return them to the pan and a 300°F (150°C) oven and bake them for another 10 to 15 minutes, then cool the pan on a rack.

STORAGE: Keep the cookies between sheets of wax paper in a tin or plastic container with a tight-fitting lid.

Makes about 50 cookies

....

1¾ cups (about 7 ounces/200 grams) pecan pieces

1½ cups light brown sugar, firmly packed

8 tablespoons (1 stick) unsalted butter, softened

1 large egg

2 teaspoons vanilla extract

1½ cups all-purpose flour
(spoon flour into a dry-measure cup and level off)

2 or 3 cookie sheets or jelly-roll pans lined
with parchment or foil

New Orleans Praline Disks

Pralines are those addictively rich New Orleans candy patties made from brown sugar, butter, and pecans. These cookies are close in flavor, but a little less rich. Please make sure the butter is really soft for these or they won't spread and become as thin as they should during baking.

1. Set racks in the upper and lower thirds of the oven and preheat to 375°F (180°C).

2. Place ½ cup of the pecans in the bowl of a food processor fitted with the metal blade. Pulse until the pecans are finely chopped, but not ground to a powder. Remove and set aside. Combine the remaining 1¼ cups of the pecan pieces and ½ cup of the brown sugar in the bowl of the food processor and pulse until the pecans and sugar are finely chopped but not ground to a powder.

3. Combine the butter, the remaining brown sugar, and the pecan and sugar mixture in the bowl of an electric mixer. Beat with the paddle on medium speed until well mixed, about 1 minute. Add the egg and vanilla and continue to beat just until smooth. Do not overbeat.

4. Decrease the speed to low and add the flour. Continue beating until the flour is just absorbed. Remove the bowl from the mixer and use a large rubber spatula to give a final mixing to the dough.

5. Roll a rounded teaspoonful of the dough (a tiny ice-cream scoop is perfect for this) between the palms of your hands to make a little sphere. Place it on one of the prepared pans. Continue with the remaining dough, keeping the cookies about 2 inches (5 cm) apart on all sides. Use a fingertip to flatten the spheres of dough slightly and sprinkle them with the reserved chopped pecans.

6. Bake the wafers until they spread and become brown around the edges, 12 to 15 minutes. After the first 7 to 8 minutes, place the pan from the lower rack on the upper one and vice versa, turning the pans back to front at the same time. If you know that your oven gives strong bottom heat, stack the pan on the lower rack on top of a second one for insulation. Slide the papers off the pans to cool the cookies. If you only have one more pan of wafers to bake, readjust one of the racks to the middle level.

....

STORAGE: Keep the wafers between sheets of wax paper in a tin or plastic container with a tight-fitting lid.

....

VARIATIONS

Substitute 1 tablespoon of Bourbon for the vanilla extract.

Make the spheres of dough slightly larger and after flattening them, top each with a pecan half that has been moistened on the bottom with a little egg white, instead of the chopped pecans.

Makes about 48 cookies

1½ cups all-purpose flour
(spoon flour into a dry-measure cup and level off)

¾ cup cornstarch

4 teaspoons baking powder

⅛ teaspoon salt

8 tablespoons (1 stick) unsalted butter, softened

1 cup confectioners' sugar

2 large eggs

1 teaspoon vanilla extract

½ teaspoon orange extract

2 teaspoons finely grated orange zest

2 or 3 cookie sheets or jelly-roll pans lined
with parchment or foil

Melting Moments

As far as I can determine, these are an old British cookie. They certainly deserve to be better known. The name is very fitting, because they are like little buttery orange-flavored clouds. Thanks to my friend Kyra Effren, who bakes every day, for sharing her wonderful recipe.

1. Set racks in the upper and lower thirds of the oven and preheat to 325°F (160°C).

2. Stir the flour, cornstarch, baking powder, and salt together and set aside.

3. Combine the butter and confectioners' sugar in the bowl of an electric mixer. Beat on low speed with the paddle until well mixed. Increase the speed to medium and continue beating until lightened, about 2 minutes.

4. Beat in the eggs one at a time, beating until smooth after each addition. Beat in the extracts and orange zest.

5. Decrease the speed to low and beat in the flour mixture. Remove the bowl from the mixer and use a large rubber spatula to give a final mixing to the dough.

6. Arrange rounded teaspoons of the dough (a tiny ice-cream scoop is perfect for this) on the prepared pans about 2 inches (5 cm) apart on all sides. After all the cookies have been placed on the pans, flour a fork and press a crisscross design into the top of each mound of dough, flattening it slightly.

7. Bake the cookies until they spread and become deep golden, about 20 minutes. After the first 10 minutes, place the pan from the lower rack on the upper one and vice versa, turning the pans back to front at the same time. If you know that your oven gives strong bottom heat, stack the pan on the lower rack on top of a second one for insulation. Slide the papers off the pans to cool the cookies. If you only have one more pan of cookies to bake, readjust one of the racks to the middle level.

STORAGE: Keep the cookies between sheets of wax paper in a tin or plastic container with a tight-fitting lid.

VARIATIONS

Substitute lemon extract and zest for the orange extract and orange zest.

Makes about 60 biscotti

3/4 cup sugar

1 1/2 cups (about 5 ounces/150 grams) whole natural
hazelnuts (skin intact)

2 cups all-purpose flour
(spoon flour into a dry-measure cup and level off)

1 1/4 teaspoons baking powder

1/2 teaspoon baking soda

1/2 teaspoon salt

2 teaspoons freshly ground black pepper

1 1/2 teaspoons ground ginger

1/2 teaspoon ground cinnamon

1/2 teaspoon ground coriander

1/4 teaspoon ground cloves

2 cups (about 8 ounces/225 grams) whole natural
hazelnuts, gently crushed into 1/2-inch (6-mm) pieces

1/3 cup water

1/3 cup honey

1 tablespoon finely grated orange zest

2 cookie sheets or jelly-roll pans lined with
parchment or foil

VARIATION

HAZELNUT BISCOTTI: If you want some
nonspicy biscotti, omit the spices except for the
cinnamon. Omit the orange zest. Add 2 teaspoons
vanilla extract to the honey and water. Almonds
also work well in this nonspicy version.

Spicy Hazelnut Biscotti

The model for this recipe is an old
Sicilian cookie called *biscotti Napoletani*
(Neapolitan biscotti). Why a Sicilian cookie
should be called "Neapolitan" is beyond
me, but the recipe was shared in the late
1980s by Salvatore Maggio when I visited
his pastry shop in Trapani, on the west coast
of Sicily. I've made a lot of adjustments to
the recipe over the years, and recently tried
spicing it up, and it worked perfectly. Please
notice that there are two quantities of
hazelnuts in the recipe—one is ground with
the sugar and the other is crushed to leave
bits of hazelnut throughout the biscotti.

1. Set a rack in the middle level of the oven and
   preheat to 350°F (180°C).

2. Combine the sugar and 1 1/4 cups hazelnuts
   in the bowl of a food processor fitted with
   the metal blade and grind to a fine powder,
   pulsing repeatedly.

3. In a large mixing bowl, stir together the
   ground hazelnut mixture, the flour, baking
   powder, baking soda, salt, and spices. Stir in
   the crushed hazelnuts.

4. Stir the water, honey, and orange zest together
   and add to the bowl. Use a large rubber
   spatula to mix the liquid into the dry
   ingredients. At first the dough will seem
   dry, but as the sugar gradually melts, the
   dough will begin to hold together.

5. Scrape the dough onto a floured work
   surface and squeeze it together. Divide it
   in half and roll each half into a cylinder a
   little shorter than one of your baking pans.
   Transfer the logs of dough to the pans,
   keeping them well apart from one another
   and from the side of the pan, and use the
   palm of your hand to flatten them slightly.

6. Bake the logs of dough until they have
   puffed and spread and feel firm when
   pressed with a fingertip, about 30 minutes.

7. Slide the baked logs on the paper to a rack to
   cool completely. Reset the racks to the upper
   and lower thirds of the oven.

8. Once the logs have cooled, use a sharp
   serrated knife to slice them 1/4- to 1/3-inch
   (6- to 8-mm) thick—if you slice them too
   thick they will be unbearably hard. Reuse the
   paper from the first pan and line up the
   biscotti, close to one another on the 2 pans,
   cut sides down.

9. Bake the biscotti until they are lightly toasted
   (you can tell when they're ready because the
   pieces of hazelnut throughout them will look
   toasted), 20 to 25 minutes. About halfway
   through the baking time, place the pan from
   the lower rack on the upper one and vice
   versa, turning the pans back to front at the
   same time. If you know that your oven gives
   strong bottom heat, stack the pan on the
   lower rack on top of a second one for
   insulation.

10. Cool the biscotti on the pans on racks.

STORAGE: Keep the biscotti between sheets of wax
paper in a tin or plastic container with a tight-
fitting lid.

Makes about 60 biscotti

1½ cups all-purpose flour
(spoon flour into a dry-measure cup and level off)

1 cup stone-ground yellow cornmeal

½ cup sugar

1 teaspoon baking powder

¼ teaspoon salt

10 tablespoons (1¼ sticks) cold unsalted butter,
cut into 12 pieces

¾ cup (about 3 ounces/75 grams) pine nuts

2 large eggs

2 teaspoons vanilla extract

1 tablespoon finely grated lemon zest

2 cookie sheets or jelly-roll pans lined with
parchment or foil

VARIATION

Add ¾ cup golden raisins or currants along with
the pine nuts.

Cornmeal & Pine Nut Biscotti

Lemon zest and vanilla bring out the sweet corn flavor in these biscotti. If you can only find the pine nuts that come in a tiny package and are outrageously expensive, substitute coarsely chopped blanched almonds.

1. Set a rack in the middle level of the oven and preheat to 350°F (180°C).

2. Combine the flour, cornmeal, sugar, baking powder, and salt in the bowl of a food processor fitted with the metal blade. Pulse several times to mix.

3. Add the butter and pulse repeatedly until the butter is completely mixed in but the mixture remains cool and powdery. Remove the blade and pour the mixture into a medium mixing bowl. Stir in the pine nuts.

4. Whisk the eggs with the vanilla and lemon zest and use a large rubber spatula to stir this into the cornmeal mixture. Continue mixing until a soft dough forms.

5. Scrape the dough onto a floured work surface and squeeze it together (the dough will be sticky). Divide it in half and roll each half into a cylinder a little shorter than one of your baking pans. Transfer the logs of dough to the pans, keeping them well apart from one another and from the sides of the pans. Use the palm of your hand to flatten them slightly.

6. Bake until the dough has puffed, spread, and feels firm when pressed with a fingertip, about 30 minutes.

7. Slide the baked logs on the paper onto a rack to cool completely. Reset the oven racks to the upper and lower thirds of the oven.

8. Once the logs have cooled, use a sharp serrated knife to slice them ⅓ to ½ inch (8 mm to 1 cm) thick. Line up the biscotti, side by side and cut side down on the 2 baking sheets.

9. Bake the biscotti until they are lightly toasted (you can tell when they're ready because the pine nuts will look toasted), 20 to 25 minutes. About halfway through the baking time, place the pan from the lower rack on the upper one and vice versa, turning the pans back to front at the same time. If you know that your oven gives strong bottom heat, stack the pan on the lower rack on top of a second one for insulation.

10. Cool the biscotti on the pans on racks.

STORAGE: Keep the biscotti between sheets of wax paper in a tin or plastic container with a tight-fitting lid at room temperature.

Makes about 40 cookies

....

3½ cups all-purpose flour
(spoon flour into a dry-measure cup and level off)

½ cup sugar

1½ teaspoons baking powder

½ teaspoon salt

12 tablespoons (1½ sticks) cold unsalted butter,
cut into 12 pieces

3 large eggs

2 teaspoons vanilla extract

Egg wash: 2 large eggs well beaten with a pinch of salt

2 cups untoasted sesame seeds

2 cookie sheets or jelly-roll pans lined with
parchment or foil

Biscotti Regina

These are a delicious Sicilian cookie, widely available in industrially made versions. I assume that the *regina* (queen) in question is Margherita di Savoia, the second and much beloved queen of a united Italy. Queen Margherita loved sweets and would often go personally to visit pastry shops with her ladies in waiting. She was known to spontaneously ennoble the owner of a pastry shop where she really liked the cookies, elevating him to the rank of *cavaliere* (knight)! Biscotti Regina are an example of Italian cookies that are not sliced and rebaked.

1. Set racks in the upper and lower thirds of the oven and preheat to 325°F (160°C).

2. Combine the flour, sugar, baking powder, and salt in the bowl of a food processor fitted with the metal blade. Pulse several times to mix.

3. Add the butter and pulse repeatedly until the butter is finely mixed in, but the mixture is still cool and powdery. Add the eggs and vanilla and pulse repeatedly until the dough forms a ball.

4. Invert the bowl onto a floured work surface and carefully remove the blade. Briefly knead the dough 2 to 3 times to make it smooth. Shape the dough into a rough cylinder. Use a bench scraper or a knife to divide the dough into 8 equal pieces.

5. Roll 1 piece of dough into a rope about 15 inches (38 cm) long. Cut the dough into 3-inch (7-cm) long cylinders. Repeat with the remaining pieces of dough, lining up the cylinders on the left side of your work surface.

6. After all the cookies have been formed, place the egg wash and sesame seeds, each in a separate shallow bowl, next to the cookies, and place the baking pans to their right.

7. Drop one of the cookies into the egg wash and use a fork to turn it over so it is completely covered. Use the fork to lift it out of the egg wash, letting the excess drip back into the bowl, and place it on the sesame seeds. Use a second fork to roll the cookie around in the sesame seeds to cover it completely. Use the same fork to transfer the coated cookie to one of the prepared pans.

8. Repeat with the remaining cookies, leaving each cookie about 1½ inches (4 cm) apart and all around on the pans.

9. Bake the cookies until they are risen, firm, and the sesame seeds are golden, about 30 minutes.

10. After the first 15 minutes, place the pan from the lower rack on the upper one and vice versa, turning the pans back to front at the same time. If you know that your oven gives strong bottom heat, stack the pan on the lower rack on top of a second one for insulation. Cool the cookies on the pans.

....

STORAGE: Keep the cookies between sheets of wax paper in a tin or plastic container with a tight-fitting lid at room temperature.

Makes about 30 cookies

....

1½ pounds (700 grams) dried Calimyrna figs

1 cup water

½ cup apricot preserves

¼ cup dark rum

1 teaspoon ground cinnamon

½ teaspoon ground cloves

1 batch dough as for Biscotti Regina, page 298

2 cookie sheets or jelly-roll pans lined with parchment or foil

Sicilian Fig Bars

Although fig bars are standard American fare, fig-filled cookies are also very traditional in Sicily, where they are called *cucidati*. I've decided to merge the two and make a fig bar that is shaped like the industrially made one, but has some typical Sicilian seasonings in it for extra flavor.

1. To make the filling, use kitchen scissors to snip the stems from the figs (they are very sharp and hard), and snip each fig into 5 or 6 pieces. In a large saucepan, combine the figs, water, apricot preserves, rum, cinnamon, and cloves. Stir to mix well.

2. Place the saucepan over medium heat and bring to a boil, stirring often. Reduce the heat to low and let the filling simmer until it is thickened, but not extremely thick, about 10 minutes. Cool the filling and purée it in the food processor with the metal blade. You can refrigerate both the dough and filling for a couple of days before continuing if you're preparing in advance.

3. When you are ready to bake the cookies, set racks in the upper and lower thirds of the oven and preheat to 350°F (180°C).

4. Divide the dough into 6 pieces and roll each into a rope about 12 inches (30 cm) long. Place 1 rope on a floured work surface and press and roll it to make a rectangle of dough about 4 inches (10 cm) wide and 12 inches (30 cm) long. Pipe or spoon about ⅙ of the filling down the middle of the dough, spreading it about 2 inches (5 cm) wide with a small offset spatula. Use a pastry brush to paint the exposed dough with water, then lift up the dough all around to enclose the filling

within a tube of dough. Pinch the seam closed where the 2 edges of dough meet. Turn the filled piece of dough over so that the seam is on the bottom, and transfer it to one of the prepared pans. Repeat with the remaining dough, placing 3 filled dough cylinders on each pan. Gently flatten the cylinders of dough with the palm of your hand.

5. Bake the cookies until the dough is set and golden, 15 to 20 minutes. About halfway through the baking, place the pan from the lower rack on the upper one and vice versa, turning the pans back to front at the same time. If you know that your oven gives strong bottom heat, place the pan on the lower rack stacked on top of a second rack for insulation.

6. Cool the cookies on the pans. When they are cool, trim the edges and use a sharp knife to cut them into 2½-inch (6-mm) lengths.

....

STORAGE: Keep the cookies at room temperature between sheets of wax paper in a tin or plastic container with a tight-fitting lid.

....

8 ounces (225 grams) canned almond paste,
cut into ½-inch (1-cm) cubes

¾ cup granulated sugar

¼ cup confectioners' sugar

2 teaspoons vanilla extract

2 large egg whites

1 cup (about 4 ounces/100 grams) untoasted pine nuts

2 cookie sheets or jelly-roll pans lined with parchment

Pine Nut Macaroons

These are a great favorite whenever they appear, and justly so—the deep, nutty flavor of the toasted pine nuts accentuates the smooth sweetness of the macaroons perfectly. Always use canned almond paste for preparing macaroons—the kind that comes packaged as a little cylinder has a lot more sugar in it and will result in macaroons that flatten out miserably while they are baking.

1. Set racks in the upper and lower thirds of the oven and preheat to 375°F (190°C).

2. Combine the almond paste, granulated sugar, and confectioners' sugar in the bowl of an electric mixer. Beat with the paddle on low speed until broken up into fine crumbs.

3. Add the vanilla and one of the egg whites and continue mixing just until smooth. Add the other egg white and mix until it is just absorbed—mixing the macaroon paste too long will cause the macaroons to flatten out while they are baking.

4. Remove the bowl from the mixer and use a large rubber spatula to give a final mixing to the paste.

5. Using a pastry bag fitted with a ½-inch (1-cm) plain tube (Ateco #806), pipe the macaroon paste into ½-inch (1-cm) high spheres on the prepared pans, keeping them about 2 inches (5 cm) apart on all sides. Hold the bag perpendicular to the pan with the tip about ½ inch (1 cm) above it and squeeze out a small sphere. Release the pressure and pull away—it doesn't matter if you leave a small point at the top.

6. Wet a clean flat-weave tea towel so that some water still drips from it and fold it into a

2-inch (5-cm) strip. Holding one of the narrow ends in each hand, position the towel over a row of macaroons. Gently lower the loosely pulled towel onto the tops of the cookies several times so they flatten slightly and are very moist on the surface. Immediately sprinkle each macaroon with some pine nuts. Repeat with the other pan.

7. Bake the macaroons until they are well risen and deep golden, about 20 minutes. After the first 10 minutes, place the pan from the lower rack on the upper one and vice versa, turning the pans back to front at the same time. If you know that your oven gives strong bottom heat, place the pan on the lower rack stacked on top of a second rack for insulation.

8. Slide the papers off the pans to cool the macaroons. To easily detach the macaroons from the paper without breaking them, sprinkle a jelly-roll pan with water. Place the paper with the macaroons on the wet pan. Wait 5 minutes, and then slide a small spatula under each macaroon to detach it.

....

STORAGE: Macaroons are best on the day they are made—after they have cooled, keep them in a single layer tightly covered with plastic wrap. Freeze for longer storage. Defrost loosely covered and bring to room temperature before serving.

Makes about 60 cookies

....

COOKIE DOUGH

3½ cups all-purpose flour
(spoon flour into a dry-measure cup and level off)

1¾ cups sugar

¼ teaspoon salt

Zest of 2 large limes removed with a Microplane® grater

12 ounces (3 sticks/350grams) unsalted butter,
cut into 24 pieces

2 large eggs

LIME SUGAR COATING

1½ cups plain or green crystal sugar or
granulated sugar

Zest of 1 large lime removed with a Microplane® grater

4 cookie sheets or jelly-roll pans lined with
parchment or foil

Tart Lime Wafers

This recipe comes from my friend Tim Brennan, chef-owner of Cravings Gourmet Desserts in Saint Louis. Tim is justly well known for his excellent cookies and these are no exception. They're also practical since you can freeze the formed logs of dough for weeks and then slice and bake the cookies whenever you need them.

1. For the dough, mix the flour, sugar, salt, and lime zest in the bowl of a food processor fitted with the metal blade. Pulse 10 times to reduce the zest to smaller particles.

2. Add the butter and pulse until it is completely mixed into the dry ingredients, but the mixture remains powdery. Add the eggs and pulse until the dough forms a ball.

3. Invert the food processor bowl over a floured work surface to turn out the dough. Carefully remove the blade and transfer any dough on it to the work surface. Divide the dough into 2 equal pieces and form each into a cylinder about 8 inches (20 cm) long.

4. Clean any flour off the work surface and combine the crystal sugar and lime zest, working it together with your fingertips for 1 minute to release the lime flavor into the sugar. Pour the sugar onto the work surface in a wide line about 8 inches (20 cm) long. Roll one of the logs of dough in it to coat the outside completely. Repeat with the other log of dough. Wrap each log of dough in plastic wrap and refrigerate until firm, about 1 hour.

5. When you are ready to bake the cookies, set racks in the upper and lower thirds of the oven and preheat to 350°F (180°C).

6. Cut one of the logs of dough into ¼-inch (6-mm) thick slices and arrange them on the prepared pans about 1 inch (2½ cm) apart on all sides. Repeat with the second log of dough, or wrap, freeze, and save it for another day.

7. Bake the cookies until they are firm and golden around the edges, 15 to 20 minutes. After the first 10 minutes, place the pan from the lower rack on the upper one and vice versa, turning the pans from back to front at the same time. If you know that your oven gives strong bottom heat, stack the pan on the lower rack on top of a second one for insulation. Slide the papers off the pans to cool the cookies. If you only have one more pan of cookies to bake, readjust one of the racks to the middle level.

....

STORAGE: Keep the cookies at room temperature between sheets of wax paper in a tin or plastic container with a tight-fitting lid.

....

VARIATIONS

Substitute lemon zest for the lime zest and yellow sugar for the green, if you are using colored sugar crystals.

fig. a

fig. b

fig. c

fig. d

a. Roll half of the dough into a cylinder 8 inches (20 cm) long.

b. Place the cylinder in the middle of a piece of parchment paper cut to the same length and carefully wrap the paper around the dough.

c. Using a bench scraper, place the blade on the paper against the cylinder of dough to tighten the paper against it.

d. Cut the logs into ¼-inch (6-mm) thick slices.

....

COOKIE DOUGH

8 ounces (2 sticks) unsalted butter, softened

½ cup granulated sugar

2 teaspoons vanilla extract

½ teaspoon lemon extract

2 large egg yolks

3 cups all-purpose flour
(spoon flour into a dry-measure cup and level off)

1 (12-ounce/350-gram) jar seedless blackberry
preserves for finishing

LEMON ICING

2 cups confectioners' sugar, sifted after measuring

1 tablespoon fresh lemon juice

1 tablespoon water

2 cookie sheets or jelly-roll pans lined with
parchment or foil

Blackberry Jam Sandwiches
with Lemon Icing

The success of these cookies mostly depends on the quality of the preserves you use. If the blackberry preserves you buy contain seeds, take the time to strain them out after you have heated the preserves. Blueberry preserves are also an excellent alternative choice for these cookies.

....

1. For the dough, combine the butter, sugar, and vanilla and lemon extracts in the bowl of an electric mixer. Beat with the paddle on medium speed until soft and light, about 3 minutes. Beat in the yolks, one at a time, beating smooth after each. Decrease the speed to low and beat in the flour just until blended.

2. Remove the bowl from the mixer and use a large rubber spatula to give the dough a final mixing. Scrape the dough out onto a piece of plastic wrap and cover with more wrap. Press the dough with the palm of your hand to make it about ½ inch (5 mm) thick. Slide the dough onto a cookie sheet and refrigerate it until firm, 1 to 2 hours, or up to 3 days.

3. When you are ready to bake the cookies, set racks in the upper and lower thirds of the oven and preheat to 350°F (180°C).

4. Remove the dough from the refrigerator and divide it into 3 pieces. Place 1 piece of dough on a floured work surface and return the other pieces to the refrigerator. Lightly flour the dough and gently press it with the rolling pin to soften slightly before rolling.

5. Roll the dough to a 9-inch (22½-cm) square. Use a 3-inch (7-cm) fluted round cutter to cut the dough into disks, lifting them with a small spatula and arranging them about 2 inches (5 cm) apart all around on the prepared pans. Place the leftover scraps of dough in a small bowl and refrigerate. Repeat with the remaining dough, then re-roll the chilled scraps to make more cookies.

6. Bake the cookies until firm and no longer shiny looking, 15 to 20 minutes. After the first 7 to 8 minutes, place the pan from the lower rack on the upper one and vice versa, turning the pans back to front at the same time. If you know that your oven gives strong bottom heat, stack the pan on the lower rack on top of a second one for insulation. Slide the papers off the pans to cool.

7. While the cookies are baking, heat the preserves in a small saucepan and bring to a simmer. Let the preserves simmer for about 5 minutes to reduce and thicken slightly.

8. To fill the cookies, turn half the bases over so that the flattest sides are facing upward. Spoon about 1 teaspoon of the reduced preserves on a cookie base and spread it to within ⅛ inch (3 mm) of the edge. Top with a second cookie, gently pressing them together. Repeat with all the cookies.

9. For the icing, combine the confectioners' sugar, lemon juice, and water in a medium saucepan and stir until smooth. Cook over low heat until it is just lukewarm, about 110°F (45°C). Use a spoon to streak the cookies with the icing.

....

STORAGE: Keep the cookies in a cool place, and between sheets of wax paper in a tin or plastic container with a tight-fitting lid.

....

8 ounces (2 sticks/225 grams) unsalted butter, very soft

6 ounces (175 grams) semisweet chocolate
(no more than 55% cocoa solids), melted and cooled

2½ cups all-purpose flour
(spoon flour into a dry-measure cup and level off)

½ cup confectioners' sugar, sifted after measuring

⅓ cup heavy whipping cream

4 ounces (100 grams) milk chocolate,
melted and cooled

2 tablespoons unsalted butter, very soft

Confectioners' sugar for dusting

2 cookie sheets or jelly-roll pans lined
with parchment or foil

Chocolate Sandwich Cookies
with Milk Chocolate Filling

Nothing could be more tender and delicate than these chocolate cookies. That's why I like to sandwich them with milk chocolate. The dough is quite soft: I recommend rolling it, then chilling it again before cutting to make the process easier—it takes a little longer but it's much easier than dealing with the frustration of trying to handle a really soft dough. There's very little sugar in the dough, so it's imperative to use a semisweet, not bittersweet, chocolate in the dough so the cookies will be sweet enough.

1. For the dough, place the butter in a bowl and use a large rubber spatula to beat it until smooth. Add the chocolate and stir it into the butter. (If the chocolate is still warm, the butter will melt and the dough will be ruined.) Stir in the flour and confectioners' sugar to form a soft dough.

2. Scrape the dough out onto a piece of plastic wrap and cover with more wrap. Press the dough with the palm of your hand to make it about ½ inch (1 cm) thick. Slide the dough onto a cookie sheet and refrigerate until firm, 1 to 2 hours, or up to 3 days.

3. When you are ready to bake the cookies, set racks in the upper and lower thirds of the oven and preheat to 350°F (180°C).

4. Remove the dough from the refrigerator and divide it into 3 equal pieces. Place 1 piece of dough on a floured work surface and return the remaining pieces to the refrigerator. Lightly flour the dough and gently press it with the rolling pin to soften slightly before rolling.

5. Roll the dough about ¼ inch (6 mm) thick to a 10-inch (25-cm) square. Use a 2- to 2½-inch (5- to 6-cm) fluted round cutter to cut the dough into disks, lifting them with a small spatula and arranging them about 2 inches (5 cm) apart on all sides on the prepared pans. Place the dough scraps in a small bowl and refrigerate. Repeat rolling and cutting with the remaining dough, then reroll the scraps to make more cookies.

6. Bake the cookies until they are firm and no longer shiny looking, 15 to 20 minutes. After the first 7 to 8 minutes, place the pan from the lower rack on the upper one and vice versa, turning the pans back to front at the same time. If you know that your oven gives strong bottom heat, stack the pan on the lower rack on top of a second one for insulation. Slide the papers off the pans to cool the cookies.

7. While the cookies are baking, heat the cream in a small saucepan to a simmer. Pour it into a bowl and let it cool. Add the cooled cream to the melted chocolate and whisk smooth. Distribute pieces of the butter all over the surface and whisk smooth. Let the filling stand until it is firm enough to spread.

8. To fill the cookies, turn half the bases over so that the flattest sides are facing upward. Pipe or spoon a dab of the filling on each cookie. Top with the other cookies, gently pressing them together. Immediately before serving, dust very lightly with confectioners' sugar.

....

STORAGE: Keep the cookies in a cool place between sheets of wax paper in a tin or plastic container with a tight-fitting lid.

COOKIE DOUGH

8 ounces (2 sticks/225 grams) unsalted butter, softened

⅔ cup granulated sugar

1 cup (about 4 ounces/100 grams) slivered almonds, finely ground in the food processor

2⅔ cups all-purpose flour
(spoon flour into a dry-measure cup and level off)

1 teaspoon ground cinnamon

½ teaspoon ground cloves

FINISHING

1 cup seedless raspberry preserves

Confectioners' sugar for sprinkling

2 cookie sheets or jelly-roll pans lined with parchment or foil

Raspberry Linzer Disks

These delicious sandwich cookies always look festive with their "window" filled with brightly colored raspberry preserves. Be careful about one thing when preparing these: Make sure the butter is really soft, or else the dough won't pull together and will remain an unmanageable powder.

1. For the dough, combine the butter and sugar in the bowl of an electric mixer. Beat with the paddle on medium speed until soft and lightened, about 5 minutes. Decrease the speed to low and beat in the almonds.

2. Mix together the flour, cinnamon, and cloves and beat into the butter mixture, continuing to beat until the dough holds together.

3. Remove the bowl from the mixer and use a large rubber spatula to give a final mixing to the dough. Scrape the dough out onto a piece of plastic wrap and cover it with more wrap. Press the dough with the palm of your hand to make it about ½ inch (1 cm) thick. Slide the dough onto a cookie sheet and refrigerate it until firm, 1 to 2 hours, or up to 3 days.

4. When you are ready to bake the cookies, set racks in the upper and lower thirds of the oven and preheat to 350°F (180°C).

5. Remove the dough from the refrigerator and divide it into 3 equal pieces. Place 1 piece of dough on a floured work surface and return the remaining pieces to the refrigerator. Lightly flour the dough and gently press it with the rolling pin to soften slightly before rolling.

6. Roll the dough about ¼ inch (6 mm) thick to a 9-inch (22½-cm) square. Use a 3-inch (7-cm) plain round cutter to cut the dough into disks, lifting them with a small spatula and arranging them on the prepared pans about 2 inches (5 cm) apart on all sides. Place the dough scraps in a small bowl and refrigerate them. Repeat with the second and third pieces of dough, refrigerating the scraps each time. Gently knead the scraps together and reroll to cut more cookies.

7. Use a 1-inch (2½-cm) round cutter to make a hole in the center of half the cookie bases. (You can also bake the holes as plain cookies.) Bake the cookies until they are firm and golden, 15 to 20 minutes. After the first 7 to 8 minutes, place the pan from the lower rack on the upper one and vice versa, turning the pans back to front at the same time. If you know that your oven gives strong bottom heat, stack the pan on the lower rack on top of a second one for insulation. Slide the papers off the pans to cool the cookies.

8. While the cookies are baking, heat the preserves in a small saucepan over low heat, stirring occasionally. Boil gently for 3 to 4 minutes to evaporate excess moisture.

9. After the cookies have cooled, dust the pierced ones with confectioners' sugar. Turn the whole bases over so that the flatter side is facing upward. Spread about ½ teaspoon of the preserves glaze on the whole bases and place the pierced cookies on top of them. Use a small spoon to fill the area in the center of the top cookie with a little more glaze.

STORAGE: Keep the cookies at room temperature loosely covered in a single layer or the glaze in the center might be marred.

VIENNESE COOKIE DOUGH

16 tablespoons (2 sticks) unsalted butter, softened

1 cup confectioners' sugar

1 cup (about 4 ounces/100 grams) slivered almonds, finely ground in the food processor

2½ cups all-purpose flour
(spoon flour into a dry-measure cup and level off)

FILLING

Baked cookie dough scraps

⅓ cup apricot preserves, strained

2 ounces (50 grams) semisweet chocolate, melted and cooled

2 tablespoons dark rum

2 teaspoons finely grated orange zest

2 teaspoons finely grated lemon zest

RUM ICING

2 cups confectioners' sugar, sifted after measuring

2 tablespoons dark rum

2 teaspoons water

1 drop liquid red food coloring

2 cookie sheets or jelly-roll pans lined with parchment or foil

Viennese Punch Cookies

In Vienna, a Punschtorte (punch cake) is an elaborate affair of dense sponge cake filled with something akin to a rum ball mixture—cake crumbs soaked in rum and flavored with a bit of chocolate, some apricot preserves, and some grated lemon and orange zests. Then it's covered with apricot preserves, a layer of marzipan, and a pink sugar icing. It's quite sweet but also very delicate. To make this cookie version of the famous cake, I decided to bake the cookie scraps, then grind them up in the food processor, adding the rum, preserves, chocolate, and citrus zests. These are definitely an adult cookie because of the quantity of rum they contain. You can always omit the rum if you wish—just substitute more apricot preserves.

1. Set racks in the upper and lower thirds of the oven and preheat to 350°F (180°C).

2. For the dough, beat the butter and confectioners' sugar in an electric mixer fitted with the paddle on medium speed until soft and light, 2 to 3 minutes. Beat in the ground almonds.

3. Remove the bowl from the mixer and stir in the flour with a large rubber spatula, mixing until the dough is

smooth. Scrape the dough out onto a lightly floured work surface and divide it into 3 equal parts.

4. Flour the surface and the dough and gently roll it to about ³/8 inch (1 cm) thick. Use a plain cutter to cut out 2- to 2½-inch (5- to 6-inch) cookies and place them on the prepared pans 1 inch (2½ cm) apart on all sides. Reserve the scraps from cutting the cookies in a bowl. Roll and cut the remaining 2 pieces of dough, reserving the scraps from the rolling and cutting with the others.

5. Bake the cookies until they are firm and dull looking, 15 to 20 minutes. After the first 7 to 8 minutes, place the pan from the lower rack on the upper one and vice versa, turning the pans back to front at the same time. If you know that your oven gives strong bottom heat, stack the pan on the lower rack on top of a second one for insulation. Slide the parchment papers off the pans to cool the cookies.

6. While the cookies are baking, arrange the scraps in a single layer on a parchment- or foil-lined pan. Bake as for the cookies and cool on a rack.

7. To make the filling, break up the cooled scraps and place them in the bowl of a food processor fitted with the metal blade. Pulse to grind coarsely. Add the preserves, melted chocolate, rum, and orange and lemon zests and pulse until the filling holds a soft shape.

8. To fill the cookies, turn half the bases over so that the flattest sides are facing upward. Spread a little less than 1 tablespoon of the filling on the cookie base to within ⅛ inch (3 mm) of the edge. Top with the other cookies, gently pressing them together.

9. For the icing, combine the confectioners' sugar, rum, water, and food coloring in a medium saucepan. Stir until smooth. Place over low heat and cook the icing until it is just lukewarm, about 110°F (45°C). Use a small offset spatula to spread a thin coating of the icing on top of each cookie.

STORAGE: Keep the cookies in a cool place between sheets of wax paper in a tin or plastic container with a tight-fitting lid.

Sources

312

AMERICAN ALMOND
103 Walworth Street
Brooklyn, NY 11205
Telephone: (800) 825-6663
Website: www.americanalmond.com

One-pound cans of almond paste.

THE BAKER'S CATALOGUE
P.O. Box 876
Norwich, VT 05055-0876
Telephone: (800) 827-6836
Website: www.bakerscatalogue.com

General baking ingredients and
equipment.

BRIDGE KITCHENWARE
214 East 52nd Street
New York, NY 10022
Telephone: (212) 688-4220
Website: www.bridgekitchenware.com

Cookware, bakeware, including tart
and cake layer pans of all sizes,
Panibois and Flexipans.

**BONNIE SLOTNICK
COOKBOOKS**
163 West 10th Street
New York, NY 10014
Telephone: (212) 989-8962
Website:
www.bonnieslotnickcookbooks.com

CALPHALON CORPORATION
P.O. Box 583
Toledo, OH 43697
Telephone: (800) 809-7267
Website: www.calphalon.com

Cookware, bakeware, and
baking tools.

THE GINGER PEOPLE
215 Reindollar Avenue
Marina, CA 93933
Telephone: (800) 551-5284
Website: www.gingerpeople.com

A full range of ginger products.

**GUITTARD CHOCOLATE
COMPANY**
10 Guittard Road
Burlingame, CA 94010
Telephone: (650) 697-4424
Website: www.guittard.com

A range of interesting chocolate
products.

KAISER BAKEWARE
3512 Faith Church Road
Indian Trail, NC 28079
Telephone: (800) 966-3009
Website: www.kaiserbakeware.com

Bakeware, including excellent tube,
spring form, and loaf pans.

KALUSTYAN'S
123 Lexington Avenue
New York, NY 10016
Telephone: (212) 685-3451
Website: www.kalustyan.com

Herbs, spices, nuts, and seeds,
including black sesame seeds and
nigella seeds. They also carry Thai
coconut cream, jasmine rice, orange
flower water, and wheat berries for
pastiera (labeled "shelled wheat").

**NEW YORK CAKE AND
BAKING DISTRIBUTORS**
56 West 22nd Street
New York, NY 10010
Telephone: (212) 675-2253;
(800) 942-2539
Website: www.nycake.com

A full line of pans, decorating
equipment, chocolate. Also, cocoa
nibs, sanding sugar, colored sugar,
molds, Silpat nonstick baking mats,
and offset spatulas.

NIELSEN-MASSEY VANILLAS
1550 Shields Drive
Waukegan, IL 60085-8307
Telephone: (800) 525- 7873
Website: www.nielsenmassey.com

Best-quality vanilla extract.

NORDICWARE
Highway 7 at Highway 100
Minneapolis, MN 55416
Telephone: (952) 920-2888;
(800) 328-4310
Website: www.nordicware.com

Bakeware, including a variety
of Bundt pans.

PENZEY'S SPICES
P.O. Box 933
Muskego, WI 53150
Telephone: (262) 785-7678;
(800) 741-7787
Website: www.penzeys.com

Herbs, spices, extracts, and
flavoring oils.

SUR LA TABLE (MAIN STORE)
Pike Place Farmers Market
84 Pine Street
Seattle, WA 98101
Telephone: (206) 448-2245;
(800) 243-0852
Website: www.surlatable.com

Pans, molds, and assorted baking
equipment and cookware, including
layer, tart, and tartlet pans.

SWEET CELEBRATIONS
(formerly Maid of Scandinavia)
P.O. Box 39426
Edina, MN 55439
Telephone: (952) 943-1508;
(800) 328-6722
Website: www.sweetc.com

Wide variety of decorating supplies.

VALRHONA
14 Avenue du Président Roosevelt
B.P. 40
26601 Tain l'Hermitage
France
Telephone: 04 75 07 90 90
Website: www.valrhona.com

Chocolate blocks and bars for baking,
as well as cocoa.

WILLIAMS-SONOMA
100 North Point Street
San Francisco, CA 94133
Telephone: (877) 812-6235
Website: www.williams-sonoma.com

Pans, molds, and assorted baking
equipment and cookware.

Bibliography

Braker, Flo. *The Simple Art of Perfect Baking*.
San Francisco: Chronicle, 2003 (revised edition).

Darenne, Emil and Duval, Emil. *Traité de Pâtisserie
Moderne*. Paris: Flammarion, 1974.

Davidson, Alan. *The Oxford Companion to Food*.
Oxford: Oxford University Press, 1999.

Del Soldo, Marco. *Il Manuale del Pasticciere Moderno*.
Milan: DeVecchi, 1973.

Fance, Wilfred James. *The New International
Confectioner*. London and Coulsdon, England:
Virtue & Company, 1981.

_____. *The Students' Technology of Breadmaking and
Flour Confectionary*. London: Routledge & Keegan
Paul, 1976.

Ferber, Christine. *Mes Tartes Sucrées et Salées*.
Paris: Payot, 1998.

Glezer, Maggie. *Artisan Baking*. New York: Artisan,
2000.

Lacam, Pierre. *Le Memorial Historique et
Géographique de la Pâtisserie*. Paris, 1895.

Mayer, Eduard. *Wiener Suss-Speisen*. Linz, Austria:
Trauner Verlag, 1982.

Olney, Richard. *Simple French Food*. New York:
Atheneum, 1974.

Richards, Paul. *Cakes for Bakers*. Chicago: Baker's
Helper Company, 1932.

Sass, Lorna J. *Recipes From an Ecological Kitchen*.
New York: Morrow, 1992.

Sultan, William J. *Modern Pastry Chef*. Westport,
Connecticut: AVI Publishing, 1977.

Teubner, Christian, et al. *Das Grosse Buch Der
Kuchen und Torten*. Munich: Gräfe & Unzer, 1983.

Thompson, David. *Thai Food*. Berkeley: Ten Speed
Press, 2002.

Thuries, Yves. *Le Livre de Recettes d'un Compagnon
du Tour de France*, 3 vols. Gaillac, France: Societé
Editar, 1980, 1982, 1979 (Vols. 1, 2, 3).

Weber, J.M. Erich. *Schule und Praxis des Konditors*.
Radebeul-Dresden, Germany: Internationaler
Fachverlag J.M. Erich Weber, 1927.

Witzelsberger, *Richard. Das Oesterreichische
Mehlspeisen Kochbuch*. Vienna: Verlag Kremayr
& Scheriau, 1979.

Index

A

almond paste
Apricot & Almond Strudel *204,* 207
Pine Nut Macaroons 302, *303*
Raspberry Almond Tartlets 188, *191*
Roman Almond & Pine Nut Tart
176, *177*

apples
Breton Apple Pie 180, *181*
Classic Tarte Tatin with Apples 206
Deep-Dish Apple Pie 203
grating technique 48
Maida's Big Apple Pie *181,* 182
Sour-Cream Apple Pie 183
Whole Grain Apple Raisin Bread
48, *49*

apricots
Apricot & Almond Strudel *204,* 207
Sicilian Fig Bars *300,* 301
Viennese Punch Cookies 310, *311*
Armenian "Barbary" Bread 70

B

Babka with Traditional Filling 100

bacon
about 126
Bacon Bread 85
Bacon Fougasse 75
Swiss Onion Tart 140
baguettes 78–79, 80, 83
Bakery Crumb Buns 105–106, *107*

bananas
Banana Rum Coconut Layer Cake
248, *249*

Banana Walnut Tart 171
Cocoa Banana Muffins 60, *61*
Bare Bones Focaccia 114

bars
Caramel Crumb Bars *273,* 276
Cocoa Nib Brownies 272, *273*
Coconut Pecan Chocolate Chunk Bars
273, 277
Macadamia Shortbreads 292, *294*
Raisin Pecan Spice Bars *273,* 275
Sicilian Fig Bars *300,* 301
Sour Cream Brownies *273,* 274

bell peppers, Roasted Pepper & Goat
Cheese Tart *138,* 139

berries
Blackberry Jam Cake 233
Blackberry Jam Sandwiches with
Lemon Icing 306, *307*
Blueberry Crumb Cake *236,* 237
Blueberry Crumble Pie 184, *185*
Blueberry Crumb Muffins 58, *61*
cake decorating techniques 267
Chocolate Raspberry Tart 169
Cornmeal Waffles with a Hint of
Lemon & Blueberry Sauce 113
Deep Dish Peach & Raspberry Pie
203
Feuillettés with Berries & Cream
201
Parisian Fruit Tarts 166, *167*
Raspberry Almond Tartlets 188, *191*
Raspberry Cream Cake 244–245
Raspberry Linzer Disks *307,* 309
Raspberry Mille-Feuille 200

Real Strawberry Shortcake 238, *239*
Strawberry Mille-Feuille 200
Triple Chocolate Cake with Raspberry
Preserves 251

biscotti
Biscotti Regina 298, *299*
Cornmeal & Pine Nut Biscotti
297, *299*
Cornmeal & Pine Nut Biscotti with
Raisins 297
Hazelnut Biscotti 296
Spicy Hazelnut Biscotti 296, *299*

biscuits
Chicken Pie with Biscuit Topping
152, *153*
Gruyère Biscuits 51
Old-Fashioned Baking-Powder
Biscuits 51
Parmigiano-Reggiano Biscuits 51
Pecorino & Pepper Biscuits 51
Shortcake 238
Bittersweet Chocolate Tart *168,* 169
Blackberry Jam Cake 233
Blackberry Jam Sandwiches with
Lemon Icing 306, *307*
Blueberry Crumb Cake *236,* 237
Blueberry Crumble Pie 184, *185*
Blueberry Crumb Muffins 58, *61*
Bourbon-Scented Pecan Tart 175
bowls 33

breads, quick 40–41. *See also* biscuits;
loaves; muffins; rusks; scones

breads, yeast. *See also* flatbread;
specialties, yeast-risen

Bacon Bread 85
baguettes 78–79, 80, 83
Cornetti 90–91, *91*
Elegant Dinner Rolls 86–87
French Bread 78–79
Grissini 112
ingredients and techniques
66–69, 94
Instant Sandwich Bread 77
Pain de Campagne 80–81, *81*
Pain De Seigle 83
Pita Bread 72–73, *73*
Prosciutto Bread 85
Rosemary Olive Knots 88–89, *89*
Semolina Sesame Braid 82
Semolina Toast 82
Seven Grain & Seed Bread 84
sourdough 68, 104
Wheat-Sheaf Loaf 79
Breton Apple Pie 180, *181*
Brioche Loaves 95

butterscotch
Butterscotch Chocolate Chunk
Cookies 284, *285*
Butterscotch Chocolate Chunk
Scones 55
Butterscotch Scones 55

C

cabbage, Ligurian Savoy Cabbage Pie
148, *149*

cakes. See also cheesecake
Banana Rum Coconut Layer Cake
248, *249*

Blackberry Jam Cake 233

Blueberry Crumb Cake *236*, 237

Chocolate & Vanilla Cake 245

Chocolate Cream Cake 245

Cinnamon-Scented Baked Chocolate
  Mousse Cake 257

Classic Génoise 240–241, *241*

Cocoa Génoise 240

decorating ideas *266*, 266–267, *267*

Devil's Food Cake with Fluffy
  White Icing *252*, 253

Génoise Très Vanillée 240

Golden Cupcakes 261, *262*

Heirloom Chocolate Cake 256

Incredibly Moist Chocolate Cupcakes
  262, 263

Individual French Hazelnut Cakes 260

Lemon Cream Cake 245

Lemon Ginger Pound Cake 227

Milk Chocolate Mousse Cake
  254, *255*

Molten Center Chocolate Cakes
  258, *259*

Orange-Scented Olive Oil Cake
  234, 235

Pecan Pound Cake 226

Perfect Birthday Cake 243

Perfect Pound Cake 226

Plum Crumb Cake 237

Raspberry Cream Cake 244–245

Real Strawberry Shortcake 238, *239*

Rum-Scented Marble Cake 228, *229*

Sour Cherry Crumb Cake 237

Sour Cream Coffee Cake 232

Triple Chocolate Cake 250–251

Triple Chocolate Cake with
  Marmalade 251

Triple Chocolate Cake with Raspberry
  Preserves 251

types 220

Viennese Raisin Coffee Cake
  230, 231

Walnut Pound Cake 226

Whipped Cream Layer Cake *246*, 247

Yellow Cake Layers 242

Cappuccino Thumbprint Cookies
  290, 291

caramel
  Caramel Crumb Bars *273*, 276
  Chocolate Caramel Pecan Tartlets
    190, *191*
  diluting 237
  "dry" 36, 37, *37*, *236*, 237, *237*
  filling 276

"gold" nuggets 266

Caramelized Onion Tart with Gorgonzola
  212, *214*

Caraway Pain De Seigle 83

Caraway Salt Straws 216

cheese. *See also* cream cheese
  about 118, 123–125
  Caramelized Onion Tart with
    Gorgonzola 212, *214*
  Cheese Fougasse 75
  Cheese Straws 216
  Filled Ham & Cheese Focaccia 119
  Gruyère, Scallion, & Walnut Tart
    141
  Gruyère Biscuits 51
  Ham & Cheese Tart 136
  Neapolitan Easter Pie *186*, 187
  Neapolitan Meat & Cheese Pie 153
  Nonna's Pizza 118
  Parmigiano-Reggiano Biscuits 51
  Pecorino & Pepper Biscuits 51
  Roasted Pepper & Goat Cheese Tart
    138, 139
  Roasted Tomato & Cantal Tart 142
  Savory Cheese Elephant Ears 210
  Sfincione 115
  Spinach & Feta Turnovers 213, *214*
  Swiss Onion & Cheese Tart 140
  Tomato & Cantal Tart 142, *143*
  Zucchini & Ricotta Pie 150

cheesecake
  Individual Chocolate Cheesecakes
    264
  Individual New York Cheesecakes
    264, *265*

cherries
  Sour Cherry Crumb Cake 237
  Sour Cherry Crumble Pie 184

Chicken Pie with Biscuit Topping
  152, *153*

chile peppers
  Corn Pudding Tart *134*, 135
  Shrimp & Toasted Pumpkinseed
    Tart *144*, 145
  Spicy Jalapeño Cornbread 50

chocolate
  about 12, *13*, 169, 272
  Bittersweet Chocolate Tart *168*, 169
  Butterscotch Chocolate Chunk
    Cookies *284*, 285
  Butterscotch Chocolate Chunk
    Scones 55
  Chocolate & Vanilla Cake 245
  Chocolate Babka Loaf 100–101, *101*

Chocolate Caramel Pecan Tartlets
  190, *191*

Chocolate Cheese Tart 173

Chocolate Cream Cake 245

Chocolate Nut Dough 164

Chocolate Orange Hazelnut Tart
  178, 179

Chocolate Bittersweet Tart 169

Chocolate Raspberry Tart 169

Chocolate Sandwich Cookies with
  Milk Chocolate Filling *307*, 308

Chocolate Spice Bread 44, 45

Cocoa Banana Muffins 60, *61*

Cocoa Génoise 240

Cocoa Nib Brownies 272, *273*

Coconut Pecan Chocolate Chunk Bars
  273, 277

Devil's Food Cake with Fluffy White
  Icing *252*, 253

Heirloom Chocolate Cake 256

Home-Style Chocolate Babka 100

Incredibly Moist Chocolate Cupcakes
  262, 263

Marbled Chocolate Brioche Loaf
  96, *97*–98, 98

Milk Chocolate Mousse Cake
  254, *255*

Molded Chocolate-Filled Napoleons
  198, *199*

Molten Center Chocolate Cakes
  258, *259*

Perfect Birthday Cake 243

Rum-Scented Marble Cake 228, *229*

shavings adhered to side of cake
  225, 225

Sour Cream Brownies *273*, 274

techniques 12, 15, 266–267, 285

Triple Chocolate Cake 250–251

Triple Chocolate Scones *56*, 57

Cinnamon Raisin Breakfast Ring 99

Cinnamon Raisin Buns 108

Cinnamon Raisin Scones 54

Cinnamon-Scented Baked Chocolate
Mousse Cake 257

Cinnamon Walnut Meringues 282

Classic Génoise 240–241, *241*

Classic Tarte Tatin with Apples 206

Cocoa Banana Muffins 60, *61*

Cocoa Génoise 240

Cocoa Nib Brownies 272, *273*

coconut
  about 170
  Banana Rum Coconut Layer Cake
    248, *249*

Coconut Pecan Chocolate Chunk Bars
  273, 277

Mango & Rice Tart 170

coffee
  Cappuccino Thumbprint Cookies
    290, 291
  Espresso Walnut Meringues 282, *283*

cookies. *See also* bars; biscotti
  about 270–271
  Blackberry Jam Sandwiches with
    Lemon Icing 306, *307*
  Butterscotch Chocolate Chunk
    Cookies *284*, 285
  Cappuccino Thumbprint Cookies
    290, 291
  Chocolate Sandwich Cookies with
    Milk Chocolate Filling *307*, 308
  Cinnamon Walnut Meringues 282
  Espresso Walnut Meringues 282, *283*
  Honey Peanut Wafers 280, *281*
  Lemon & Almond Tuiles 288, *289*
  Lemon Poppy Seed Drops 286, *287*
  Melting Moments *294*, 295
  New Orleans Bourbon Praline Disks
    293
  New Orleans Praline Disks 293, *294*
  Pine Nut Macaroons 302, *303*
  Raspberry Linzer Disks *307*, 309
  rolling techniques 270, *270–271*
  Tart Lemon Wafers 304
  Tart Lime Wafers 304–305, *305*
  Three-Way Gingersnaps *278*, 279
  Viennese Punch Cookies 310, *311*

Cornetti 90–91, *91*

cornmeal
  cornbread for stuffing 50
  Cornmeal & Pine Nut Biscotti
    297, 299
  Cornmeal & Pine Nut Biscotti with
    Raisins 297
  Cornmeal Buttermilk Waffles 113
  cornmeal pastry dough 145
  Cornmeal Waffles with a Hint of
    Lemon & Blueberry Sauce 113
  Corn Muffins 50
  Crisp Cornmeal Flatbread 76
  Old-Fashioned Cornbread 50
  Spicy Jalapeño Cornbread 50

Corn Pudding Tart *134*, 135

cream cheese
  Chocolate Cheese Tart 173
  Danish Cheese Pockets 209
  Individual Chocolate Cheesecakes
    264

Individual New York Cheesecakes 264, *265*

Lemony Cheese Tart with Sour-Cream Glaze *172, 173*

Smoked Salmon Mille-Feuilles *214, 215*

softening 221

crème anglaise 200

Crisp Cornmeal Flatbread 76

Currant Scones 52

Curried Fish Pie 146–147

D

dairy products, about 15–16, 123–125

Danish Cheese Pockets 209

Date Walnut Bread 47

Deep-Dish Apple Pie 203

Deep-Dish Peach & Raspberry Pie 203

Deep-Dish Peach Pie with Woven Lattice Crust 202–203

Deep-Dish Plum Pie 203

Devil's Food Cake with Fluffy White Icing *252, 253*

dough

about 156

"blind" baking 130, 165

braiding techniques 82, 95

Breton Dough 180

Chocolate Nut Dough 164

cornmeal pastry 145

forming lattice crust 187, 202

No-Roll Flaky Dough 133

Nut Tart Dough 160

Olive-Oil Dough 132

Pizza & Focaccia Dough 114

Press-In Cookie Dough 165

puff pastry 193, 194, 195, *196*

Rich Pie Dough 128

rolling and forming savory crust 129–131, *129–131*

rolling and forming sweet crust 161–163, *161–163*

Sweet Tart Dough 160

E

eggs

about 16

Curried Fish Pie 146–147

egg white techniques 221–222

Gruyère, Scallion, & Walnut Tart 141

Ham & Egg Tart 136, *137*

Ligurian Savoy Cabbage Pie 148, *149*

Roasted Pepper & Goat Cheese Tart *138*, 139

Swiss Onion Tart 140

Zucchini & Ricotta Pie 150

egg wash 68, 111

Elegant Dinner Rolls 86–87

equipment 24–33.

See also food processor

Espresso Walnut Meringues 282, *283*

F

Fennel Fig & Almond Bread 42, *43*

Feuillettés with Berries & Cream 201

figs

Fennel Fig & Almond Bread 42, *43*

Sicilian Fig Bars *300*, 301

Filled Ham & Cheese Focaccia 119

fish

about 127

Curried Fish Pie 146–147

Focaccia alla Barese 116–117, *117*

Sfincione 115

Smoked Salmon Mille-Feuilles *214*, 215

flatbread

Armenian "Barbary" Bread 70

Crisp Cornmeal Flatbread 76

Fougasse 74–75, *75*

Mixed-Grain Turkish Flatbread 71

Sesame Turkish Flatbread 71

Turkish Flatbread 71

focaccia

Bare Bones Focaccia 114

dough 114

Filled Ham & Cheese Focaccia 119

Focaccia Alla Barese 116–117, *117*

Rosemary Focaccia 114

Sfincione 115

food processor 32, 52, 95, 160

Fougasse 74–75, *75*

French Bread 78–79

frostings and icings

about 223–225

Chocolate Fudge Icing 263

coloring techniques 267

Confectioners' Sugar Icing 261

decorating ideas *266*, 266–267, *267*

Fluffy White Icing 253

ganache 243, 250

Raspberry Buttercream 244

Rum Icing 310

fruit

about 158–159, 166

Parisian Fruit Tarts 166, *167*

Strudel 207

fruit, dried. *See also* raisins and currants

about 159

Fennel Fig & Almond Bread 42, *43*

Orange-Scented Dried Cranberry Scones 54

Panettone alla Milanese 104

Sicilian Fig Bars *300*, 301

G

Génoise Très Vanillée 240

Ginger-Scented Panettone 104

Ginger Scones with Almond Topping 54, *56*

Golden Cupcakes 261, *262*

grains and grain flakes

about 18, 170

Mango & Rice Tart 170

Neapolitan Easter Pie *186*, 187

Rusks for Dunking 62

Seven Grain & Seed Bread 84

Sweet Rusks for Dunking 62

Grissini 112

Gruyère, Scallion, & Walnut Tart 141

Gruyère Biscuits 51

H

Ham & Cheese Tart 136

Ham & Egg Tart 136, *137*

Hazelnut Biscotti 296

Heirloom Chocolate Cake 256

herbs

about 20, 22

Rosemary Focaccia 114

Rosemary Fougasse 75

Rosemary Olive Knots 88–89, *89*

Tomato & Cantal Tart 142, *143*

Home-Style Chocolate Babka 100

Honey Peanut Wafers 280, *281*

I

Incredibly Moist Chocolate Cupcakes *262*, 263

Individual Chocolate Cheesecakes 264

Individual French Hazelnut Cakes 260

Individual New York Cheesecakes 264, *265*

ingredients, about

butter 15, 221

flavorings and extracts 16–17

flours 17–18, 82, 194

lard 127

leaveners 39, 41, 67, 68

meat and fish 126–127

mozzarella cheese 118

overview 10–23

savory tarts and pies 123–127

serrano chiles 145

sweeteners 23, 161

sweet tarts and pies 158–159

thickeners 18

vegetables 125–126

yeast 67, 68

yogurt 16

Instant Sandwich Bread 77

Irish Soda Bread Muffins 59, *61*

K

Kouing Amman 102–103, *103*

L

lemons

Blackberry Jam Sandwiches with Lemon Icing 306, *307*

Cornmeal Waffles with a Hint of Lemon & Blueberry Sauce 113

Lemon & Almond Tuiles 288, *289*

Lemon Cream Cake 245

Lemon Ginger Pound Cake 227

Lemon Ginger Tartlets 189

Lemon Lime Tartlets 189, *191*

Lemon Melting Moments 295

Lemon Poppy Seed Drops 286, *287*

Lemony Cheese Tart with Sour-Cream Glaze *172, 173*

Meyer Lemon Tartlets 189

Tart Lemon Wafers 304

Ligurian Savoy Cabbage Pie 148, *149*

limes

Lemon Lime Tartlets 189, *191*

Tart Lime Wafers 304–305, *305*

liquors and liqueurs

about 18

Banana Rum Coconut Layer Cake 248, *249*

Bourbon-Scented Pecan Tart 175

Molded Chocolate-Filled Napoleons 198, *199*

New Orleans Bourbon Praline Disks 293

Raspberry Cream Cake 244–245

Raspberry Mille-Feuille 200

Rum-Scented Marble Cake 228, *229*

Sicilian Fig Bars *300*, 301

Swiss Walnut Crescents 208

Triple Chocolate Cake 250–251

Viennese Punch Cookies 310, *311*

316

loaves

Brioche Loaves 95

Chocolate Babka Loaf 100–101, *101*

Chocolate Spice Bread 44, 45

Date Walnut Bread 47

Fennel Fig & Almond Bread 42, *43*

Marbled Chocolate Brioche Loaf
96, 97–98, *98*

Spicy Jalapeño Cornbread 50

Whole Grain Apple Raisin Bread
48, *49*

Whole Wheat Currant Bread 46

yeast bread 67–68

M

Macadamia Shortbreads *292*, 294

Maida's Big Apple Pie *181*, 182

Mango & Rice Tart 170

Marbled Chocolate Brioche Loaf
96, 97–98, *98*

meat 126–127. *See also* chicken;
fish; pork

Melting Moments *294*, 295

Meyer Lemon Tartlets 189

milk

Cornmeal Buttermilk Waffles 113

Pumpkin-Pecan Buttermilk Tart with
Cinnamon Whipped Cream 174

types 15–16, 170

Milk Chocolate Mousse Cake 254, *255*

Mixed-Grain Turkish Flatbread 71

Molded Chocolate-Filled Napoleons
198, *199*

Molten Center Chocolate Cakes 258, *259*

mousse

Cinnamon-Scented Chocolate
Mousse 257

Milk Chocolate Mousse 254

muffins

Blueberry Crumb Muffins 58, *61*

Cocoa Banana Muffins 60, *61*

Corn Muffins 50

Irish Soda Bread Muffins 59, *61*

Whole Wheat Raisin Muffins 58

N

Neapolitan Easter Pie *186*, 187

Neapolitan Meat & Cheese Pie 153

New Orleans Bourbon Praline Disks 293

New Orleans Praline Disks 293, *294*

Nonna's Pizza 118

No-Roll Flaky Dough 133

nuts. *See also* almond paste

about 19–20, *21*

adhered to side of cake 225, *225*, 266

Babka with Traditional Filling 100

Banana Walnut Tart 171

Bourbon-Scented Pecan Tart 175

Chocolate Caramel Pecan Tartlets
190, *191*

Chocolate Nut Dough 164

Chocolate Orange Hazelnut Tart
178, 179

Coconut Pecan Chocolate Chunk Bars
273, 277

Cornmeal & Pine Nut Biscotti
297, 299

Date Walnut Bread 47

Espresso Walnut Meringues 282, *283*

Fennel Fig &Almond Bread 42, *43*

Ginger Scones with Almond Topping
54, *56*

Gruyère, Scallion, & Walnut Tart
141

Hazelnut Biscotti 296

Honey Peanut Wafers 280, *281*

Individual French Hazelnut Cakes 260

Lemon & Almond Tuiles 288, *289*

Lemon Poppy Seed Drops 286, *287*

Macadamia Shortbreads 292, *294*

New Orleans Bourbon Praline Disks
293

New Orleans Praline Disks 293, *294*

Nut Tart Dough 160

Pecan Pound Cake 226

Pecan Stickiest Buns *107*, 108

Pine Nut Macaroons 302, *303*

Pumpkin-Pecan Buttermilk Tart with
Cinnamon Whipped Cream 174

Raisin Pecan Spice Bars *273*, 275

Roman Almond & Pine Nut Tart
176, *177*

Sour Cream Brownies *273*, 274

Spicy Hazelnut Biscotti 296, *299*

Swiss Walnut Crescents 208

Triple Chocolate Scones with
Almond Topping 57

Viennese Punch Cookies 310, *311*

Walnut Pound Cake 226

Walnut Tart 175

Whole Wheat Currant Bread 46

O

oils

about 20

Olive-Oil Dough 132

Orange-Scented Olive Oil Cake
234, 235

Old-fashioned Baking-Powder
Biscuits 51

Old-Fashioned Cornbread 50

Olive-Oil Dough 132

olives

Focaccia alla Barese 116–117, *117*

Olive Fougasse 75

pitting technique 116

Rosemary Olive Knots 88–89, *89*

One-Step Croissants 109–111, *110*, *111*

onions

Caramelized Onion Tart with
Gorgonzola 212, *214*

Focaccia alla Barese 116–117, *117*

Gruyère, Scallion, & Walnut Tart
141

Sfincione 115

Swiss Onion & Cheese Tart 140

Swiss Onion Tart 140

oranges

Chocolate Orange Hazelnut Tart
178, 179

Melting Moments *294*, 295

Neapolitan Easter Pie *186*, 187

Orange-Scented Dried Cranberry
Scones 54

Orange-Scented Olive Oil Cake
234, 235

Orange Tartlets 189

Triple Chocolate Cake with
Marmalade 251

oven items 32

P

Pain de Campagne 80–81, *81*

Pain de Seigle 83

Panettone alla Milanese 104

pans 26, 27, 28, 222, 231

paper goods, towels, and liners 32

Parisian Fruit Tarts 166, *167*

Parmigiano-Reggiano Biscuits 51

passion-fruit, Chocolate Bittersweet
Tart 169

pastries. *See* pastry cream; puff pastry

pastry cream 166, 187, 200. *See also*
crème anglaise

peaches

Deep-Dish Peach and Raspberry Pie
203

Deep-Dish Peach Pie with Woven
Lattice Crust 202–203

Pecan Pound Cake 226

Pecan Stickiest Buns *107*, 108

Pecorino & Pepper Biscuits 51

peppers. *See* bell peppers; chile peppers

Perfect Birthday Cake 243

Perfect Elephant Ears 210, *211*

Perfect Pound Cake 226

pies. *See* tarts and pies, savory; tarts
and pies, sweet

Pineapple Tarte Tatin *204*, 205–206

Pine Nut Macaroons 302, *303*

Pita Bread 72–73, *73*

pizza

dough 114

Nonna's Pizza 118

Pizza Chiena 151

Plain Mille-Feuille 200

plums

Deep-Dish Plum Pie 203

Plum Crumb Cake 237

pork

about 126–127

Filled Ham & Cheese Focaccia 119

Ham & Cheese Tart 136

Ham & Egg Tart 136, *137*

Neapolitan Meat & Cheese Pie 153

Prosciutto Bread 85

Quiche Lorraine 136

salt pork, about 127

Press-In Cookie Dough 165

Prosciutto Bread 85

puff pastry

about 193, 194

Apricot & Almond Strudel *204*, 207

Baked Layer 197

Caramelized Onion Tart with
Gorgonzola 212, *214*

Caraway Salt Straws 216

Cheese Straws 216

Classic Tarte Tatin with Apples 206

Danish Cheese Pockets 209

Deep-Dish Apple Pie 203

Deep-Dish Peach & Raspberry Pie
203

Deep-Dish Peach Pie with Woven
Lattice Crust 202–203

Deep-Dish Plum Pie 203

Feuillettés with Berries & Cream
201

Instant Puff Pastry 195, *196*

Molded Chocolate-Filled Napoleons
198, *199*

Perfect Elephant Ears 210, *211*

Pineapple Tarte Tatin *204*, 205–206

Plain Mille-Feuille 200

Raspberry Mille-Feuille 200

Salt & Pepper Straws 216–217, *217*

317

Savory Cheese Elephant Ears 210

Smoked Salmon Mille-Feuilles *214*, 215

Spinach & Feta Turnovers 213, *214*

Strawberry Mille-Feuille 200

Swiss Walnut Crescents 208

Pumpkin-Pecan Buttermilk Tart with Cinnamon Whipped Cream 174

Q

Quiche Lorraine 136

Quick Brioche Braid 95

R

Raisin Pecan Spice Bars *273*, 275

raisins and currants

Babka with Traditional Filling 100

Cinnamon Raisin Breakfast Ring 99

Cinnamon Raisin Buns 108

Cinnamon Raisin Scones 54

Cornmeal & Pine Nut Biscotti with Raisins 297

Ginger-Scented Panettone 104

Panettone alla Milanese 104

Raisin Pecan Spice Bars *273*, 275

Raisin Scones 52

Semolina Fennel & Raisin Bread 82

Viennese Raisin Coffee Cake *230*, 231

Whole Grain Apple Raisin Bread 48, *49*

Whole Wheat Currant Bread 46

Whole Wheat Raisin Muffins 58

Raspberry Almond Tartlets 188, *191*

Raspberry Cream Cake 244–245

Raspberry Linzer Disks *307*, 309

Raspberry Mille-Feuille 200

Real Strawberry Shortcake 238, *239*

Real Welsh Scones 52–53, *53*

Rich Pie Dough 128

Roasted Pepper & Goat Cheese Tart *138*, 139

Roasted Tomato & Cantal Tart 142

Roman Almond & Pine Nut Tart 176, *177*

Rosemary Focaccia 114

Rosemary Fougasse 75

Rosemary Olive Knots 88–89, *89*

Rum-Scented Marble Cake 228, *229*

rusks, sweet for dunking 62

S

Salt & Pepper Straws 216–217, *217*

Savory Cheese Elephant Ears 210

scones

Butterscotch Chocolate Chunk Scones 55

Butterscotch Scones 55

Cinnamon Raisin Scones 54

Ginger Scones with Almond Topping 54, *56*

Orange-Scented Dried Cranberry Scones 54

Real Welsh Scones 52–53, *53*

Triple Chocolate Scones *56*, 57

seeds

about 20, *21*

Biscotti Regina 298, *299*

Caraway Pain de Seigle 83

Caraway Salt Straws 216

crushing technique 42

Elegant Dinner Rolls 87

Fennel Fig & Almond Bread 42, *43*

Lemon Poppy Seed Drops 286, *287*

Semolina Fennel & Raisin Bread 82

Semolina Sesame Braid 82

Sesame Turkish Flatbread 71

Seven Grain & Seed Bread 84

Shrimp & Toasted Pumpkinseed Tart *144*, 145

Semolina Fennel & Raisin Bread 82

Semolina Sesame Braid 82

Semolina Toast 82

Sesame Turkish Flatbread 71

Seven Grain & Seed Bread 84

Sfincione 115

Shrimp & Toasted Pumpkinseed Tart *144*, 145

Sicilian Fig Bars *300*, 301

Smoked Salmon Mille-Feuilles *214*, 215

Sour Cherry Crumb Cake 237

Sour Cherry Crumble Pie 184

sour cream

custard 183

glaze 173

Golden Cupcakes 261, *262*

Individual New York Cheesecakes 264, *265*

Sour-Cream Apple Pie 183

Sour-Cream Brownies *273*, 274

Sour-Cream Coffee Cake 232

specialties, yeast-risen. *See also* focaccia; pizza

Babka with Traditional Filling 100

Bakery Crumb Buns 105–106, *107*

Brioche Loaves 95

Chocolate Babka Loaf 100–101, *101*

Cinnamon Raisin Breakfast Ring 99

Cinnamon Raisin Buns 108

Cornmeal Buttermilk Waffles 113

Cornmeal Waffles with a Hint of Lemon & Blueberry Sauce 113

Ginger-Scented Panettone 104

Grissini 112

Home-Style Chocolate Babka 100

Kouing Amman 102–103, *103*

Marbled Chocolate Brioche Loaf 96, 97–98, *98*

One-Step Croissants 109–111, *110, 111*

Panettone Alla Milanese 104

Pecan Stickiest Buns *107*, 108

Quick Brioche Braid 95

Sfincione 115

spices

about 20, 22

Babka with Traditional Filling 100

Chocolate Spice Bread 44, 45

Cinnamon Raisin Breakfast Ring 99

Cinnamon Raisin Buns 108

Cinnamon Raisin Scones 54

Cinnamon-Scented Baked Chocolate Mousse Cake 257

cinnamon sugar 58

Cinnamon Walnut Meringues 282

Cinnamon Whipped Cream 174

Ginger-Scented Panettone 104

Ginger Scones with Almond Topping 54, *56*

Lemon Ginger Pound Cake 227

Lemon Ginger Tartlets 189

Raisin Pecan Spice Bars *273*, 275

Spicy Hazelnut Biscotti 296, *299*

Three-Way Gingersnaps *278*, 279

Walnut Tart 175

Spicy Hazelnut Biscotti 296, *299*

Spicy Jalapeño Cornbread 50

Spinach & Feta Turnovers 213, *214*

storage items 33

Strawberry Mille-Feuille 200

surfaces 33

Sweet Rusks for Dunking 62

Swiss Onion & Cheese Tart 140

Swiss Onion Tart 140

Swiss Walnut Crescents 208

syrup, moistening 244, 250, 254

T

Tangerine Tartlets 189

Tart Lemon Wafers 304

Tart Lime Wafers 304–305, *305*

tarts and pies, savory

about 122

Caramelized Onion Tart with Gorgonzola 212, *214*

Chicken Pie with Biscuit Topping 152, *153*

Corn Pudding Tart *134*, 135

Curried Fish Pie 146–147

Gruyère, Scallion, & Walnut Tart 141

Ham & Cheese Tart 136

Ham & Egg Tart 136, *137*

ingredients 123–127

Ligurian Savoy Cabbage Pie 148, *149*

Neapolitan Meat & Cheese Pie 153

No-Roll Flaky Dough 133

Olive-Oil Dough 132

Quiche Lorraine 136

Rich Pie Dough 128

Roasted Pepper and Goat Cheese Tart *138*, 139

Roasted Tomato & Cantal Tart 142

rolling and forming crust 129–131, *129–131*

Shrimp & Toasted Pumpkin-seed Tart *144*, 145

Spinach & Feta Turnovers 213, *214*

Swiss Onion and Cheese Tart 140

Swiss Onion Tart 140

Tomato & Cantal Tart 142, *143*

Zucchini & Ricotta Pie 150

tarts and pies, sweet

about 156–159

Banana Walnut Tart 171

Bittersweet Chocolate Tart *168*, 169

Blueberry Crumble Pie 184, *185*

Bourbon-Scented Pecan Tart 175

Breton Apple Pie 180, 181

Chocolate Caramel Pecan Tartlets 190, *191*

Chocolate Cheese Tart 173

Chocolate Nut Dough 164

Chocolate Orange Hazelnut Tart *178*, 179

Chocolate Passion-Fruit Tart 169

Chocolate Raspberry Tart 169

Deep-Dish Apple Pie 203

Deep-Dish Peach & Raspberry Pie 203

Deep-Dish Peach Pie with Woven Lattice Crust 202–203

Deep-Dish Plum Pie 203

Lemon Ginger Tartlets 189

Lemon Lime Tartlets 189, *191*

318

Lemony Cheese Tart with Sour-Cream
      Glaze *172*, 173
Maida's Big Apple Pie *181*, 182
Mango & Rice Tart 170
Meyer Lemon Tartlets 189
Neapolitan Easter Pie *186*, 187
Nut Tart Dough 160
Orange Tartlets 189
Parisian Fruit Tarts 166, *167*
pastry cream 166, 187
Press-In Cookie Dough 165
Pumpkin-Pecan Buttermilk Tart with
Cinnamon Whipped Cream 174
Raspberry Almond Tartlets 188, *191*
Roman Almond & Pine Nut Tart
      176, *177*
Sour Cherry Crumble Pie 184
Sour-Cream Apple Pie 183
Sweet Tart Dough 160
Tangerine Tartlets 189
Walnut Tart 175

techniques
braiding dough 82, 95
cake decorating *225, 266*,
      266–267, 267
cake making 221–225, *224, 225*
chocolate 12, 15, 266–267, 285
cooking sugar 37
crushing seeds 42
cutting puff pastry 194
cutting round scones 52
egg wash 68, 111
egg whites 221–222
food processor 52, 95, 160
fruit preparation 48, 158–159
handling chiles 50
lattice crust 187, 202
measuring 36
oven 36
pitting olives 116
quick breads 40
rolled cookies 270, *270–271*
savory crust 129–131, *129–131*
sweet crust 161–163, *161–163*
testing for doneness 40, 68, 223
unmolding and cooling 36–37
yeast bread 66–69, 94
Three-Way Gingersnaps *278*, 279

tomatoes
about 142
Nonna's Pizza 118
Roasted Tomato & Cantal Tart 142
Tomato & Cantal Tart 142, *143*
tools and utensils 28–30, *31*

toppings
almond 54
cinnamon sugar 58
crumb 58, 105, 183, 184, 237
fruit glaze 157, 166
ganache glaze 243, 250
sour-cream glaze 173
whipped cream 174, 223
Triple Chocolate Cake 250–251
Triple Chocolate Scones *56*, 57
Turkish Flatbread 71

V
vanilla
Chocolate & Vanilla Cake 245
Génoise Très Vanillée 240
vegetables
about 125–126
Chicken Pie with Biscuit Topping
      152, *153*
Viennese Punch Cookies 310, *311*
Viennese Raisin Coffee Cake *230*, 231

W
waffles
Cornmeal Buttermilk Waffles 113
Cornmeal Waffles with a Hint of
      Lemon & Blueberry Sauce 113
Walnut Tart 175
Wheat-Sheaf Loaf 79
whipped cream
about 223
caramel 247
cinnamon 174
rum 248
vanilla 201, 238, 253
Whipped Cream Layer Cake *246*, 247
Whole Grain Apple Raisin Bread 48, 49
Whole Grain Fougasse, Part 75
Whole Wheat Currant Bread 46
Whole Wheat Raisin Muffins 58

Y
Yellow Cake Layers 242

Z
Zucchini & Ricotta Pie 150

Acknowledgments

320

Moving to a new publishing house isn't always an easy transition, but I thank my editor, Anja Schmidt, for making the process of doing this book not only easy, but a real pleasure. Anja has been a joy to work with and her unerring sense of taste and practicality has shaped every aspect of *The Modern Baker*. A big thank you to my agent, Phyllis Wender, who always makes me feel as though I'm her only client. For close to 20 years I have benefited from Phyllis' sound advice and vast experience in publishing at every stage of the books and other projects I have done. Natalie Danford edited, re-wrote, and polished the manuscript and helped with every aspect of writing this book. Thank you, Natalie, this book wouldn't exist without you.

At DK Publishing I've enjoyed working with and wish to thank the great team of in-house and freelance people who worked on *The Modern Baker*: former assistant editor Nichole Morford, copy editor Peggy Fallon, and proofreader Ann Cahn; on the production end, executive managing editor Sharon Lucas, art director Dirk Kaufman, managing art editor Michelle Baxter, designer Gary Tooth, photographer Charles Schiller and his wife, Denise Schiller, studio assistant Armando Moutela, model Sebastian Royo, prop stylist Pamela Duncan Silver and her assistant, Yvonne Moutela, and food stylist Karen Tack and her assistant, Ellie Ritt.

For publicity, promotions, and marketing, thanks go to director of publicity and marketing Judi Powers, associate director of publicity Rachel Kempster, and marketing manager Kristen O'Connell.

Special thanks to Cara Tannenbaum and Andrea Tutunjian not only for recipe testing but also for so many years of unwavering friendship and generosity, as well as to the "moral support team," my partner Sandy Lustig, my second mother Ann Nurse, my mentor Maida Heatter, and the dearest friends, Nancy Nicholas, Miriam Brickman, and Sandy Leonard. And a big thank you to owner Rick Smilow and my many friends and colleagues at the Institute of Culinary Education.

My thanks to generous friends who shared precious personal recipes: Fritz Blank, Flo Braker, Tim Brennan, Anna Teresa Callen, Kyra Effren, Fran Gage, Dorie Greenspan, Maida Heatter, Anita Jacobson, Loretta Keller, Albert Kumin, the late Peter Kump, Sandy Leonard, Karen Ludwig, Mary Lou McGrath, Jennifer Morris, Ann Amendolara Nurse, Roberto Santibañez, Loretta Sartori, the late Mildred Shapiro, Bonnie Stern, Michelle Tampakis, Cara Tannenbaum, Reina Teeger, Stephanie Weaver, and Vicky Zeph.

A last special thank you to Susan Wyler for introducing me to DK Publishing, and to Carl Raymond for first welcoming me there.